KB086786

적중100

영어 기출 문제집

중3

능률 | 김성곤

Best Collection

구성과 특징

교과서의 주요 학습 내용을 중심으로 학습 영역별 특성에 맞춰 단계별로 다양한 학습 기회를 제공하여
단원별 학습능력 평가는 물론 중간 및 기말고사 시험 등에 완벽하게 대비할 수 있도록 내용을 구성

Words & Expressions

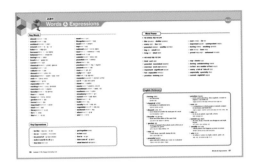

Step1	Key Words 단원별 핵심 단어 설명 및 풀이
	Key Expression 단원별 핵심 숙어 및 관용어 설명
	Word Power 반대 또는 비슷한 뜻 단어 배우기
	English Dictionary 영어로 배우는 영어 단어
Step2	실력평가 단원별 수시평가 대비 주관식, 객관식 문제풀이
Step3	서술형 대비 학업성취도 및 수행능력평가 대비 서술형 문제풀이

Conversation

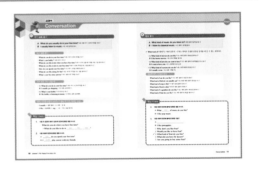

Step1	핵심 의사소통 소통에 필요한 주요 표현 방법 요약
	핵심 Check 기본적인 표현 방법 및 활용능력 확인
Step2	대화문 익히기 교과서 대화문 심층 분석 및 확인
Step3	교과서 확인학습 빈칸 채우기를 통한 문장 완성 능력 확인
Step4	기본평가 시험대비 기초 학습 능력 평가
Step5	실력평가 단원별 수시평가 대비 주관식, 객관식 문제풀이
Step6	서술형 대비 학업성취도 및 수행능력평가 대비 서술형 문제풀이

Grammar

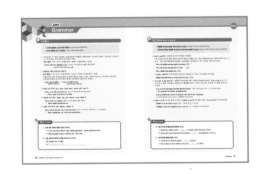

Step1	주요 문법 단원별 주요 문법 사항과 예문을 알기 쉽게 설명
	핵심 Check 기본 문법사항에 대한 이해 여부 확인
Step2	기본평가 시험대비 기초 학습 능력 평가
Step3	실력평가 단원별 수시평가 대비 주관식, 객관식 문제풀이
Step4	서술형 대비 학업성취도 및 수행능력평가 대비 서술형 문제풀이

Reading

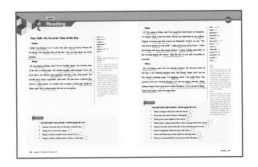

Step1	구문 분석 단원별로 제시된 문장에 대한 구문별 분석과 내용 설명
	확인문제 문장에 대한 기본적인 이해와 인지능력 확인
Step2	확인학습A 빈칸 채우기를 통한 문장 완성 능력 확인
Step3	확인학습B 제시된 우리말을 영어로 완성하여 작문 능력 키우기
Step4	실력평가 단원별 수시평가 대비 주관식, 객관식 문제풀이
Step5	서술형 대비 학업성취도 및 수행능력평가 대비 서술형 문제풀이
	교과서 구석구석 교과서에 나오는 기타 문장까지 완벽 학습

Composition

영역별 핵심문제

단어 및 어휘, 대화문, 문법, 독해 등 각 영역별 기출문제의 출제 유형을 분석하여 실전에 대비하고 연습할 수 있도록 문제를 배열

단원별 예상문제

기출문제를 분석한 후 새로운 시험 출제 경향을 더하여 새롭게 출제될 수 있는 문제를 포함하여 시험에 완벽하게 대비할수 있도록 준비

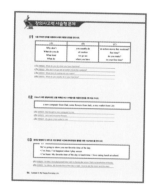

서술형 실전 및 창의사고력 문제

학교 시험에서 점차 늘어나는 서술형 시험에 집중 대비하고 고득점을 취득하는데 만전을 기하기 위한 학습 코너

단원별 모의고사

영역별, 단계별 학습을 모두 마친 후 실전 연습을 위한 모의고사

교과서 파헤치기

- **단어Test1~3** 영어 단어 우리말 쓰기, 우리말을 영어 단어로 쓰기, 영영풀이에 해당하는 단어와 우리말 쓰기
- **대화문Test1~2** 대화문 빈칸 완성 및 전체 대화문 쓰기
- **본문Test1~5** 빈칸 완성, 우리말 쓰기, 문장 배열연습, 영어 작문하기 복습 등 단계별 반복 학습을 통해 교과서 지문에 대한 완벽한 습득
- **구석구석지문Test1~2** 지문 빈칸 완성 및 전문 영어로 쓰기

Lesson **1**

A Life Full of Experiences

🎙 의사소통 기능

- 바람에 대해 묻고 답하기
  A: What would you like to do this year?
  B: I'd like to travel to other countries.

- 만족이나 불만족에 대해 묻기
  How do you like hiking?

🎙 언어 형식

- 현재완료진행형
  I **have been writing** my shopping lists in Spanish!

- 관계대명사 what
  Find **what** keeps you motivated.

Words & Expressions

Key Words

- **ask** [æsk] 동 묻다, 요청하다
- **awesome** [ɔ́:səm] 형 엄청난
- **case** [keis] 명 사례, 경우, 상자
- **confident** [kánfədənt] 형 자신 있는
- **creative** [kriéitiv] 형 창조적인
- **culture** [kʌ́ltʃər] 명 문화
- **exactly** [igzǽktli] 부 정확하게
- **experience** [ikspíəriəns] 명 경험
- **finally** [fáinəli] 부 마침내
- **finish** [fíniʃ] 동 끝내다
- **foreign** [fɔ́:rən] 형 외국의
- **furniture** [fɔ́:rnitʃər] 명 가구
- **guess** [ges] 동 추측하다
- **hold** [hould] 동 쥐다, 들다
- **improve** [imprúːv] 동 개선하다, 향상시키다
- **join** [dʒɔin] 동 가입하다
- **meaningful** [míːniŋfəl] 형 의미 있는, 중요한
- **memorize** [méməraiz] 동 암기하다
- **motivate** [móutəvèit] 동 동기를 부여하다
- **nervous** [nɔ́:rvəs] 형 불안한
- **own** [oun] 형 ~ 자신의 동 소유하다

- **perfect** [pɔ́:rfikt] 형 완벽한
- **perform** [pərfɔ́:rm] 동 공연하다, 수행하다
- **post** [poust] 동 (웹사이트에 정보 · 사진을) 올리다[게시하다]
- **recommend** [rèkəménd] 동 추천하다
- **requirement** [rikwáiərmənt] 명 필요조건, 요건
- **responsibility** [rispànsəbíləti] 명 책임감
- **review** [rivjúː] 명 검토, 후기
- **share** [ʃɛər] 동 공유하다
- **shelf** [ʃelf] 명 선반, 책꽂이
- **shopping list** 쇼핑 목록
- **social media** 소셜 미디어
- **spend** [spend] 동 쓰다
- **subtitle** [sʌ́btaitəl] 명 자막
- **talent** [tǽlənt] 명 재능
- **translation** [trænsléiʃən] 명 번역[통역](된 것), 번역문
- **travel** [trǽvəl] 동 여행하다
- **treasure** [tréʒər] 명 보물
- **vocabulary** [voukǽbjulèri] 명 어휘
- **volunteer** [vàləntíər] 명 자원봉사자 동 자원봉사하다
- **weakness** [wíːknis] 명 약점

Key Expressions

- **a review of a match** 경기 논평
- **be good at ~** ~을 잘하다
- **be interested in ~** ~에 관심을 가지다
- **be proud of ~** ~을 자랑스러워하다
- **be related to ~** ~에 관련되다
- **be struck by** ~에 감동받다
- **become familiar with ~** ~에 친숙해지다
- **first of all** 첫째로
- **get better at ~** ~에 능숙해지다
- **get used to ~** ~에 익숙해지다
- **give up** 포기하다

- **go shopping** 쇼핑하러 가다
- **in any case** 어쨌든
- **keep A motivated** A가 계속 의욕을 가지게 하다
- **not ~ at all** 전혀 ~가 아닌
- **run a race** 경주를 하다
- **spend time -ing** ~하면서 시간을 보내다
- **take a swimming class** 수영 수업을 받다
- **take care of** ~을 돌보다
- **try -ing** 시험 삼아 ~해 보다
- **what's most important** 가장 중요한 것
- **would like to ~** ~하고 싶다

Word Power

※ 서로 비슷한 뜻을 가진 어휘

- □ **confident** 자신 있는 : **convinced** 확신하는
- □ **improve** 개선하다 : **develop** 발달시키다
- □ **exactly** 정확하게 : **correctly** 정확하게
- □ **travel** 여행하다 : **tour** 여행하다
- □ **finally** 마침내 : **at last** 마침내
- □ **guess** 추측하다 : **infer** 추론하다

- □ **recommend** 추천하다 : **suggest** 제안하다
- □ **nervous** 불안한 : **annoyed** 짜증이 난
- □ **awesome** 엄청난 : **amazing** 놀랄만한
- □ **spend** 쓰다 : **use** 사용하다
- □ **finish** 끝내다 : **complete** 완성하다

※ 서로 반대의 뜻을 가진 어휘

- □ **confident** 자신 있는 ↔ **unconfident** 자신감이 없는
- □ **responsibility** 책임감 ↔ **irresponsibility** 무책임
- □ **perfect** 완벽한 ↔ **imperfect** 불완전한
- □ **exactly** 정확하게 ↔ **inexactly** 정확하지 않게

- □ **weakness** 약점 ↔ **strength** 강점
- □ **meaningful** 의미 있는 ↔ **meaningless** 의미 없는
- □ **finish** 끝내다 ↔ **begin** 시작하다

English Dictionary

- □ **motivate** 동기를 부여하다
  → to make someone want to achieve something and make them willing to work hard in order to do this
  누군가가 무엇인가를 이루도록 만들거나 그것을 위하여 열심히 노력하도록 만들다
- □ **perfect** 완벽한
  → not having any mistakes, faults, or damage
  아무런 실수, 결점 또는 손상이 없는
- □ **post** (웹사이트에 정보·사진을) 올리다[게시하다]
  → add a message to an online message board
  메시지를 온라인 게시판에 올리다
- □ **recommend** 추천하다
  → to advise someone to do something
  어떤 사람에게 무엇인가를 하도록 조언하다
- □ **requirement** 필요조건, 요건
  → something that someone needs or asks for
  누군가가 필요하거나 요구하는 어떤 것
- □ **responsibility** 책임감
  → a duty to be in charge of someone or something
  어떤 사람 또는 무엇인가를 담당하는 의무

- □ **review** 검토
  → a careful examination of a situation or process
  어떤 상황이나 과정에 대한 신중한 조사
- □ **share** 공유하다
  → to have or use something with other people
  다른 사람과 함께 어떤 것을 가지거나 사용하다
- □ **shelf** 선반
  → a long flat narrow board attached to a wall
  벽에 붙은 길고 평평한 좁은 판자
- □ **talent** 재능
  → a natural ability to do something well
  어떤 일을 잘 하는 천부적인 능력
- □ **treasure** 보물
  → a group of valuable things such as gold, silver, jewels
  금, 은, 보석 같은 귀중한 것의 집합
- □ **volunteer** 자원봉사자
  → someone who does a job willingly without being paid
  보수를 받지 않고 기꺼이 일하는 사람

 01 다음 문장의 빈칸에 들어가기에 적절한 것은?

> What's most important is to become familiar with the language first. I suggest watching Spanish movies often. It will help you get _____ to the sound of the language.

① known   ② used   ③ closed
④ learned   ⑤ convinced

02 다음 영영풀이에 해당하는 단어를 고르시오.

> a long flat narrow board attached to a wall

① shelf   ② culture
③ responsibility   ④ subtitle
⑤ door

 03 다음 대화의 빈칸에 들어갈 말로 적절한 것을 고르시오.

> B: We are finally on top of the mountain! How do you like hiking?
> G: It isn't easy at all, but now I understand why not _____ up is so important.

① looking   ② running
③ giving   ④ hanging
⑤ filling

04 다음 중 밑줄 친 부분의 뜻풀이가 바르지 <u>않은</u> 것은?

① I'd like to learn how to make my <u>own</u> mobile game. (소유하다)
② What did the girl learn <u>through</u> the experience? (~을 통해서)
③ Many people learn languages for <u>fun</u>. (재미)
④ They are my <u>favorite</u> players. (아주 좋아하는)
⑤ How can I <u>improve</u> my Spanish? (개선하다)

05 다음 중 〈보기〉에 있는 단어를 사용하여 자연스러운 문장을 만들 수 <u>없는</u> 것은?

> ┤ 보기 ├
> match   familiar   suggest   practice

① The best way to learn a new language is to _____ it every day.
② I have _____ the language of my phone to Spanish.
③ What's most important is to become _____ with the language first.
④ I can't wait to see the final _____.
⑤ I _____ watching Spanish movies often.

서답형
06 다음 주어진 단어를 이용해 빈칸을 완성하시오.

> Can you tell me about one of your _____ experiences? (mean)

➡ _____

01 다음 밑줄 친 부분을 알맞은 어형으로 고치시오.

> Furthermore, they had to <u>memory</u> the long poem.

➡ _____

02 다음 우리말에 맞게 빈칸에 알맞은 말을 쓰시오.

(1) 어쨌든, 학생들은 새로운 언어를 배우는 재미있는 방법을 가지고 있다.
➡ In any _____, students have interesting ways to study new languages.

(2) 나는 무언가를 만들고 난 후에 자신감을 느낀다.
➡ I feel _____ after I finish making something.

(3) 너를 동기 부여되도록 하는 것을 찾아라. 그러면 배우는 것을 더 즐길 수 있을 거야.
➡ Find what keeps you _____; then you will enjoy learning more.

(4) 만약 사람들의 말이 너무 빠르면 먼저 스페인 어린이 영화 보기를 시도해 보아라.
➡ If the people talk too fast, try _____ Spanish children's movies first.

03 주어진 단어를 이용해 빈칸을 완성하시오.

> Many students learn new languages because of school _____s. (require)

➡ _____

04 다음 짝지어진 단어의 관계가 같도록 빈칸에 알맞은 말을 쓰시오. (주어진 철자로 시작할 것)

> exactly : correctly = f_____ : complete

05 빈칸에 공통으로 들어갈 단어를 쓰시오.

> • You have to _____ used to other cultures.
> • Watching Chinese dramas with Chinese subtitles is a good way to _____ better at listening.

06 빈칸에 알맞은 단어를 〈보기〉에서 골라 쓰시오.

> ┤ 보기 ├
> experiences   talents   review   joined subtitles

(1) She _____ a skateboarding club last month.
(2) Having new experiences lets us find new _____.
(3) Also, why don't you try writing a _____ of a match in Spanish?
(4) It's also a good idea to print out the _____ and read them first.
(5) I am sure that these new _____ in Jeju Island would help me understand Korea better.

Conversation

1 바람에 대해 묻고 답하기

> **A** What would you like to do this year? 올해 너는 무엇을 할 거니?
>
> **B** I'd like to travel to other countries. 나는 다른 나라들을 여행하고 싶어.

- 상대방이 바라는 것에 대해 물을 때는 '~하고 싶다'는 의미인 'would like to'를 써서 'What would you like to ~?'로 나타내거나 'What do you want to ~?' 등의 표현을 쓸 수 있다. 바라는 것은 to do, to drink, to eat 등의 to부정사 형태로 쓴다. 이에 답할 때는 'I'd like to ~.', 'I want to ~.' 등의 표현 또는 'I am going to ~'나 'I'm looking forward to -ing'을 쓸 수 있다.

- 상대방이 무엇을 하고 싶은지 바라는 것을 물어볼 때, 실현 가능성이 낮은 경우 'I wish I could ~'라고 대답할 수 있다.

바람 묻기

- What would you like to do? 너는 무엇을 하고 싶으니?
- What do you want to eat? 너는 무엇을 먹기를 원하니?
- What are you going to do? 너는 무엇을 할 거니?

바람 · 소망을 나타내는 여러 표현

- I'm willing to V (기꺼이) …하겠다
- I can't wait to V …하고 싶어 기다릴 수 없다
- I am dying to V …하고 싶어서 죽겠다
- I am eager to V …하고 싶어 하다

- My wish is to V …이 내 바람이다
- I look forward to V-ing …하기를 기대하다
- I hope that … …이기를 바라다

핵심 Check

1. 다음 우리말과 일치하도록 빈칸에 알맞은 말을 쓰시오.

   A: _____ would you _____ to do this year? (올해 무엇을 하고 싶니?)

   B: I would like to learn a new language. (나는 새로운 언어를 배우고 싶어.)

2. 다음 대화의 순서를 바르게 배열하시오.

   B: What are you doing?

   (A) That's nice. What would you like to do this year?

   (B) Well, first of all, I'd like to spend time volunteering with my friends during summer vacation.

   (C) I'm writing a list of things that I want to do this year.

   ➡ _____

2 만족이나 불만족에 관해 묻기

• **How do you like hiking?** 하이킹은 마음에 드니?

■ 'How do you like ~?'는 '~은 어떻습니까?' '~는 마음에 드나요?'의 의미로 상대방이 어떤 대상에 만족하는지 혹은 불만족하는지를 물어보는 표현이다. 'How do you like ~?'는 '(음식 등을) 어떻게 해드릴까요?'의 의미를 나타내기도 한다.

■ 'How do you like ~?'에 대하여 대답할 때는 만족하는지 아닌지를 직접적으로 나타내어 'It is great.', 'It is nice.', 'It wasn't bad.' 등으로 대답하거나 'It isn't easy.' 'It isn't interesting.' 등으로 대답한다.

■ 만족이나 불만족에 대하여 물을 때는 'Are you satisfied with ~?' 또는 'Are you happy with ~?'를 사용하여 '~에 만족하니?'라고 물어보기도 한다. 'Do you like ~?'와 'Is this the one that you want(ed)?'와 같은 표현도 만족이나 불만족을 물어보는 표현이다.

만족이나 불만족에 관해 묻기

• How do you like it? 그것이 마음에 드니?

• Are you satisfied with it? 그것이 만족스럽니?
  = Are you happy with it?

• Do you like it? 너는 그것을 좋아하니?

• Is this what you wanted? 이것이 네가 원한 것이니?
  = Is this the one that you wanted?

만족이나 불만족에 대한 대답

• It is great. = It is nice. 그것은 좋다.

• It wasn't bad. 그것은 나쁘지 않았어.

핵심 Check

3. 다음 대화의 순서가 바르게 배열된 것을 고르시오.

B: Hey, Suji! What are you holding?

G: Hi, Ben. It's a skateboard. I'm going skateboarding.

B: Wow! I didn't know that you could skateboard. How did you learn to skateboard?

(A) It's really fun! It helps me make new friends, too.

(B) I joined a local skateboarding club last month.

(C) I see. So how do you like it?

B: How?

G: I go skateboarding with other members of the club, and we share tips with one another.

① (A) – (C) – (B)　　　② (B) – (A) – (C)　　　③ (B) – (C) – (A)
④ (C) – (A) – (B)　　　⑤ (C) – (B) – (A)

Listen & Talk 1 C

B: What are you doing?

G: I'm writing a list of things ❶that I want to do this year.

B: That's nice. ❷What would you like to do this year?

G: Well, first of all, I'd like to ❸spend time volunteering with my friends during summer vacation.

B: That sounds great.

G: ❹What about you? What would you like to do this year?

B: I'm thinking of ❺taking a swimming class.

G: That's really cool.

B: 너는 무엇을 하고 있니?
G: 올해 하고 싶은 일의 목록을 작성하고 있는 중이야.
B: 멋있다. 너는 올해 무엇을 하기를 원하니?
G: 음, 우선 여름 방학 동안 친구들과 자원봉사를 하면서 시간을 보내고 싶어.
B: 그거 좋겠다.
G: 너는 어떠니? 너는 올해 무엇을 하고 싶어?
B: 나는 수영 수업 받는 것을 생각하고 있어.
G: 그거 정말 멋있구나.

❶ that은 주격 관계대명사로 선행사는 a list of things이다.
❷ 'What would you like to do this year?'는 상대방에게 바람이 무엇인지 물어보는 말이다.
❸ 'spend 시간 -ing'는 '~하면서 시간을 보내다'의 의미이다.
❹ 'What about you?'는 '너는 어떠니?'의 의미로 상대방의 의견을 묻고 있다.
❺ 'take a class'는 '수업을 듣다'의 의미이다.

Check(√) True or False

(1) The girl would like to spend time volunteering this winter.　　T ☐ F ☐

(2) The boy wants to take a swimming class this year.　　T ☐ F ☐

Listen & Talk 2 B

B: Hey, Suji! What are you holding?

G: Hi, Ben. It's a skateboard. I'm going skateboarding.

B: Wow! I didn't know ❶that you could skateboard. How did you learn to skateboard?

G: I joined a local skateboarding club last month.

B: I see. So ❷how do you like it?

G: It's really fun! It ❸helps me make new friends, too.

B: How?

G: I go skateboarding with other members of the club, and we share tips with one another.

B: 안녕, 수지야! 들고 있는 것이 뭐니?
G: 안녕, Ben. 그것은 스케이트보드야. 나는 스케이트보드를 타러 가는 중이야.
B: 와우! 네가 스케이트보드를 탈줄 아는지 몰랐어. 스케이트보드는 어떻게 배웠니?
G: 지난달에 지역 스케이트보드 클럽에 가입했어.
B: 알겠다. 너는 그것이 마음에 드니?
G: 정말로 좋아! 그것은 또한 새로운 친구를 사귀도록 도와줘.
B: 어떻게?
G: 나는 클럽의 다른 회원들과 스케이트보드를 타러 가는데, 우리는 서로 방법을 공유해.

❶ that은 동사 know의 목적어가 되는 명사절을 유도하는 접속사이다.
❷ 'how do you like it?'은 만족하는지 여부를 묻는 말로 '그것이 마음에 드니?'의 의미이다.
❸ 동사 help는 목적격보어로 to부정사 또는 원형부정사를 쓴다.

Check(√) True or False

(3) Suji is satisfied with going skateboarding.　　T ☐ F ☐

(4) Ben joined a local skateboarding club last month.　　T ☐ F ☐

(5) Going skateboarding helps Ben make new friends.　　T ☐ F ☐

Listen & Talk 1 B

G: ❶What would you like to do this year?

B: I'd like to learn the guitar. I listened to the song "Cavatina," and I ❷was struck by the sound of the guitar.

G: That's great. ❸Where are you going to learn it?

B: My friend Jinsu is a very good guitar player. I'll ❹ask him to teach me.

❶ 상대방에게 하고 싶어하는 것이 무엇인지 물어보는 표현이다.

❷ be struck by = ~에 감동을 받다

❸ 'Where are you going to learn it?'은 현재진행형을 사용하여 미래의 계획을 묻는 질문이다.

❹ 'ask+목적어+to부정사'로 '~에게 …하도록 요청하다'의 의미이다

Listen & Talk 2 C

G: Did you make this shelf ❶yourself? It's amazing!

B: Thanks. I started making furniture last year.

G: Cool! ❷How do you like it?

B: It was hard at first, but now I love it. I feel so confident after I finish making something.

G: That's great. I think you're really good at it.

B: Thanks. I guess I found a new talent. I think ❸it's good to try new things.

G: Exactly. ❹Having new experiences lets us find new talents.

❶ yourself는 강조 용법의 재귀대명사이다.

❷ '그것이 마음에 드니?'의 의미로 상대방이 만족하는지를 묻고 있다.

❸ 가주어 it, 진주어 to부정사의 구문이다.

❹ 동명사가 주어로 쓰였다.

Listen & Talk 2 D

A: I ❶ran a race last year.

B: How did you like it?

A: I liked it a lot. It helped me ❷build confidence.

❶ run a race = 경주하다, 달리기하다

❷ 동사 help의 목적격보어로 쓰인 원형부정사이다.

Presentation Time Step 1

A: Can you tell me about ❶one of your meaningful experiences?

B: I cooked dinner for my family last Sunday.

A: How did you like it?

B: It was not easy, but I learned ❷that I could ❸make people happy with my cooking.

❶ one of the/소유격+복수명사 = ~ 중의 하나

❷ that은 동사 learned의 목적어 역할을 하는 명사절을 유도하는 접속사이다.

❸ 'make+목적어+목적격보어(형용사)'의 형태로 5형식 구문이다.

Presentation Time Step 3

Our group ❶recommends cooking dinner for your family. It is a meaningful experience ❷because you will learn that cooking for others can make them ❸happy. After this experience, ❹you will feel great.

❶ recommends의 목적어로 동명사가 쓰였다.

❷ because+주어+동사 cf. because of+명사(구)

❸ happy는 목적격보어로 쓰인 형용사이다.

❹ 동사 feel의 보어로 형용사 great를 썼다.

Do It Yourself A

B: My band ❶performed at the school festival yesterday.

G: Cool. ❷How did you like that?

B: It wasn't bad, but I made some mistakes.

G: It's okay. ❸I'm sure you sounded fine.

B: Thanks for ❹saying so. It was my first time playing the drums in front of so many people.

G: How did you feel about that?

B: I was very nervous, but I felt great, too!

G: That's awesome. ❺I'm so proud of you.

❶ perform = 공연하다, 연주하다

❷ '그것이 마음에 들었니?'의 의미로 상대방이 만족하는지 물어보는 표현이다.

❸ 'I'm sure' 뒤에는 접속사 that이 생략되었다.

❹ saying은 전치사의 목적어로 쓰인 동명사이다.

❺ be proud of ~ = ~을 자랑스러워하다. = pride oneself on ~

● 다음 우리말과 일치하도록 빈칸에 알맞은 말을 쓰시오.

Listen & Talk 1 B

G: What _____ you _____ to do this year?

B: I'd _____ to _____ the guitar. I _____ to the song "Cavatina," and I _____ _____ by the _____ of the guitar.

G: That's great. _____ are you _____ to learn it?

B: My friend Jinsu is a very _____ guitar _____. I'll _____ him to teach me.

Listen & Talk 1 C

B: _____ are you _____?

G: I'm _____ a list of _____ _____ I want to _____ this year.

B: That's nice. _____ would you _____ to do this year?

G: Well, _____ of all, I'd _____ to _____ time _____ with my friends _____ summer vacation.

B: That _____ great.

G: _____ _____ you? _____ would you _____ to do this year?

B: I'm _____ of _____ a swimming _____.

G: That's really _____.

Listen & Talk 2 B

B: Hey, Suji! _____ are you _____?

G: Hi, Ben. It's a _____. I'm going _____.

B: Wow! I didn't _____ _____ you could skateboard. _____ did you _____ to _____?

G: I _____ a _____ skateboarding club _____ _____.

B: I _____. So _____ do you _____ it?

G: It's _____ fun! It _____ me _____ new friends, too.

B: How?

G: I _____ _____ with other _____ of the club, and we _____ _____ with one another.

Listen & Talk 2 C

G: Did you _____ this _____ _____? It's _____!
B: Thanks. I _____ _____ _____ last year.
G: Cool! _____ do you _____ it?
B: It was _____ at first, but now I _____ it. I _____ so _____ after I finish _____ something.
G: That's _____. I think you're _____ _____ _____ it.
B: Thanks. I _____ I _____ a new _____. I think it's _____ to _____ new things.
G: _____. _____ new _____ lets us _____ new talents.

Listen & Talk 2 D

A: I _____ a _____ last year.
B: _____ did you _____ it?
A: I _____ it a lot. It _____ me build _____.

Presentation Time Step 1

A: Can you _____ me about _____ of your _____ experiences?
B: I _____ dinner _____ my family last Sunday.
A: _____ did you _____ it?
B: It was _____ _____, but I learned _____ I could _____ people _____ with my _____.

Presentation Time Step 3

Our group _____ _____ dinner for your family. It is a _____ _____ _____ you will learn that _____ for _____ can _____ them happy. After this _____, you will _____ great.

Do It Yourself A

B: My band _____ at the school _____ yesterday.
G: Cool. _____ did you _____ that?
B: It _____ _____, but I _____ some _____.
G: It's okay. I'm sure you _____ _____.
B: Thanks _____ _____ so. It was my first time _____ the drums in _____ of so many people.
G: How did you _____ about that?
B: I was very _____, but I _____ great, too!
G: That's _____. I'm _____ _____ of you.

해석

G: 그 책꽂이를 직접 만들었니? 멋있다!
B: 고마워. 나는 작년에 가구 만들기를 시작했어.
G: 멋있어! 그것이 마음에 드니?
B: 처음에는 어려웠어. 그러나 지금 나는 그것을 아주 좋아해. 무엇인가를 만들고 나면 매우 자신감을 느껴.
G: 좋겠다. 나는 네가 그것을 정말 잘한다고 생각해.
B: 고마워. 나는 새로운 재능을 발견했다고 생각해. 새로운 것을 시도하는 것은 좋다고 생각해.
G: 그렇지. 새로운 경험을 하는 것이 우리에게 새로운 재능을 발견하도록 해.

A: 나는 작년에 달리기를 했어.
B: 그것이 마음에 들었니?
A: 굉장히 좋았어. 그것이 자신감을 가지도록 도와주었어.

A: 너에게 의미 있던 경험 중 하나를 말해주겠니?
B: 나는 지난 일요일에 가족을 위하여 저녁을 요리했어.
A: 그것이 마음에 들었니?
B: 그것은 쉽지 않았어. 하지만 나는 내가 요리한 것을 가지고 사람을 행복하게 만들 수 있다는 것을 배웠어.

우리 모둠은 여러분의 가족을 위하여 저녁을 요리할 것을 추천합니다. 그것은 여러분이 다른 사람을 위하여 요리하는 것이 그들을 행복하게 만들 수 있다는 것을 배울 것이기 때문에 의미 있는 경험입니다. 이 경험 이후에 여러분은 기분 좋게 느낄 것입니다.

B: 우리 밴드가 어제 학교 축제에서 연주를 했어.
G: 멋있네. 너는 그것이 마음에 들었니?
B: 나쁘지 않았어. 하지만 내가 몇 가지 실수를 저질렀어.
G: 괜찮아. 네 연주는 확실히 좋았어.
B: 그렇게 말해주니 고마워. 그것이 그토록 많은 사람들 앞에서 처음으로 드럼을 연주한 것이었어.
G: 그것에 대하여 어떻게 느꼈니?
B: 나는 매우 불안했어. 그러나 또한 기분 좋기도 했어.
G: 훌륭하구나. 나는 네가 정말 자랑스러워.

01 다음 대화의 밑줄 친 부분이 의도하는 것을 고르시오.

> **B:** We are finally on top of the mountain! <u>How do you like hiking?</u>
>
> **G:** It isn't easy at all, but now I understand why not giving up is so important.

① 계획 묻기   ② 초대하기

③ 취미 묻기   ④ 하고 싶은 일 권유하기

⑤ 만족이나 불만족에 대해 묻기

[02~03] 다음 대화를 읽고 물음에 답하시오.

> **G:** What would you like   __(A)__   this year?
>
> **B:** I'd like to learn the quitar. I listened to the song "Cavatina," and I was (B)<u>strike</u> by the sound of the guitar.
>
> **G:** That's great. Where are you going to learn it?
>
> **B:** My friend Jinsu is a very good guitar player. I'll ask him to teach me.

02 위 대화의 빈칸 (A)에 알맞은 것은?

① to do   ② do

③ doing   ④ for doing

⑤ to doing

03 위 대화의 밑줄 친 (B)를 알맞은 형으로 고치시오.

➡ _____

04 다음 대화의 문맥상 또는 어법상 어색한 것을 찾아 고치시오.

> **A:** I took care of my friend's pet.
>
> **B:** What did you like it?
>
> **A:** I liked it a lot. It helped me develop responsibility.

_____ ➡ _____

[01~03] 다음 대화를 읽고 물음에 답하시오.

Lina: Can you tell me about one of your meaningful experiences?

Bill: I cooked dinner for my family last Sunday.

Lina: _____ (A)

Bill: It was not easy, but (B)나는 나의 요리를 가지고 사람들을 행복하게 만들 수 있다는 것을 알게 되었어. (that / I / I / happy / people / learned / could make / with my cooking).

01 빈칸 (A)에 들어가기에 적절하지 <u>않은</u> 것은?

① Were you satisfied with it?

② How did you like it?

③ Do you think it tasted good?

④ Did you like cooking food for your family?

⑤ Were you happy with the experience?

02 주어진 어구를 배열하여 (B)의 밑줄 친 우리말을 영어로 옮길 때 5번째 오는 단어는?

① that ② could ③ make

④ people ⑤ happy

03 위 대화를 읽고 대답할 수 <u>없는</u> 질문은?

① What was Bill's meaningful experience?

② When did Bill cook dinner for his family?

③ How did Bill like his experience?

④ What did Bill learn from his experience?

⑤ Why did Lina ask Bill about meaningful experience?

[04~05] 다음 대화를 읽고 물음에 답하시오.

B: Hey, Suji! What are you ___(A)___ ?

G: Hi, Ben. It's a skateboard. I'm going skateboarding.

B: Wow! I didn't know that you could skateboard. How did you learn to skateboard?

G: I joined a local skateboarding club last month.

B: I see. So how do you like it?

G: It's really fun! It helps me make new friends, too.

B: How?

G: I go skateboarding with other members of the club, and we share tips with one another.

04 빈칸 (A)에 들어갈 가장 알맞은 말을 고르시오.

① looking at ② holding

③ going ④ reading

⑤ driving

05 위 대화의 내용과 일치하는 것은?

① Ben is learning skateboarding.

② Suji learned skateboarding by video.

③ Suji will go skateboarding with Ben.

④ Suji and Bed share tips with each other.

⑤ Ben asks Suji how she learned skateboarding.

06 다음 글의 내용과 일치하지 <u>않는</u> 것은?

Today was my school festival! My band was okay, but I made some mistakes. It was my first time playing the drums in front of so many people! I was very nervous but I felt great, too!

① The writer made some mistakes.
② The writer felt good about his or her band.
③ The writer played the guitar.
④ There were many people at the festival.
⑤ The writer played the drums for the first time in front of so many people.

[07~09] 다음 대화를 읽고 물음에 답하시오.

> B: My band performed at the school festival yesterday.
> G: Cool. How did you like that?
> B: It wasn't bad, but I made some mistakes.
> G: It's okay. I'm sure you sounded ___(A)___ .
> B: Thanks for saying so. It was my first time playing the drums in front of so many people.
> G: How did you feel about that?
> B: I was very nervous, but I felt great, too!
> G: That's awesome. (B)나는 네가 너무 자랑스러워. (so)

07 빈칸 (A)에 들어가기에 가장 적절한 것은?

① terrible　　② fine　　③ cold
④ slow　　⑤ loud

서답형

08 밑줄 친 (B)를 주어진 단어를 써서 영어로 쓰시오.

➡ _____

09 다음 중 위 대화를 읽고 대답할 수 없는 질문은?

① Is the boy a member of the school band?
② Did the girl like the performance?
③ How did the boy feel after the performance?
④ How many times did the boy play the drums in front of many people?
⑤ How many mistakes did the boy make at the festival?

10 다음 빈칸 ⓐ~ⓔ에 들어갈 대화로 어색한 것은?

> B: _____ⓐ_____
> G: I'm writing a list of things that I want to do this year.
> B: That's nice. _____ⓑ_____
> G: Well, first of all, I'd like to spend time volunteering with my friends during summer vacation.
> B: _____ⓒ_____
> G: _____ⓓ_____ What would you like to do this year?
> B: I'm thinking of taking a swimming class.
> G: _____ⓔ_____

① ⓐ What are you doing?
② ⓑ What would you like to do this year?
③ ⓒ That sounds great.
④ ⓓ What about her?
⑤ ⓔ That's really cool.

11 다음 대화의 흐름상 어색한 문장은?

> G: Did you make this shelf yourself? It's amazing!
> B: Thanks. ⓐI started making furniture last year.
> G: Cool! ⓑHow do you like it?
> B: It was hard at first, but now I love it. I feel so confident after I finish making something.
> G: ⓒThat's too bad. I think you're really good at it.
> B: Thanks. ⓓI guess I found a new talent. I think it's good to try new things.
> G: Exactly. ⓔHaving new experiences lets us find new talents.

① ⓐ　② ⓑ　③ ⓒ　④ ⓓ　⑤ ⓔ

[01~03] 다음 대화를 읽고 물음에 답하시오.

B: Hey, Suji! What are you holding?

G: Hi, Ben. It's a skateboard. I'm going skateboarding.

B: Wow! I didn't know that you could skateboard. (A) did you learn to skateboard?

G: I joined a local skateboarding club last month.

B: I see. (B)So how do you like it?

G: It's really fun! (C)그것은 또한 새로운 친구를 사귀도록 나에게 도움을 줘. [helps / new friends / too]

B: How?

G: I go skateboarding with other members of the club, and we share tips with one another.

01 빈칸 (A)에 들어갈 의문사를 쓰시오.

➡ _____

02 밑줄 친 (B)와 바꿔 쓸 수 있는 말을 완성하기 위하여 빈칸에 적절한 말을 쓰시오. (주어진 철자로 시작)

➡ So are you s_____ with it?

03 밑줄 친 (C)의 우리말을 영작하시오. (주어진 단어를 반드시 포함)

➡ _____

[04~05] 다음 대화를 읽고 물음에 답하시오.

G: Did you make this shelf yourself? It's amazing!

B: Thanks. I started making furniture last year.

G: Cool! How do you like it?

B: It was hard at first, but now I love it. 나는 무엇인가를 만들고 난 후에 매우 자신감을 느낀다. [so, confident, make, finish, something]

G: That's great. I think you're really good at it.

B: Thanks. I guess I found a new talent. I think it's good to try new things.

G: Exactly. Having new experiences let us find new talents.

04 밑줄 친 우리말을 "I"로 시작하는 영어 문장으로 옮겨 쓰시오. (주어진 단어 포함 및 필요하면 어형 변화)

➡ I _____.

05 위 대화의 문맥상 또는 어법상 어색한 것을 찾아 고치시오.

_____

➡ _____

06 다음 대화의 흐름상 어색한 문장을 찾아 바로잡아 쓰시오.

B: What are you doing?

G: I'm writing a list of things that I want to do this year.

B: That's nice. How would you like to do this year?

G: Well, first of all, I'd like to spend time volunteering with my friends during summer vacation.

B: That sounds great.

G: What about you? What would you like to do this year?

B: I'm thinking of taking a swimming class.

G: That's really cool.

➡ _____

Grammar

① 현재완료진행형

> • I **have been writing** my shopping lists in Spanish!
> 제가 사야 할 목록을 스페인어로 적어 오고 있어요!
>
> • My brother **has been studying** Spanish since last year.
> 내 남동생은 지난해부터 스페인어를 공부해 오고 있다.

- 현재완료진행형은 'have[has] been+동사원형-ing'의 형태로 보통 for(~ 동안)나 since(~ 이래로)와 함께 쓰여 '~ 이래로[~ 동안] …해 오고 있다'라고 해석한다.

  • He **has been waiting** for her for two hours. 그는 두 시간 동안 그녀를 기다리고 있다.

- 현재완료진행형은 어떤 상태나 행위가 과거 어느 때부터 시작되어 현재까지 계속 진행되고 있음을 나타내거나 현재까지 계속적으로 반복되고 있는 것을 나타낸다.

  • Imelda **has been cleaning** her house for 2 hours. Imelda는 두 시간 동안 그녀의 집을 청소하고 있다.

- 현재완료진행형에서 진행형이 가능한 동사는 현재완료진행형으로 동작의 계속을 표현하고, 진행형으로 쓸 수 없는 동사(have(소유), belong, know, like, hate 등)는 현재완료형으로 상태의 계속을 표현한다. 즉, 현재완료진행은 '상태'가 아닌 '동작'만을 나타낸다.

  • It **has been raining** since yesterday. 어제부터 계속 비가 내리고 있다.: 동작의 계속

  • He **has had** poor crops this year. 그는 올해 적은 농작물을 수확했다.: 상태의 계속

- **현재완료 / 현재완료진행형**

  현재완료는 동작의 결과에 초점을 맞춘다고 생각할 수 있지만, 현재완료진행형은 계속되고 있는 동작 그 자체에 초점을 맞춘다고 생각할 수 있다.

  • She **has done** the dishes. 그녀는 설거지를 했다. → 결과에 초점

  • She **has been doing** the dishes. 그녀는 설거지를 하고 있다. → 동작에 초점

핵심 Check

1. 주어진 어휘를 빈칸에 어법에 맞게 쓰시오.

(1) I have been _____ French for four hours. (study)

(2) Andy has _____ playing soccer since he was eight. (like)

(3) They have been _____ Christmas since 2016. (celebrate)

---

② 관계대명사 what

- Find **what** keeps you motivated. 당신에게 계속 동기 부여가 되는 것을 찾아라.
- This book is **what** I wanted to buy. 이 책은 내가 사고자 원했던 것이다.

■ 관계대명사 what은 다른 관계대명사와 다르게 선행사를 포함하는 관계대명사로 '~하는 것'으로 해석하며, the thing(s) which[that]의 의미이다.

■ 관계대명사 what이 이끄는 절은 명사절로 문장에서 주어, 보어, 목적어의 역할을 한다.

(1) 주어 역할

- **What** you need is something to eat. 당신한테는 먹을 것이 필요해요.

(2) 보어 역할

- This is **what** they said. 이것이 그들이 말한 것이다.

(3) 목적어 역할

- If I do not understand **what** he says, I always ask him.
  난 그가 하는 말이 이해가 안 될 때는 언제나 그에게 물어본다. (동사의 목적어)
- Listen to **what** he says on the matter. 그 일에 대해 그가 하는 말을 잘 들어라. (전치사의 목적어)

■ **관계대명사 what의 관용적인 표현**

- They experience **what is called** jet lag. 그들은 시차로 인한 피로라고 불리는 것을 경험합니다.
- I respect him, not for **what he has**, but for **what he is**.
  내가 그를 존경하는 것은 그의 재산 때문이 아니라 그의 인격 때문이다.
- **What's worse**, I have a muscle pain. 설상가상으로, 나는 근육통을 겪고 있어.

핵심 Check

2. 다음 빈칸에 들어갈 알맞은 말을 쓰시오.

(1) Michelle은 그녀가 하고 있는 것을 정말 좋아합니다.

➡ Michelle loves _____ she is doing.

(2) 내가 해줄 수 있는 건 이 정도야.

➡ This is _____ I could do for you.

(3) 그녀의 말은 완전히 허튼 소리야.

➡ _____ she says is pure nonsense.

01 다음 두 문장이 같은 의미가 되도록 할 때 빈칸에 알맞은 것은?

> These are the things which she bought.
> = These are _____ she bought.

① how   ② which   ③ who
④ that   ⑤ what

02 다음 괄호 안에서 알맞은 말을 고르시오.

(1) He has been (waiting / waited) for her for an hour.

(2) I (am living / have been living) in Seoul for 10 years.

(3) The book is (what / that) she bought yesterday.

(4) (What / That) he wants to do is to play the guitar.

03 다음 두 문장을 한 문장으로 바꾸어 쓸 때 알맞게 표현한 것을 고르시오.

> • It started snowing the day before yesterday.
> • It is still snowing.

① It is snowing now.

② It snowed two days ago.

③ It has been snowing for three days.

④ It was snowing the day before yesterday.

⑤ It will be snowing tomorrow.

04 다음 우리말에 맞게 주어진 어휘를 바르게 배열하시오.

(1) 네가 어젯밤에 한 것을 내게 말해 줘.

    (you, me, tell, did, night, what, last)

    ➡ _____

(2) 내가 어제 네게 말했던 것을 기억해라.

    (I, you, yesterday, told, remember, what)

    ➡ _____

(3) 요즘은 허리가 영 시원찮다.

    (me, my, back, bothering, been, lately, has)

    ➡ _____

 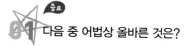
01 다음 중 어법상 올바른 것은?

① He has been planting apple trees for 2010.
② I've been looked for this book for an hour.
③ Megan has been write letters all day long.
④ It has been raining heavily for more than three hours.
⑤ He has been reading the book since about two hours.

02 다음 중 어법상 어색한 것은?

① What Jumi wants to do after school is to go shopping with her friends.
② It made me think what I liked.
③ Do you understand that he says?
④ What I want is something cold to drink.
⑤ What is the thing that she brought to the party?

03 다음 빈칸에 알맞은 말이 바르게 짝지어진 것은?

• She _____ ballet since she was eight.
• This brush is _____ Kate bought yesterday.

① learns – which
② learned – that
③ is learning – what
④ has learned – that
⑤ has been learning – what

04 다음 괄호 안에서 알맞은 말을 고르시오.

(1) How long have you (wear / been wearing) this dress?
(2) Mary has been teaching English (since / for) two years.
(3) He has been practicing the violin (since / for) he was a little boy.
(4) The restaurant didn't sell (that / what) I wanted to eat.
(5) He lost all (that / what) he owned.

05 다음 대화의 빈칸에 들어갈 말로 알맞은 것은?

M: What are you looking for there?
W: _____ I'm looking for is my smart phone.

① What   ② That
③ This   ④ Which
⑤ It

06 다음 문장의 빈칸에 들어갈 알맞은 것은?

My wife has been studying Chinese _____ five years.

① since   ② for
③ at   ④ during
⑤ with

07 밑줄 친 부분의 쓰임이 올바른 것은?

① I have been studying Chinese last year.
② They have been knowing her for a long time.
③ We have been meeting them 5 years ago.
④ It has been raining since last Friday.
⑤ Amy have been reading the book for an hour.

서답형

08 다음 문장에서 어법상 틀린 부분을 찾아 바르게 고쳐 쓰시오.

Jamie's uncle is that is called a walking dictionary.

_____ ➡ _____

서답형

09 주어진 어휘를 이용하여 다음 우리말을 영작하시오.

가격이 몇 달째 꾸준히 오르고 있다. (7단어)
(months, prices, increase, steadily, for)

➡ _____

10 다음 주어진 문장의 밑줄 친 what과 같은 용법으로 쓰인 것을 모두 고르시오.

What I want to experience in Andong is to try Andong-jjimdak.

① I didn't know what to do next.
② Sophie showed me what was in her backpack.
③ What he said on the phone made his mom upset.
④ What are you talking about?
⑤ You don't know what it means to me.

11 다음 우리말에 맞게 빈칸에 알맞은 것을 고르시오.

하루 종일 계속 비가 오고 있다.
→ It _____ all day long.

① rained   ② rains
③ is raining   ④ has been raining
⑤ has been rained

12 다음 빈칸에 들어갈 말이 나머지와 다른 하나는?

① I disagree with _____ you say about that matter.
② I think _____ you say is logically wrong.
③ Could you name the person _____ you respect most?
④ She was very passionate about _____ she was doing.
⑤ You'd better just ignore _____ she says.

13 다음 두 문장을 한 문장으로 바르게 연결한 것은?

• Elena told me that she wanted to buy the things.
• They looked nice but cheap.

① Elena told me that she wanted to buy looked nice but cheap.
② Elena told me that she wanted to buy the things looked nice but cheap.
③ Elena told me that she wanted to buy which looked nice but cheap.
④ Elena told me that she wanted to buy that looked nice but cheap.
⑤ Elena told me that she wanted to buy what looked nice but cheap.

14 다음 우리말과 일치하도록 빈칸에 알맞은 단어로 묶은 것은?

> 저런 낡은 의자를 참고 사용해 온 것이 얼마나 오래됐니?
> → How long _____ you been _____ up with that old chair?

① had – putting
② had – put
③ have – putting
④ have – put
⑤ had – puts

15 다음 문장에서 어법상 <u>어색한</u> 것을 바르게 고쳐 다시 쓰시오.

(1) The man has been taken care of the children for a few years.

➡ _____

_____

(2) Melina has been teaching English at the school two years ago.

➡ _____

_____

(3) She has been reading a book for 3 p.m.

➡ _____

(4) Ron has been watching the play since two hours.

➡ _____

_____

(5) This is the movie what I want to see.

➡ _____

_____

(6) Let me look at which you took with your camera in Canada.

➡ _____

_____

16 다음 중 어법상 <u>어색한</u> 것을 고르시오. (2개)

① Rose has been having a stomachache yesterday.
② I have been taking flute lessons since March.
③ The baby has been crying for two hours.
④ I read the book what you bought the other day.
⑤ I am sure that that was not what was intended.

17 다음 우리말에 맞게 영작한 것을 <u>모두</u> 고르시오.

> 나는 네가 요전날 한 말을 이해할 수 없다.

① I can't understand that you said the other day.
② I can't understand what you said the other day.
③ I can't understand the things that you said the other day.
④ I can't understand the things what you said the other day.
⑤ I can't understand you said the other day.

18 다음 중 빈칸에 들어갈 말로 알맞은 것을 고르시오.

> _____ I am listening to now is classical music.

① When   ② Which
③ That   ④ Who
⑤ What

01 괄호 안의 단어 수대로 주어진 두 문장을 하나의 문장으로 쓰시오.

(1) • Oliver arrivéd at the bus stop at one o'clock to meet his friend.
• He is still waiting for his friend. (10 단어)

➡ _____

_____

(2) • James started doing yoga an hour ago.
• He is still doing it. (8 단어)

➡ _____

_____

(3) • I have taken tennis lessons over the last 5 years.
• I am still taking tennis lessons. (11 단어)

➡ _____

_____

02 다음 우리말에 맞게 주어진 어구를 바르게 배열하시오.

(1) 네가 무슨 짓을 하는지 내가 모를 줄 아는구나. (I, you, you're, don't, doing, know, think, what, that)

➡ _____

(2) 내가 가장 하고 싶은 일은 콘서트에 가는 거야. (I, a concert, most, do, want, go, is, what, to, to, to)

➡ _____

_____

(3) 그들은 그를 수년 동안 이탈리아인으로 생각해 왔다. (an Italian, they, him, years, thinking, been, have, as, for, of)

➡ _____

03 다음 그림을 보고, 주어진 어휘를 이용하여 빈칸을 알맞게 채우시오.

(1) _____ are some flowers. (what, want, receive, she)

(2) The Bible is _____ read. (I, want, what)

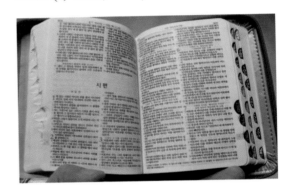

04 다음 〈보기〉에 주어진 단어를 이용하여 문맥에 맞게 문장을 완성하시오.

┤ 보기 ├
| since | for |

(1) I have been reading this book _____ three hours.

(2) Jolly has been living in Seoul _____ she was born.

05 주어진 두 문장을 what을 이용하여 하나의 문장으로 쓰시오.

(1) • Find the thing.
   • The thing keeps you motivated.
   ➡ _____

(2) • It made me think the thing.
   • I liked it.
   ➡ _____

(3) • You said the thing.
   • It made me surprised.
   ➡ _____

(4) • Something is done.
   • It cannot be undone.
   ➡ _____

06 다음 문장에서 어법상 <u>어색한</u> 것을 바르게 고치시오.

(1) How long have you been lived in Korea?

_____ ➡ _____

(2) Mr. McDonald has been working in the restaurant since 10 years.

_____ ➡ _____

(3) Ben has been reading a book for this morning.

_____ ➡ _____

(4) That can I do now is to build a strong house.

_____ ➡ _____

(5) Let me tell you that I saw last night.

_____ ➡ _____

(6) You're the only one what really understands me.

_____ ➡ _____

(7) That he did with his wealth was quite unique.

_____ ➡ _____

07 현재완료진행형을 사용하여, 주어진 두 문장을 한 문장으로 바꾸시오.

(1) • Harold is reading the book.
   • He started reading the book this morning.
   ➡ _____
   _____

(2) • Taehee started talking on the phone at one p.m.
   • She is still talking on the phone at 3 p.m.
   ➡ _____
   _____

08 다음 우리말을 괄호 안에 주어진 어휘를 이용하여 영작하시오.

(1) 그들은 4대째 계속 여기 살고 있다. (here, four generations, live, for, 8 단어)
   ➡ _____

(2) 과학자들은 토성의 고리를 연구해 오고 있다. (study, Saturn's rings, 6 단어)
   ➡ _____

(3) 그 영화는 3개월째 상영되고 있어요. (the movie, show, for, 8 단어)
   ➡ _____

(4) 일전에 한 약속을 잊지 마라. (forget, promise, the other day, 8 단어)
   ➡ _____
   _____

Learn a New Language, Find a New World

Why Do People Learn Foreign Languages?

Many students learn new languages because of school requirements.
because of+명사구

Many others learn them for fun. In any case, students everywhere
= new languages *어쨌든(= anyway. anyhow. at any rate)*

have found interesting ways to study new languages. Let's meet
현재완료 *형용사적 용법의 to부정사*

these students and listen to their ideas.
= students everywhere who have found interesting ways to study new languages

I Love Soccer!

I'm a big fan of a Spanish soccer team. I want to understand
명사적 용법의 to부정사

interviews with my favorite players. However, it's not easy because I
= to understand interviews with my favorite players *because+절*

don't know Spanish that well. How can I improve my Spanish?
지시부사(수량·정도를 나타내는 형용사·부사를 수식)

- Owen, 16

The best way to learn a new language is to practice it every day. I
형용사적 용법의 to부정사 *명사적 용법의 to부정사*

have changed the language of my phone to Spanish, and I have been
change A to B: A를 B로 바꾸다

writing my shopping lists in Spanish!
현재완료진행형(특정 행위가 과거의 어느 시점에 시작하여 현재까지도 계속 진행 중임을 나타냄.)

- Julie, 15

foreign 외국의, 타국의
requirement 필요 조건, (학교에서의) 필수 수업
case 경우, 상자
interview 인터뷰, 면접
improve 향상시키다, 나아지다
practice 연습하다

확인문제

● 다음 문장이 본문의 내용과 일치하면 T, 일치하지 <u>않으면</u> F를 쓰시오.

1 Many students learn new languages because of school requirements. ☐

2 Owen wants to have interviews with his favorite soccer players. ☐

3 Owen doesn't know Spanish well. ☐

4 Julie says the best way to learn a new language is to practice it with native speakers. ☐

5 Julie has changed the language of her phone to Spanish. ☐

6 Julie has been writing her homework lists in Spanish. ☐

What's most important is to become familiar with the language first. I
선행사를 포함한 관계대명사   명사적 용법의 to부정사

suggest watching Spanish movies often. It will help you get used to the
suggest는 목적어로 동명사를 취한다.   help+목적어+to부정사 혹은 원형부정사   get used to:
                                                                        ~에 익숙해지다.

sound of the language. If the people talk too fast, try watching Spanish
                                            try ~ing: (시험 삼아) ~해 보다

children's movies first.   - Inho, 14

Some words are used only in soccer, not in everyday life. Learn some
              수동태(사용된다)

soccer vocabulary and memorize it. Also, why don't you try writing a
                                        = soccer vocabulary   = how about trying?

review of a match in Spanish? It will help you improve your writing
                  스페인어로   help+목적어+원형부정사 혹은 to부정사

skills.   - Rohan, 16

No More Subtitles!

DREAM4 is back! I'm so excited to see my favorite Korean boy
                              부사적 용법의 to부정사(감정의 원인)

band perform. Their singing and their dancing are just perfect. I want
지각동사 see+목적어+원형부정사

to understand their songs without subtitles or translations though. Any
명사적 용법의 to부정사   (문장 끝이나 중간에서 단독으로) 그렇지만[하지만](부사)

tips?   - Marisa, 14

You should find friends who are interested in DREAM4 and start a
                        who는 주격 관계대명사로 선행사 friends를 수식

club. In my club, we motivate one another. We translate songs and sing
                              서로

together. Doing these things is fun and really improves our Korean!
          주어로 쓰인 동명사   are(×)

                                                            - Lori, 15

familiar 익숙한, 친숙한

get used to …에 익숙해지다

vocabulary 어휘

memorize 암기하다

review 후기, 검토

match 경기, 시합

skill 기능, 기술

subtitle 자막

perform 수행하다, 공연하다

perfect 완벽한, 완전한

translation 번역[통역](된 것), 번역문

though 그렇지만, (비록) …이긴 하지만

be interested in …에 관심[흥미]이 있다

motivate 동기를 부여하다

translate 번역[통역]하다, 옮기다

확인문제

● 다음 문장이 본문의 내용과 일치하면 T, 일치하지 않으면 F를 쓰시오.

1 Inho suggests watching Spanish movies often. ☐

2 Inho thinks watching Spanish children's movies isn't good. ☐

3 Rohan suggests learning some soccer vocabulary and memorizing it. ☐

4 Rohan also suggests reading a review of a match in Spanish. ☐

5 Marisa is so excited to see her favorite Korean boy band perform. ☐

6 Lori should find friends who are interested in DREAM4 and start a club. ☐

Follow DREAM4 on social media. They often post short messages

= The members of DREAM4

in Korean about how they are doing. They also post pictures with the

한국어로   간접의문문(의문사+주어+동사)   ~와 함께

messages, so you can understand the posts more easily.   - Aishah, 14

I recommend watching Korean dramas. I've been watching Korean

recommend는 목적어로 동명사를 취한다.   현재완료진행형

dramas for a year, and they're really interesting! You can use Korean

for+숫자(~ 동안)

subtitles for help with listening. It's also a good idea to print out the

가주어   진주어

subtitles and read them first.   - Brandon, 16

to print out과 (to) read가 등위접속사 and로 병렬 연결되어 있다.

What Works for You?

There are hundreds of good tips out there, but everyone has their

수백의

own way of learning. Find what keeps you motivated; then you will

동격의 전치사   선행사를 포함한 관계대명사   •   동기가 부여된

enjoy learning more. Remember, every language is hard at first, but a

enjoy는 목적어로 동명사를 취한다.   처음에는

new language can make your world much bigger!

비교급 강조(= even. still. far. a lot)

follow 따르다. (사회관계망 서비스 등에서) 팔로하다
social media 소셜 미디어
post (웹 사이트에 정보 · 사진을) 올리다
recommend 추천하다
print out (프린터로) 출력하다

📎 **확인문제**

● 다음 문장이 본문의 내용과 일치하면 T, 일치하지 <u>않으면</u> F를 쓰시오.

1   The members of DREAM4 often post short messages in Korean about how they are doing. ☐

2   The members of DREAM4 also post pictures with the messages in many foreign languages. ☐

3   Brandon recommends watching Korean dramas. ☐

4   Brandon has been watching Korean dramas for many years. ☐

5   The writer says every language is hard at first. ☐

6   The writer says a new language can make your world much more exciting. ☐

● 우리말을 참고하여 빈칸에 알맞은 말을 쓰시오.

1 Learn _____ _____ _____, Find a New World

2 Why Do People Learn _____ _____?

3 Many students learn new languages _____ _____ _____ _____.

4 Many others learn them _____ _____.

5 _____ _____ _____, students everywhere have found interesting ways to study new languages.

6 Let's meet these students and _____ _____ _____ _____.

7 I _____ Soccer!

8 I'm _____ _____ _____ of a Spanish soccer team.

9 I want to _____ _____ with my favorite players.

10 _____, it's not easy because I don't know _____ _____ _____.

11 How can I _____ _____ _____? - Owen, 16

12 The best way to learn a new language is _____ _____ _____ every day.

13 I _____ _____ _____ _____ of my phone to Spanish, and I _____ _____ _____ my shopping lists in Spanish! - Julie, 15

14 What's most important is to _____ _____ _____ the language first.

1 새로운 언어를 배우고, 새로운 세상을 찾아라

2 왜 사람들은 외국어를 배울까?

3 많은 학생들이 학교 필수 수업 이기 때문에 새로운 언어를 배운다.

4 다른 많은 이들은 재미를 위해 그것을 배운다.

5 어떤 경우에도, 모든 곳의 학생들은 새로운 언어를 공부하는 데 흥미로운 방법들을 찾아낸다.

6 이 학생들을 만나서 그들의 생각을 들어보자.

7 저는 축구를 정말 좋아해요!

8 전 스페인 축구 팀의 엄청난 팬 이랍니다.

9 저는 제가 정말 좋아하는 선수들의 인터뷰를 이해하고 싶어요.

10 그런데 스페인어를 그렇게 잘 알지 못하기 때문에 그것이 쉽지 않아요.

11 어떻게 하면 제가 스페인어 실력을 늘릴 수 있을까요? – 오언, 16세

12 새로운 언어를 배울 수 있는 가장 좋은 방법은 그 언어를 매일 연습하는 것이랍니다.

13 저는 제 휴대 전화의 설정을 스페인어로 바꿨고, 제가 사야 할 목록을 스페인어로 적어 오고 있어요! – 줄리, 15세

14 가장 중요한 것은 우선 그 언어와 친해지는 것이에요.

15 I _____ _____ Spanish movies often.

16 It will help you _____ _____ _____ the sound of the language.

17 If the people talk too fast, _____ _____ Spanish children's movies first. - Inho, 14

18 Some words _____ _____ only in soccer, not in everyday life.

19 Learn some _____ _____ and _____ it.

20 Also, _____ _____ _____ try writing a review of a match _____ _____?

21 It will help you _____ _____ _____ _____. - Rohan, 16

22 _____ _____ Subtitles!

23 DREAM4 _____ _____!

24 I'm _____ _____ to see my favorite Korean boy band perform.

25 Their singing and their dancing are _____ _____.

26 I want to understand their songs _____ _____ or _____ though.

27 _____ _____? - Marisa, 14

28 You should find friends who _____ _____ _____ DREAM4 and start a club.

29 In my club, we motivate _____ _____.

30 We _____ songs and _____ _____.

15 전 스페인 영화들을 자주 볼 것을 제안하는데요.

16 그것은 당신이 언어의 소리에 익숙해지도록 도울 거예요.

17 만약 사람들이 너무 빨리 말한다면, 어린이를 위한 스페인 영화들을 먼저 보는 것을 시도해 보세요. – 인호, 14세

18 어떤 단어들은 일상생활에서가 아니라 오직 축구에서만 쓰인답니다.

19 몇몇 축구 어휘들을 배우고 기억하세요.

20 또한, 스페인어로 경기에 대한 후기를 써 보는 건 어때요?

21 그것은 당신이 작문 실력을 향상하도록 도울 거예요. – 로한, 16세

22 더는 자막 없이!

23 DREAM4가 돌아왔어요!

24 저는 제가 정말 좋아하는 한국의 젊은 남성 밴드가 공연하는 것을 보는 게 너무 신이 나요.

25 그들의 노래와 춤은 정말 완벽하답니다.

26 그렇지만 자막이나 번역이 없이 그들의 노래를 이해하고 싶어요.

27 어떤 조언들이 있을까요? – 마리사, 14세

28 당신은 DREAM4에 관심이 있는 친구들을 찾아 모임을 시작해야 해요.

29 우리 모임에서 우리는 서로 동기를 부여한답니다.

30 우리는 함께 노래를 번역하고 노래해요.

31 _____ these things is fun and really _____ _____ _____! - Lori, 15

32 Follow DREAM4 _____ _____ _____.

33 They often _____ _____ _____ in Korean about how they are doing.

34 They also post pictures _____ _____ _____, so you can understand the posts _____ _____.- Aishah, 14

35 I _____ _____ Korean dramas.

36 _____ _____ _____ Korean dramas for a year, and they're really interesting!

37 You can use Korean subtitles _____ _____ _____ _____.

38 It's also a good idea to _____ _____ _____ _____ and read them first. - Brandon, 16

39 What _____ for You?

40 There are _____ _____ good tips out there, but everyone has _____ _____ _____ of learning.

41 Find _____ keeps you _____; then you will enjoy learning more.

42 Remember, every language is hard _____ _____, but a new language can make your world _____ _____!

31 이런 것들을 하는 것은 재미있고 정말로 우리의 한국어 실력을 향상해요! – 로리, 15세

32 소셜 미디어에서 DREAM4를 팔로하세요.

33 그들은 종종 자신들이 어떻게 지내는지에 대해 한국어로 짧은 메시지를 올려요.

34 그들은 또한 메시지와 함께 사진들을 올려서 당신은 더 쉽게 게시물을 이해할 수 있어요. – 아이샤, 14세

35 저는 한국 드라마들을 볼 것을 추천해요.

36 저는 1년 동안 한국 드라마들을 시청해 왔고, 그것들은 정말 재미있어요!

37 듣기에 도움이 되도록 한국어 자막을 사용할 수 있고요.

38 먼저 자막들을 출력해서 읽는 것도 좋은 생각이랍니다. – 브랜던, 16세

39 무엇이 당신에게 효과가 있는 걸까?

40 세상에는 수백 가지 좋은 조언들이 있지만, 모든 사람이 학습에 대한 그들만의 방법을 가지고 있다.

41 당신에게 계속 동기 부여가 되는 것을 찾아라. 그러면 당신은 학습을 더욱 즐길 것이다.

42 기억해라, 모든 언어는 처음에는 어렵지만, 새로운 언어가 당신의 세상을 더욱 넓혀줄 수 있다!

● 우리말을 참고하여 본문을 영작하시오.

1 ▶ 새로운 언어를 배우고, 새로운 세상을 찾아라

➡ _____

2 ▶ 왜 사람들은 외국어를 배울까?

➡ _____

3 ▶ 많은 학생들이 학교 필수 수업이기 때문에 새로운 언어를 배운다.

➡ _____

4 ▶ 다른 많은 이들은 재미를 위해 그것을 배운다.

➡ _____

5 ▶ 어떤 경우에도, 모든 곳의 학생들은 새로운 언어를 공부하는 데 흥미로운 방법들을 찾아낸다.

➡ _____

6 ▶ 이 학생들을 만나서 그들의 생각을 들어보자.

➡ _____

7 ▶ 저는 축구를 정말 좋아해요!

➡ _____

8 ▶ 전 스페인 축구 팀의 엄청난 팬이랍니다.

➡ _____

9 ▶ 저는 제가 정말 좋아하는 선수들의 인터뷰를 이해하고 싶어요.

➡ _____

10 ▶ 그런데 스페인어를 그렇게 잘 알지 못하기 때문에 그것이 쉽지 않아요.

➡ _____

11 ▶ 어떻게 하면 제가 스페인어 실력을 늘릴 수 있을까요? – 오언, 16세

➡ _____

12 ▶ 새로운 언어를 배울 수 있는 가장 좋은 방법은 그 언어를 매일 연습하는 것이랍니다.

➡ _____

13 ▶ 저는 제 휴대 전화의 설정을 스페인어로 바꿨고, 제가 사야 할 목록을 스페인어로 적어 오고 있어요!
– 줄리, 15세

➡ _____

_____

14 ▶ 가장 중요한 것은 우선 언어와 친해지는 것이에요.

➡ _____

15 전 스페인 영화들을 자주 볼 것을 제안하는데요.

➡ _____

16 그것은 당신이 언어의 소리에 익숙해지도록 도울 거예요.

➡ _____

17 만약 사람들이 너무 빨리 말한다면, 어린이를 위한 스페인 영화들을 먼저 보는 것을 시도해 보세요.
– 인호, 14세

➡ _____

18 어떤 단어들은 일상생활에서가 아니라 오직 축구에서만 쓰인답니다.

➡ _____

19 몇몇 축구 어휘들을 배우고 기억하세요.

➡ _____

20 또한, 스페인어로 경기에 대한 후기를 써 보는 건 어때요?

➡ _____

21 그것은 당신이 작문 실력을 향상하도록 도울 거예요. – 로한, 16세

➡ _____

22 더는 자막 없이!

➡ _____

23 DREAM4가 돌아왔어요!

➡ _____

24 저는 제가 정말 좋아하는 한국의 젊은 남성 밴드가 공연하는 것을 보는 게 너무 신이 나요.

➡ _____

25 그들의 노래와 춤은 정말 완벽하답니다.

➡ _____

26 그렇지만 자막이나 번역이 없이 그들의 노래를 이해하고 싶어요.

➡ _____

27 어떤 조언들이 있을까요? – 마리사, 14세

➡ _____

28 당신은 DREAM4에 관심이 있는 친구들을 찾아 모임을 시작해야 해요.

➡ _____

29 우리 모임에서 우리는 서로 동기를 부여한답니다.

➡ _____

30 우리는 함께 노래를 번역하고 노래해요.

➡ _____

31 이런 것들을 하는 것은 재미있고 정말로 우리의 한국어 실력을 향상해요! – 로리, 15세

➡ _____

32 소셜 미디어에서 DREAM4를 팔로하세요.

➡ _____

33 그들은 종종 자신들이 어떻게 지내는지에 대해 한국어로 짧은 메시지를 올려요.

➡ _____

34 그들은 또한 메시지와 함께 사진들을 올려서 당신은 더 쉽게 게시물을 이해할 수 있어요.

– 아이샤, 14세

➡ _____

_____

35 저는 한국 드라마들을 볼 것을 추천해요.

➡ _____

36 저는 1년 동안 한국 드라마들을 시청해 왔고, 그것들은 정말 재미있어요!

➡ _____

37 듣기에 도움이 되도록 한국어 자막을 사용할 수 있고요.

➡ _____

38 맨 먼저 자막들을 출력해서 읽는 것도 좋은 생각이랍니다. – 브랜던, 16세

➡ _____

39 무엇이 당신에게 효과가 있는 걸까?

➡ _____

40 세상에는 수백 가지 좋은 조언들이 있지만, 모든 사람이 학습에 대한 그들만의 방법을 가지고 있다.

➡ _____

41 당신에게 계속 동기 부여가 되는 것을 찾아라, 그러면 당신은 학습을 더욱 즐길 것이다.

➡ _____

42 기억해라, 모든 언어는 처음에는 어렵지만, 새로운 언어가 당신의 세상을 더욱 넓혀줄 수 있다!

➡ _____

[01~03] 다음 글을 읽고 물음에 답하시오.

_____ ⓐ _____ is most important is to become familiar with the language first. I suggest watching Spanish movies often. It will help you get used to the sound of the language. If the people talk too fast, try watching Spanish children's movies first.   - Inho, 14

Some words are used only in soccer, not in everyday life. Learn some soccer vocabulary and memorize it. Also, why don't you try writing a review of a match in Spanish? ⓑ그것은 당신이 작문 실력을 향상하도록 도울 거예요.
                                        - Rohan, 16

서답형

01 Fill in the blank ⓐ with a suitable word.

➡ _____

서답형

02 위 글의 밑줄 친 ⓑ의 우리말에 맞게 주어진 어휘를 이용하여 8단어로 영작하시오.

improve, writing skills

➡ _____

중요

03 위 글의 주제로 알맞은 것을 고르시오.

① how to become familiar with Spanish movies
② various ways of improving your Spanish
③ the useful way of watching Spanish children's movies
④ some words used only in sports
⑤ how to write a review of a match in Spanish

[04~06] 다음 글을 읽고 물음에 답하시오.

I Love Soccer!
I'm a big fan of a ①Spanish soccer team. I want to understand interviews with my favorite players. _____ ⓐ _____, it's not easy because I don't know ②Spanish that well. How can I improve my ③Spanish?   - Owen, 16

The best way to learn a new language is to practice it every day. I have changed the language of my phone to ④Spanish, and I ⓑhave been writing my shopping lists in ⑤ Spanish!
                                        - Julie, 15

중요

04 위 글의 빈칸 ⓐ에 들어갈 알맞은 말을 고르시오.

① Therefore   ② However
③ Besides   ④ In other words
⑤ For instance

05 밑줄 친 ①~⑤ 중에서 단어의 뜻이 나머지 넷과 다른 것은?

①   ②   ③   ④   ⑤

06 위 글의 밑줄 친 ⓑhave been writing과 현재완료의 용법이 같은 것을 모두 고르시오.

① He has watched the movie twice.
② She has been sick since last Friday.
③ I have just finished reading the book.
④ He has lived in Busan for 10 years.
⑤ Have you ever seen a lion?

[07~09] 다음 글을 읽고 물음에 답하시오.

> (A)[How / Why] Do People Learn Foreign Languages?
>
> Many students learn new languages (B) [because / because of] school requirements. Many others learn @them for fun. In any case, students everywhere have (C)[found / founded] interesting ways to study new languages. Let's meet these students and listen to their ideas.

서답형

07 위 글의 괄호 (A)~(C)에서 문맥이나 어법상 알맞은 낱말을 골라 쓰시오.

➡ (A) _____ (B) _____ (C) _____

서답형

08 위 글의 밑줄 친 @them이 가리키는 것을 본문에서 찾아 쓰시오.

➡ _____

중요

09 위 글의 뒤에 올 내용으로 가장 알맞은 것을 고르시오.

① 새로운 언어를 배우는 이유
② 학교 필수 수업에 해당하는 새로운 언어
③ 전 세계의 재미있는 언어의 종류
④ 새로운 언어를 공부하는 흥미로운 방법들
⑤ 전 세계 학생들이 선호하는 외국어

[10~13] 다음 글을 읽고 물음에 답하시오.

> Follow DREAM4 on social media. They often post short messages in Korean about @자신들이 어떻게 지내는지. They also post pictures with the messages, so you can understand the posts more easily.
>
> - Aishah, 14

> I recommend watching Korean dramas. I've been watching Korean dramas for a year, and they're really interesting! You can use Korean subtitles for help with listening. ⓑIt's also a good idea to print out the subtitles and read them first.
>
> - Brandon, 16

서답형

10 위 글의 밑줄 친 @의 우리말에 맞게 주어진 어휘를 알맞게 배열하시오.

> doing / are / they / how

➡ _____

11 위 글의 밑줄 친 ⓑIt과 문법적 쓰임이 같은 것을 고르시오.

① It is 2 miles from here to the airport.
② I make it a rule to get up early.
③ It's Jim who will marry Ann.
④ How's it going with you?
⑤ It's impossible to get there in time.

서답형

12 다음 문장에서 위 글의 내용과 다른 부분을 찾아서 고치시오.

> As the members of DREAM4 post comments with the messages, it is possible to understand the posts more easily.

_____ ➡ _____

서답형

13 다음 빈칸 (A)와 (B)에 알맞은 단어를 넣어 한국어를 배우기 위한 아이샤와 브랜던의 조언을 완성하시오.

> Aishah recommends (A)_____ DREAM4 on social media and Brandon recommends watching (B)_____ _____.

[14~15] 다음 글을 읽고 물음에 답하시오.

(A)What's most important is to become familiar with the language first. I suggest watching Spanish movies often. It will help you get used to the sound of the language. If the people talk too fast, try watching Spanish children's movies first.　　　　- Inho, 14

Some words 　(B)　 only in soccer, not in everyday life. Learn some soccer vocabulary and memorize it. Also, why don't you try writing a review of a match in Spanish? It will help you improve your writing skills.

- Rohan, 16

14 위 글의 밑줄 친 (A)What과 같은 의미로 쓰인 것을 모두 고르시오.

① What kind of music do you like?
② What a genius he is!
③ He will do what he can do for you.
④ I pointed to what looked like a bird.
⑤ What are you looking for?

서답형

15 위 글의 빈칸 (B)에 use를 알맞은 형태로 쓰시오.

➡ _____

[16~18] 다음 글을 읽고 물음에 답하시오.

ⓐ _____

DREAM4 is back! I'm so excited to see my favorite Korean boy band perform. Their singing and their dancing are just perfect. I want to understand their songs without subtitles or translations though. Any tips?

- Marisa, 14

You should find friends who are interested in DREAM4 and start a club. In my club, we motivate one another. We translate songs and sing together. ⓑDoing these things is fun and really improves our Korean!　　- Lori, 15

중요

16 위 글의 빈칸 ⓐ에 들어갈 제목으로 알맞은 것을 고르시오.

① DREAM4 Is My Favorite Band
② Do You Like Perfect Singing?
③ No More Subtitles!
④ How to Start a Club
⑤ The Easy Way to Master Korean

서답형

17 위 글의 밑줄 친 ⓑ를 다음과 같이 바꿔 쓸 때 빈칸에 들어갈 알맞은 말을 두 단어로 쓰시오.

➡ It is fun and really improves our Korean _____ _____ these things!

중요

18 Which question CANNOT be answered after reading the passage?

① Why is Marisa so excited?
② What's the name of Marisa's favorite Korean boy band?
③ Can Marisa understand her favorite Korean band's songs without subtitles or translations?
④ What does Lori recommend to Marisa?
⑤ How many members are there in Lori's club?

[19~22] 다음 글을 읽고 물음에 답하시오.

Many students learn new languages because of school requirements. Many others learn them for fun. ⓐIn any case, students everywhere have found interesting ways ⓑto study new languages. Let's meet these students and listen to their ideas.

19 위 글의 밑줄 친 ⓐIn any case와 바꿔 쓸 수 없는 말을 고르시오.

① Anyway
② Anyhow
③ By the way
④ At any rate
⑤ At all events

20 위 글의 밑줄 친 ⓑto study와 to부정사의 용법이 같은 것을 모두 고르시오.

① He went abroad to study new languages.
② It's time for you to study new languages.
③ She is clever enough to study new languages.
④ I decided to to study new languages.
⑤ We need the place to study new languages in.

중요

21 위 글의 제목으로 알맞은 것을 고르시오.

① How Do People Learn Foreign Languages?
② Many Kinds of Languages
③ The Difficulty of Learning Foreign Languages
④ Why Do People Learn Foreign Languages?
⑤ Wonderful Ways to Communicate with Foreigners

서답형

22 본문의 내용과 일치하도록 다음 빈칸 (A)와 (B)에 알맞은 단어를 쓰시오.

Many students learn new languages because of (A)_____ _____ or (B)_____ _____.

[23~25] 다음 글을 읽고 물음에 답하시오.

I Love Soccer!
I'm a big fan of a Spanish soccer team. I want to understand interviews with my favorite players. However, it's not easy because I don't know Spanish that well. How can I improve my Spanish?　- Owen, 16
The best way (A)to learn a new language is (B)to practice it every day. I have changed the language of my phone ⓐ Spanish, and I have been writing my shopping lists ⓑ Spanish!　- Julie, 15

23 위 글의 빈칸 ⓐ와 ⓑ에 들어갈 전치사가 바르게 짝지어진 것은?

　　　ⓐ　ⓑ　　　　　　ⓐ　ⓑ
① by – in　　　② to – in
③ in – from　　④ in – by
⑤ to – by

서답형

24 아래 〈보기〉에서 위 글의 밑줄 친 (A)to learn, (B)to practice와 to부정사의 용법이 같은 것을 각각 고르시오.

보기
① I have many friends to talk with.
② It is important to use your time well.
③ He awoke to find himself famous.
④ I want something cold to drink.
⑤ Her dream is to be a doctor.

➡ (A)와 같은 것: _____
　 (B)와 같은 것: _____

25 According to the passage, which is NOT true?

① Owen is a big fan of a Spanish soccer team.

② Owen speaks Spanish well enough to understand interviews with his favorite players.

③ According to Julie, the best way to learn a new language is to practice it every day.

④ Julie has changed the language of her phone to Spanish.

⑤ Julie has been writing her shopping lists in Spanish.

[26~28] 다음 글을 읽고 물음에 답하시오.

I recommend ⓐwatching Korean dramas. I've been ⓑwatching Korean dramas for a year, and they're really interesting! You can use Korean subtitles for help with listening. It's also a good idea to print out the subtitles and read them first. - Brandon, 16

What Works for You?

There are hundreds of good tips out there, but everyone has their own way of learning. ⓒFind what keeps you motivated; then you will enjoy learning more. Remember, every language is hard at first, but a new language can make your world ⓓmuch bigger!

서답형

26 아래 〈보기〉에서 위 글의 밑줄 친 ⓐwatching, ⓑwatching 과 문법적 쓰임이 같은 것을 각각 모두 고르시오.

┌─ 보기 ─
① I like watching Korean dramas.
② Watching Korean dramas makes me happy.
③ She is watching Korean dramas.
④ My hobby is watching Korean dramas.
⑤ I saw him watching Korean dramas.
└

➡ ⓐ: _____ , ⓑ: _____

서답형

27 위 글의 밑줄 친 ⓒ를 다음과 같이 바꿔 쓸 때 빈칸에 들어갈 알맞은 말을 두 단어로 쓰시오.

➡ _____ _____ find what keeps you motivated, you will enjoy learning more.

28 위 글의 빈칸 ⓓmuch와 바꿔 쓸 수 없는 말을 고르시오.

① still   ② a lot   ③ far

④ even   ⑤ very

[29~30] 다음 글을 읽고 물음에 답하시오.

I Love Soccer!

I'm a big fan of a ___ⓐ___ soccer team. (①) I want to understand interviews with my favorite players. (②) How can I improve my Spanish? (③)   - Owen, 16

The best way to learn a new language is to practice it every day. (④) I have changed the language of my phone to Spanish, and I have been writing my shopping lists in Spanish! (⑤)   - Julie, 15

서답형

29 위 글의 빈칸 ⓐ에 Spain을 알맞은 형태로 쓰시오.

➡ _____

30 위 글의 흐름으로 보아, 주어진 문장이 들어가기에 가장 적절한 곳은?

However, it's not easy because I don't know Spanish that well.

①   ②   ③   ④   ⑤

[01~03] 다음 글을 읽고 물음에 답하시오.

I Love Soccer!

I'm a big fan of a Spanish soccer team. I want to understand interviews with my favorite players. However, (A)it's not easy because I don't know Spanish that well. How can I improve my Spanish?　　- Owen, 16

The best way to learn a new language is to practice it every day. I have changed the language of my phone to Spanish, and I ____(B)____ my shopping lists in Spanish!
- Julie, 15

01 위 글의 밑줄 친 (A)it이 가리키는 것을 본문에서 찾아 쓰시오.

➡ _____

02 Fill in the blanks (B) with suitable words to match the meaning of the sentence below.

> I started to write my shopping lists in Spanish and I am still writing them in Spanish!

➡ _____

03 위 글의 내용을 다음과 같이 정리하고자 한다. 빈칸 (A)~(C)에 들어갈 알맞은 단어를 본문에서 찾아 쓰시오.

How to Learn a New Language	
Interests	Spanish (A)_____ team
Wants	To (B)_____ the players' interviews
Useful Tip	Practice (C)_____ every day.

[04~06] 다음 글을 읽고 물음에 답하시오.

I recommend watching Korean dramas. I've been watching Korean dramas for a year, and they're really (A)[interesting / interested]! You can use Korean subtitles for help with listening. It's also a good idea to print out the subtitles and (B)[read / reading] them first.
- Brandon, 16

※ You = Marisa

What Works for You?

There are hundreds of good tips out there, but everyone has their own way of learning. Find ____ⓐ____ keeps you (C)[motivating / motivated]; then you will enjoy learning more. Remember, every language is hard at first, but a new language can make your world much bigger!

04 Fill in the blank ⓐ with a suitable word.

➡ _____

05 위 글의 괄호 (A)~(C)에서 어법상 알맞은 낱말을 골라 쓰시오.

➡ (A) _____ (B) _____ (C) _____

06 다음 빈칸 (A)~(C)에 알맞은 단어를 넣어, 브랜던이 마리사에게 추천하는 한국 드라마들을 보는 방법을 완성하시오.

> He recommends using (A)_____ _____ for help with listening, (B)_____ _____ the subtitles, and (C)_____ them first.

[07~09] 다음 글을 읽고 물음에 답하시오.

What's most important is to become familiar with the language first. ⓐI suggest to watch Spanish movies often. It will help you ⓑ소리에 익숙해지도록 of the language. If the people talk too fast, try watching Spanish children's movies first.   - Inho, 14

Some words are used only in soccer, not in everyday life. Learn some soccer vocabulary and memorize it. Also, why don't you try writing a review of a match in Spanish? It will help you improve your writing skills.

- Rohan, 16

※ you = Owen

07 위 글의 밑줄 친 ⓐ에서 어법상 틀린 부분을 찾아 고치시오.

_____ ➡ _____

08 위 글의 밑줄 친 ⓑ의 우리말에 맞게 5단어로 영작하시오.

➡ _____

09 위 글의 내용과 일치하도록 다음 빈칸 (A)와 (B)에 알맞은 단어를 쓰시오.

Rohan suggests that Owen should learn and memorize some (A)_____ _____. Rohan also suggests writing a review of a match (B)_____.

[10~12] 다음 글을 읽고 물음에 답하시오.

No More Subtitles!
   DREAM4 (A)[is / are] back! I'm so excited to see my favorite Korean boy band perform. Their singing and their dancing (B)[is / are] just perfect. I want to understand their songs without subtitles or translations though. Any tips?   - Marisa, 14

   You should find friends who are interested in DREAM4 and start a club. In my club, we motivate one another. We translate songs and sing together. ⓐDoing these things (C)[is / are] fun and really improves our Korean!

- Lori, 15

10 위 글의 괄호 (A)~(C)에서 문맥과 어법상 알맞은 낱말을 골라 쓰시오.

➡ (A) _____ (B) _____ (C) _____

11 위 글의 밑줄 친 ⓐDoing these things가 가리키는 것을 영어로 쓰시오.

➡ _____

12 주어진 영영풀이를 참고하여 아래 빈칸에 철자 m으로 시작하는 단어를 넣어 로리의 모임에 대한 소개를 완성하시오.

영영풀이: provide with a motive

Lori and her friends _____ each club member to learn and improve Korean, and they translate songs and sing together.

해석

After You Read B

A: I want to improve my Chinese. Do you have any tips?
자신이 바라는 것을 표현 = I'd like to ~

B: Learn vocabulary which is related to your interests.
which는 주격 관계대명사이며 선행사는 vocabulary

C: Watching Chinese dramas with Chinese subtitles is a good way to get better
동명사가 문장의 주어이다. 동명사는 단수 취급한다.

at listening.

A: Thanks a lot!

구문해설 • improve: 증가시키다, 늘리다 • subtitle: 자막
• a good way to ~: ~하기 위한 좋은 방법 • a lot: 많이, 매우

A: 나는 중국어 실력을 늘리고 싶어. 좋은 방법이 있니?

B: 네가 관심 있는 것들과 관련된 어휘를 배워.

C: 중국어 자막이 있는 중국 드라마를 보는 것이 듣기를 잘하게 하는 좋은 방법이야.

A: 정말 고마워!

After You Read C

How to Learn a New Language
의문사+to부정사: 명사적 용법

Interests Spanish soccer team
스페인의(형용사)

Wants To understand the players' interviews

Useful Tips • Practice Spanish every day.
스페인어(명사)
• Become familiar with Spanish.
~와 친해지다
• Learn soccer vocabulary and write a review of a match
축구 어휘　　　　　　　후기　　　　경기
in Spanish.
스페인어로
Find what keeps you motivated; then you will enjoy learning more.
관계대명사　　　동기가 부여된

구문해설 • Spanish: 스페인의(형용사); 스페인어(명사) • practice: 연습하다
• become familiar with: ~와 친해지다 • vocabulary 어휘 • motivated: 동기가 부여된

새로운 언어를 배울 수 있는 방법

관심: 스페인 축구 팀

원하는 것: 선수들의 인터뷰를 이해하기

• 유용한 조언들: 스페인어를 매일 연습해라.

• 스페인어와 친해져라.

• 축구 어휘들을 배우고 스페인어로 경기에 대한 후기를 써 보아라.

당신에게 계속 동기 부여가 되는 것을 찾아라. 그러면 당신은 학습을 더욱 즐길 것이다.

Do It Yourself B

I'm so excited to see my favorite Korean boy band perform. I want to
부정사의 부사적 용법(원인)　　　　　　　지각동사 see의 목적격보어로 동사원형(현재분사형도 가능)
understand their songs without subtitles or translations though. Any tips?
부사: 그러나, 그래도　　　= Can you give me any tips?

- *Marisa*

구문해설 • perform: 공연[연주]하다 • translation: 번역

나는 내가 가장 좋아하는 한국의 소년 밴드가 공연하는 것을 보아서 매우 신나요. 그러나 나는 자막이나 번역이 없이 그들의 노래를 이해하고 싶어요. 어떤 조언들이 있을까요?

Words & Expressions

01 다음 짝지어진 단어의 관계가 같도록 빈칸에 들어갈 알맞은 말을 고르시오.

> improve : develop = _____ : finish

① recommend ② complete
③ practice ④ translate
⑤ perform

02 다음 문장의 빈칸에 적절한 것은?

> Some words are used only in soccer, not in everyday life. Learn some soccer _____ and memorize it.

① rule ② idiom ③ phrase
④ subtitle ⑤ vocabulary

03 다음 대화의 빈칸에 들어갈 말로 적절한 것을 고르시오.

> A: What _____ you like to do this year?
> B: I'd like to travel to other countries.

① would ② should
③ could ④ might
⑤ did

04 다음 우리말에 맞게 빈칸에 알맞은 말을 쓰시오.

(1) 나는 자원봉사하면서 시간을 쓰고 싶어.
➡ I'd like to _____ time volunteering.

(2) 그 경험을 통해서 소녀는 무엇을 배웠나?
➡ What did the girl learn _____ the experience?

Conversation

[05~07] 다음 대화를 읽고 물음에 답하시오.

B: What are you doing?
G: I'm writing a list of things that I want to do this year.
B: That's nice. _____(A)_____
G: Well, first of all, I'd like to spend time volunteering with my friends during summer vacation.
B: That sounds great.
G: _____(B)_____ What would you like to do this year?
B: (C)나는 수영 수업을 받는 것을 생각하고 있어.(am thinking of, take)
G: That's really cool.

05 빈칸 (A)에 들어갈 가장 알맞은 말을 고르시오.

① What would you like to do this year?
② What are you looking at right now?
③ What does she want to do?
④ Where do you like to go?
⑤ What does she want to have?

06 Which one is most suitable for the blank (B)?

① Really?
② What about you?
③ Do you think so?
④ How nice!
⑤ Where are you going?

07 주어진 단어를 써서 밑줄 친 (C)에 해당하는 영어 문장을 쓰시오.

➡ _____

[08~10] 다음 대화를 읽고 물음에 답하시오.

G: ___(A)___ would you like to do this year?

B: I'd like to learn the guitar. I listened to the song "Cavatina," and (B)나는 기타 소리에 감동을 받았어.

G: That's great. Where are you going to learn it?

B: My friend Jinsu is a very good guitar player. I'll ask him to teach me.

08 빈칸 (A)에 들어갈 의문사를 쓰시오.

➡ _____

09 밑줄 친 (B)의 우리말을 영작하시오. (was struck, sound 포함)

➡ _____

10 위 대화의 내용과 일치하는 것은?

① The girl plays the guitar very well.
② The boy learned to play the piano.
③ The boy listened to the song "Cavatina."
④ Jinsu is poor at playing the guitar.
⑤ The boy will learn to play the guitar from the girl.

11 다음 대화의 순서가 바르게 배열된 것은?

A: Can you tell me about one of your meaningful experiences?

(A) It was not easy, but I learned that I could make people happy with my cooking.

(B) How did you like it?

(C) I cooked dinner for my family last Sunday.

① (A) – (C) – (B)   ② (B) – (A) – (C)
③ (B) – (C) – (A)   ④ (C) – (A) – (B)
⑤ (C) – (B) – (A)

12 다음 대화의 빈칸에 들어갈 말로 알맞은 것은?

B: Hey, Suji! What are you holding?

G: Hi, Ben. It's a skateboard. I'm going skateboarding.

B: Wow! I didn't know that you could skateboard. _____

G: I joined a local skateboarding club last month.

B: I see. So how do you like it?

G: It's really fun! It helps me make new friends, too.

① Where did you buy the skateboard?
② Why are you holding the skateboard?
③ How about making some new friends?
④ Who made you join the club?
⑤ How did you learn to skateboard?

13 다음 대화의 흐름상 어색한 문장은?

B: My band performed at the school festival yesterday.

G: Cool. ⓐWhy did you like that?

B: It wasn't bad, but ⓑI made some mistakes.

G: It's okay. ⓒI'm sure you sounded fine.

B: Thanks for saying so. It was my first time playing the drums in front of so many people.

G: ⓓHow did you feel about that?

B: I was very nervous, but I felt great, too!

G: That's awesome. ⓔI'm so proud of you.

① ⓐ   ② ⓑ   ③ ⓒ   ④ ⓓ   ⑤ ⓔ

Grammar

14 다음 문장의 빈칸에 알맞은 말이 바르게 짝지어진 것은?

> • My sister has been surfing the Internet _____ 2 hours.
> • My little brother has been taking a swimming class _____ last month.

① for – for
② since – for
③ since – since
④ for – since
⑤ since – during

15 다음 중 어색한 문장을 <u>모두</u> 고르시오.

① Please tell me that you bought for Jane's birthday.
② What Jake wants to do after school is to play soccer with his friends.
③ My mom has been growing vegetables last year.
④ Long time ago, they believed what the earth was flat.
⑤ I have been writing a report for two hours.
⑥ Julie has been teaching French for three years.

16 다음 그림을 참고하여 괄호 안에 주어진 어휘를 이용하여 빈칸에 알맞게 쓰시오.

Mariko _____ _____ _____
_____ an hour. (cook)

17 다음 두 문장의 의미가 같도록 빈칸에 알맞은 말을 쓰시오.

(1) Mina shows me the thing that she painted. (3 단어)
= Mina shows me _____.

(2) Hugh bought his son something that looked really nice. (6 단어)
= Hugh bought _____

_____.

(3) Some people believe something that they want to believe. (6 단어)
= Some people _____

_____.

18 다음 빈칸에 들어갈 말이 나머지와 <u>다른</u> 하나는?

① _____ surprised Taeho was the ending of the movie.
② I know _____ you did something wrong.
③ The students couldn't understand _____ the instructor said.
④ She showed me _____ she had in her bag.
⑤ That is _____ I have been looking for.

19 다음 ⓐ~ⓖ 중 어법상 옳은 것을 <u>모두</u> 고르시오.

> ⓐ I knew what you did it.
> ⓑ Please show me that you will wear to the party.
> ⓒ What I have to do right now is to call my mom.
> ⓓ Do you always believe what you see?
> ⓔ He has been studying science for 1997.
> ⓕ I have been writing my shopping lists in Spanish!
> ⓖ It has been snowing last week.

➡ _____

Reading

[20~21] 다음 글을 읽고 물음에 답하시오.

I Love Soccer!

I'm a big fan of a Spanish soccer team. I want to understand interviews with my favorite players. However, it's not easy because I don't know Spanish ⓐthat well. How can I improve my Spanish? - Owen, 16

ⓑ새로운 언어를 배울 수 있는 가장 좋은 방법은 그 언어를 매일 연습하는 것이랍니다. I have changed the language of my phone to Spanish, and I have been writing my shopping lists in Spanish! - Julie, 15

20 위 글의 밑줄 친 ⓐthat과 문법적 쓰임이 같은 것을 고르시오.

① What's <u>that</u> over there?
② This is the book <u>that</u> you lent me.
③ I am so tired <u>that</u> I cannot go on.
④ I can't go <u>that</u> far.
⑤ She said <u>that</u> the story was true.

21 위 글의 밑줄 친 ⓑ의 우리말에 맞게 주어진 어휘를 알맞게 배열하시오.

> to practice it / a new language / the best way / every day / is / to learn / .

➡ _____

_____

[22~24] 다음 글을 읽고 물음에 답하시오.

What's most important is to become familiar ____ⓐ____ the language first. I suggest (A) watching Spanish movies often. It will help you get used ____ⓑ____ the sound of the language. If the people talk too fast, try watching Spanish children's movies first.
- Inho, 14

Some words are used only in soccer, not in everyday life. Learn some soccer vocabulary and memorize it. Also, why don't you try writing a review of a match in Spanish? It will help you improve your writing skills.
- Rohan, 16

※ you = Owen

22 위 글의 빈칸 ⓐ와 ⓑ에 들어갈 전치사가 바르게 짝지어진 것은?

	ⓐ	ⓑ		ⓐ	ⓑ
①	with	– to	②	in	– by
③	to	– for	④	with	– by
⑤	in	– to			

23 위 글의 밑줄 친 (A)watching과 문법적 쓰임이 <u>다른</u> 것을 <u>모두</u> 고르시오.

① I know the girl <u>watching</u> TV there.
② He is fond of <u>watching</u> TV.
③ <u>Watching</u> TV always makes me happy.
④ My hobby is <u>watching</u> TV.
⑤ He is <u>watching</u> TV now.

24 According to the passage, which is NOT true?

① Inho says that becoming familiar with Spanish first is the most important.

② Inho recommends watching Spanish movies often as it will help Owen get used to the sound of Spanish.

③ Inho suggests Owen should get used to the fast sound of Spanish before watching a children's movie.

④ Rohan advises Owen to learn some soccer vocabulary and memorize it.

⑤ Rohan advises Owen to write a review of a match in Spanish.

[25~26] 다음 글을 읽고 물음에 답하시오.

No More Subtitles!

DREAM4 is back! I'm so excited ⓐto see my favorite Korean boy band perform. Their singing and their dancing are just perfect. ⓑ I want to understand their songs with subtitles or translations though. Any tips?   - Marisa, 14

25 아래 〈보기〉에서 위 글의 밑줄 친 ⓐto see와 to부정사의 용법이 다른 것의 개수를 고르시오.

┌─── 보기 ───┐
① I need a friend to talk with.
② My dream is to see the band perform.
③ She felt sorry to see what happened.
④ This is the best chance to see the show.
⑤ He ran fast to see the design first.
└──────────┘

① 1개   ② 2개   ③ 3개   ④ 4개   ⑤ 5개

26 위 글의 밑줄 친 ⓑ에서 흐름상 어색한 부분을 찾아 고치시오.

_____ ➡ _____

[27~29] 다음 글을 읽고 물음에 답하시오.

Follow DREAM4 on social media. They often post short messages in Korean about how they are doing. They also post pictures with the messages, so you can understand the posts more easily.   - Aishah, 14

I recommend watching Korean dramas. ⓐ I've been watching Korean dramas for a year, and ⓑthey're really interesting! You can use Korean subtitles for help with listening. ⓒIt's also a good idea to print out the subtitles and read them first.   - Brandon, 16

27 According to Aishah, why is it possible to understand the posts of DREAM4 more easily? Fill in the blanks below with suitable words.

➡ Because they also post _____ _____

_____ _____.

28 위 글의 밑줄 친 ⓐ를 다음과 같이 바꿔 쓸 때 빈칸에 들어갈 알맞은 말을 두 단어로 쓰시오.

➡ I started to watch Korean dramas a year _____, and I'm still _____ them.

29 위 글의 밑줄 친 ⓑthey와 ⓒIt이 가리키는 것을 각각 본문에서 찾아 쓰시오.

➡ ⓑ _____

ⓒ _____

01 출제율 90%

짝지어진 단어의 관계가 같도록 빈칸에 알맞은 것은?

| weakness : strength = _____ : forget |

① remember   ② realize

③ motivate   ④ join

⑤ convince

02 출제율 95%

다음 단어의 영영풀이가 어색한 것은?

① shelf – a long flat narrow board attached to a wall

② confident – sure that something will happen in the way that you want or expect

③ responsibility – a duty to be in charge of someone or something

④ recommend – to advise someone to do something

⑤ perfect – having some mistakes, faults, or damage

[03~05] 다음 대화를 읽고 물음에 답하시오.

G: Did you make this shelf yourself? It's amazing!

B: Thanks. I started ____(A)____ furniture last year.

G: Cool! How do you like it?

B: It was hard at first, but now I love it. I feel so confident after I finish making something.

G: That's great. (B)나는 네가 그것을 정말 잘한다고 생각해. (really, good)

B: Thanks. I guess I found a new talent. I think it's good to try new things.

G: Exactly. Having new experiences lets us to find new talents.

03 출제율 95%

빈칸 (A)에 들어가기에 적절한 것을 고르시오.

① making   ② buying   ③ moving

④ dealing   ⑤ selling

04 출제율 85%

밑줄 친 (B)에 주어진 단어를 써서 해당하는 영어 문장을 완성하시오.

➡ _____

05 출제율 90%

위 대화에서 어법이 어색한 문장을 찾아 바로 잡으시오.

_____

➡ _____

[06~08] 다음 대화를 읽고 물음에 답하시오.

B: What are you doing?

G: I'm writing a list of things that I want to do this year.

B: That's nice. (A)너는 올해 무엇을 하고 싶니? (would, like)

G: Well, first of all, I'd like to spend time volunteering with my friends during summer vacation.

B: That sounds great.

G: What about you? What would you like to do this year?

B: I'm thinking of taking a swimming class.

G: That's really cool.

06 출제율 90%

밑줄 친 (A)의 우리말을 영어로 옮겨 쓰시오. (주어진 표현 포함)

➡ _____

07 What would the boy like to do this year?

① He would like to write a shopping list.

② He would like to do volunteering.

③ He would like to spend time with his friends.

④ He would like to take a swimming class.

⑤ He would like to go hiking with his family.

08 위 대화를 읽고 대답할 수 있는 것은?

① What will the boy do this week?

② What does the girl plan to do this summer?

③ Why does the boy ask the girl her plan?

④ Where are they talking at the moment?

⑤ How will the girl go volunteering with her friends?

09 다음 빈칸에 알맞은 말이 순서대로 짝지어진 것은?

> • _____ is most important is to become familiar with the language first.
> • He has been talking on the phone _____ 3 p.m.

① What – since   ② That – for

③ What – for   ④ That – since

⑤ Which – for

10 다음 중 어법상 적절한 문장은? (2개)

① It has been snowed for three days.

② She has been cleaning her room last night.

③ He has been building his house since two months.

④ Anne has been swimming for an hour.

⑤ Tom has been to Paris several times.

11 다음 두 문장이 같도록 할 때 빈칸에 알맞은 말을 쓰시오.

> • Yuna gave me the things that she had kept for years.
> = Yuna gave me _____ she had kept for years.

12 다음 중 어법상 바르지 <u>않은</u> 것은?

① I have been doing my homework for two hours.

② Cathy has been listening to the music 3 hours ago.

③ Is eating healthy food what they want to do?

④ We have known her since she was a little child.

⑤ That's what is keeping you up so late.

13 다음 문장의 빈칸에 알맞은 말은?

> Grace has been _____ for her daughter since this morning.

① look   ② looked

③ looking   ④ to look

⑤ to looking

[14~16] 다음 글을 읽고 물음에 답하시오.

What's most important is ⓐto become familiar with ⓑthe language first. I suggest watching Spanish movies often. It will help you get used to the sound of the language. If the people talk too fast, try watching Spanish children's movies first.   - Inho, 14

ⓒSome words are used only in soccer, not in everyday life. Learn some soccer vocabulary and memorize ⓓit. Also, why don't you try writing a review of a match in Spanish? It will help you improve your writing skills.
    - Rohan, 16

14 아래 〈보기〉에서 위 글의 밑줄 친 ⓐto become과 to부정사의 용법이 같은 것의 개수를 고르시오.

> ┤ 보기 ├
> ① He wanted me to study English hard.
> ② He was the last man to tell a lie.
> ③ I was excited to see the show.
> ④ This book is easy to read.
> ⑤ What do you want to be in the future?

① 1개   ② 2개   ③ 3개   ④ 4개   ⑤ 5개

15 위 글의 밑줄 친 ⓑthe language와 ⓓit이 가리키는 것을 본문에서 찾아 쓰시오.

➡ ⓑ _____ ⓓ _____

16 위 글의 밑줄 친 ⓒ를 다음과 같이 바꿔 쓸 때 빈칸에 들어갈 알맞은 단어를 쓰시오.

➡ Some words are used not in everyday life _____ only in soccer.

[17~19] 다음 글을 읽고 물음에 답하시오.

No More Subtitles!

DREAM4 is back! I'm so excited to see my favorite Korean boy band perform. Their singing and their dancing are just perfect. I want to understand their songs without subtitles or translations (A)though. Any tips?
    - Marisa, 14

You should find friends __ⓐ__ are interested in DREAM4 and start a club. In my club, we motivate one another. We translate songs and sing together. (B)Doing these things is fun and really improve our Korean!   - Lori, 15

17 Fill in the blank ⓐ with a suitable word.

➡ _____

18 위 글의 밑줄 친 (A)though와 같은 의미로 쓰인 것을 고르시오.

① Though it stopped raining, the wind was still blowing.
② He supported his family though he was young.
③ Our team lost. It was a good game though.
④ Though she was tired, she worked hard.
⑤ Though he tried very hard, he failed the course.

19 위 글의 밑줄 친 (B)에서 어법상 틀린 부분을 찾아 고치시오.

➡ _____ ➡ _____

[20~21] 다음 글을 읽고 물음에 답하시오.

Follow DREAM4 on social media. They often post short messages in Korean about how they are doing. They also post pictures with the messages, so you can understand the posts more easily.　　　　- Aishah, 14

I recommend watching Korean dramas. I've been watching Korean dramas for a year, and they're really interesting! You can use Korean subtitles for help with listening. It's also a good idea to print out the subtitles and read them first.　　　　- Brandon, 16

What Works for You?

There are hundreds of good tips out there, but everyone has their own way of learning. Find what keeps you motivated; then you will enjoy learning more. Remember, every language is hard at first, but a new language can make your world much bigger!

✏️ 출제율 90%

20 How long has Brandon been watching Korean dramas? Answer in English in a full sentence. (8 words)

➡️ _____

✏️ 출제율 100%

21 According to the passage, which is NOT true?

① The members of DREAM4 often post short messages in Korean about how they are doing.

② The members of DREAM4 also post pictures with the messages.

③ Brandon recommends watching Korean dramas.

④ Everyone has their own way of learning a new language.

⑤ Every language is easy at first, and a new language can make your world much bigger.

[22~24] 다음 글을 읽고 물음에 답하시오.

What I Want to Experience in Andong

What city do you want to go to in Korea? (①) I want to go to Andong. (②) I'd also like to make my own Hahoe mask and learn how to dance the *talchum*. (③) Also, I want to visit Hahoe Village. (④) I am sure that ⓐthese new experiences in Andong would help me understand Korea better. (⑤)

✏️ 출제율 95%

22 위 글의 흐름으로 보아, 주어진 문장이 들어가기에 가장 적절한 곳은?

In Andong, I want to try Andong-jjimdak.

①　　　②　　　③　　　④　　　⑤

✏️ 출제율 90%

23 위 글의 밑줄 친 ⓐ가 가리키는 것 세 가지를 본문에서 찾아 쓰시오.

➡️ (1) _____

(2) _____

(3) _____

✏️ 출제율 100%

24 위 글을 읽고 알 수 없는 것을 고르시오.

① 한국에서 가 보고 싶은 도시

② 그 도시에서 먹고 싶은 음식

③ 하회탈 만드는 법

④ 그 도시에서 배우고 싶은 춤

⑤ 그 도시에서 방문하고 싶은 마을

[01~02] 다음 대화를 읽고 물음에 답하시오.

> A: I want to ___(A)___ my Chinese. Do you have any tips?
> B: Learn vocabulary which is related to your interests.
> C: (B)중국어 자막이 있는 중국 드라마를 보는 것이 듣기를 더 잘하는 좋은 방법이야. (watch, dramas, subtitles, get better)
> A: Thanks a lot!

01 빈칸 (A)에 들어갈 알맞은 말을 주어진 철자로 시작하여 쓰시오.

➡ i_____

02 밑줄 친 (B)의 우리말을 영어로 쓰시오. (주어진 단어를 포함할 것)

➡ _____

_____

03 다음 우리말에 맞게 빈칸에 알맞은 말을 쓰시오. (주어진 철자로 시작할 것)

(1) 나는 기타 소리에 감동을 받았어.
➡ I was s_____ by the sound of the guitar.

(2) 나는 수영 수업 듣는 것을 생각하고 있어.
➡ I'm thinking of t_____ a swimming class.

(3) 우리는 서로 방법을 공유하고 있어.
➡ We s_____ tips with one another.

04 관계대명사 what을 사용하여 주어진 두 문장을 한 문장으로 바꾸시오.

(1) • This is something.
• I wanted to buy it.
➡ _____

(2) • I enjoyed the food.
• You cooked it for me last night.
➡ _____

(3) • Do you remember the dress?
• Bella wore it at the party last night.
➡ _____

_____

05 현재완료진행형을 사용하여 주어진 두 문장을 한 문장으로 바꾸시오.

(1) • The alarm started ringing 5 minutes ago.
• It is still ringing.
➡ _____

(2) • Mary began chatting with her friends at two o'clock.
• She is still chatting.
➡ _____

_____

(3) • He is writing a book.
• He started writing the book last month.
➡ _____

06 다음 우리말을 주어진 어휘를 이용하여 영작하시오.

(1) 그 보고서는 내가 알고 싶어하는 것을 보여 주었다. (the report, show, want)
➡ _____

(2) 그는 그녀가 한 말의 많은 것에 묵시적으로 동의했다. (much of, silently, agree, had said)
➡ _____

(3) 나는 그 신문에서 읽은 것을 전혀 믿지 않는다.
(never, believe, in the newspaper)

➡ _____

(4) 엄마는 몇 주 동안 계속 쇼핑을 하고 계신다.
(mom, weeks, shop, been)

➡ _____

(5) 누군가가 계속해서 부엌에서 사탕을 훔쳐 가고 있다. (someone, candies, from the kitchen, steal, been)

➡ _____

(6) 이 영화는 많은 사람들이 기다려 온 것이다.
(this movie, been, what, wait)

➡ _____

[07~09] 다음 글을 읽고 물음에 답하시오.

ⓐ가장 중요한 것은 우선 언어와 친해지는 것이에요. I suggest watching Spanish movies often. It will help you get used to the sound of the language. If the people talk too fast, try watching Spanish children's movies first.
- Inho, 14

Some words are used only in soccer, not in everyday life. Learn some soccer vocabulary and memorize it. Also, ⓑwhy don't you try writing a review of a match in Spanish? It will help you improve your writing skills.
- Rohan, 16

07 위 글의 밑줄 친 ⓐ의 우리말에 맞게 주어진 어휘를 이용하여 11 단어로 영작하시오.

what's, become familiar with, first

➡ _____
_____

08 위 글의 밑줄 친 ⓑ를 다음과 같이 바꿔 쓸 때 빈칸에 들어갈 알맞은 말을 두 단어로 쓰시오.

➡ _____ _____ trying

09 위 글의 내용과 일치하도록 다음 빈칸 (A)와 (B)에 알맞은 단어를 쓰시오.

Inho suggests watching (A)_____ _____ often because it will be helpful in getting used to (B)_____ _____ of the language.

[10~11] 다음 글을 읽고 물음에 답하시오.

No More Subtitles!

DREAM4 is back! I'm so excited to see my favorite Korean boy band perform. Their singing and their dancing are just perfect. I want to understand their songs without subtitles or translations though. Any tips?
- Marisa, 14

You should find friends who are interested in DREAM4 and start a club. In my club, we motivate one another. We translate songs and sing together. Doing these things is fun and really improves our ___ⓐ___!
- Lori, 15

10 위 글의 빈칸 ⓐ에 들어갈 알맞은 말을 본문에서 찾아 쓰시오.

➡ _____

11 위 글의 내용을 다음과 같이 정리하고자 한다. 빈칸 (A)와 (B)에 들어갈 알맞은 단어를 본문에서 찾아 쓰시오.

Marisa asks for advice about the ways to understand the songs of DREAM4, her favorite Korean boy band, without (A)_____ or (B)_____.

창의사고력 서술형 문제

01 다음 〈보기 A〉와 〈보기 B〉에서 알맞은 말을 하나씩 골라 완전한 문장을 만드시오.

┌─ 보기A ─────────────┐ ┌─ 보기B ─────────────────┐
- She has been
- I have been
- They have
- It has been

- working here since 2018.
- known her for two years.
- swimming for half an hour.
- raining since last night.

(1) _____

(2) _____

(3) _____

(4) _____

02 A와 B에 주어진 어구를 활용하여, 관계대명사 what이 들어간 문장을 어법에 맞게 3문장 이상 쓰시오.

A	Jumi/want to do	I/bought	he/like the most	I/like
B	take a walk in the park	*the Little Prince*	play the guitar	she gave me

┌─ 보기 ──┐
What Jumi wants to do after school is to take a walk in the park with her friends.

(1) _____

(2) _____

(3) _____

03 다음 내용을 바탕으로 특정 지역에 가서 경험해 보고 싶은 일을 계획하는 글을 쓰시오.

┌──┐
Andong
- Food that I want to try: Andong-jjimdak
- Activities that I want to try or learn: – make a Hahoe mask
                                 – learn how to dance the *talchum*
- Place that I want to visit: Hahoe Village

┌──┐
What I Want to Experience in Andong

What city do you want to go to in Korea? I want to go to (A)_____ . In Andong, I want to try (B)_____ . I'd also like to make my own (C)_____ and learn how to dance (D)_____ . Also, I want to visit (E)_____ . I am sure that these new experiences in Andong would help me understand Korea better.

단원별 모의고사

01 다음 〈보기〉의 단어가 빈칸에 들어갈 수 <u>없는</u> 것은?

> 보기
> camping advise good how understand

① She would like to learn _____ to make her own mobile game.
② My friend Jinsu is a very _____ guitar player.
③ I'd like to _____ a swimming class
④ I'd like to go _____ with my family.
⑤ I _____ why not giving up is so important.

02 다음 짝지어진 단어의 관계가 같도록 빈칸에 알맞은 말을 쓰시오. (주어진 철자로 시작할 것)

> ask : reply = perfect : i_____

03 다음 중 밑줄 친 부분의 뜻풀이가 바르지 <u>않은</u> 것은?

① I <u>joined</u> a local skateboarding club last month. (가입했다)
② She is <u>nervous</u> when she goes skateboarding. (불안한)
③ I started making <u>furniture</u> last year. (가구)
④ I guess I found a new <u>talent</u>. (배우)
⑤ My band <u>performed</u> at the school festival yesterday. (공연했다)

04 다음 대화의 문맥상 또는 어법상 <u>어색한</u> 것을 찾아 고치시오.

> A: I want to improve my Chinese. Do you have any tips?
> B: Learn vocabulary what is related to your interests.
> C: Watching Chinese dramas with Chinese subtitles is a good way to get better at listening.
> A: Thanks a lot!

_____

➡ _____

[05~07] 다음 대화를 읽고 물음에 답하시오.

> G: Did you make this shelf yourself? It's amazing!
> B: Thanks. I started making furniture last year.
> G: Cool! How do you like it?
> B: It was hard at first, but now ___(A)___ . I feel so confident after I finish making something.
> G: That's great. I think you're really good at it.
> B: Thanks. I guess I found a new talent. I think it's good to try new things.
> G: Exactly. (B)새로운 경험을 하는 것은 우리에게 새로운 재능을 발견하도록 해준다. (have, experiences, let, talents)

05 밑줄 친 (A)에 들어가기에 적절한 것을 고르시오.

① I love it
② I don't make it
③ I buy it
④ I have a problem
⑤ I am worried

06 밑줄 친 (B)의 우리말을 적절한 영어 문장으로 옮기시오.
(주어진 단어를 적절한 형태로 바꾸어 포함할 것)

➡ _____

07 위 대화의 내용과 일치하지 <u>않는</u> 것은?

① 소녀는 소년이 가구를 잘 만든다고 생각한다.
② 소년은 직접 가구를 만들었다.
③ 소년은 가구 만들기가 어려워 좋아하지 않는다.
④ 소년은 무엇인가를 만들고 난 후 자신감을 느낀다.
⑤ 소년은 새로운 재능을 발견했다고 생각한다.

08 다음 대화의 빈칸에 들어갈 말을 〈보기〉에서 골라 순서대로 배열하시오.

> B: What are you doing?
> G: I'm writing a list of things that I want to do this year.
> B: _____
> G: Well, first of all, I'd like to spend time volunteering with my friends during summer vacation.
> B: _____
> G: _____
> B: _____
> G: That's really cool.

┌─── 보기 ───┐
(A) That sounds great.
(B) I'm thinking of taking a swimming class.
(C) That's nice. What would you like to do this year?
(D) What about you? What would you like to do this year?
└──────────┘

➡ _____

09 짝지어진 대화가 <u>어색한</u> 것을 고르시오.

① A: What would you like to do this year?
   B: I'd like to travel to other countries.
② A: I bought a bag for you. Is this what you wanted?
   B: Yes. That's exactly what I wanted.
③ A: Hey, Suji! What are you holding?
   B: It's a skateboard. I'm going skateboarding.
④ A: How did you like it?
   B: I will like it a lot.
⑤ A: Do you like action movies?
   B: No, I don't. I don't have much interest in them.

10 다음 대화의 순서가 바르게 배열된 것을 고르시오.

> G: What would you like to do this year?
> (A) My friend Jinsu is a very good guitar player. I'll ask him to teach me.
> (B) That's great. Where are you going to learn it?
> (C) I'd like to learn the guitar. I listened to the song "Cavatina," and I was struck by the sound of the guitar.

① (A) – (C) – (B)　　② (B) – (A) – (C)
③ (B) – (C) – (A)　　④ (C) – (A) – (B)
⑤ (C) – (B) – (A)

11 주어진 표현을 사용하여 질문에 대한 대답을 완성하시오.

(1) Q: How long has Vivian been listening to the music?
   A: She _____
   _____. (2 hours)
(2) Q: Since when has Charlie been cooking bulgogi?
   A: He _____
   _____. (6:00 p.m.)

12 다음 중 〈보기〉의 문장과 의미가 같은 것을 고르시오.

┌─── 보기 ───┐

Emily is sleeping in her room now. She began sleeping at ten o'clock.

① Emily is sleeping in her room at ten o'clock.
② Emily has been sleeping in her room since ten o'clock.
③ Emily slept in her room at ten o'clock.
④ Emily has slept in her room for ten o'clock.
⑤ Emily had slept in her room since ten o'clock.

13 다음 빈칸에 들어갈 말을 순서대로 묶은 것은?

- You should be satisfied with _____ you have.
- If the facts are true, that is all _____ counts.

① which – what
② that – that
③ that – what
④ what – that
⑤ what – what

14 다음 문장에서 어법상 어색한 것을 바르게 고쳐 다시 쓰시오.

(1) This ring is that my mom gave me.

➡ _____

(2) You can look up that you need on the computer.

➡ _____

(3) Is this the thing what you were looking for?

➡ _____

(4) Russia has been belonging to such a category.

➡ _____

15 다음 중 어법상 옳은 문장을 모두 고르시오.

① I could not understand that the teacher talked about.
② Judy has been having the hairpin for 10 years.
③ I have been cleaning my room for two hours.
④ This dress is what she bought it last weekend.
⑤ I remember what he did last month.

[16~17] 다음 글을 읽고 물음에 답하시오.

I Love Soccer!

I'm a big fan of a Spanish soccer team. I want to understand interviews with my favorite players. However, it's not easy because I don't know Spanish that well. How can I improve my Spanish?　　　　　　- Owen, 16

The best way to learn a new language is to practice it every day. I have changed the language of my phone to Spanish, and I have been writing my shopping lists in Spanish!

- Julie, 15

16 Why does Owen have difficulty in understanding interviews with his favorite players? Answer in English. (7 words)

➡ _____

17 줄리가 새로운 언어를 매일 연습하기 위해 실천해 온 두 가지를 우리말로 쓰시오.

➡ (1) _____
   (2) _____

[18~19] 다음 글을 읽고 물음에 답하시오.

What's most important is to become familiar with the language first. I suggest watching Spanish movies often. ⓐIt will help you get used to the sound of the language. If the people talk too fast, try watching Spanish children's movies first. - Inho, 14

ⓑSome words are used only in soccer, not in everyday life. Learn some soccer vocabulary and memorize it. Also, why don't you try writing a review of a match in Spanish? ⓒIt will help you improve your writing skills.
- Rohan, 16

18 위 글의 밑줄 친 ⓐIt과 ⓒIt이 가리키는 것을 각각 본문에서 찾아 쓰시오.

➡ ⓐ _____
   ⓒ _____

19 위 글의 밑줄 친 ⓑ를 능동태로 고치시오.

➡ _____

[20~21] 다음 글을 읽고 물음에 답하시오.

No More Subtitles!
DREAM4 is back! ⓐI'm so excited to see my favorite Korean boy band to perform. Their singing and their dancing are just perfect. I want to understand their songs without subtitles or translations though. Any tips?
- Marisa, 14

You should find friends who are interested in DREAM4 and start a club. In my club, we motivate one another. We translate songs and sing together. Doing these things is fun and really improves our Korean! - Lori, 15

20 위 글의 밑줄 친 ⓐ에서 어법상 틀린 부분을 찾아 고치시오.

_____ ➡ _____

21 According to the passage, which is NOT true?

① Marisa's favorite Korean boy band is DREAM4.
② Marisa wants to understand DREAM4's songs without subtitles or translations.
③ Marisa is looking for friends who are interested in DREAM4.
④ Lori and her friends motivate one another in their club.
⑤ Lori and her friends translate songs and sing together.

[22~23] 다음 글을 읽고 물음에 답하시오.

I recommend ___ⓐ___ Korean dramas. I've been watching Korean dramas for a year, and they're really interesting! You can use Korean subtitles for help with listening. It's also a good idea to print out the subtitles and read them first. - Brandon, 16

22 위 글의 빈칸 ⓐ에 watch를 알맞은 형태로 쓰시오.

➡ _____

23 주어진 영영풀이에 해당하는 단어를 본문에서 찾아 쓰시오.

translation of foreign dialogue of a movie or TV program

➡ _____

Lesson 2

Take Care of Yourself

🎙 의사소통 기능

- 알고 있는지 묻기
  Have you heard the term *body image*?
- 놀람 표현하기
  I'm surprised that this small band can do all that.

🎙 언어 형식

- 관계대명사의 계속적 용법
  Walnuts also have wrinkles, **which** the brain has too.
- 명사의 뒤에서 명사를 수식하는 분사
  We all know that a diet **containing** a variety of food keeps our bodies healthy.

Words & Expressions

Key Words

- **accept** [æksépt] 동 받아들이다
- **active** [ǽktiv] 형 활발한
- **advice** [ædváis] 명 충고
- **awesome** [ɔ́:səm] 형 엄청난
- **beneficial** [bènəfíʃəl] 형 유익한
- **benefit** [bénəfit] 명 이득
- **brain** [brein] 명 뇌
- **cell** [sel] 명 세포
- **check** [tʃek] 동 검토하다
- **chemical** [kémikəl] 명 화학물질
- **chew** [tʃuː] 동 씹다
- **clue** [kluː] 명 단서
- **compared** [kəmpéərd] 형 비교되는
- **contain** [kəntéin] 동 포함하다
- **convenient** [kənvíːnjənt] 형 편리한
- **damage** [dǽmidʒ] 동 손상을 주다
- **deep sleep** 숙면
- **diet** [dáiət] 명 음식
- **function** [fʌ́ŋkʃən] 명 기능
- **ginger** [dʒíndʒər] 명 생강
- **healthy** [hélθi] 형 건강한
- **hollow** [hálou] 형 속이 빈
- **however** [hauévər] 부 그러나
- **improve** [imprúːv] 동 개선하다
- **increase** [inkríːs] 동 증가하다
- **lower** [lóuər] 동 낮추다
- **meaningful** [míːniŋfəl] 형 의미 있는
- **midnight** [mídnait] 명 자정
- **mirror** [mírər] 동 반사하다
- **moved** [muːvd] 형 감동받은
- **multiple** [mʌ́ltəpl] 형 복합적인
- **negative** [négətiv] 형 부정적인
- **pillow** [pílou] 명 베개
- **positive** [pázətiv] 형 긍정적인
- **prevent** [privént] 동 방해하다, 가로 막다
- **process** [práses] 동 처리하다
- **productive** [prədʌ́ktiv] 형 생산적인
- **risk** [risk] 명 위험
- **search** [səːrtʃ] 동 조사하다
- **sensitive** [sénsətiv] 형 민감한
- **similar** [símələr] 형 비슷한
- **slice** [slais] 동 얇게 자르다
- **smart band** 스마트 밴드
- **stomach** [stʌ́mək] 명 위장
- **thirsty** [θɔ́ːrsti] 형 목마른
- **track** [træk] 동 진행과정을 추적하다
- **upset** [ʌ́pset] 형 불편한
- **vision** [víʒən] 명 시력
- **walnut** [wɔ́ːlnʌt] 명 호두
- **wrinkle** [ríŋkl] 명 주름

Key Expressions

- **a variety of** 다양한
- **as it is** 있는 그대로
- **as usual** 평소처럼
- **at least** 적어도
- **be divided into** ~로 나뉘어지다
- **be good for ~** ~에 좋다
- **by oneself** 혼자서
- **come to mind** 생각이 떠오르다
- **compare A to B** A를 B에 비교하다
- **feel like -ing** ~하고 싶다
- **for this reason** 이런 이유로
- **from now on** 지금부터
- **give praise** 칭찬하다
- **in addition** 게다가
- **keep -ing** 계속 ~하다
- **look like** ~처럼 보이다
- **move on to** (새로운 일·주제로) 넘어가다
- **not only A but also B** A뿐만 아니라 B도
- **on the other hand** 반면에
- **prevent A from -ing** A가 ~하지 못하게 하다
- **stay healthy** 건강을 유지하다
- **that's why** 그런 이유로
- **throw up** 토하다
- **work out** 운동하다

Word Power

※ 서로 비슷한 뜻을 가진 어휘

- □ **contain** 포함하다 : **involve** 포함하다
- □ **sensitive** 민감한 : **touchy** 민감한
- □ **improve** 개선하다 : **develop** 발전하다
- □ **however** 그러나 : **yet** 그러나
- □ **convenient** 편리한 : **handy** 편리한
- □ **function** 기능 : **role** 역할
- □ **hollow** 속이 빈 : **empty** 빈
- □ **risk** 위험 : **danger** 위험

- □ **damage** 손상을 주다 : **harm** 손상시키다
- □ **advice** 충고 : **tip** 충고
- □ **positive** 긍정적인 : **affirmative** 긍정적인
- □ **check** 검토하다 : **review** 검토하다
- □ **awesome** 엄청난 : **amazing** 굉장한
- □ **benefit** 이득 : **advantage** 이득
- □ **lower** 낮추다 : **reduce** 줄이다
- □ **beneficial** 유익한 : **helpful** 도움이 되는

※ 서로 반대의 뜻을 가진 어휘

- □ **contain** 포함하다 ↔ **exclude** 제외하다
- □ **sensitive** 민감한 ↔ **insensitive** 무감각한
- □ **prevent** 가로 막다 ↔ **allow** 허용하다
- □ **increase** 증가하다 ↔ **decrease** 감소하다
- □ **multiple** 복합적인 ↔ **uniform** 단일한
- □ **lower** 낮추다 ↔ **raise** 올리다

- □ **healthy** 건강한 ↔ **ill** 아픈, 병든
- □ **positive** 긍정적인 ↔ **negative** 부정적인
- □ **convenient** 편리한 ↔ **inconvenient** 불편한
- □ **similar** 비슷한 ↔ **different** 다른
- □ **hollow** 속이 빈 ↔ **full** 꽉 찬
- □ **beneficial** 유익한 ↔ **harmful** 해로운

English Dictionary

- □ **active** 활발한
  → always busy doing things, especially physical or mental activities
  무엇인가를, 특히 육체적인 또는 정신적인 활동을 하느라 언제나 바쁜

- □ **brain** 뇌
  → the organ inside your head that controls how you think, feel, and move
  머릿속에 있는 생각, 감정, 동작을 조절하는 기관

- □ **convenient** 편리한
  → useful to you because it saves you time
  시간을 덜어 주어 유용한

- □ **hollow** 속이 빈
  → having an empty space inside
  내부에 빈 공간을 가진

- □ **improve** 개선하다
  → to make something better, or to become better
  무엇인가를 더 좋게 만들거나 더 좋아지다

- □ **pillow** 베개
  → a cloth bag filled with soft material that you put your head on
  머리를 올려놓는 부드러운 물질로 채워진 포대

- □ **risk** 위험
  → the possibility that something bad, unpleasant, or dangerous may happen
  나쁘거나 불쾌하거나 위험한 일이 일어날 가능성

- □ **slice** 얇게 자르다
  → to cut meat, bread, vegetables, etc into thin flat pieces
  고기, 빵, 채소를 얇은 조각으로 자르다

- □ **thirsty** 목마른
  → feeling that you want or need a drink
  음료를 원하거나 필요하다고 느끼는

- □ **vision** 시력
  → the ability to see
  보는 능력

- □ **walnut** 호두
  → a nut that you can eat, shaped like a human brain
  인간의 뇌처럼 생긴 먹을 수 있는 견과류

- □ **wrinkle** 주름
  → lines on your face and skin that you get when you are old
  나이가 들어 얼굴과 피부에 생기는 선

01 다음 대화의 빈칸에 들어갈 말로 적절한 것을 고르시오.

> B: Have you heard that chewing ice is bad for your teeth?
> G: No, I haven't. Why is that?
> B: It can _____ your teeth. It can also make them too sensitive.

① damage
② clean
③ produce
④ lower
⑤ check

02 다음 중 밑줄 친 부분의 뜻풀이가 바르지 <u>않은</u> 것은?

① A diet <u>containing</u> a variety of foods keeps our bodies healthy. (포함하는)
② Slice open a tomato and <u>compare</u> it with the human heart. (비교하다)
③ Eating tomatoes can <u>lower</u> your risk of heart disease. (낮추다)
④ Walnuts help our brains stay healthy and <u>active</u>. (활발한)
⑤ You may not like ginger's strong <u>taste</u> or smell. (취향)

03 다음 문장의 빈칸에 들어갈 말로 적절한 것을 고르시오.

> To stay _____, you need to exercise regularly.

① harmful
② multiple
③ similar
④ sensitive
⑤ healthy

04 다음 영영풀이에 해당하는 단어를 고르시오.

> a cloth bag filled with soft material that you put your head on

① pillow
② walnut
③ wrinkle
④ sofa
⑤ furniture

05 다음 문장에 공통으로 들어갈 말은?

> • Each of these foods looks _____ a certain body part.
> • A walnut is divided into two parts, just _____ the brain.
> • You may not _____ ginger's strong taste or smell.

① as
② for
③ like
④ about
⑤ alike

06 다음 중 〈보기〉에 있는 단어를 사용하여 자연스러운 문장을 만들 수 <u>없는</u> 것은?

> ┌─── 보기 ───┐
> preventing   lower   shape   clue

① Nature, however, gives us a big _____.
② For this _____, ginger can be good for your stomach.
③ They are also good for _____ Alzheimer's disease.
④ Look at the _____ of a walnut.
⑤ Eating tomatoes can _____ your risk of heart disease.

01 주어진 단어를 이용해 빈칸을 완성하시오.

> Can you tell me about one of your
> _____ experiences?

➡ _____ (mean)

02 다음 짝지어진 단어의 관계가 같도록 빈칸에 알맞은 말을 쓰시오. (주어진 철자로 시작할 것)

> improve : develop = p_____ : profitable

03 빈칸에 알맞은 단어를 〈보기〉에서 골라 쓰시오.

> ┌─ 보기 ─┐
> usual   healthy   advice   what

(1) Which picture shows a _____ habit?
(2) What _____ does the boy give the girl?
(3) That's probably _____ is making you tired.
(4) I went to bed after midnight, as _____.

04 다음 우리말에 맞게 빈칸에 알맞은 말을 쓰시오.

(1) 너는 body image라는 용어를 들어본 적이 있니?
 ➡ Have you heard the _____ *body image*?
(2) 너는 얼음을 씹는 것이 이에 나쁘다는 것을 들어본 적이 있니?
 ➡ Have you heard that _____ ice is bad for your teeth?

(3) 토마토를 얇게 잘라 내서 그것을 인간의 심장과 비교해 보아라.
 ➡ Slice open a tomato and _____ it with the human heart.
(4) 그것은 인간의 두뇌 형태와 매우 비슷하다.
 ➡ It's very similar to the _____ of the human brain

05 다음 영어 설명에 해당하는 단어를 쓰시오. (주어진 철자로 시작할 것)

> feeling that you want or need a drink

➡ t_____

06 다음 우리말을 주어진 단어를 이용하여 영작하시오.

> 몇몇 음식들은 그 음식이 유익한 신체 부위의 생김새를 반영한다. (mirror, good for)

➡ _____
_____

07 다음 대화의 빈칸에 들어갈 말로 적절한 말을 쓰시오.

> G: What's this?
> B: It's a smart band. It lets me check my health information on my smartphone.
> G: What kind of information?
> B: It shows how far I _____ during the day and how well I _____ at night.
> G: Interesting. I'm surprised that this small band can do all that.

Conversation

① 알고 있는지 묻기

> • Have you heard the term *body image*? body image라는 용어를 들어본 적이 있니?

■ 'Have you heard ~?'는 '~을 들어본 적이 있니?'라는 의미로 상대방이 지금 이야기하는 것에 대해 알고 있는지를 물어보는 말이다. '~에 관하여 들어본 적이 있니?'라는 의미로 'Have you heard about ~?' 또는 'Have you heard of ~?'라고 할 수도 있다. 접속사 that을 사용하여 'Have you heard that 주어+동사?' 형태로 말할 수도 있다.

■ 'Have you heard ~?'는 현재완료를 사용하여 어떤 일에 대하여 과거에 들어본 적이 있어서 현재에 그것을 알고 있는지 물어보는 것으로, 현재완료의 용법 중에서 '경험'에 해당한다. 'Do you know ~?'라고 해도 비슷한 의미의 질문이 될 수 있지만 좀 더 직설적인 느낌을 준다.

■ 'Have you heard ~?'에 대한 대답은 'Yes, I have.' 'No, I haven't.'라고 하여야 하지만 경우에 따라서는 'Have you heard ~?'로 질문하는 경우에 그 의도가 새로운 정보를 전달하는 것일 때도 있기 때문에 'I knew that.' 'I didn't know that.' 등으로 대답하기도 한다.

알고 있는지 묻기

- Have you heard about/of ~? ~에 대하여 들어본 적이 있습니까?
- Have you heard that 주어+동사? ~이라는 것을 들어본 적이 있습니까?
- Do you know that 주어+동사 ~? ~이라는 것을 아십니까?
- Did you know about ~? ~에 대해서 알고 있었습니까?

알고 있는지 대답하기

- Yes, I have. 네. 들어본 적이 있습니다.
- I've never heard of it. 전혀 들어본 적 없어.
- Oh, really? 아, 진짜로?
- I didn't know that. 그건 몰랐어요.
- No, that's new to me. 아니. 그건 처음 들어봐.
- I think I have. 들어본 적 있는 것 같은데.

▶ 핵심 Check

1. 다음 대화의 빈칸에 들어갈 말을 고르시오.

B: Have you heard that chewing ice is bad for your teeth?

G: _____ Why is that?

B: It can damage your teeth. It can also make them too sensitive.

① Have you heard?
② No, I haven't.
③ Did you know that?
④ Yes, I did.
⑤ No way.

❷ 놀람 표현하기

> • I'm surprised that this small band can do all that.
> 이 작은 밴드가 그 모든 것을 할 수 있다니 놀랍다.

■ 상대방이 말하는 사실에 대하여 놀라움을 표현할 때는 'I'm surprised that 주어+동사 ~.'의 형태를 사용하여 '~라는 사실에 놀랐다.'라는 의미를 나타낸다. surprised 대신 shocked, amazed를 사용해서 'I'm shocked that ~.' 'I'm amazed that ~.'이라고 할 수도 있다.

■ 단순히 상대의 말에 '놀랐다'는 의미로 'I can't believe it.' 'It's amazing.' 등을 사용하기도 한다. '놀랍지 않다' '당연하다'의 의미로는 'No wonder (that) 주어+동사 ~.'를 쓸 수 있다. 'No wonder (that) ~'은 'It is no wonder that ~.'에서 It is를 생략한 것이다.

나는 ~에 놀랐다.

- I'm surprised that ~.
- I'm shocked that ~.
- I'm amazed that ~.

놀람 표현하기

- How could that be possible? 그게 어떻게 가능해?
- It can't be true. 그게 사실일 리 없어.
- I can't believe it. 믿을 수 없어.
- It's[That's] surprising. 놀라워.
- What a surprise! 놀랍다!

믿을 수 없어., 정말이야?, 농담이지?

- You're kidding (me).
- You must be joking.
- You have got to be kidding me.
- Really?

핵심 Check

2. 다음 대화의 빈칸에 들어갈 말로 가장 자연스러운 것은?

B: It's a smart band. It lets me check my health information on my smartphone.

G: What kind of information?

B: It shows how far I walk during the day and how well I sleep at night.

G: Interesting. _____ this small band can do all that.

① No wonder that
② I'm surprised that
③ It is believed that
④ You're surprised that
⑤ It is disappointing that

Listen & Talk 1 B

B: You look tired. Did you get enough sleep?

G: Yes, I did. I slept ❶for over seven hours.

B: Okay. When did you go to bed?

G: I went to bed after midnight, ❷as usual.

B: That's probably what is making you tired. Have you heard that ❸when you go to bed is very important?

G: No, I haven't. Why is that?

B: Scientists say that ❹going to bed late can make you feel tired the next day.

G: I didn't know that.

B: On the other hand, going to bed early can improve your memory and help you be more productive. From now on, try to go to bed earlier.

B: 너 피곤해 보인다. 잠은 충분히 잤니?

G: 응, 그래. 나는 일곱 시간 이상 잤어.

B: 알았어. 너는 언제 잠들었니?

G: 평소처럼 자정이 넘어서 잠들었어.

B: 아마 그것이 너를 피곤하게 만드는 것일 거야. 네가 언제 잠드는지가 아주 중요하다는 말을 들어본 적이 있니?

G: 아니. 왜 그렇지?

B: 과학자들은 늦게 잠자리에 드는 것은 그 다음날 피곤함을 느끼게 할 수 있다고 말해.

G: 나는 몰랐어.

B: 반면에 일찍 잠자리에 드는 것은 기억력을 향상시키고, 더 생산적이 되도록 도와줄 수 있어. 지금부터는 일찍 자도록 노력해 봐.

❶ 전치사 for는 기간을 나타내어 '~ 동안'이라는 뜻이다.　　❷ as usual = 평소처럼
❸ that절에서 'when you go to bed'가 주어로 쓰였다.　　❹ going은 동명사로 can make의 주어 역할을 한다.

Check(√) True or False

(1) The boy advises the girl to go to bed early.　　　　T ☐ F ☐

(2) Going to bed late can help to be more productive.　　T ☐ F ☐

Listen & Talk 2 B

B: What are you doing in the living room?

G: I'm doing yoga.

B: You're working out by yourself?

G: Yes, I'm following this online video. It shows me all the steps.

B: Let me see. Wow, ❶it's been watched two million times! I'm surprised that so many people have watched this video.

G: I know! These kinds of programs are becoming popular right now.

B: It looks very convenient. You don't have to go out to exercise.

G: That's right. ❷That's why I love these programs. You should try them, too.

B: 너 거실에서 무엇을 하고 있니?

G: 나는 요가를 하는 중이야.

B: 혼자서 운동한다는 말이니?

G: 그래. 이 온라인 비디오를 따라하는 중이야. 그것이 나에게 모든 단계를 보여줘.

B: 어디 보자. 와, 2백만 번이나 시청되었구나! 그렇게 많은 사람이 이 비디오를 보았다니 놀라워.

G: 알아! 이런 종류의 프로그램이 지금 인기를 얻는 중이야.

B: 그것은 매우 편리해 보여. 너는 운동하러 밖에 나갈 필요가 없어.

G: 맞아. 그런 이유로 나는 이런 프로그램을 아주 좋아해. 너도 한번 시도해 봐.

❶ 'it's been watched'는 현재완료 수동태이다.
❷ That's why ~. = 그것이 ~하는 이유이다., 그런 이유로 ~하다.

Check(√) True or False

(3) The girl is doing yoga with the boy.　　　　T ☐ F ☐

(4) Online video program is becoming popular.　　T ☐ F ☐

Listen & Talk 1 A

B: Have you heard that ❶chewing ice is bad for your teeth?
G: No, I haven't. Why is that?
B: It can damage your teeth. It can also make them too ❷sensitive.

❶ 'chewing ice'는 is의 주어인 동명사이다.
❷ sensitive는 동사 make의 목적격보어이다.

Listen & Talk 1 C

G: ❶Have you heard the term *body image*? It means "the way you see your own body." A lot of teens have a negative body image. They think they're too fat or too thin ❷compared to others. However, I want you to build a positive body image. Accept your body as it is and give ❸yourself praise every day. Remember, there is only one you, so don't compare yourself to others. Loving yourself can make a big difference in your life.

❶ 상대방이 body image라는 용어를 아는지 묻는 말이다.
❷ compared to = ~와 비교하여
❸ yourself는 재귀 용법의 재귀대명사이다.

Listen & Talk 1 D-1

A: Have you heard that ❶writing by hand is good for your health?
B: Oh, really?
A: Yes, it improves your memory.

❶ 'writing by hand'는 주어 역할을 하는 동명사이다.

Listen & Talk 1 D-2

A: Have you heard that ❶using a cell phone before bed is bad for your health?
B: Oh, really?
A: Yes, ❷it prevents deep sleep.

❶ 'using a cell phone before bed'가 동사 is의 주어인 동명사이다.
❷ it = using a cell phone before bed

Listen & Talk 2 A

G: What's this?
B: It's a smart band. ❶It lets me check my health information on my smartphone.
G: What kind of information?
B: It shows ❷how far I walk during the day and how well I sleep at night.
G: Interesting. I'm surprised that this small band can do all that.

❶ 사역동사 let이 쓰여서 목적격보어 check는 원형부정사이다.
❷ 'how far ~'와 'how well ~'은 간접의문문으로 show의 목적어이다.

Listen & Talk 2 C

B: What is that? It looks nice.
G: This is a magic cup. I carry it everywhere with me.
B: What's special about it?
G: It's awesome. ❶It tells me to drink water every two hours.
B: Really? I'm surprised that it can talk to you.
G: It even asks me questions like "Aren't you thirsty?"
B: That's so cool! But why are you trying to drink more water?
G: Because ❷drinking a lot of water can increase your energy and help your blood flow.
B: That's amazing. I should buy one!

❶ 'tell+목적어+to부정사'의 구문으로 to부정사가 목적격보어이다.
❷ 'drinking a lot of water'는 주어 역할을 하는 동명사구이다.

Do It Yourself A

B: Oh, I'm so hungry.
G: Why don't you eat some snacks before dinner?
B: ❶I don't want to. I'll wait until dinner.
G: Okay, but have you heard that eating little and often is good for your health?
B: Really? I thought eating three meals a day was fine.
G: If you keep waiting until dinner, you will eat too much and too quickly. Eating little and often ❷prevents you from eating like that.
B: I see. Then I'll go eat an apple right now.

❶ 'I don't want to.' 뒤에는 'eat some snacks before dinner'가 생략되었다.
❷ prevent A from -ing= A가 ~하지 못하게 하다

● 다음 우리말과 일치하도록 빈칸에 알맞은 말을 쓰시오.

Listen & Talk 1 A

B: _____ you _____ that _____ ice is bad for your _____?

G: No, I haven't. _____ is that?

B: It can _____ your teeth. It can also _____ them too _____.

Listen & Talk 1 B

B: You _____ tired. Did you _____ _____ sleep?

G: Yes, I did. I _____ _____ _____ seven hours.

B: Okay. _____ _____ you _____ to bed?

G: I _____ _____ _____ after midnight, _____ _____.

B: That's probably _____ is _____ you tired. _____ you heard that _____ you go to bed is very important?

G: No, I haven't. _____ is _____?

B: Scientists say that _____ _____ _____ _____ can make you _____ _____ the next day.

G: I didn't know that.

B: On the _____ hand, going to bed early can _____ your _____ and help you be more _____. From _____ on, try to go to bed earlier.

Listen & Talk 1 D-1

A: _____ you heard that _____ by hand is _____ for your _____?

B: Oh, _____?

A: Yes, it _____ your memory.

Listen & Talk 2 A

G: What's this?

B: It's a _____ band. It lets me _____ my _____ information on my _____.

G: What _____ of information?

B: It shows _____ _____ I walk during the day and _____ _____ I sleep at night.

G: Interesting. I'm _____ that this _____ band can do all that.

해석

B: 너는 얼음을 씹는 것이 이에 나쁘다는 말을 들어보았니?
G: 아니. 왜 그런데?
B: 그것이 이에 손상을 줄 수 있어. 그것은 또한 이를 너무 예민하게 만들 수 있어.

B: 너 피곤해 보인다. 잠은 충분히 잤니?
G: 응, 그래. 나는 일곱 시간 이상 잤어.
B: 알았어. 너는 언제 잠들었니?
G: 평소처럼 자정이 넘어서 잠들었어.
B: 아마 그것이 너를 피곤하게 만드는 것일 거야. 네가 언제 잠자리에 드는지가 아주 중요하다는 말을 들어본 적이 있니?
G: 아니. 왜 그렇지?
B: 과학자들은 늦게 잠자리에 드는 것은 그 다음날 피곤함을 느끼게 할 수 있다고 말해.
G: 나는 몰랐어.
B: 반면에 일찍 잠자리에 드는 것은 기억력을 향상시키고, 더 생산적이 되도록 도와줄 수 있어. 지금부터는 일찍 자도록 노력해 봐.

A: 손으로 글을 쓰는 것이 건강에 좋다는 말을 들어본 적이 있니?
B: 오, 정말?
A: 그래, 그것이 기억력을 높여주는데.

G: 이것이 뭐니?
B: 그것은 스마트밴드야. 그것은 나에게 스마트폰으로 건강 정보를 점검할 수 있도록 해줘.
G: 어떤 종류의 정보니?
B: 그것은 내가 낮에 얼마나 멀리 걷는지, 밤에 얼마나 잘 자는지를 보여줘.
G: 흥미롭다. 나는 이 작은 밴드가 그 모든 일을 할 수 있다는 것이 놀라워.

Listen & Talk 2 B

B: _____ are you doing in the _____ room?

G: I'm _____ _____.

B: You're _____ out by _____?

G: Yes, I'm _____ this online video. It shows me all the _____.

B: _____ me see. Wow, it's _____ _____ two million times! I'm _____ that so many people _____ _____ this video.

G: I know! These kinds of _____ are becoming _____ right now.

B: It looks very _____. You don't have to go _____ to _____.

G: That's right. _____ _____ I love these programs. You should _____ them, too.

Listen & Talk 2 C

B: What is that? It _____ nice.

G: This is a _____ cup. I carry it _____ with me.

B: What's _____ about it?

G: It's _____. It tells me to _____ water _____ two hours.

B: Really? I'm _____ that it can _____ to you.

G: It even _____ me questions like "Aren't you _____?"

B: That's so cool! But _____ are you _____ to drink more water?

G: Because _____ a lot of water can _____ your energy and _____ your blood _____.

B: That's amazing. I should _____ one!

Do It Yourself A

B: Oh, I'm so _____.

G: Why _____ you eat some snacks _____ dinner?

B: I don't _____ to. I'll _____ until dinner.

G: Okay, but have you heard that _____ little and _____ is good for your _____?

B: _____? I thought _____ three meals a day was fine.

G: If you keep _____ until dinner, you will _____ too much and _____ quickly. _____ and _____ prevents you _____ _____ like that.

B: I see. Then I'll go _____ an apple _____ now.

B: 너 거실에서 무엇을 하고 있니?

G: 나는 요가를 하는 중이야.

B: 혼자서 운동한다는 말이니?

G: 그래, 이 온라인 비디오를 따라하는 중이야. 그것이 나에게 모든 단계를 보여줘.

B: 어디 보자. 와, 2백만 번이나 시청되었구나! 그렇게 많은 사람이 이 비디오를 보았다니 놀라워.

G: 알아! 이런 종류의 프로그램이 지금 인기를 얻는 중이야.

B: 그것은 매우 편리해 보여. 너는 운동하러 밖에 나갈 필요가 없어.

G: 맞아. 그런 이유로 나는 이런 프로그램을 아주 좋아해. 너도 한번 시도해 봐.

B: 저것이 뭐니? 그것은 좋아 보인다.

G: 이것은 매직 컵이야. 나는 어디든지 그것을 가지고 다녀.

B: 그것은 무엇이 특별하니?

G: 정말 끝내줘. 그것은 두 시간마다 물을 마시라고 나에게 말을 해.

B: 정말? 그것이 너에게 말을 할 수 있다는 것이 놀라워.

G: 심지어 그것은 "목마르지 않니?'와 같은 질문도 해.

B: 정말 멋지구나! 그런데 왜 너는 물을 더 마시려고 애쓰니?

G: 왜냐하면 물을 많이 마시는 것이 에너지를 높여주고, 피가 잘 흐르게 도와줘.

B: 정말 놀랍구나. 하나 사야겠다!

B: 오, 나는 너무 배가 고파.

G: 저녁 먹기 전에 간식을 좀 먹는 것이 어떠니?

B: 나는 그것을 원하지 않아. 나는 저녁 식사까지 기다릴 거야.

G: 알았어. 하지만 너는 조금 자주 먹는 것이 건강에 좋다는 말을 들어본 적이 있니?

B: 정말이니? 나는 하루에 세끼 식사하는 것이 좋다고 생각했는데.

G: 만약 네가 저녁식사까지 계속 기다리면 너무 많이 그리고 너무 빨리 먹을 거야. 조금 자주 먹는 것이 네가 그렇게 먹는 것을 막아 줄 거야.

B: 알았어. 그러면 지금 당장 사과를 먹으러 가야겠다.

Conversation 시험대비 기본평가

01 다음 대화의 빈칸에 들어갈 말로 알맞은 것은?

> A: This running app can track your running course. It can suggest many different training plans, too.
> B: I'm _____ that it can do all that.

① worried　　　② disappointed　　　③ surprised
④ happy　　　⑤ concerned

02 다음 중 밑줄 친 말 대신 쓰기에 <u>어색한</u> 것을 고르시오.

> B: Have you heard that chewing ice is bad for your teeth?
> G: <u>No, I haven't.</u> Why is that?
> B: It can damage your teeth. It can also make them too sensitive.

① I think I have.　　② Oh, really?　　③ I didn't know that.
④ No, that's new to me.　　⑤ No. I've never heard of it.

[03~04] 다음 대화를 읽고 물음에 답하시오.

> B: What are you doing in the living room?
> G: I'm doing yoga.
> B: You're working out by yourself?
> G: Yes, I'm following this online video. It shows me all the steps.
> B: Let me see. Wow, it's been watched two million times! I'm surprised that so many people have watched this video.
> G: I know! These kinds of programs are becoming popular right now.
> B: It looks very convenient. You don't have to go out to exercise.
> G: That's right. <u>그런 이유로 나는 이 프로그램을 아주 좋아해.</u> (that's, these programs, why, love, I) You should try them, too.

03 밑줄 친 우리말 의미에 어울리도록 주어진 단어를 배열하시오.

➡ _____

04 위 대화의 내용과 일치하는 것은?

① The boy and the girl are doing yoga.
② The boy is showing the online video.
③ The girl follows all the steps of the video.
④ The girl didn't know many people watched the video.
⑤ Because of the video, the girl wants to go out.

[01~03] 다음 대화를 읽고 물음에 답하시오.

> B: You look tired. Did you get enough sleep?
> G: Yes, I did. I slept ____(A)____ over seven hours.
> B: Okay. When did you go to bed?
> G: I went to bed after midnight, (B)평소처럼.
> B: That's probably what is making you tired. Have you heard that when you go to bed is very important?
> G: No, I haven't. Why is that?
> B: Scientists say that going to bed late can make you feel tired the next day.
> G: I didn't know that.
> B: On the other hand, going to bed early can improve your memory and help you be more productive. From now on, try to going to bed earlier.

01 빈칸 (A)에 들어갈 전치사를 고르시오.

① with   ② on   ③ in   ④ for   ⑤ by

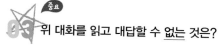
02 밑줄 친 (B)의 우리말을 영어로 쓰시오.

➡ _____

03 위 대화를 읽고 대답할 수 없는 것은?

① Did the girl get enough sleep?
② Why does the girl go to bed late?
③ How many hours did the girl sleep?
④ Why does the girl look tired?
⑤ What does the boy advise the girl to do?

04 밑줄 친 ①~⑤ 중 문맥상이나 어법상 어색한 것을 찾아 고치시오.

> B: Oh, ①I'm so hungry.
> G: Why don't you eat some snacks before dinner?
> B: I don't want to. ②I'll wait until dinner.
> G: Okay, but have you heard that ③eat little and often is good for your health?
> B: Really? I thought eating three meals a day was fine.
> G: If you keep waiting until dinner, ④you will eat too much and too quickly. Eating little and often prevents you from eating like that.
> B: I see. ⑤Then I'll go eat an apple right now.

➡ _____

05 다음 대화의 빈칸에 들어갈 말을 고르시오.

> A: Have you heard that using a cell phone before bed is bad for your health?
> B: Oh, really?
> A: _____

① Yes, it prevents deep sleep.
② I'm surprised that you know that.
③ Didn't you have a cell phone?
④ Why don't you buy a new cell phone?
⑤ How many hours do you use your cell phone?

06 다음 문장에서 어법상 어색한 부분을 찾아 올바른 형태로 고치시오.

> Have you heard that swimming is good for your back? Our group made a plan go swimming together every Tuesday and Thursday at World Sports Park. We are sure it will help us stay healthy.

➡ _____

[07~10] 다음 대화를 읽고 물음에 답하시오.

B: What is that? It looks nice.
G: This is a magic cup. I carry it everywhere with me. (ⓐ)
B: What's special about it?
G: It's awesome. (ⓑ)
B: Really? I'm surprised that it can talk to you.
G: It even asks me questions like "Aren't you thirsty?" (ⓒ)
B: That's so cool! But ___(A)___ are you trying to drink more water? (ⓓ)
G: Because drinking a lot of water can ___(B)___ your energy and help your blood flow. (ⓔ)
B: That's amazing. I should buy one!

07 ⓐ~ⓔ 중에서 다음 문장이 들어가기에 적절한 곳은?

> It tells me to drink water every two hours.

① ⓐ　② ⓑ　③ ⓒ　④ ⓓ　⑤ ⓔ

08 빈칸 (A)에 들어가기에 적절한 의문사를 쓰시오.

➡ _____

09 위 대화의 빈칸 (B)에 다음 영영풀이에 해당하는 단어를 철자 i로 시작하여 쓰시오.

> to make something larger or greater in size, amount, number, etc.

➡ _____

10 위 대화의 내용과 일치하지 않는 것은?

① The girl carries a cup everywhere.
② The cup makes the girl drink water every three hours.
③ The boy is surprised that the cup can talk.
④ Drinking a lot of water increases our energy.
⑤ The cup can ask questions like "Aren't you thirsty?"

11 밑줄 친 ⓐ~ⓔ 중 대화의 흐름상 어색한 문장은?

B: What are you doing in the living room?
G: I'm doing yoga.
B: ⓐYou're working out by yourself?
G: Yes, ⓑI'm following this online video. It shows me all the steps.
B: Let me see. Wow, ⓒit's been watched two million times! I'm surprised that so many people have watched this video.
G: I know! ⓓThese kinds of programs are becoming popular right now.
B: It looks very convenient. You don't have to go out to exercise.
G: That's right. That's why I love these programs. ⓔYou should avoid them, too.

① ⓐ　② ⓑ　③ ⓒ　④ ⓓ　⑤ ⓔ

[01~03] 다음 대화를 읽고 물음에 답하시오.

> B: Have you heard that chewing ice is bad ___(A)___ your teeth?
> G: No, I haven't. ___(B)___?
> B: It can damage your teeth. (C)그것은 또한 그것들을 너무 민감하게 만들 수 있어.

01 빈칸 (A)에 들어갈 전치사를 쓰시오.

➡ _____

02 빈칸 (B)에 들어갈 적절한 내용의 의문문을 쓰시오. (that을 포함하는 3단어)

➡ _____

03 밑줄 친 (C)의 우리말을 영작하시오.

➡ _____

04 다음 대화의 빈칸에 들어갈 말을 〈보기〉에서 골라 순서대로 배열하시오.

> B: Oh, I'm so hungry.
> G: _____
> B: _____
> G: Okay, but have you heard that eating little and often is good for your health?
> B: Really? _____
> G: If you keep waiting until dinner, you will eat too much and too quickly.
> _____
> B:

┤ 보기 ├
> (A) Eating little and often prevents you from eating like that.
> (B) Why don't you eat some snacks before dinner?
> (C) I see. Then I'll go eat an apple right now.
> (D) I thought eating three meals a day was fine.
> (E) I don't want to. I'll wait until dinner.

➡ _____

[05~06] 다음 대화를 읽고 물음에 답하시오.

> B: What are you doing in the living room?
> G: I'm doing yoga.
> B: You're ___(A)___ out by yourself?
> G: Yes, I'm following this online video. It shows me all the steps.
> B: Let me see. Wow, it's been watched two million times! (B)그렇게 많은 사람들이 이 비디오를 보았다는 사실에 놀랐다. (have watched)
> G: I know! These kinds of programs are becoming popular right now.
> B: It looks very convenient. You don't have to go out to exercise.
> G: That's right. That's why I love these programs. You should try them, too.

05 내용상 (A)에 들어가기에 적절한 말을 쓰시오.

➡ _____

06 밑줄 친 (B)의 우리말을 영어 문장으로 옮겨 쓰시오.

➡ _____
_____

Grammar

① 관계대명사의 계속적 용법

- Walnuts also have wrinkles, **which** the brain has too.
  호두에는 또한 주름이 있는데, 이 주름은 인간의 뇌에도 있다.
- Stadler, **who** is 33 years old, was the 2004 winner. Stadler는 33세인데, 2004년 우승자였다.

■ 관계대명사의 계속적 용법은 관계대명사 앞에 콤마(,)를 붙인 형태로 선행사를 부연 설명한다. 제한적 용법과 마찬가지로 선행사가 사람이면 who, 사물이면 which를 쓴다. 제한적 용법은 관계사가 이끄는 절부터 해석하고, 계속적 용법은 앞에서부터 해석한다.

- He has two daughters **who** are teachers. 그는 교사인 딸이 둘 있다.: 제한적 용법 → 딸이 둘인지 더 있는지 모름.
- He has two daughters, **who** are teachers. 그는 딸이 둘인데, 그들은 교사이다.: 계속적 용법 → 딸이 둘만 있음.

■ 계속적 용법의 관계대명사는 '접속사(and, but, for, though 등)+대명사'로 고쳐 쓸 수 있다.

- I bought a book, **which** was written by Roald Dahl.
  = I bought a book, **and it** was written by Roald Dahl.
  나는 책을 한 권 샀는데 그 책은 Roald Dahl에 의해 씌여진 것이다.

■ 관계대명사 that과 what은 계속적 용법으로 사용할 수 없으며, 관계대명사가 계속적 용법으로 쓰였을 때는 생략하지 않는다.

- The swing, **which** I rode when I was a child, gathered rust. (○)
- The swing, that I rode when I was a child, gathered rust. (×)
  그 그네는 내가 어렸을 때 타고 놀았던 것인데, 녹이 슬었다.

■ which는 선행사로 구나 절을 가질 수도 있다.

- People say that I found my level, **which** I don't agree.
  사람들이 내가 알맞은 곳에 자리잡았다고 하지만, 나는 그렇게 생각하지 않는다.

핵심 Check

1. 빈칸에 알맞은 관계대명사를 쓰시오.
   (1) This story is about a man, _____ had two daughters.
   (2) I was offered another position, _____ I accepted.
   (3) He has a car, _____ is expensive.

2 명사의 뒤에서 명사를 수식하는 분사

- We all know that a diet **containing** a variety of food keeps our bodies healthy. 우리는 모두 다양한 음식을 포함하는 식사가 우리의 몸을 건강하게 유지시켜 준다는 것을 알고 있다.
- Frank took part in a meeting **held** in Seoul. Frank는 서울에서 열린 회의에 참석했다.

■ 분사는 명사의 앞이나 뒤에서 명사를 꾸며 주는 형용사 역할을 한다. 현재분사는 '능동' 이나 '진행'의 의미가 있고, 과거분사는 '수동'이나 '완료'의 의미가 있다.
- There is a baby **sleeping** in the cradle. 요람에서 자고 있는 아기가 있다.: 뒤에서 수식하는 현재분사 '진행'
- The **sleeping** baby is very cute. 자고 있는 그 아기는 매우 귀엽다.: 앞에서 수식하는 현재분사 '진행'
- I met a little girl **named** Lily. 나는 Lily라는 이름의 어린 소녀를 만났다.: 뒤에서 수식하는 과거분사 '수동'
- Many of the **invited** guests will not attend the party.
  초대 받은 손님 중 상당수가 파티에 참석하지 않을 것이다.: 앞에서 수식하는 과거분사 '수동'

■ 분사에 다른 어구(목적어나 보어, 수식어구 등)가 함께 있을 때는 뒤에서 명사를 수식한다.
- Look at the boy **dancing** on the stage. 무대 위에서 춤추는 소년을 보세요.
- I entered the hall **crowded** with people. 나는 사람들이 붐비는 복도로 들어갔다.

■ 명사를 뒤에서 수식하는 경우에는 그 앞에 '주격 관계대명사+be 동사'가 생략된 것으로 생각할 수 있다.
- Look at the boy (who is) **dancing** on the stage.
- I entered the hall (which was) **crowded** with people.

핵심 Check

2. 괄호 안에 주어진 어휘를 이용하여 빈칸을 알맞게 채우시오.

(1) I would love to have a room _____ with books. (fill)

(2) This photo is about a woman _____ a bag. (carry)

(3) There was a young man _____ tea in the living room. (have)

01 다음 빈칸에 들어갈 말로 알맞은 것은?

> Bill had some books, _____ he read again and again.

① who   ② which   ③ how
④ that   ⑤ what

02 다음 괄호 안에서 알맞은 말을 고르시오.

(1) It is a fact (knowing / known) to everybody.

(2) There were some pictures (painting / painted) by herself.

(3) The girl (wearing / worn) a blue hat is my sister.

(4) A bright light brought the (sleeping / slept) baby into view.

03 다음 두 문장을 한 문장으로 바꾸어 쓸 때 알맞게 표현한 것을 고르시오.

> • Ms. Green is an English teacher.
> • She lives in this house.

① Ms. Green, which is an English teacher, lives in this house.
② Ms. Green, what is an English teacher, lives in this house.
③ Ms. Green, who is an English teacher, lives in this house.
④ Ms. Green, whom is an English teacher, lives in this house.
⑤ Ms. Green, that is an English teacher, lives in this house.

04 다음 우리말에 맞게 주어진 어휘를 바르게 배열하시오.

(1) 나는 그 책을 읽기 시작했는데 그것은 매우 재미있었다.
    (I, the book, interesting, read, began, was, very, which, to)
    ➡ _____

(2) TV를 보고 있는 소년은 Jane의 아들입니다.
    (the boy, Jane's son, TV, watching, is)
    ➡ _____

(3) 그는 한국에서 만들어진 스마트폰을 샀다.
    (he, Korea, smart phone, bought, made, a, in)
    ➡ _____

01 다음 중 어법상 어색한 것은?

① Walnuts also have wrinkles, which the brain has too.
② Amy lives in a house, that has a nice pool.
③ These are the books, which I bought yesterday.
④ Mike, who is a thief, is in the jail now.
⑤ The Eiffel Tower, which is made of steel, is in France.

02 중요 다음 중 어법상 바르지 않은 것은?

① The castle attacked by the enemy was finally destroyed.
② There was only one book remaining in the box.
③ Saint Exupery wrote many touched stories.
④ The little girl taking a walk in the park is my daughter.
⑤ We all know that a diet containing a variety of food keeps our bodies healthy.

03 다음 빈칸에 알맞은 말이 바르게 짝지어진 것은?

| • The students _____ the movie looked so bored. |
| • He likes Kate, _____ is very kind. |

① watching – who
② watching – that
③ watched – who
④ watched – that
⑤ watch – what

서답형
04 다음 괄호 안에서 알맞은 말을 고르시오.

(1) I know Ms. Chalsey, (who / that) is from Canada.
(2) Tom visited his house, (who / which) was in London.
(3) He said nothing, (that / which) made his mom get angrier.
(4) Look at the man (playing / played) the flute.
(5) Can you show me the article (posting / posted) on the site?
(6) Shirley couldn't get into the house because of the fiercely (barking / barked) dog.

05 중요 주어진 문장의 밑줄 친 부분의 쓰임이 나머지 넷과 다른 것은?

① *The Kiss* is a famous picture <u>painted</u> by Klimt.
② Mr. Kim is a Korean artist <u>known</u> to everyone in Korea.
③ Noah read a newspaper <u>written</u> in English.
④ Everyone <u>invited</u> to the party is expected to bring a gift.
⑤ Someone had already <u>made</u> coffee by the time I arrived at my office.

06 다음 밑줄 친 부분을 바꿔 쓸 때, 의미상 가장 적절한 것은?

> This is *The Old Man and the Sea*, which was written by Hemingway.

① as it
② but it
③ or it
④ and it
⑤ because it

07 〈중요〉 Which is suitable for the blank?

> Mina is appreciating a painting _____ by Pierre-Auguste Renoir.

① draw
② drew
③ drawn
④ drawing
⑤ to draw

〈서답형〉

08 다음 빈칸에 알맞은 관계대명사를 쓰시오.

(1) This is Sarah, _____ is the kindest girl in our school.
(2) Carrots have some chemicals that can make vitamin A, _____ improves your vision.
(3) She went to the party with Hannah, _____ is her best friend.
(4) We visited a museum, _____ is in Jeonju.

09 다음 우리말을 바르게 영작한 것을 고르시오.

> 나를 기다리는 사람들이 있었다.

① There were waiting people for me.
② There were people waiting for me.
③ There were people waited for me.
④ There were waited people for me.
⑤ There were people wait for me.

10 〈중요〉 다음 문장의 밑줄 친 부분 중 어법상 <u>어색한</u> 것은?

> This is the picture of Leopard Cat, ⓐthat ⓑis ⓒeasily ⓓfound ⓔin Thailand and Southeast Asia

① ⓐ
② ⓑ
③ ⓒ
④ ⓓ
⑤ ⓔ

11 다음 문장의 빈칸에 들어갈 수 <u>없는</u> 것은?

> *Yesterday* is a famous song _____ by many singers.

① sung
② singing
③ loved
④ which is sung
⑤ which is loved

〈서답형〉

12 다음 밑줄 친 부분을 바꿔 쓸 때, 빈칸에 적절한 말을 쓰시오.

> • To buy some food, she went to the store, for it was the cheapest.
> = To buy some food, she went to the store, _____ was the cheapest.

13 〈중요〉 다음 문장의 빈칸에 들어갈 수 <u>없는</u> 말은?

> The boy _____ is my friend.

① dancing to music
② invited to the party
③ talking to Sumi
④ reading a book
⑤ wears glasses

14 다음 빈칸에 알맞은 것은?

> Yesterday I met Clare, _____ I haven't seen for long.

① whom ② which
③ that ④ what
⑤ when

15 다음 빈칸에 알맞은 말이 순서대로 바르게 짝지어진 것을 고르시오.

> • The curry _____ at this restaurant tastes good.
> • The lady _____ a pretty bag is talking on the phone with her friend.

① served – held
② served – holding
③ serves – holds
④ serving – held
⑤ serving – holding

서답형

16 다음 문장에서 어법상 어색한 것을 바르게 고쳐 다시 쓰시오.

(1) I didn't like the students, which ran here and there in the library.

➡ _____

_____

(2) I put the picture on the wall, that made me remember my best friend.

➡ _____

_____

(3) There was a little baby cried on the bed.

➡ _____

_____

(4) People all over the world love to eat food making out of potatoes.

➡ _____

_____

17 다음 중 어법상 어색한 것을 고르시오. (2개)

① Sam liked the present, that Bella gave to her.
② Mick is the boy singing on the stage.
③ I will visit my friend in Suwon, who is a teacher.
④ The woman nicknaming Black Swan is working at the bank.
⑤ I opened the box, which was filled with a lot of books.

18 다음 우리말에 맞게 영작한 것을 고르시오.

> 나는 그 방에서 상자 하나를 발견했는데, 그것은 녹색 천으로 덮여 있었다.

① I discovered a box in the room, that was covered with a green cloth.
② I discovered a box in the room, to cover with a green cloth.
③ I discovered a box in the room, which was covered with a green cloth.
④ I discovered a box in the room, which was covering with a green cloth.
⑤ I discovered a box in the room, covering with a green cloth.

서답형

19 다음 문장에서 생략되어 있는 것을 찾아 어법에 맞게 다시 쓰시오.

(1) Kim Yuna loved by many Koreans was a famous figure skater.

➡ _____

_____

(2) People in Germany want to buy smart phones made in Korea.

➡ _____

_____

01 빈칸에 알맞은 관계대명사를 쓰시오.

(1) Emily, _____ is five years old, can play the flute.

(2) Help yourself to the food, _____ is very delicious.

(3) My best friend, _____ wants to be a B-boy dancer, is Jackson.

(4) Mom let me play computer games, _____ made me surprised.

02 다음 우리말에 맞게 주어진 어구를 바르게 배열하시오.

(1) 무명 작가에 의해 씌여진 그 소설은 작년에 영화로 만들어졌다. (an, author, written, was, the novel, a movie, unknown, made, last year, into, by)

➡ _____

(2) 한국은 10위를 차지했는데 그것은 인도와 브라질보다 앞선 순위였다. (Korea, India and Brazil, ahead, 10th place, ranked, was, which, of)

➡ _____

(3) 개를 산책시키고 있는 그 남자는 내 친구이다. (the man, of, his dog, a friend, walking, is, is, mine, who)

➡ _____

03 다음 문장에서 생략된 것을 넣어 다시 쓰시오.

(1) A lot of people like cars made in Korea.

➡ _____

(2) The man reading a book at the table is my father.

➡ _____

(3) The little girl holding the woman's hand is crying loudly.

➡ _____

04 다음 두 문장을 해석하고 그 차이를 설명하시오.

(1) Jacob has two sons who are farmers.
(2) Jacob has two sons, who are farmers.

➡ 해석: _____

차이: _____

05 괄호 안에 있는 단어를 어법에 맞게 고쳐 쓰시오.

(1) The second story is about a woman (bake) bread.

➡ _____

(2) I got a message (write) in numbers.

➡ _____

06 다음 그림을 보고, 주어진 어휘를 이용하여 빈칸을 알맞게 채우시오.

(1) All the actors _____

make the musical interesting. (sing and dance)

(2) Do not bother the _____ trees. (plant)

07 다음 〈보기〉에 주어진 단어를 이용하여 문맥에 맞게 문장을 완성하시오.

┌─── 보기 ───┐
| lie   wrap |
└──────────┘

(1) Do you see a little box _____ in silver _____ paper?

(2) Look at the big snake _____ in a coil.

08 관계대명사의 계속적 용법을 이용하여 주어진 두 문장을 하나의 문장으로 쓰시오.

(1) • The new library can hold many people.
　　• And it made them happy.
　➡ _____
　　_____

(2) • Ella carried a box.
　　• It looked very heavy for her.
　➡ _____
　　_____

(3) • I like Jane.
　　• I like her, for she is kind and wise.
　➡ _____
　　_____

09 다음 문장에서 어법상 <u>어색한</u> 것을 바르게 고치시오.

(1) Snow White lived in the palace, who had a nice and beautiful garden.
　_____ ➡ _____

(2) The owner, which is a scary person, will be angry at you.
　_____ ➡ _____

(3) I visited my grandfather, that wasn't home.
　_____ ➡ _____

(4) The sleeping in the bed baby is Emma's daughter.
　_____ ➡ _____

(5) Frank has a nice car making in Germany.
　_____ ➡ _____

(6) The shop sold toy cars became popular.
　_____ ➡ _____

Beneficial Foods for Our Bodies

We all know that a diet containing a variety of foods keeps our
<small>that은 명사절을 이끄는 접속사로 생략 가능   현재분사로 앞의 명사 a diet를 수식</small>

bodies healthy. But sometimes we are not sure which foods are good
<small>의문형용사</small>

for which body parts. Nature, however, gives us a big clue. Look at the
<small>= gives a big clue to us (4형식)</small>

following examples. Each of these foods not only looks like a certain
<small>= not merely[just/simply]</small>

body part but is also good for that body part.
<small>not only A but also B = B as well as A: 'A뿐만 아니라 B도</small>

Slice open a tomato and compare it with the human heart. You will
<small>얇게 썰어 열다   compare A with B: A와 B를 비교하다</small>

see that they look similar. They both have multiple hollow spaces and
<small>= a tomato (which is sliced open) and the human heart</small>

are red. Researchers say that the chemicals that make tomatoes red are
<small>선행사 the chemicals를 수식하는 주격 관계대명사</small>

good for your heart and blood. In addition, eating tomatoes can lower
<small>= Besides   동명사 주어</small>

your risk of heart disease.

Look at the shape of a walnut. Do you notice anything? Yes, it's very
<small>= the shape of a walnut</small>

similar to the shape of the human brain! A walnut is divided into two
<small>A is similar to B: A는 B와 유사하다   be divided into: ~로 나뉘다</small>

parts, just like the brain. Walnuts also have wrinkles, which the brain
<small>꼭 ~처럼   콤마(,)와 함께 쓰인 계속적 용법의 목적격 관계대명사</small>

has too. Studies show that walnuts help our brains stay healthy and
<small>help+목적어+원형부정사 또는 to부정사</small>

active. They are also good for preventing Alzheimer's disease.
<small>be good for: ~에 좋다</small>

---

beneficial 유익한, 이로운
diet 식사, 식습관
contain …이 함유되어 있다
a variety of 여러 가지의
nature 자연, 본성
clue 단서, 실마리
slice (얇게) 썰다
compare 비교하다
multiple 많은, 다수의, 다양한
hollow 속이 빈, 텅 빈
researcher 연구원, 조사원
chemical 화학 물질, 화학제품
risk 위험
disease 질병, 병
in addition 게다가, 덧붙여
similar 유사한, 닮은
wrinkle 주름, 주름을 잡다
active 활동적인, 활발한
prevent 예방하다, 막다

확인문제

● 다음 문장이 본문의 내용과 일치하면 T, 일치하지 <u>않으면</u> F를 쓰시오.

1   A diet containing a variety of foods keeps our bodies healthy. ☐

2   We are sure which foods are good for which body parts. ☐

3   A tomato and the human heart have multiple hollow spaces and are red. ☐

4   Eating tomatoes can increase your risk of heart disease. ☐

5   The chemicals that make tomatoes red are good for your heart and blood. ☐

6   Walnuts help our stomach stay healthy and active. ☐

A slice of carrot looks like the human eye. Carrots have some
look like+명사: …인 것처럼 보이다

chemicals that can make vitamin A, which improves your vision. It
선행사 some chemicals를 수식하는 주격 관계대명사   which는 계속적 용법의 주격 관계대명사이며, 선행사 vitamin A를 부연 설명

helps your eyes process light and send a clear image to the brain. So if
help+목적어+원형부정사 또는 to부정사

you want healthy eyes, eat carrots.

Cutting onions is not fun because it makes you cry. But try slicing
동명사 주어   are(×)   사역동사(make)+목적어+원형부정사   잘라 보아라

one anyway. You can see that the inside looks a little like a human cell.
= anyhow = at any rate = in any case = at all events   └ ~처럼 보인다 ┘

Scientists say that onions contain vitamin B, which helps make new,
계속적 용법의 주격 관계대명사로, 선행사 vitamin B를 부연 설명   help+원형부정사 또는 to부정사

healthy cells.

Now, let's move on to ginger. What body part comes to mind when
어떤(의문형용사)

you see it? Doesn't it look like a stomach? You may not like ginger's
= ginger   ~하지 않을지도 모른다

strong taste or smell, but these come from a special chemical that
~로부터 나오다

prevents you from feeling sick and throwing up. For this reason, ginger
prevent A from ~ing: A가 ~하는 것을 막다

can be good for your stomach.

Isn't it amazing that some foods mirror the body parts that they
가주어   진주어가 되는 명사절 이끄는 접속사   목적격 관계대명사

are good for? Interestingly, there are many other such foods. Find
수사의문문: 강한 반어적 표현(It is amazing의 뜻을 더 강하게 표현한 것임.)

as many as you can and try to eat a variety of them.
as+원급+as+주어+can[could] = as+원급+as possible: '가능한 한 …한'

---

improve 개선하다, 향상시키다

vision 시력, 눈

process 과정; 처리하다

cell 작은 방, 세포

move on (새로운 일 · 주제로) 넘어가다

ginger 생강

come to mind 생각이 떠오르다, 생각나다

stomach 위, 위장, 복부

throw up 토하다

mirror 거울; 잘 보여주다, 반영하다

📎 **확인문제**

● 다음 문장이 본문의 내용과 일치하면 T, 일치하지 않으면 F를 쓰시오.

1 A slice of carrot is similar to the human eye. ☐

2 Vitamin B helps your eyes process light. ☐

3 It is not fun to cut onions because it makes you cry. ☐

4 Vitamin A in onions helps make new, healthy cells. ☐

5 Ginger looks like a stomach. ☐

6 It isn't amazing that some foods mirror the body parts that they are good for. ☐

● 우리말을 참고하여 빈칸에 알맞은 말을 쓰시오.

1 _____ Foods for Our Bodies

2 We all know that a diet _____ a variety of foods _____ our bodies _____.

3 But sometimes we are not sure which foods _____ _____ _____ which body parts.

4 Nature, however, gives us _____ _____ _____.

5 Look at the _____ examples.

6 Each of these foods _____ _____ looks like a certain body part _____ is _____ good for that body part.

7 Slice open a tomato and _____ it _____ the human heart.

8 You will see that they _____ _____.

9 They both have _____ _____ _____ and are red.

10 Researchers say _____ the chemicals _____ make tomatoes red _____ good for your heart and blood.

11 _____ _____, eating tomatoes can _____ your risk of heart disease.

12 Look at _____ _____ of a walnut.

13 Do you notice _____?

14 Yes, it's very _____ _____ the shape of the human brain!

15 A walnut _____ _____ _____ two parts, just like the brain.

16 Walnuts also have wrinkles, _____ the brain has too.

17 Studies show that walnuts help our brains _____ _____ and active.

18 They are also good for _____ Alzheimer's disease.

19 _____ _____ _____ _____ looks like the human eye.

20 Carrots have some chemicals _____ can make vitamin A, _____ improves your vision.

21 It helps your eyes _____ light and _____ a clear image _____ the brain.

22 So if you want _____ _____, eat carrots.

23 _____ _____ is not fun because it _____ _____ _____.

24 But _____ _____ one anyway.

25 You can see that the inside _____ _____ _____ _____ a human cell.

26 Scientists say that onions contain vitamin B, _____ _____ _____ new, healthy cells.

27 Now, let's _____ _____ _____ ginger.

28 What body part _____ _____ _____ when you see it?

29 _____ it look like a stomach?

30 You may not like ginger's _____ _____ or smell, but these _____ _____ a special chemical that _____ you _____ sick and _____ up.

31 _____ _____ _____, ginger can be good for your stomach.

32 Isn't it amazing that some foods _____ the body parts _____ they are good for?

33 Interestingly, there are _____ _____ _____ _____ _____.

34 Find _____ _____ _____ _____ _____ and try to eat a variety of them.

18 호두는 또한 알츠하이머병을 예방하는 데도 좋다.

19 썰어 놓은 당근의 모양은 사람의 눈과 비슷해 보인다.

20 당근에는 비타민 A를 만들 수 있는 화학 성분이 있는데, 그것이 시력을 개선한다.

21 비타민 A는 눈이 빛을 처리하여 뇌에 선명한 이미지를 보낼 수 있도록 돕는다.

22 그러므로 건강한 눈을 원한다면, 당근을 먹어라.

23 양파를 써는 것은 즐겁지 않은데 왜냐하면 그것이 당신을 울게 만들기 때문이다.

24 그렇지만 어쨌든 하나를 잘라 보아라.

25 당신은 양파의 내부가 약간 인간의 세포처럼 보인다는 것을 알 수 있다.

26 과학자들은 양파가 비타민 B를 함유하는데, 이 비타민 B가 새롭고 건강한 세포를 만드는 데 도움이 된다고 주장한다.

27 이제 생강으로 넘어가 보자.

28 생강을 보면 몸의 어떤 부위가 생각나는가?

29 생강이 마치 위장처럼 생기지 않았는가?

30 당신은 어쩌면 생강의 강한 맛과 냄새를 좋아하지 않을지도 모르지만, 이러한 맛과 냄새는 복통과 구토를 예방하는 생강의 특별한 성분에서 나온다.

31 이러한 이유로 생강은 당신의 위장에 좋을 수 있다.

32 어떤 음식이 그 음식이 유익한 신체 부위의 생김새를 반영하고 있다는 점이 놀랍지 않은가?

33 흥미롭게도 그러한 음식은 상당히 많다.

34 가능한 한 그러한 음식을 많이 찾아서 다양한 음식을 먹도록 하라.

● 우리말을 참고하여 본문을 영작하시오.

1 우리 몸에 이로운 음식

➡ _____

2 우리는 다양한 음식을 포함하는 식사가 우리의 몸을 건강하게 유지해 준다는 것을 알고 있다.

➡ _____

3 그러나 때때로 우리는 어떤 음식이 어떤 신체 부위에 좋은지 잘 모를 때가 있다.

➡ _____

4 하지만 자연은 우리에게 확실한 단서를 제시해 준다.

➡ _____

5 다음의 예들을 살펴보자.

➡ _____

6 각각의 이 음식들은 우리 신체의 특정 부분과 비슷해 보일 뿐만 아니라 그 신체 부위에도 좋다.

➡ _____

7 토마토 한 개를 잘라내서 그것을 사람의 심장과 비교해 보자.

➡ _____

8 당신은 그 둘이 비슷해 보인다는 것을 알게 될 것이다.

➡ _____

9 둘 다 여러 개의 빈 공간이 있고 붉은 색이다.

➡ _____

10 연구원들은 토마토를 붉게 만드는 화학 물질이 사람의 심장과 피에 유익하다고 한다.

➡ _____

11 게다가, 토마토를 먹는 것이 심장병에 걸릴 위험성을 낮출 수 있다.

➡ _____

12 호두의 모양을 살펴보자.

➡ _____

13 뭔가를 알아차릴 수 있는가?

➡ _____

14 그렇다, 호두의 모양은 인간의 뇌 형태와 매우 유사하다!

➡ _____

15 호두는 마치 인간의 뇌처럼 두 부분으로 나뉜다.

➡ _____

16 호두에는 또한 주름이 있는데, 이는 인간의 뇌에도 있는 것이다.

➡ _____

17 연구 결과는 호두가 사람의 뇌가 건강하고 활동적인 상태를 유지하는 데 도움을 준다는 것을 보여준다.

➡ _____

18 호두는 또한 알츠하이머병을 예방하는 데도 좋다.

➡ _____

19 썰어 놓은 당근의 모양은 사람의 눈과 비슷해 보인다.

➡ _____

20 당근에는 비타민 A를 만들 수 있는 화학 성분이 있는데, 그것이 시력을 개선한다.

➡ _____

21 비타민 A는 눈이 빛을 처리하여 뇌에 선명한 이미지를 보낼 수 있도록 돕는다.

➡ _____

22 그러므로 건강한 눈을 원한다면, 당근을 먹어라.

➡ _____

23 양파를 써는 것은 즐겁지 않은데 왜냐하면 그것이 당신을 울게 만들기 때문이다.

➡ _____

24 그렇지만 어쨌든 하나를 잘라 보아라.

➡ _____

25 당신은 양파의 내부가 약간 인간의 세포처럼 보인다는 것을 알 수 있다.

➡ _____

26 과학자들은 양파가 비타민 B를 함유하는데, 이 비타민 B가 새롭고 건강한 세포를 만들어 내는 데 도움이 된다고 주장한다.

➡ _____

27 이제 생강으로 넘어가 보자.

➡ _____

28 생강을 보면 몸의 어떤 부위가 생각나는가?

➡ _____

29 생강이 마치 위장처럼 생기지 않았는가?

➡ _____

30 당신은 어쩌면 생강의 강한 맛과 냄새를 좋아하지 않을지도 모르지만, 이러한 맛과 냄새는 복통과 구토를 예방하는 생강의 특별한 성분에서 나온다.

➡ _____

_____

31 이러한 이유로 생강은 당신의 위장에 좋을 수 있다.

➡ _____

32 어떤 음식이 그 음식이 유익한 신체 부위의 생김새를 반영하고 있다는 점이 놀랍지 않은가?

➡ _____

33 흥미롭게도 그러한 음식은 상당히 많다.

➡ _____

34 가능한 한 그러한 음식을 많이 찾아서 다양한 음식을 먹도록 하라.

➡ _____

[01~03] 다음 글을 읽고 물음에 답하시오.

We all know that a diet ⓐcontaining a variety of foods keeps our bodies healthy. But sometimes we are not sure which foods are good (A)[at / for] which body parts. Nature, however, gives us a big clue. Look at the following examples. Each of these foods not only (B)[look / looks] like a certain body part but (C)[is / are] also good for that body part.

01 위 글의 밑줄 친 ⓐcontaining과 문법적 쓰임이 같은 것을 모두 고르시오.

① I won't give up playing soccer.
② He kept me waiting all day.
③ My job is selling cars.
④ Do you mind opening the window?
⑤ Jane was listening to music.

서답형

02 위 글의 괄호 (A)~(C)에서 문맥이나 어법상 알맞은 낱말을 골라 쓰시오.

➡ (A) _____ (B) _____ (C) _____

03 According to the passage, which is NOT true?

① A diet containing various foods keeps our bodies healthy.
② Nobody knows which foods are good for which body parts.
③ Nature gives us a big clue about which foods are good for which body parts.
④ Some foods look like a certain body part.
⑤ Some foods are also good for those body parts.

[04~07] 다음 글을 읽고 물음에 답하시오.

Slice open a tomato and compare it with the human heart. You will see that they look similar. They both have multiple hollow spaces and are red. (A)Researchers say that the chemicals that makes tomatoes red is good for your heart and blood. _____ⓐ_____, eating tomatoes can lower your risk of heart disease.

04 위 글의 빈칸 ⓐ에 들어갈 알맞은 말을 고르시오.

① Instead
② However
③ Still
④ On the other hand
⑤ In addition

서답형

05 위 글의 밑줄 친 (A)에서 어법상 틀린 부분을 찾아 고치시오. (두 군데)

_____ ➡ _____, _____ ➡ _____

06 위 글의 제목으로 알맞은 것을 고르시오.

① Food Similar to Your Heart Is Good for Your Heart
② Various Foods That Keep Our Bodies Healthy
③ Which Foods Are Good for Which Body Parts?
④ Let's Compare Foods with Our Body Parts
⑤ The Chemicals That Make Tomatoes Red

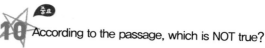

중요

07 Which question CANNOT be answered after reading the passage?

① Which food looks like the human heart?

② What's the similarity between a tomato and the human heart?

③ What chemicals make tomatoes red?

④ Do tomatoes have any chemicals that are good for your heart and blood?

⑤ Can eating tomatoes lower your risk of heart disease?

[08~10] 다음 글을 읽고 물음에 답하시오.

A slice of carrot looks like the human eye. Carrots have some chemicals that can make vitamin A, (A)which improves your _____ⓐ_____ . It helps your eyes process light and send a clear image to the brain. So if you want healthy eyes, eat carrots.

08 위 글의 빈칸 ⓐ에 들어갈 알맞은 말을 고르시오.

① heart   ② brain

③ stomach   ④ vision

⑤ hearing

서답형

09 위 글의 밑줄 친 (A)를 다음과 같이 바꿔 쓸 때 빈칸에 들어갈 알맞은 단어를 쓰시오.

➡ Carrots have some chemicals that can make vitamin A, _____ improves your vision.

중요

10 According to the passage, which is NOT true?

① A slice of carrot looks like the human eye.

② There are some chemicals that can lower the effect of vitamin A in carrots.

③ Vitamin A helps your eyes process light.

④ Vitamin A helps your eyes send a clear image to the brain.

⑤ Eating carrots helps you have healthy eyes.

[11~13] 다음 글을 읽고 물음에 답하시오.

Look at the shape of a walnut. (①) Do you notice anything? (②) A walnut is divided into two parts, just like the brain. (③) Walnuts also have wrinkles, which the brain has too. (④) Studies show that walnuts help our brains stay healthy and active. (⑤) ⓐThey are also good for protecting Alzheimer's disease.

11 위 글의 흐름으로 보아, 주어진 문장이 들어가기에 가장 적절한 곳은?

Yes, it's very similar to the shape of the human brain!

①   ②   ③   ④   ⑤

서답형

12 위 글의 밑줄 친 ⓐ에서 흐름상 어색한 부분을 찾아 고치시오.

_____ ➡ _____

서답형

13 다음 빈칸 (A)와 (B)에 알맞은 단어를 넣어 호두와 인간의 뇌의 모양에 있어 서로 유사한 점을 완성하시오.

They are divided into (A)_____ _____ and have (B)_____ .

[14~15] 다음 글을 읽고 물음에 답하시오.

> Now, let's move on ___ⓐ___ ginger. What body part comes ___ⓐ___ mind when you see it? Doesn't it look like a stomach? You may not like ginger's strong taste or smell, but these come ___ⓑ___ a special chemical that prevents you ___ⓑ___ feeling sick and throwing up. For this reason, ginger can be good for your stomach.

14 위 글의 빈칸 ⓐ와 ⓑ에 각각 공통으로 들어갈 전치사가 바르게 짝지어진 것은?

	ⓐ	ⓑ		ⓐ	ⓑ
①	for	from	②	on	in
③	to	from	④	to	for
⑤	for	in			

서답형

15 Why can ginger be good for your stomach? Fill in the blanks (A) and (B) with suitable words.

> It's because a (A)___ ___ of ginger prevents you from feeling sick and (B)___ ___.

[16~19] 다음 글을 읽고 물음에 답하시오.

> Cutting onions is not fun because ⓐit makes you cry. But try slicing one ⓑanyway. You can see that the inside looks a little like a human cell. ⓒScientists say that onions contain vitamin B, which helps make new, healthy cells.

서답형

16 위 글의 밑줄 친 ⓐit이 가리키는 것을 본문에서 찾아 쓰시오.

➡ _____

17 위 글의 밑줄 친 ⓑanyway와 바꿔 쓸 수 없는 말을 고르시오.

① anyhow
② at any rate
③ by the way
④ in any case
⑤ at all events

서답형

18 위 글의 밑줄 친 ⓒ를 다음과 같이 바꿔 쓸 때 빈칸에 들어갈 알맞은 말을 두 단어로 쓰시오.

> ➡ Scientists say that onions contain vitamin B, which helps ___ new, healthy cells.

서답형

19 위 글의 내용을 다음과 같이 정리하고자 한다. 빈칸 ①~③에 들어갈 알맞은 단어를 쓰시오.

> Food: ①___
> Similar Body Part: ②___ ___
> ___
> Benefit: ③___ ___ in this food helps make new, healthy cells.

20 주어진 글 다음에 이어질 글의 순서로 가장 적절한 것은?

> We all know that a diet containing a variety of foods keeps our bodies healthy.
> (A) Nature, however, gives us a big clue. Look at the following examples.
> (B) Each of these foods not only looks like a certain body part but is also good for that body part.
> (C) But sometimes we are not sure which foods are good for which body parts.

① (A) – (C) – (B)
② (B) – (A) – (C)
③ (B) – (C) – (A)
④ (C) – (A) – (B)
⑤ (C) – (B) – (A)

[21~23] 다음 글을 읽고 물음에 답하시오.

Isn't it amazing that some foods mirror the body parts that (A)they are good for? Interestingly, there are many other such foods. Find ⓐ many ⓑ you can and try (B)to eat a variety of them.

서답형

21 위 글의 빈칸 ⓐ와 ⓑ에 공통으로 들어갈 알맞은 단어를 쓰시오.

➡ _____

서답형

22 위 글의 밑줄 친 (A)they가 가리키는 것을 본문에서 찾아 쓰시오.

➡ (A) _____

23 위 글의 밑줄 친 (B)to eat과 to부정사의 용법이 같은 것을 모두 고르시오.

① She came here to ask questions.
② It began to rain hard.
③ To remember all the names is not easy.
④ There is no one to do it.
⑤ I was surprised to hear the news.

[24~25] 다음 글을 읽고 물음에 답하시오.

We all know that a diet containing a variety of foods ⓐ우리의 몸을 건강하게 유지해 준다. But sometimes we are not sure which foods are good for which body parts. Nature, however, gives us a big clue. Look at the following examples. Each of these foods not only looks like a certain body part but is also good for that body part.

서답형

24 위 글의 밑줄 친 ⓐ의 우리말에 맞게 주어진 어휘를 이용하여 4단어로 영작하시오.

keeps

➡ _____

서답형

25 다음 빈칸 (A)와 (B)에 알맞은 단어를 넣어 위 글의 요지를 완성하시오.

Some foods that (A)_____ _____ certain body parts are (B)_____ _____ those body parts.

[26~27] 다음 글을 읽고 물음에 답하시오.

Now, let's move on to ginger. What body part comes to mind when you see it? Doesn't it look like a stomach? You may not like ginger's strong taste or smell, but ⓐthese come from a special chemical that prevents you from feeling sick and throwing up. For this reason, ginger can be good for your stomach.

서답형

26 위 글의 밑줄 친 ⓐthese가 가리키는 것을 우리말로 쓰시오.

➡ _____

중요

27 위 글을 읽고 알 수 없는 것을 고르시오.

① What body part does ginger look like?
② Is ginger's taste strong?
③ Is ginger's smell strong?
④ Where does ginger's strong taste come from?
⑤ How does a special chemical prevent you from feeling sick and throwing up?

[01~03] 다음 글을 읽고 물음에 답하시오.

We all know that a diet ⓐcontaining a variety of foods keeps our bodies healthy. But sometimes we are not sure which foods are good for which body parts. ⓑNature, however, gives us a big clue. Look at the following examples. ⓒEach of these foods not only looks a certain body part but is also good for that body part.

중요

01 위 글의 밑줄 친 ⓐcontaining을 관계대명사를 사용하여 두 단어로 고치시오.

➡ _____

고난이도

02 다음 빈칸 (A)와 (B)에 알맞은 단어를 넣어 ⓑ가 의미하는 내용을 완성하시오.

The shapes of some foods are naturally (A)_____ to those of the body parts which they are (B)_____ for.

03 위 글의 밑줄 친 ⓒ에서 어법상 틀린 부분을 찾아 고치시오.

_____ ➡ _____

[04~05] 다음 글을 읽고 물음에 답하시오.

Isn't it amazing that some foods mirror the body parts that they are good for? Interestingly, there are many other ⓐsuch foods. Find as many as ⓑyou can and try to eat a variety of them.

04 다음 빈칸에 알맞은 단어를 넣어 위 글의 밑줄 친 ⓐsuch foods가 가리키는 것을 완성하시오.

some foods that _____ the body parts that they are good for

중요

05 위 글의 밑줄 친 ⓑyou can을 한 단어로 바꿔 쓰시오.

➡ _____

[06~08] 다음 글을 읽고 물음에 답하시오.

A slice of carrot looks like the human eye. Carrots have some chemicals that can make vitamin A, which improves your vision. It helps your eyes process light and send a clear image to the brain. So if you want healthy eyes, eat ____ⓐ____.

06 위 글의 빈칸 ⓐ에 들어갈 알맞은 한 단어를 쓰시오.

➡ _____

07 다음 문장에서 위 글의 내용과 다른 부분을 찾아서 고치시오.

The shape of a slice of carrot is similar to that of the human brain.

_____ ➡ _____

고난이도

08 다음 빈칸 (A)~(C)에 알맞은 단어를 넣어 비타민 A의 역할을 완성하시오.

Vitamin A (A)_____ your vision, and helps your eyes (B)_____ _____ and send a (C)_____ _____ to the brain.

[09~11] 다음 글을 읽고 물음에 답하시오.

Look at the shape of a walnut. Do you notice anything? Yes, it's very similar ⓐ the shape of the human brain! A walnut is divided ⓑ two parts, just like the brain. ⓒWalnuts also have wrinkles, which the brain has too. Studies show that walnuts help our brains stay healthy and active. They are also good for preventing Alzheimer's disease.

09 Fill in the blanks ⓐ and ⓑ with suitable words.

➡ ⓐ _____ ⓑ _____

10 위 글의 밑줄 친 ⓒ를 다음과 같이 바꿔 쓸 때 빈칸에 들어갈 알맞은 단어를 쓰시오.

➡ Walnuts also have wrinkles, _____ the brain has _____ too.

11 위 글의 연구 결과를 다음과 같이 정리하고자 한다. 빈칸 (A)와 (B)에 들어갈 알맞은 단어를 본문에서 찾아 쓰시오.

(A)_____ are good for preventing Alzheimer's disease as well as help (B)_____ _____ stay healthy and active.

[12~13] 다음 글을 읽고 물음에 답하시오.

Now, let's move on to ginger. What body part comes to mind when you see it? Doesn't it look like a stomach? You may not like ginger's strong taste or smell, but these come from a special chemical that prevents you from ⓐ sick and ⓑ up. For this reason, ginger can be good for your stomach.

12 위 글의 빈칸 ⓐ와 ⓑ에 feel과 throw를 각각 알맞은 형태로 쓰시오.

➡ ⓐ _____ ⓑ _____

13 You may not like ginger. Why? Fill in the blanks with suitable words.

➡ Because of its _____ _____ or _____ .

[14~15] 다음 글을 읽고 물음에 답하시오.

Slice open a tomato and compare it with the human heart. You will see that ⓐthey look similar. They both have multiple hollow spaces and are red. Researchers say that ⓑ토마토를 붉게 만드는 화학 물질이 사람의 심장과 피에 유익하다. ⓒIn addition, eating tomatoes can lower your risk of heart disease

14 다음 빈칸 (A)와 (B)에 알맞은 단어를 넣어, 위 글의 밑줄 친 ⓐthey가 가리키는 것을 완성하시오.

(A)_____ _____ which is sliced open and the (B)_____ _____

15 위 글의 밑줄 친 ⓑ의 우리말에 맞게 한 단어를 보충하여, 주어진 어휘를 알맞게 배열하시오.

tomatoes / good / make / the chemicals / your heart and blood / for / red / are

➡ _____
_____

구석구석

해석

Presentation Time

Have you heard that swimming is good for your back? Our group made a plan
현재완료의 용법 중에서 경험을 나타내는 용법   be good for ~ = ~에 좋다   made a plan to ~ = ~할 계획을 세우다
to go swimming together every Tuesday and Thursday at World Sports Park.

We are sure it will help us stay healthy.
We are sure (that)   'help+목적어+원형부정사'
~ = 우리는 ~을 확신한다

구문해설 • back: 등, 허리   • make a plan to ~ = ~할 계획을 세우다

수영을 하는 것이 허리에 좋다는 말을 들어본 적이 있니? 우리 모둠은 매주 화요일과 목요일에 World Sports Park에 함께 수영을 가기로 계획을 세웠어. 우리는 그것이 우리가 건강하게 지내는 데 도움이 될 것이라고 확신하고 있어.

Wrap Up READING

Eat Chicken Sandwiches, Be Healthier

A chicken sandwich is a healthy food that I recommend. I'd like to talk about
= which(목적격 관계대명사)   want to의 공손한 표현
some of its ingredients that are good for our health. First, chicken breast is
주격 관계대명사+be동사: 생략 가능
meat with a lot of protein and little fat. Onions contain lots of vitamin B. Also,
= much   거의 없는   = a lot of
walnuts are good for the brain. So why don't you try a chicken sandwich this
= how[what] about trying
weekend?

구문해설 • recommend: 추천하다   • ingredient: (특히 요리 등의) 재료[성분]
• chicken breast: 닭 가슴살   • protein: 단백질   • fat: 지방

치킨 샌드위치를 먹고 더 건강해 지세요

치킨 샌드위치는 제가 추천하는 건강에 좋은 음식입니다. 저는 건강에 좋은 그것의 재료 몇 가지에 대해 이야기하고 싶습니다. 먼저 닭 가슴살은 많은 단백질을 가지고 있고 지방은 거의 없는 고기입니다. 양파는 비타민 B를 많이 포함하고 있습니다. 또한, 호두는 뇌에 좋습니다. 그러니, 이번 주말에 치킨 샌드위치를 드시는 것이 어떠세요?

Culture Link

Yoga in India

Indian people practice yoga to better understand their minds, bodies, thoughts,
better가 동사를 수식하는 부사로 쓰인 to부정사의 부사적 용법
and emotions. They use it to guide themselves to a healthier life.
= yoga   to부정사의   주어와 목적어가 같으므로 재귀대명사 사용
부사적 용법

구문해설 • thought: 생각, 사색   • guide A to B: A를 B로 안내하다[인도하다]

인도의 요가

인도사람들은 그들의 마음, 신체, 생각과 감정을 더 잘 이해하기 위해 요가를 한다. 그들은 자신들을 더 건강한 삶으로 인도하기 위해 그것을 사용한다.

01 다음 중 밑줄 친 부분의 뜻풀이가 바르지 <u>않은</u> 것은?

① Form now on, <u>try</u> to go to bed earlier. (애쓰다)

② Did you get <u>enough</u> sleep? (충분한)

③ I went to bed after <u>midnight</u>, as usual. (정오)

④ You will see that they look <u>similar</u>. (비슷한)

⑤ So if you want <u>healthy</u> eyes, eat carrots. (건강한)

02 다음 중 〈보기〉에 있는 단어를 사용하여 자연스러운 문장을 만들 수 <u>없는</u> 것은?

┌─── 보기 ───┐
stay   contain   notice   variety
└────────────┘

① He didn't even _____ I was sitting here.

② A walnut is _____ into two parts, just like the brain.

③ Walnuts help our brains _____ healthy and active.

④ Scientists say that onions _____ vitamin B.

⑤ Find as many as you can and try to eat a _____ of them.

03 주어진 내용으로 보아 다음 빈칸에 들어갈 말로 적절한 것을 고르시오.

> Studies show that walnuts help our brains stay healthy and active. They are also good for _____ Alzheimer's disease.

① preventing   ② giving   ③ producing
④ containing   ⑤ finding

04 다음 밑줄 친 단어와 의미가 같은 단어를 고르시오.

> B: Have you heard that chewing ice is bad for your teeth?
> G: No, I haven't. Why is that?
> B: It can <u>damage</u> your teeth. It can also make them too sensitive.

① harm   ② chew   ③ contain
④ improve   ⑤ compare

05 다음 대화의 순서가 바르게 배열된 것을 고르시오.

> B: What are you doing in the living room?
> G: I'm doing yoga.
> B: You're working out by yourself?
> G: Yes, I'm following this online video. It shows me all the steps.
> B: Let me see. Wow, it's been watched two million times! I'm surprised that so many people have watched this video.
> (A) It looks very convenient. You don't have to go out to exercise.
> (B) That's right. That's why I love these programs. You should try them, too.
> (C) I know! These kinds of programs are becoming popular right now.

① (A) – (C) – (B)   ② (B) – (A) – (C)
③ (B) – (C) – (A)   ④ (C) – (A) – (B)
⑤ (C) – (A) – (B)

[06~07] 다음 글을 읽고 물음에 답하시오.

G: Have you heard the term *body image*? It means "the way you see your own body." A lot of teens have a negative body image. They think they're too fat or too thin compared ___(A)___ others. However, I want you to build a positive body image. Accept your body as (B)it is and give yourself praise every day. Remember, there is only one you, so don't compare yourself ___(C)___ others. Loving yourself can make a big difference in your life.

06 위 글의 (A)와 (C)에 공통으로 알맞은 것은?

① at   ② of   ③ to
④ for   ⑤ from

07 위 글의 (B)it이 가리키는 것을 영어로 쓰시오.

➡ _____

08 위 글의 내용과 일치하지 <u>않는</u> 것은?

① The term '*body image*' means 'the way you see your own body.'
② Most teens have a bright body image.
③ Some teens think they are too thin.
④ Some teens think they are too fat.
⑤ You had better not compare yourself to others.

[09~10] 다음 대화를 읽고 물음에 답하시오.

B: Oh, I'm so hungry.
G: Why don't you eat some snacks before dinner?
B: ___(A)___ I'll wait until dinner.
G: Okay, but have you heard that eating little and often is good for your health?
B: Really? I thought eating three meals a day was fine.
G: If you keep waiting until dinner, you will eat too much and too quickly. Eating little and ___(B)___ prevents you from eating like that.
B: I see. Then I'll go eat an apple right now.

09 빈칸 (A)에 들어가기에 적절한 내용을 고르시오.

① Would you give me some?
② I already had some.
③ Let's have some snacks together.
④ I don't want to.
⑤ I'd like to have some snacks.

10 대화의 내용으로 보아 (B)에 들어가기에 적절한 것을 고르시오.

① none   ② often
③ three times   ④ apples
⑤ fruit

[11~12] 다음 대화를 읽고 물음에 답하시오.

G: What's this?
B: It's a smart band. It lets me check my health information on my smartphone.
G: What kind of information?
B: It shows how far I walk during the day and how well I sleep at night.
G: Interesting. I'm surprised that this small band can do all that.

11 위 대화를 읽고 알 수 없는 것은?

① A smart band is related with health.
② A smart band shows health information on the smartphone.
③ A smart band shows us how far we walk during the day.
④ A smart band is a kind of app for the smartphone.
⑤ The smart band lets him know how well he sleeps at night.

12 위 대화에서 a smart band가 구체적으로 하는 일을 우리말로 쓰시오.

➡ _____

_____

13 다음 대화의 빈칸 ⓐ~ⓔ에 들어갈 말로 어색한 것은?

B: You look tired. _____ ⓐ _____
G: Yes, I did. I slept for over seven hours.
B: Okay. When did you go to bed?
G: _____ ⓑ _____
B: That's probably what is making you tired. Have you heard that when you go to bed is very important?
G: _____ ⓒ _____
B: Scientists say that going to bed late can make you feel tired the next day.
G: _____ ⓓ _____
B: On the other hand, going to bed early can improve your memory and help you be more productive. _____ ⓔ _____

① ⓐ Did you get enough sleep?
② ⓑ I went to bed after midnight, as usual.
③ ⓒ No, I haven't. Why is that?
④ ⓓ I already knew that.
⑤ ⓔ From now on, try to go to bed earlier.

Grammar

14 다음 빈칸에 들어갈 말로 알맞은 것은?

Our art room, _____ is on the third floor, is very big.

① where   ② who   ③ what
④ that   ⑤ which

15 다음 중 어법상 어색한 문장을 모두 고르시오.

① The injured man was lain on the ground.
② Jim gave me the photos taken last week.
③ This is the most expensive car making in England.
④ The place was full of people enjoying themselves at the party.
⑤ I am looking for a girl wearing a blue skirt.

16 다음 그림을 참고하여 빈칸에 알맞게 쓰시오.

I met Jenny and Jack, _____ _____ I picked up garbage.

17 다음 두 문장의 의미가 같도록 빈칸에 알맞은 말을 쓰시오.

(1) Let's pick up the leaves fallen on the pavement.

= Let's pick up the leaves _____ fallen on the pavement.

(2) The boy listening to music is holding a spoon.

= The boy _____ listening to music is holding a spoon.

18 다음 문장을 의미에 맞게 바르게 바꿔 쓴 문장을 고르시오.

> I love Isabella, who is making it very hard for me to do so.

① I love Isabell, for she is making it very hard for me to do so.

② I love Isabella, though she is making it very hard for me to do so.

③ I love Isabella, and she is making it very hard for me to do so.

④ I love Isabella, so she is making it very hard for me to do so.

⑤ I love Isabella unless she is making it very hard for me to do so.

19 다음 ⓐ～ⓖ 중 어법상 옳은 것을 모두 고르시오.

> ⓐ My parents were moved by the letter written by my sister and me.
>
> ⓑ I ate freshly baking bread and jam this morning.
>
> ⓒ Abigail sitting on the sofa is reading a book.
>
> ⓓ Is the girl jumped rope with Daniel Amanda?
>
> ⓔ I'd like to see the movie *The Help*, which many people recommended.

> ⓕ I want to go to the party with Jia, that is a close friend of mine.
>
> ⓖ I know a girl, whose elder sister is a famous singer.

➡ _____

Reading

[20~22] 다음 글을 읽고 물음에 답하시오.

> (A)We all know that a diet containing a variety of foods keeps our bodies healthily. But sometimes we are not sure which foods are good for which body parts. Nature, ⓐ , gives us a big clue. Look at the following examples. Each of these foods (B) not only looks like a certain body part but is also good for that body part.

20 위 글의 빈칸 ⓐ에 들어갈 알맞은 말을 고르시오.

① therefore ② in addition

③ however ④ similarly

⑤ for instance

21 위 글의 밑줄 친 (A)에서 어법상 틀린 부분을 찾아 고치시오.

_____ ➡ _____

22 위 글의 밑줄 친 (B)not only와 바꿔 쓸 수 없는 말을 모두 고르시오.

① not just ② not merely

③ not mainly ④ not simply

⑤ not mostly

[23~24] 다음 글을 읽고 물음에 답하시오.

Look at the shape of a walnut. Do you notice anything? Yes, it's very similar to the shape of the human brain! A walnut is divided into two parts, just like the brain. ⓐWalnuts also have wrinkles, that the brain has too. Studies show that walnuts help our brains stay healthy and active. They are also good for preventing Alzheimer's disease.

23 위 글의 밑줄 친 ⓐ에서 어법상 틀린 부분을 찾아 고치시오.

_____ ➡ _____

24 Which question canNOT be answered after reading the passage?

① What does the shape of a walnut look like?
② How many parts are a walnut and the human brain divided into?
③ Why do walnuts and the human brain have wrinkles?
④ What food helps our brains stay healthy and active?
⑤ What food is good for preventing Alzheimer's disease?

[25~27] 다음 글을 읽고 물음에 답하시오.

ⓐCutting onions (A)[is / are] not fun because it makes you (B)[cry / to cry]. But ⓑ어쨌든 하나를 잘라 보아라. You can see that the inside looks (C)[a few / a little] like a human cell. Scientists say that onions contain vitamin B, which helps make new, healthy cells.

25 위 글의 밑줄 친 ⓐCutting과 문법적 쓰임이 다른 것을 모두 고르시오.

① I don't like cutting onions.
② Cutting onions needs much patience.
③ She is cutting onions.
④ I saw him cutting onions.
⑤ Are you good at cutting onions?

26 위 글의 괄호 (A)~(C)에서 문맥이나 어법상 알맞은 낱말을 골라 쓰시오.

➡ (A) _____ (B) _____ (C) _____

27 위 글의 밑줄 친 ⓑ의 우리말에 맞게 4단어로 영작하시오.

➡ _____

[28~29] 다음 글을 읽고 물음에 답하시오.

Now, let's move on to ginger. What body part comes to mind when you see it? Doesn't it look like a stomach? You may not like ginger's strong taste or smell, ⓐbut these come from a special chemical that prevents you from feeling sick and overeating. For this reason, ginger can be good for your stomach.

28 위 글의 요지로 알맞은 것을 고르시오.

① Ginger and a stomach have some similarity.
② Ginger that looks like a stomach is good for a stomach.
③ Some people may not like ginger.
④ Ginger has strong taste or smell.
⑤ Ginger has a special chemical.

29 위 글의 밑줄 친 ⓐ에서 문맥상 낱말의 쓰임이 적절하지 않은 것을 찾아 알맞게 고치시오.

_____ ➡ _____

출제율 90%

01 다음 짝지어진 단어의 관계가 같도록 빈칸에 알맞은 것은?

> prevent : allow = _____ : refuse

① chew　　② contain　　③ search
④ accept　　⑤ increase

출제율 95%

02 다음 중 밑줄 친 단어 대신 쓸 수 있는 것을 모두 고르시오.

> The strong taste or smell of the ginger come from a special chemical that <u>prevents</u> you from feeling sick and throwing up.

① keeps　　② tries　　③ stops
④ helps　　⑤ accepts

출제율 90%

03 다음 영영풀이에 해당하는 단어를 고르시오.

> the organ inside your head that controls how you think, feel, and move

① brain　　② stomach　　③ eye
④ heart　　⑤ mouth

출제율 85%

04 빈칸에 알맞은 단어를 〈보기〉에서 골라 쓰시오.

> ┌─ 보기 ─┐
> hollow　process　popular　chewing

(1) Have you heard that _____ ice is bad for your teeth?

(2) These kinds of programs are becoming _____ right now.

(3) They both have multiple _____ spaces and are red.

(4) Vitamin A helps your eyes _____ light.

출제율 100%

05 다음 빈칸에 들어갈 말이 순서대로 바르게 짝지어진 것은?

> B: You look tired. Did you get __(A)__ sleep?
> G: Yes, I did. I slept for over seven hours.
> B: Okay. __(B)__ did you go to bed?
> G: I went to bed after midnight, as usual.

　　(A)　　(B)　　　　　(A)　　(B)
① enough – What　　② much – How
③ much　 – Why　　④ little – Where
⑤ enough – When

[06~08] 다음 대화를 읽고 물음에 답하시오.

> B: What is that? It looks nice.
> G: This is a magic cup. I carry it everywhere with me.
> B: _____(A)_____
> G: It's awesome. It tells me to drink water every two hours.
> B: Really? I'm (B)<u>surprised</u> that it can talk to you.
> G: It even asks me questions like "Aren't you thirsty?"
> B: That's so cool! But why are you trying to drink more water?
> G: Because drinking a lot of water can increase your energy and (C)<u>혈액이 흐르는 것을 도와준다</u>. (your blood)
> B: That's amazing. I should buy one!

출제율 90%

06 빈칸 (A)에 들어가기에 적절한 것을 고르시오.

① What's the name of this cup?
② What's special about it?
③ How long have you used this?
④ How much does it hold?
⑤ Is it good for your health?

07 밑줄 친 (B)와 바꿔 쓸 수 있는 것을 고르시오.

① worried   ② pleased

③ amazed   ④ frightened

⑤ convinced

08 밑줄 친 (C)의 우리말을 영작하시오.

➡ _____

[09~10] 다음 대화를 읽고 물음에 답하시오.

B: _____ ⓐ _____
G: I'm doing yoga.
B: _____ ⓑ _____
G: Yes, I'm following this online video. It shows me all the steps.
B: Let me see. _____ ⓒ _____
(A)I'm surprised that so many people have watched this video.
G: I know! These kinds of programs are becoming popular right now.
B: _____ ⓓ _____ You don't have to go out to exercise.
G: _____ ⓔ _____ That's why I love these programs. You should try them, too.

09 빈칸 ⓐ~ⓔ에 들어갈 말로 어색한 것은?

① ⓐ What are you doing in the living room?

② ⓑ You're working out by yourself?

③ ⓒ Wow, it's hardly been watched!

④ ⓓ It looks very convenient.

⑤ ⓔ That's right.

10 밑줄 친 (A)를 다음과 같이 바꾸어 쓸 때 빈칸에 들어가기에 적절한 단어를 쓰시오. (주어진 철자로 시작할 것)

How could it be p_____ that so many people have watched this video?

11 다음 빈칸에 들어갈 수 있는 말이 나머지와 다른 하나는?

① I want to go to the party with Jinwoo, _____ is a close friend of mine.

② I have a friend, _____ can speak English well.

③ I know a man, _____ helps lots of people in need in his town.

④ I will visit Moscow with Mariah, _____ makes me excited.

⑤ I visited my grandfather, _____ wasn't home.

12 다음 중 어법상 적절한 문장은?

① I found a box filling with many letters at the basement.

② I bought a new laptop manufacturing in Korea.

③ The man selling ice cream looks friendly.

④ Mom bought me a new camera, with whom I took lots of photos.

⑤ Sumin loves her new cap, who she bought on sale.

13 다음 밑줄 친 말 대신 쓸 수 있는 말을 두 단어로 쓰시오.

> • Thomas, <u>who</u> is old, is in good shape.
> = Thomas, _____ is old, is in good shape.

14 다음 문장의 빈칸에 알맞은 말은?

> Grace _____ in a shower came quite late.

① catching   ② to catch
③ catch   ④ catches
⑤ caught

15 다음 빈칸에 들어갈 말을 순서대로 묶은 것은?

> • Lou Gehrig _____ the "iron horse" played 2,130 consecutive games.
> • I'd like to visit the National Museum of Korea, _____ is located in Seoul.

① called – who
② called – which
③ calling – who
④ calling – which
⑤ call – that

[16~18] 다음 글을 읽고 물음에 답하시오.

> Slice open a tomato and compare it with the human heart. You will see that they look similar. They both have multiple (A)<u>hollow</u> spaces and are red. Researchers say (B)<u>that</u> the chemicals (C)<u>that</u> make tomatoes red are good for your heart and blood. In addition, eating tomatoes can lower your risk of _____ ⓐ _____.

16 위 글의 빈칸 ⓐ에 들어갈 알맞은 말을 고르시오.

① stomachache
② heart disease
③ eye disease
④ unhealthy cells
⑤ Alzheimer's disease

17 위 글의 밑줄 친 (A)hollow와 바꿔 쓸 수 있는 말을 모두 고르시오.

① vacant   ② unclear
③ full   ④ empty
⑤ useful

18 위 글의 밑줄 친 (B)that, (C)that과 문법적 쓰임이 같은 것을 각각 모두 고르시오.

> ① He is the greatest novelist that has ever lived.
> ② The trouble is that we are short of money.
> ③ Look at the bird that is flying in the sky.
> ④ He was the first man that came here.
> ⑤ I can't believe that Ann loved Jake.

➡ (B)와 같은 것: _____
    (C)와 같은 것: _____

[19~21] 다음 글을 읽고 물음에 답하시오.

> ⓐ썰어 놓은 당근 한 조각 looks like the human eye. Carrots have some chemicals that can make vitamin A, which improves your vision. ⓑ<u>It helps your eyes process light and send a clear image to the brain.</u> So if you want healthy eyes, eat carrots.

19 위 글의 밑줄 친 ⓐ의 우리말에 맞게 4단어로 영작하시오.

➡ _____

20 위 글의 밑줄 친 ⓑ를 다음과 같이 바꿔 쓸 때 빈칸에 들어갈 알맞은 말을 각각 두 단어로 쓰시오.

➡ It helps your eyes _____ light and _____ a clear image to the brain.

21 Fill in the blanks (A) and (B) with suitable words to match the content of the paragraph above.

> Food: (A)_____
> Similar Body Part: eyes
> Benefits: They help improve your (B)_____.

[22~23] 다음 글을 읽고 물음에 답하시오.

Isn't (A)it amazing ___ⓐ___ some foods mirror the body parts ___ⓑ___ they are good for? Interestingly, there are many other such foods. Find as many as you can and try to eat a variety of them.

22 위 글의 빈칸 ⓐ와 ⓑ에 공통으로 들어갈 알맞은 단어를 쓰시오.

➡ _____

23 위 글의 밑줄 친 (A)it과 문법적 쓰임이 같은 것을 고르시오.

① Did you hear it?
② I find it strange that she doesn't want to go.
③ It's impossible to get there in time.
④ It's ten past twelve.
⑤ Look! It's climbing up that tree.

[24~26] 다음 글을 읽고 물음에 답하시오.

Eat Chicken Sandwiches, Be Healthier

A chicken sandwich is a healthy food that I recommend. I'd like to talk about some of ⓐits ingredients that are good for our health. First, chicken breast is meat with a lot of protein and little fat. Onions contain lots of vitamin B. Also, walnuts are good for the brain. So ⓑwhy don't you try a chicken sandwich this weekend?

24 위 글의 종류로 알맞은 것을 고르시오.

① review   ② book report
③ summary   ④ recommendation
⑤ essay

25 위 글의 밑줄 친 ⓐ에 해당하는 재료 세 가지와 그것들이 건강에 좋은 이유를 우리말로 쓰시오.

➡ _____
_____
_____

26 위 글의 밑줄 친 ⓑ를 동명사를 사용하여 고치시오.

➡ _____
_____

[01~03] 다음 대화를 읽고 물음에 답하시오.

> B: It's a smart band. It lets me check my ___(A)___ information on my smartphone.
> G: What kind of information?
> B: It shows (B)하루 동안 얼마나 걷는지 밤에 잠을 얼마나 잘 자는지.(how far, during the day, at night)
> G: Interesting. I'm ___(C)___ that this small band can do all that.

01 위 대화의 내용으로 보아 빈칸 (A)에 들어가기에 적절한 단어를 주어진 철자로 시작하여 쓰시오.

➡ h_____

02 밑줄 친 (B)의 우리말을 영어로 쓰시오. (주어진 단어를 반드시 포함할 것)

➡ _____
_____

03 빈칸 (C)에 들어가기에 적절한 단어를 주어진 철자로 시작하여 쓰시오.

➡ s_____

04 다음 주어진 단어를 이용해 빈칸을 완성하시오.

> A lot of teens have a negative body image. They think they're too fat or too thin _____ to others.

➡ _____ (compare)

05 다음 우리말에 맞게 빈칸에 알맞은 말을 쓰시오.

(1) 호두의 모양을 보아라.
➡ Look at the _____ of a walnut.

(2) 그러나 자연은 우리에게 큰 단서를 준다.
➡ Nature, however, gives us a big _____.

(3) 과학자들은 양파가 비타민 B를 포함하고 있다고 말한다.
➡ Scientists say that onions _____ vitamin B.

06 계속적 용법의 관계대명사를 사용하여 주어진 두 문장을 한 문장으로 바꾸시오.

(1) • I want to meet Jon Kim in person someday.
   • He is my favorite actor.
➡ _____
_____

(2) • Have you read the book, *The Last Leaf*.
   • It was written by O. Henry.
➡ _____
_____

07 다음 문장에서 틀린 것을 고쳐 다시 쓰시오.

(1) The men given out flyers are wearing caps.
➡ _____
_____

(2) The soldier injuring in the war was lying on the bed.
➡ _____
_____

(3) Last week I bought a new computer, that I like a lot.
➡ _____
_____

08 다음 우리말을 주어진 어휘를 이용하여 영작하시오.

(1) 그는 Huong과 결혼했는데, 그녀는 베트남 출신이다. (got married, is, Vietnam)

➡ _____

(2) 그녀는 그 옷을 사고 싶어 했는데, 그것은 너무 비쌌다. (the dress, buy, want, too)

➡ _____

_____

(3) 정원에 심겨진 그 꽃은 매우 빠르게 자랐다. (plant, grow up, fast)

➡ _____

_____

[09~11] 다음 글을 읽고 물음에 답하시오.

We all know that a diet containing (A)a variety of foods keeps our bodies healthy. But sometimes we are not sure which foods are good for which body parts. Nature, however, gives us a big ____ⓐ____. Look at the following examples. (B)Each of these foods not only looks like a certain body part but is also good for that body part.

09 주어진 영영풀이를 참고하여 빈칸 ⓐ에 철자 c로 시작하는 단어를 쓰시오.

something that helps you to find the answer to a problem or mystery

➡ _____

10 위 글의 밑줄 친 (A)a variety of와 바꿔 쓸 수 있는 단어를 철자 v로 시작하여 쓰시오.

➡ _____

11 위 글의 밑줄 친 (B)를 다음과 같이 바꿔 쓸 때 빈칸에 들어갈 알맞은 말을 세 단어로 쓰시오.

➡ Each of these foods is also good for that body part _____ looks like a certain body part.

[12~14] 다음 글을 읽고 물음에 답하시오.

Slice open a tomato and compare it with the human heart. You will see that they look (A) [different / similar]. They both have multiple hollow spaces and are red. Researchers say that the chemicals (B)[that / what] make tomatoes red are good for your heart and blood. In addition, eating tomatoes can (C) [increase / lower] your risk of heart disease.

12 위 글의 괄호 (A)~(C)에서 문맥이나 어법상 알맞은 낱말을 골라 쓰시오.

➡ (A) _____ (B) _____ (C) _____

13 What do a tomato and a human heart have in common? Fill in the blanks (A) and (B) with suitable words.

They both have multiple (A)_____ _____ and are (B)_____.

14 What makes tomatoes good for your heart and blood? Answer in English. (6 words)

➡ _____

창의사고력 서술형 문제

01 Look at the tips about the body image and fill in the blanks.

> **Tips for Building a Positive Body Image**
> • _____ your body as it is. (여러분의 몸을 있는 그대로 받아들여라.)
> • Give yourself _____ every day. (매일 스스로를 칭찬하라.)
> • Don't _____ yourself to others. (자신을 다른 사람들과 비교하지 마라.)

02 다음 주어진 〈보기〉와 같이, 분사를 사용하여 빈칸에 자기 자신의 문장을 쓰시오.

> ┌ 보기 ┐
> I have a scarf <u>made in Italy</u>.

(1) I received a letter _____ from a strange girl.
(2) I'm excited when I walk on a road _____.
(3) I like the lady _____.

03 다음 내용을 바탕으로 반 친구들에게 건강에 좋은 음식을 추천하는 글을 쓰시오.

> **Food:** What food do you recommend?
> — fruit yogurt salad
> **Healthy Ingredients:** What are its healthy ingredients?
> — bananas, blueberries, yogurt
> **Benefits:** Why are these ingredients good for your health?
> — • bananas: plenty of potassium, which helps lower blood pressure
>   • blueberries: lots of vitamin C
>   • yogurt: a lot of calcium, which is good for our bones

> **Eat Fruit Yogurt Salad, Be Healthier**
> (A)_____ is a healthy food that I recommend. I'd like to talk about some of its ingredients that are good for our health. First, (B)_____ have plenty of potassium, which helps (C)_____. Blueberries have lots of (D)_____, and yogurt has a lot of calcium, which is good for our (E)_____. So why don't you try fruit yogurt salad this weekend?

단원별 모의고사

01 다음 문장의 빈칸에 들어갈 말로 적절한 것을 고르시오.

> However, I want you to build a positive body image. Accept your body as it is and give yourself praise every day. Remember, there is only one you, so don't _____ yourself to others. Loving yourself can make a big difference in your life.

① compare
② improve
③ lower
④ check
⑤ prevent

02 다음 대화의 빈칸에 들어갈 말로 적절한 것을 고르시오.

> B: You look tired. Did you get enough sleep?
> G: Yes, I did. I slept for over seven hours.
> B: Okay. When did you go to bed?
> G: I went to bed _____, as usual.

① by myself
② with the light off
③ after midnight
④ in the dark
⑤ regularly

03 다음 영영풀이에 해당하는 단어를 고르시오.

> having an empty space inside

① hollow
② sensitive
③ productive
④ positive
⑤ moved

[04~05] 다음 대화를 읽고 물음에 답하시오.

> B: What are you doing in the living room?
> G: I'm doing yoga.
> B: (A)혼자서 운동하고 있구나?
> G: Yes, I'm following this online video. It shows me all the steps.
> B: Let me see. Wow, it's been watched two million times! I'm surprised that so many people have watched this video.
> G: I know! These kinds of programs are becoming popular right now.
> B: It looks very convenient. You don't have to go out to exercise.
> G: That's right. That's why I love these programs. You should try them, too.

04 밑줄 친 (A)를 영어로 옮길 때 빈칸에 철자 w로 시작하는 단어를 쓰시오.

➡ You're _____ out by yourself?

05 위 대화를 읽고, 다음 질문에 해당하는 대답의 빈칸에 들어가기에 적절한 것을 고르시오.

> Q. Why does the girl love those programs?
> A. Because they are very _____ to follow and she doesn't have to go out to exercise.

① famous
② convenient
③ interesting
④ surprising
⑤ sensitive

06 다음 중 짝지어진 대화가 <u>어색한</u> 것을 고르시오.

① A: This is your birthday gift. It's a new phone.
　B: Really? Thanks a lot.

② A: There's no class tomorrow.
　B: It can't be true. Tomorrow is Tuesday.

③ A: The book says pigs are smarter than the dog.
　B: Really? That's hard to believe.

④ A: It's snowing outside.
　B: It's no wonder. It's April now.

⑤ G: Look, Eric. It's raining.
　B: I can't believe it. It was completely sunny when I left home.

[07~09] 다음 대화를 읽고 물음에 답하시오.

B: You look tired. Did you get enough sleep?
G: Yes, I did. I slept for over seven hours.
B: Okay. When did you go to bed?
G: I went to bed after midnight, as usual.
B: That's probably that is making you tired. Have you heard that when you go to bed is very important?
G: No, I haven't. Why is that?
B: (A)과학자들은 늦게 자는 것이 너를 다음날 피곤하게 느끼도록 만들 수 있다고 말해. (going to bed, scientists, can, feel, make, say, that, late, tired, you, the next day).
G: I didn't know that.

07 위 대화에서 문맥상 또는 어법상 <u>어색한</u> 것을 찾아 고치시오.

➡ ＿＿＿＿＿＿＿＿＿ ➡ ＿＿＿＿＿＿＿＿＿

08 밑줄 친 (A)의 우리말을 주어진 어구를 배열하여 영어로 옮기시오.

➡ ＿＿＿＿＿＿＿＿＿＿＿＿＿＿＿＿
　＿＿＿＿＿＿＿＿＿＿＿＿＿＿＿＿

09 According to the passage, which one is true?

① The boy didn't get enough sleep.
② The girl slept for over seven hours.
③ The girl went to bed before midnight.
④ When you go to bed isn't important.
⑤ The girl will go to bed late as usual.

10 다음 빈칸 (A)와 (B)에 들어갈 말이 순서대로 바르게 짝지어진 것은?

B: Oh, I'm so hungry.
G: Why don't you eat some snacks before dinner?
B: I don't want to. I'll wait until dinner.
G: Okay, but have you heard that eating ＿＿(A)＿＿ is good for your health?
B: Really? I thought eating three meals a day was fine.
G: If you keep ＿＿(B)＿＿ until dinner, you will eat too much and too quickly. Eating little and often prevents you from eating like that.
B: I see. Then I'll go eat an apple right now.

　　　(A)　　　　　　(B)
① little and often　　waiting
② various foods　　counting
③ three times　　　watching
④ much food　　　eating
⑤ in the house　　suggesting

11 다음 주어진 단어의 형태를 알맞게 바꿔 문장을 완성하시오.

(1) Is the car _____ next to mine Ann's car? (park)

(2) The man _____ his car on the street is my English teacher. (park)

12 다음 빈칸에 들어갈 말을 순서대로 묶은 것은?

> • Suyeon is my best friend, _____ works at an animal hospital.
> • It is *The Mona Lisa*, _____ was painted by Leonardo da Vinci.

① that – that
② which – who
③ which – which
④ who – who
⑤ who – which

13 다음 밑줄 친 부분과 바꿔 쓸 수 있는 것은?

> I broke the promise, and it made Megan upset.

① which
② that
③ what
④ who
⑤ where

14 다음 문장에서 어법상 어색한 것을 바르게 고쳐 다시 쓰시오.

(1) I can't find the books, that Evelyn gave them to me.

➡ _____

_____

(2) She is my friend, Sophia, that is from Hungary.

➡ _____

_____

(3) I got a C in my test, what made my mom disappointed.

➡ _____

_____

(4) The girl who cleaning the room is my sister.

➡ _____

_____

(5) You can find a nice beach covering with white sand.

➡ _____

_____

[15~16] 다음 글을 읽고 물음에 답하시오.

> We all know that a diet _____ⓐ_____ a variety of foods keeps our bodies healthy. But sometimes we are not sure ⓑ어떤 음식이 어떤 신체 부위에 좋은지. Nature, however, gives us a big clue. Look at the following examples. Each of these foods not only looks like a certain body part but is also good for that body part.

15 위 글의 빈칸 ⓐ에 contain을 알맞은 형태로 쓰시오.

➡ _____

16 위 글의 밑줄 친 ⓑ의 우리말에 맞게 한 단어를 보충하여, 주어진 어휘를 알맞게 배열하시오.

> are / body parts / which / good / foods / which

➡ _____

[17~19] 다음 글을 읽고 물음에 답하시오.

(①) Slice open a tomato and compare it with the human heart. (②) They both have multiple hollow spaces and are red. (③) Researchers say that the chemicals that make tomatoes red are good for your heart and blood. (④) In addition, ⓐeating tomatoes can lower your risk of heart disease. (⑤)

17 위 글의 흐름으로 보아, 주어진 문장이 들어가기에 가장 적절한 곳은?

> You will see that they look similar.

①   ②   ③   ④   ⑤

18 아래 〈보기〉에서 위 글의 밑줄 친 ⓐeating과 문법적 쓰임이 같은 것의 개수를 고르시오.

> ┤ 보기 ├
> ① She left without saying a word.
> ② Look at the smiling girl.
> ③ I heard him speaking English.
> ④ Telling a lie is not good.
> ⑤ Seeing is believing.

① 1개   ② 2개   ③ 3개   ④ 4개   ⑤ 5개

19 위 글의 내용을 다음과 같이 정리하고자 한다. 빈칸 (A)~(C)에 들어갈 알맞은 단어를 본문에서 찾아 쓰시오.

> Food: tomatoes
> Similar Body Part: (A)_____
> Benefit: They are good for the
>   (B)_____ and (C)_____.

[20~22] 다음 글을 읽고 물음에 답하시오.

A slice of carrot ⓐlooks like the human eye. Carrots have some chemicals that can make vitamin A, which improves your vision. It helps your eyes ⓑprocess light and send a clear image to the brain. So if you want healthy eyes, eat carrots.

20 위 글의 밑줄 친 ⓐlooks like와 바꿔 쓸 수 있는 말을 모두 고르시오.

① resembles   ② looks for
③ is similar to   ④ is alike
⑤ looks after

21 위 글의 밑줄 친 ⓑprocess와 같은 의미로 쓰인 것을 고르시오.

① It's a normal part of the learning process.
② I want to know the manufacturing process.
③ We're in the process of selling our house.
④ This machine can quickly process the data.
⑤ The process of making steel is complex.

22 Which vitamin helps improve your vision? Answer in English. (3 words)

➡ _____

Lesson 3

Always Aware, Always Prepared

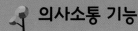 **의사소통 기능**

- 궁금증 표현하기
  I'm curious about how that happened.
- 경고하기 · 주의 주기
  Make sure you don't take the elevators in a real fire.

언어 형식

- 과거완료
  One night in February, after I **had gone** to bed, an earthquake hit.
- 여러 가지 접속사
  Since it was my first time experiencing an earthquake, I didn't know how to react.

Words & Expressions

교과서

Key Words

- **actually** [ǽktʃuəli] 부 실제로
- **affect** [əfékt] 동 영향을 주다
- **avoid** [əvɔ́id] 동 ~을 피하다
- **amusement park** 놀이 공원
- **aware** [əwéər] 형 인식하는
- **cause** [kɔːz] 동 초래하다
- **character** [kǽriktər] 명 등장인물
- **chest** [tʃest] 명 가슴
- **collapse** [kəlǽps] 동 붕괴되다, 무너지다
- **common** [kámən] 형 흔한
- **confusion** [kənfjúːʒən] 명 혼란, 혼동
- **crawl** [krɔːl] 동 기어가다
- **curious** [kjúəriəs] 형 호기심이 많은
- **damage** [dǽmidʒ] 명 손상
- **destroy** [distrɔ́i] 동 파괴하다
- **disaster** [dizǽstər] 명 재난
- **drill** [dril] 명 훈련
- **earthquake** [ə́ːrθkweik] 명 지진
- **exactly** [igzǽktli] 부 정확하게
- **exit** [égzit] 동 나가다, 퇴장하다
- **flood** [flʌd] 명 홍수
- **heat wave** 폭염
- **heavy rain** 폭우
- **hit** [hit] 동 치다, 때리다, 부딪치다
- **immediately** [imíːdiətli] 부 즉시
- **include** [inklúːd] 동 포함하다
- **mention** [ménʃən] 동 언급하다
- **missing** [mísiŋ] 형 실종된
- **natural disaster** 자연 재해
- **nervously** [nə́ːrvəsli] 부 불안하게
- **occur** [əkə́ːr] 동 (일·사건 등이) 일어나다, 발생하다
- **panic** [pǽnik] 명 극심한 공포, 공황
- **perform** [pərfɔ́ːrm] 동 공연하다, 수행하다
- **prepared** [pripɛ́ərd] 형 준비된
- **press** [pres] 동 누르다
- **properly** [prápərli] 부 제대로, 적절하게
- **reaction** [riǽkʃən] 명 반응
- **realize** [ríːəlàiz] 동 깨닫다
- **recently** [ríːsntli] 부 최근에
- **scary** [skɛ́əri] 형 무서운
- **serious** [síəriəs] 형 심각한
- **shake** [ʃéikiŋ] 동 흔들리다, 흔들다
- **smash** [smæʃ] 동 세게 부딪치다
- **special effect** 특수 효과
- **suddenly** [sʌ́dnli] 부 갑자기, 급작스럽게
- **survival kit** 생존 장비
- **swing** [swiŋ] 동 흔들리다, 흔들다
- **tap** [tæp] 동 두들기다
- **urgently** [ə́ːrdʒəntli] 부 긴급하게
- **violently** [váiələntli] 부 격렬하게, 심하게
- **weight** [weit] 명 무게
- **whole** [houl] 형 전체의
- **wildfire** [wáildfaiər] 명 들불, 산불
- **worse** [wəːrs] 형 더 나쁜

Key Expressions

- **a large number of** 매우 많은
- **as well** 역시, 또한
- **at any time** 어느 때든지
- **a variety of** 다양한
- **based on ~** ~에 바탕을 둔
- **break into pieces** 산산조각이 나다
- **get a discount** 할인을 받다
- **in case of ~** ~의 경우에
- **in the middle of** ~의 한가운데에
- **keep ~ing** 계속해서 ~하다
- **make one's way** 가다, 나아가다
- **make sure** 확실하게 하다
- **pull over** 길 한쪽으로 차를 대다
- **put in** 집어넣다
- **pull out** 끌어내다
- **roll off** 굴러 떨어지다
- **take ~ seriously** 진지하게 받아들이다
- **tip over** 넘어지다, 기울어지다

Word Power

※ 서로 비슷한 뜻을 가진 어휘

□ **damage** 손상 : **harm** 손해

□ **include** 포함하다 : **involve** 포함하다

□ **exactly** 정확하게 : **correctly** 정확하게

□ **nervously** 불안하게 : **anxiously** 불안하게

□ **affect** 영향을 주다 : **influence** 영향을 주다

□ **properly** 적절하게 : **rightly** 적절하게

□ **recently** 최근에 : **lately** 최근에

□ **actually** 실제로 : **really** 실제로

※ 서로 반대의 뜻을 가진 어휘

□ **aware** 아는, 인식하는 ↔ **unaware** 알지 못하는

□ **destroy** 파괴하다 ↔ **construct** 건설하다

□ **exit** 나가다 ↔ **enter** 들어가다

□ **violently** 격렬하게 ↔ **nonviolently** 비폭력적으로

□ **common** 흔한 ↔ **rare** 드문

□ **include** 포함하다 ↔ **exclude** 제외하다

□ **whole** 전체의 ↔ **partial** 부분적인

□ **avoid** 피하다 ↔ **face** 마주하다

※ 명사 – 동사

□ **confuse** 혼란을 주다 – **confusion** 혼란

□ **weigh** 무게가 나가다 – **weight** 무게

□ **destroy** 파괴하다 – **destruction** 파괴

□ **perform** 공연하다 – **performance** 공연, 수행

English Dictionary

□ **cause** 초래하다
→ to make something happen, especially something bad
어떤 일, 특히 나쁜 일이 일어나게 만들다

□ **collapse** 붕괴하다
→ to break apart and fall down suddenly
갑자기 부서지거나 무너지다

□ **common** 흔한
→ happening often and to many people or in many places
너무 많은 사람에게 또는 너무 많은 장소에서 자주 일어나는

□ **crawl** 기어가다
→ to move along on your hands and knees with your body close to the ground
바닥에 몸을 가까이 하고 손이나 무릎으로 이동하다

□ **curious** 호기심이 많은
→ wanting to know about something
어떤 것에 대해 알기를 원하는

□ **destroy** 파괴하다
→ to damage something so badly that it no longer exists or cannot be used or repaired
더 이상 존재하거나 사용할 수 없거나 고칠 수 없도록 심하게 손상시키다

□ **disaster** 재난
→ a sudden event such as a flood, storm, or accident which causes great damage or suffering
큰 손상이나 고통을 초래하는 홍수, 폭풍 또는 사고와 같은 갑작스러운 사건

□ **earthquake** 지진
→ a sudden shaking of the Earth's surface that often causes a lot of damage
종종 많은 손상을 가져오는 지표면의 갑작스러운 흔들림

□ **exit** 나가다, 퇴장하다
→ to leave a place
어떤 장소를 떠나다

□ **flood** 홍수
→ a very large amount of water that covers an area that is usually dry
대개는 건조한 한 지역을 덮는 아주 많은 양의 물

□ **include** 포함하다
→ to make someone or something part of a larger group
어떤 사람 또는 어떤 것을 더 큰 집단의 구성원이 되도록 만들다

□ **properly** 적절하게
→ correctly, or in a way that is considered right
정확하게 또는 올바르다고 여겨지는 방식으로

01 다음 짝지어진 단어의 관계가 같도록 빈칸에 알맞은 말을 고르시오.

> damage : harm = _____ : correct

① exact
② aware
③ serious
④ legal
⑤ worse

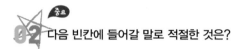

02 다음 빈칸에 들어갈 말로 적절한 것은?

> I was driving home when the shaking started. But I _____ immediately. I'm listening to the radio to find out what's going on.

① pulled in
② pulled out
③ pulled down
④ pulled off
⑤ pulled over

03 다음 중 영영풀이가 어색한 것은?

① flood: a very large amount of water that covers an area that is usually dry
② storm: a sudden shaking of the Earth's surface that often causes a lot of damage
③ disaster: a sudden event such as a flood, storm, or accident which causes great damage or suffering
④ common: happening often and to many people or in many places
⑤ exit: to leave a place

04 다음 중 밑줄 친 부분의 뜻풀이가 바르지 않은 것은?

① We nervously made our way down the stairs. (내려갔다)
② What natural disasters have you experienced? (재난)
③ Make sure you place your hands in the middle of the person's chest. (한 가운데에)
④ Make sure that you exit the building immediately. (들어가다)
⑤ Soon the whole room began to shake violently. (전체의)

05 다음 중 〈보기〉에 있는 단어를 사용하여 자연스러운 문장을 만들 수 없는 것은? (대 · 소문자 무시)

> ┌─── 보기 ├──
> rang   based   crawling   destroyed

① We started _____ toward the door.
② _____ on the report, earthquakes are fourth.
③ Many houses and building were _____ by the earthquake.
④ Then suddenly the _____ seemed to stop.
⑤ At that moment, my mom's cell phone _____.

서답형

06 다음 밑줄 친 단어와 의미가 같은 단어를 쓰시오. (주어진 철자로 시작할 것)

> Although I had done many earthquake drills in school, I had never thought I'd experience a real earthquake.

➡ t_____

01 다음 주어진 단어를 이용해 빈칸을 완성하시오.

> Performing CPR _____ can save someone's life. Here are the steps for proper CPR.

➡ _____ (proper)

02 다음 빈칸에 공통으로 들어가기에 적절한 단어를 쓰시오.

> • In case of yellow dust, make sure that you wear a mask when you go _____.
> • I'm listening to the radio right now to find _____ what's going on.

➡ _____

03 다음 문장의 빈칸에 들어가기에 적절한 단어를 주어진 철자로 시작하여 쓰시오.

> 나는 건물이 붕괴될까봐 걱정이 되기 시작했다.
> ➡ I started to worry that the building would c_____.

04 다음 우리말에 맞게 빈칸에 알맞은 말을 쓰시오.

(1) 나는 여전히 정확하게 무엇이 일어나고 있는지 몰랐다.
   ➡ I still didn't know what _____ was happening.
(2) 엄마는 나와 동생을 침대 밖으로 끌어내셨다.
   ➡ My mom _____ me and my brother _____ bed.
(3) 화재가 났을 경우에는 무엇을 해야 할까요?
   ➡ _____ _____ _____ a fire, what should I do?

05 다음 짝지어진 단어의 관계가 같도록 빈칸에 알맞은 말을 쓰시오.

> destroy : construct = _____ : exclude

06 빈칸에 알맞은 단어를 〈보기〉에서 골라 쓰시오.

> ┌─ 보기 ─┐
> scared   seriously   prepared
> made our way

(1) We nervously _____ down the stairs and outside.
(2) I still get _____ when I remember that night.
(3) After that night, I began to take earthquake drills _____.

07 다음 영영풀이에 해당하는 단어를 주어진 철자로 쓰시오.

> to damage something so badly that it no longer exists or cannot be used or repaired

➡ d_____

08 밑줄 친 단어의 반대말을 쓰시오. (주어진 철자로 시작할 것)

> A: In case of a fire, what should I do?
> B: Make sure that you cover your mouth with a wet cloth.
> A: Anything else?
> B: Make sure that you <u>exit</u> the building immediately.

➡ e_____

Conditional

교과서

Conversation

1 궁금증 표현하기

• **I'm curious about how that happened.** 나는 어떻게 그것이 일어났는지 궁금하다.

■ 'curious'는 '호기심이 생기는, 궁금한'이라는 뜻이다. 상대방에게 궁금한 것을 질문으로 표현하는 대신 '나는 ~에 관하여 호기심이 생긴다, ~에 관하여 궁금하다'라는 뜻으로 'I'm curious about ~'의 형태로 궁금증이나 호기심을 표현할 수 있다. '나는 ~이 궁금하다.'라는 뜻의 'I wonder ~.' 또는 'I would like to know ~.'를 쓸 수도 있다.

■ '나는 ~에 대하여 궁금하다'의 의미는 '나는 ~을 알고 싶다'의 의미로 'I want to know ~'의 의미이기도 하다. 좀 더 직접적으로 'Do you know ~?'라는 형태로 물어볼 수도 있다. 보통 '~에 대하여 궁금하다.'는 표현을 들었을 때 그 내용을 알면 자세한 설명을 해주고 그렇지 않을 때는 '같이 알아보자'는 표현 등이 따라 온다.

궁금증 표현하기

• I am curious about ~. 나는 ~이 궁금하다.
• I wonder ~. 나는 ~인지 궁금하다.
• I would like/want to know ~. 나는 ~이 알고 싶다.

궁금증을 나타내는 유사 표현

• Do you know ~? 너는 ~을 알고 있니?
• I'd be very interested to know ~. 나는 ~이 알고 싶다.
• Can you tell me about ~? ~에 대해 말해 줄 수 있니?

핵심 Check

1. 다음 대화의 순서를 바르게 배열하시오.

A: I heard that there have been many wildfires in Korea.

(A) I'm curious about when it happened.

(B) Yes. There was a big one in Yangyang.

(C) It happened in 2005.

① (A) – (C) – (B)　　　② (B) – (A) – (C)
③ (B) – (C) – (A)　　　④ (C) – (A) – (B)
⑤ (C) – (B) – (A)

② **경고하기 · 주의 주기**

> • Make sure you don't take the elevators in a real fire.
> 실제 화재에서는 절대로 엘리베이터를 타지 않도록 해라.

■ 상대방에게 주의 사항을 알려주어서 경고할 때는 'Make sure ~'를 사용한다. 'make sure ~'는 '반드시 ~하도록 하다' '~임을 확인하다'의 의미로 상대에게 '반드시 확인하라.'의 의미로 경고하는 경우에 자주 쓰인다. 'Be sure ~'도 마찬가지 의미가 될 수 있다. 우리말로 해석할 때는 '~을 확실하게 해라' '반드시 ~해라'가 된다.

■ 'Make sure' 또는 'Be sure' 뒤에는 접속사 that이 이끄는 절이 온다. 그래서 'Make sure that 주어+동사 ~', 'Be sure that 주어+동사 ~'의 형태가 되지만 접속사 that은 대부분 생략하고 'Make sure 주어+동사 ~', 'Be sure 주어+동사 ~'의 형태가 된다.

■ 보통 상대방에게 직접적인 경고를 할 때는 '~을 조심해라.'의 의미로 'Watch out for ~', 'Look out for ~'를 쓴다. 'Make sure you don't ~' 'Be sure you don't ~'은 '절대로 ~하지 마라'의 의미이다.

경고하기 · 주의하기 표현

- Make sure (that) ~. : 반드시 ~해라.
- Watch out for ~. : ~을 조심해라.
- Make sure you don't ~. : ~하지 않도록 명심해라.
- You need to keep in mind that ~ : ~라는 사실을 명심해라.

- Be sure (that) ~. : ~을 확실하게 해라.
- Look out for ~. : ~을 잘 살펴라.
- Be careful not to ~. : ~하지 않도록 조심해라.

핵심 Check

2. 다음 대화의 밑줄 친 말 대신 쓸 수 있는 것을 고르시오.

B: Mom, what else do we need to put in the natural disaster survival kit?

W: Well, we need water, some food, and radio.

B: Anything else, Mom?

W: Oh, <u>make</u> sure that you include batteries for the radio.

① be   ② keep   ③ need   ④ watch   ⑤ look

3. 우리말과 일치하도록 주어진 어구를 배열하여 문장을 만드시오.

A: In case of yellow dust, what should I do?

B: _____ (밖에 나갈 때는 반드시 마스크를 착용하도록 해라.)

(that / make / you / you / sure / a mask / when / wear / go out)

Listen & Talk 1 B

G: There seem to be many natural disasters in Korea these days.

B: I agree. There was an earthquake in the south last week. Also a storm is coming this week.

G: I'm curious about ❶which type of natural disaster causes the most damage in Korea.

B: Actually I read a report yesterday about the damage from each type of natural disaster. Number one is storms.

G: I see. I guess earthquakes are second.

B: No, second is heavy rain, and third is heavy snow.

G: What about earthquakes?

B: Based on the report, earthquakes are fourth. But the damage from earthquakes ❷has been increasing recently because they have been happening more often in Korea.

G: I see. It seems like we have to be prepared for a variety of natural disasters in Korea.

G: 요즈음 한국에서 많은 자연 재해가 있는 것 같아.

B: 동의해. 지난주에 남부에서 지진이 있었어. 또한 이번 주에는 태풍이 올 거야.

G: 나는 어떤 종류의 자연 재해가 한국에서 가장 큰 피해를 주는지 궁금해.

B: 사실 나는 어제 각 유형의 자연 재해로 인한 피해에 관한 보고서를 읽었어. 첫 번째가 폭풍이야.

G: 그렇구나. 지진이 두 번째인 것 같아.

B: 아니야. 두 번째는 폭우이고 세 번째는 폭설이야.

G: 지진은?

B: 보고서에 따르면, 지진은 네 번째야. 하지만 최근 한국에서 지진이 더 자주 일어나기 때문에 지진으로 인한 피해가 증가하고 있어.

G: 그렇구나. 한국에서는 다양한 자연 재해에 대비를 해야 할 것 같아.

❶ 'which type of ∼'는 간접의문문으로 전치사 about의 목적어이다.
❷ 'has been increasing'은 현재완료진행형으로 과거로부터 시작해서 지금도 계속되는 일을 나타낸다.

Check(√) True or False

(1) Storms cause the most damage in Korea. T ☐ F ☐

(2) The damage from heavy rain is increasing recently. T ☐ F ☐

 Listen & Talk 2 B

W: Performing ❶CPR properly can save someone's life. Here are the steps for proper CPR. First, check that the person needs help. Tap the person and shout, "Are you okay?" If there's no reaction, call 119 for help. Second, ❷listen, look, and feel for breathing. If the person's not breathing, begin CPR. Make sure you place your hands in the middle of the person's chest. Use your body weight to press harder on the chest. After 30 presses, give the person two breaths. ❸Keep doing CPR until help arrives.

W: 제대로 심폐소생술을 수행하는 것은 누군가의 생명을 구할 수 있습니다. 여기 적절한 심폐소생술을 위한 단계가 있습니다. 첫째, 그 사람이 도움을 필요로 하는지 확인하십시오. 그 사람을 두드리며 "괜찮으세요?"라고 큰소리로 외치세요. 반응이 없으면 119에 전화를 걸어 도움을 요청하세요. 둘째, 호흡을 하는지 듣고, 보고, 느끼세요. 그 사람이 숨을 쉬지 않으면 심폐소생술을 시작하세요. 손을 반드시 그 사람의 가슴 가운데에 놓도록 하세요. 가슴을 더 세게 누르기 위해 체중을 이용하세요. 30번 누른 후, 그 사람에게 두 번 바람을 불어 넣으시오. 도움이 올 때까지 심폐소생술을 계속하세요.

❶ CPR = 심폐소생술 (cardiopulmonary resuscitation)
❷ 호흡이 있는지 살피라는 의미로 귀, 눈, 촉감을 모두 동원해서 확인한다는 의미로 'listen, look, feel'을 사용했다.
❸ keep ∼ing = ∼을 계속하다

Check(√) True or False

(3) When someone needs help, first begin CPR. T ☐ F ☐

(4) You should place your hands in the middle of the person's chest to perform CPR. T ☐ F ☐

Listen & Talk 1 A

B: There was a big flood in Europe. Did you hear about it?

G: No, I didn't. But floods aren't that common in winter, ❶are they? I'm curious about how that happened.

B: ❷Me too. Let's do some online research.

❶ be동사가 있는 문장의 부가의문문이다.
❷ Me too. = I agree.

Listen & Talk 1 C

B: Hey, did you hear about the big fires in California?

G: No, I didn't. How serious are they?

B: They've destroyed ❶a large number of houses and other buildings.

G: Are the fires still going on?

B: Yes, actually the wind has made the fires worse. I hope all the people ❷living there are okay.

G: ❸So do I. I'm curious about how many people had to leave their homes.

B: Actually more than 20,000 people had to leave their homes, and about 400 people are missing in that area.

G: That's terrible. I hope they're somewhere safe.

❶ 'a number of'를 강조하여 'a large number of'라고 했다.
❷ 현재분사 living은 people을 뒤에서 수식한다.
❸ 'So do I.'는 '나도 마찬가지야.'의 의미로 'Me, too.' 또는 'I agree.'에 해당한다.

Listen & Talk 1 D

A: I heard that there have been many wildfires in Korea.

B: Yes. There was a big ❶one in Yangyang.

A: I'm curious about ❷when it happened.

B: It happened in 2005.

❶ one = wildfire
❷ 전치사 about의 목적어로 간접의문문이다.

Listen & Talk 2 A

B: Mom, what else do we need to put in the natural disaster survival kit?

W: Well, we need water, some food, and a radio.

B: ❶Anything else, Mom?

W: Oh, ❷make sure that you include batteries for the radio.

❶ Anything else? = Is there anything else?
❷ 접속사 that은 생략 가능하다.

Listen & Talk 2 D

A: ❶In case of a fire, what should I do?

B: Make sure that you cover your mouth with a wet cloth.

A: Anything else?

B: Make sure that you exit the building immediately.

❶ In case of ~ = ~의 경우에

Do It Yourself A

G: Did you hear that earthquakes ❶are occurring more often in Korea than before?

B: Oh, really? I've never felt an earthquake in Korea.

G: They usually occur in the southern part of Korea, but now they are occurring in other places as well.

B: I didn't know that. I'm curious about ❷why earthquakes have occurred so often in Korea recently.

G: ❸Why don't we do some research to find out?

B: Sounds good, but where do we look first?

G: How about asking our science teacher first? I think she can help us.

B: Okay. ❹Let's go and find her.

❶ 현재진행시제를 사용하여 현재에 계속되는 일을 나타내고 있어서 시제 일치를 시키지 않았다.
❷ 전치사 about의 목적어가 되는 간접의문문이다.
❸ Why don't we ~? = ~하는 게 어때?
❹ go and find = go to find

● 다음 우리말과 일치하도록 빈칸에 알맞은 말을 쓰시오.

Listen & Talk 1 A

B: There _____ a big _____ in Europe. Did you _____ about it?

G: No, I didn't. But _____ aren't that _____ in winter, _____ they? I'm _____ about _____ that happened.

B: Me too. Let's do some online _____.

Listen & Talk 1 B

G: There _____ to be many _____ _____ in Korea _____ days.

B: I agree. There was an _____ in the _____ last week. Also a _____ is coming this week.

G: I'm _____ about _____ type of _____ causes the _____ _____ in Korea.

B: Actually I read a _____ yesterday about the _____ from _____ _____ of natural disaster. Number one is storms.

G: I see. I _____ earthquakes are _____.

B: No, second is _____ rain, and third is heavy _____.

G: _____ about earthquakes?

B: _____ on the report, _____ are fourth. But the _____ from earthquakes has _____ _____ recently _____ they have _____ happening more often in Korea.

G: I see. It _____ _____ we have to be _____ for a _____ of _____ _____ in Korea.

Listen & Talk 1 C

B: Hey, did you _____ _____ the big _____ in California?

G: No, I didn't. How _____ are they?

B: They've _____ a large number of _____ and buildings.

G: _____ the fires still _____ _____?

B: Yes, _____ the wind has made the fires _____. I hope all the people _____ _____ are okay.

G: _____ _____ I. I'm _____ about how many people had to _____ their homes.

B: _____ more than 20,000 people had to _____ their homes, and about 400 people are _____ in that area.

G: That's _____. I hope they're _____ safe.

B: 유럽에 큰 홍수가 있었어. 그것에 대해 들었니?
G: 아니. 하지만 겨울에는 홍수가 그렇지 않아, 그렇지 않니? 나는 어떻게 그런 일이 일어났는지 궁금해.
B: 나도 그래. 온라인 검색을 해보자.

G: 요즈음 한국에서 많은 자연 재해가 있는 것 같아.
B: 동의해. 지난주에 남부에서 지진이 있었어. 또한 이번 주에는 태풍이 올 거야.
G: 나는 어떤 종류의 자연 재해가 한국에서 가장 큰 피해를 주는지 궁금해.
B: 사실 나는 어제 각 유형의 자연 재해로 인한 피해에 관한 보고서를 읽었어. 첫 번째가 폭풍이야.
G: 그렇구나. 지진이 두 번째인 것 같아.
B: 아니야. 두 번째는 폭우이고 세 번째는 폭설이야.
G: 지진은?
B: 보고서에 따르면, 지진은 네 번째야. 하지만 최근 한국에서 지진이 더 자주 일어나기 때문에 지진으로 인한 피해가 증가하고 있어.
G: 그렇구나. 한국에서는 다양한 자연 재해에 대비를 해야 할 것 같아.

B: 안녕. 너 캘리포니아에서 일어난 큰 화재에 대해 들었니?
G: 아니. 얼마나 심각하니?
B: 많은 집들과 다른 건물들을 파괴했어.
G: 아직도 화재가 진행되고 있니?
B: 그래. 사실 바람이 화재를 더 악화시켰어. 나는 거기 사는 모든 사람들이 괜찮기를 바라.
G: 나도 그래. 얼마나 많은 사람들이 집을 떠나야 했는지 궁금해.
B: 사실 2만 명 이상이 집을 떠나야 했고, 약 400명이 실종되었어.
G: 끔찍하구나. 나는 그들이 안전한 곳에 있기를 바라.

Listen & Talk 2 A

B: Mom, _____ _____ do we need to _____ _____ the natural disaster _____ _____?

W: Well, we need _____, some food, and a _____.

B: _____ else, Mom?

W: Oh, _____ sure that you _____ batteries for the _____.

Listen & Talk 2 B

W: _____ CPR properly can _____ someone's life. _____ are the _____ for _____ CPR. First, check that the person _____ help. _____ the person and shout, "_____ you okay?" If there's no _____, call 119 for help. Second, _____, look, and _____ for breathing. If the person's not _____, begin CPR. Make _____ you _____ your hands _____ the middle of the person's _____. Use your body _____ to press _____ on the chest. After 30 presses, give the person two _____. Keep doing CPR until _____ arrives.

Listen & Talk 2 D

A: _____ _____ of a fire, _____ should I _____?

B: _____ sure that you _____ your mouth with a _____ cloth.

A: Anything _____?

B: Make sure that you _____ the building _____.

Do It Yourself A

G: Did you _____ that earthquakes are _____ more _____ in Korea than _____?

B: Oh, _____? I've never _____ an earthquake in Korea.

G: They _____ occur in the _____ part of Korea, but now they are occurring in _____ _____ as well.

B: I didn't know that. I'm _____ about _____ earthquakes have _____ so often in Korea recently.

G: Why don't we do some _____ to find out?

B: Sounds good, but where _____ we look first?

G: _____ _____ asking our science teacher first? I think she can _____ us.

B: Okay. _____ go and _____ her.

해석

B: 엄마, 자연 재해 생존 장비에 무엇을 더 넣어야 할까요?

W: 글쎄. 우리는 물, 약간의 식량 그리고 라디오가 필요해.

B: 다른 것은요, 엄마?

W: 오, 라디오 건전지를 반드시 포함하도록 해.

W: 제대로 심폐소생술을 수행하는 것은 누군가의 생명을 구할 수 있습니다. 여기 적절한 심폐소생술을 위한 단계가 있습니다. 첫째, 그 사람이 도움을 필요로 하는지 확인하십시오. 그 사람을 두드리며 "괜찮으세요?" 라고 큰소리로 외치세요. 반응이 없으면 119에 전화를 걸어 도움을 요청하세요. 둘째, 호흡을 하는지 듣고, 보고, 느끼세요. 그 사람이 숨을 쉬지 않으면 심폐소생술을 시작하세요. 손을 반드시 그 사람의 가슴 가운데에 놓도록 하세요. 가슴을 더 세게 누르기 위해 체중을 이용하세요. 30번 누른 후, 그 사람에게 두 번 바람을 불어 넣으시오. 도움이 올 때까지 심폐소생술을 계속하세요.

A: 화재가 발생하면 어떻게 해야 하나요?

B: 반드시 젖은 천으로 입을 가리도록 해.

A: 다른 것은 뭐가 있을까요?

B: 즉시 건물 밖으로 나가도록 해야 해.

G: 한국에서 지진이 전보다 자주 일어나고 있다는 말을 들었니?

B: 오, 정말? 나는 한국에서 지진을 느껴본 적이 없어.

G: 보통 지진이 한국의 남부에서 발생하지만, 이제는 다른 지역에서도 발생하고 있어.

B: 그건 몰랐어. 나는 왜 최근에 한국에서 지진이 그렇게 자주 발생하는지 궁금해.

G: 알아내기 위해 조사를 해보는 게 어떨까?

B: 좋은 것 같아. 하지만 먼저 어디에서 찾아야 하지?

G: 먼저 과학 선생님께 여쭤보면 어떨까? 나는 선생님께서 우리를 도울 수 있을 거라고 생각해.

B: 알았어. 가서 선생님을 찾아보자.

[01~02] 다음 대화의 빈칸에 들어갈 말로 알맞은 것을 고르시오.

01

B: Hey, did you hear about the big fires in California?

G: No, I didn't. How serious are they?

B: They've destroyed a large number of houses and other buildings.

G: _____

B: Yes, actually the wind has made the fires worse. I hope all the people living there are okay.

① Are the fires still going on?

② Have you been there?

③ How did you know about that?

④ How many houses were destroyed?

⑤ Do you know anyone living there?

02

A: In case of a fire, what should I do?

B: Make sure that you cover your mouth with a wet cloth.

A: Anything else?

B: _____ you exit the building immediately.

① I have wondered   ② Make sure that

③ Run before   ④ I want to ask

⑤ I have heard

03 우리말과 일치하도록 주어진 어구를 배열하여 문장을 만드시오.

B: Mom, what else do we need to put in the natural disaster survival kit?

W: Well, we need water, some food, and a radio.

B: Anything else, Mom?

W: Oh, 라디오를 위한 건전지를 반드시 포함하도록 해라. (batteries, for, sure, make, that, include, the radio, you)

➡ _____

[01~03] 다음 대화를 읽고 물음에 답하시오.

B: Hey, did you hear about the big fires in California?

G: No, I didn't. How serious are they?

B: They've destroyed a large number of houses and other buildings.

G: Are the fires still going on?

B: Yes, (A)actual the wind has made the fires worse. I hope all the people living there are okay.

G: So do I. (B)I'm curious about how many people had to leave their homes.

B: Actually more than 20,000 people had to leave their homes, and about 400 people are missing in that area.

G: That's terrible. I hope they're somewhere safe.

서답형

01 밑줄 친 (A)를 알맞은 형으로 고치시오.

➡ _____

02 밑줄 친 (B)를 다음과 같이 바꾸어 쓸 때 빈칸에 적절한 것은?

➡ I _____ how many people had to leave their homes.

① know   ② find   ③ wonder
④ believe   ⑤ worry

중요

03 위 대화의 내용과 일치하지 않는 것은?

① There were big fires in California.

② The fires were caused by the wind.

③ People who left their homes were more than 20,000.

④ About 400 people are missing in that area.

⑤ Many houses and buildings were destroyed.

[04~07] 다음 대화를 읽고 물음에 답하시오.

G: (A)There seem to be many natural disasters in Korea these days.

B: I agree. There was an earthquake in the south last week. (ⓐ) Also a storm is coming this week.

G: I'm curious about which type of natural disaster causes the most damage in Korea.

B: (ⓑ) Number one is storms.

G: I see. I guess earthquakes are second.

B: No, second is heavy rain, and third is heavy snow. (ⓒ)

G: What about earthquakes?

B: Based on the report, earthquakes are fourth. (ⓓ) But the damage from earthquakes has been increasing recently because they have been happening more often in Korea.

G: I see. (ⓔ) It seems like we have to be (B)prepare for a variety of natural disasters in Korea.

중요

04 ⓐ~ⓔ 중에서 다음 문장이 들어가기에 적절한 곳은?

Actually I read a report yesterday about the damage from each type of natural disaster.

① ⓐ   ② ⓑ   ③ ⓒ   ④ ⓓ   ⑤ ⓔ

서답형

05 위 대화의 밑줄 친 (A)와 같은 뜻이 되도록 빈칸에 알맞은 말을 쓰시오.

➡ _____ seems _____ there _____ many natural disasters in Korea these days.

서답형

06 위 대화의 밑줄 친 (B)prepare를 알맞은 형으로 고치시오.

➡ _____

07 위 대화를 읽고, 대답할 수 없는 것은?

① What kinds of natural disasters are occurring in Korea?
② What did the boy read yesterday?
③ Which type of natural disaster causes the most damage in Korea?
④ What disaster occurred in the south last week?
⑤ Why have earthquakes been happening more often in Korea?

08 다음 대화의 순서가 바르게 배열된 것을 고르시오.

> A: I heard that there have been many wildfires in Korea.
> (A) Yes. There was a big one in Yangyang.
> (B) It happened in 2005.
> (C) I'm curious about when it happened.

① (A) – (C) – (B)
② (B) – (A) – (C)
③ (B) – (C) – (A)
④ (C) – (A) – (B)
⑤ (C) – (B) – (A)

[09~10] 다음 대화를 읽고 물음에 답하시오.

> G: Did you hear that earthquakes are occurring more often in Korea than before?
> B: Oh, really? _____ ⓐ _____
> G: They usually occur in the southern part of Korea, but _____ ⓑ _____ .
> B: I didn't know that. I'm curious about why earthquakes have occurred so often in Korea recently.
> G: _____ ⓒ _____
> B: Sounds good, but where do we look first?
> G: _____ ⓓ _____ I think she can help us.
> B: _____ ⓔ _____

09 위 대화의 빈칸 ⓐ~ⓔ에 들어갈 대화로 가장 어색한 것은?

① ⓐ I've never felt an earthquake in Korea.
② ⓑ now they are occurring in other places as well
③ ⓒ Why don't we do some research to find out?
④ ⓓ How about searching the Internet before asking our science teacher first?
⑤ ⓔ Okay. Let's go and find her.

중요

10 위 대화를 읽고 다음 중 대답할 수 없는 것은?

① Are earthquakes occurring more often in Korea?
② Has the boy felt an earthquake before?
③ Where do earthquakes usually occur in Korea?
④ Why have earthquakes occurred so often in Korea?
⑤ Will they search the Internet at once?

[01~03] 다음 대화를 읽고 물음에 답하시오.

G: There seem to be many natural disasters in Korea these days.

B: I agree. There was an earthquake in the south last week. Also a storm is coming this week.

G: (A)나는 궁금하다 which type of natural disaster causes the most damage in Korea.

B: Actually I read a report yesterday about the damage from each type of natural disaster. Number one is storms.

G: I see. I guess earthquakes are second.

B: No, second is heavy rain, and third is heavy snow.

G: ____(B)____ earthquakes?

B: Based on the report, earthquakes are fourth. But the damage from earthquakes has been increasing recently because they have been happening more often in Korea.

G: I see. (C)한국에서는 다양한 자연 재해에 대하여 준비가 되어야 할 것 같다.(it, like, seems, have to, prepared for, be, we, natural disasters, a variety of, in Korea)

01 밑줄 친 (A)의 우리말에 맞게 영어로 쓰시오. (about 포함)

➡ _____

02 대화의 내용으로 보아 빈칸 (B)에 들어가기에 적절한 말을 2단어로 쓰시오.

➡ _____

03 밑줄 친 (C)의 우리말을 주어진 어구를 배열하여 영작하시오.

➡ _____
_____

[04~06] 다음 글을 읽고 물음에 답하시오.

W: Performing CPR properly can save someone's life. Here are the steps for proper CPR. First, check that the person needs help. Tap the person and shout, "Are you okay?" If there's no ___(A)___ , call 119 for help. Second, listen, look, and feel for breathing. If the person's not breathing, begin CPR. (B)반드시 그 사람의 가슴 가운데에 손을 놓도록 하세요.(sure, place, your hands, you, make, the person's chest, in the middle of). Use your body weight to press harder on the chest. After 30 presses, give the person two breaths. Keep doing CPR until help arrives.

04 빈칸 (A)에 들어가기에 적절한 단어를 쓰시오.

➡ _____

05 주어진 어구를 배열하여 밑줄 친 (B)의 우리말을 영작하시오.

➡ _____
_____

06 When should we start CPR on the person? Answer in English. (9 words)

➡ _____
_____

Grammar

교과서

① 과거완료

> • One night in February, after I **had gone** to bed, an earthquake hit.
> 2월 어느 날 밤, 내가 잠자리에 든 후에 지진이 일어났다.
>
> • It was more beautiful than I **had imagined**. 그건 내가 상상했던 것보다 더 아름답더군요.

■ 과거완료는 과거 이전에 일어난 일이 과거의 어느 시점까지 영향을 미칠 때 쓰며, 'had+과거분사'의 형태로 쓴다. 과거완료도 현재완료처럼 완료, 계속, 경험, 결과의 용법이 있다. 또한 과거의 어느 시점보다 먼저 일어난 일이나 상태를 나타낼 때도 쓰이며 이것을 보통 '대과거'라고 한다.

• I **had** just **finished** my homework when he called me. 〈완료〉 그가 내게 전화했을 때 나는 막 숙제를 마쳤다.

• She **had cleaned** her house for two hours before I visited her. 〈계속〉
그녀는 내가 그녀를 방문하기 전에 2시간 동안 그녀의 집을 청소했다.

• He **had** never **seen** a live tiger before.. 〈경험〉 그는 전에 살아 있는 호랑이를 한 번도 본 적이 없었다.

• He **had gone** to Seoul when I visited him. 〈결과〉 내가 그를 방문했을 때 그는 서울로 가고 없었다.

• He realized that he **had met** her before. 〈대과거〉 그는 전에 그녀를 만난 적이 있다는 것을 깨달았다. 〈대과거〉

■ 한 문장에 두 가지 과거의 일이 나올 때, 두 동작이 거의 동시에 일어났거나 시간차가 거의 없이 연속적으로 일어났을 경우에는 단순과거로 표현한다. 또, 접속사 after나 before가 쓰여 두 동작의 전후 관계가 명백할 때도 단순과거로 표현할 수 있다.

• I **showed** them how to do it and they **tried**. 나는 그들에게 그것을 어떻게 하는지 보여주었고, 그들은 해 보았다.
〈시간차가 거의 없는 연속 동작〉

• The village **was** quiet before they **came**. 그들이 오기 전에는 마을이 조용했다. 〈전후 관계가 명백함〉

핵심 Check

1. 다음 괄호 안에서 알맞은 말을 고르시오.

(1) When she came home, her husband (had done / does) the dishes already.

(2) Judy knew that Megan (had finished / finished) her homework the previous day.

(3) The train (has / had) just left when I arrived at the station.

② 여러 가지 접속사

> • **Since** it was my first time experiencing an earthquake, I didn't know how to react. 지진을 경험한 것이 처음이었기 때문에, 나는 어떻게 반응해야 할지 몰랐다.

■ 접속사란 단어와 단어, 구와 구, 절과 절을 연결시켜 주는 말이다.

(1) 이유를 나타내는 since

■ since는 '~이기 때문에'라는 의미로 이유를 나타내는 접속사로 쓰인다. since가 이끄는 부사절이 이유를 나타내고, 주절이 그 결과를 나타내며, 이때의 since는 as나 because로 바꿔 쓸 수 있다.

- He couldn't go out **since** he was sick. 그는 아파서 나갈 수 없었다.
  = He couldn't go out **as[because]** he was sick.

cf. since와 같은 의미인 due to나 because of 등은 뒤에 (대)명사나 동명사가 온다.

- He quit the job **because of** his health. 그는 건강상의 이유로 직장을 그만 두었다.

■ since는 이외에도 전치사나 접속사로 '~한 이래로'의 뜻으로 쓰인다.

- He has worked **since** he left school. 그는 학교를 나온 이래 일하고 있다.

(2) 양보절을 이끄는 although

■ although는 '비록 ~일지라도'라는 의미로 양보절을 이끌며 이끄는 절의 내용과 주절의 내용은 서로 상반되고 even though나 though로 바꿔 쓸 수 있다.

- **Although** he is rich, he is not happy. 그는 부자지만 행복하지는 않다.

cf. although와 비슷한 의미인 despite는 전치사이므로 뒤에 (대)명사나 동명사가 나온다.

- He is very strong **despite** his age. 그는 노령임에도 불구하고 매우 정정하다.

cf. even if는 '만일 ~라고 할지라도(가정)' 정도의 뜻이다.

■ 기타 접속사

(1) 시간 관계를 나타내는 접속사: after, before, as soon as, when, while, until 등
(2) 조건을 나타내는 접속사: if, unless, in case (that), in the event (that) 등
(3) 목적을 나타내는 접속사: so that, in order that 등

핵심 Check

2. 다음 빈칸에 들어갈 말을 〈보기〉에서 골라 쓰시오.

> ┤ 보기 ├
> although   after   since

(1) _____ I'm broke, I don't need your help.

(2) We don't worry _____ we are armed with effective tools.

(3) Several years _____ they'd split up, they met again by chance in Paris.

01 다음 빈칸에 들어갈 말로 알맞은 것은?

> I recognized her at once as I _____ her before.

① see   ② saw   ③ seen
④ have seen   ⑤ had seen

02 다음 괄호 안에서 알맞은 말을 고르시오.

(1) When I called, he (already started / had already started).
(2) I admitted to her that I (lied / had lied) to her.
(3) (Although / When) the sun was shining, it wasn't very warm.
(4) I was here a bit early (after / since) my watch gained time.

03 다음 두 문장을 한 문장으로 바꾸어 쓸 때 알맞게 표현한 것을 고르시오.

> • Mike is not honest.
> • I don't believe him.

① Although Mike is not honest, I don't believe him.
② Mike is not honest although I don't believe him.
③ Since Mike is not honest, I don't believe him.
④ Mike is not honest since I don't believe him.
⑤ Mike is not honest after I don't believe him.

04 다음 우리말에 맞게 주어진 어휘를 바르게 배열하시오.

(1) 작년까지 Linda는 Paris를 방문한 적이 전혀 없었다. (until로 시작할 것)
     (year, Linda, Paris, had, last, until, visited, never)
     ➡ _____

(2) 그는 부자였지만, 사람들은 그가 가난한 줄 알았다. (접속사로 시작할 것)
     (he, he, people, was, was, thought, poor, rich, although)
     ➡ _____

(3) 나는 간밤에 너무 무서워서 잠을 잘 수 없었다. ('주절+종속절'의 구조로 쓸 것)
     (I, I, night, couldn't, afraid, sleep, was, last, so, since)
     ➡ _____

01 다음 중 어법상 어색한 것은?

① Our little friends had finished the shoes when we got up.
② They talked about the accident that happened there a few hours before.
③ When I arrived at the bus stop, the bus had already left.
④ He had never been abroad before he became thirty.
⑤ The plane had already taken off when I reached the airport.

02 다음 중 어법상 바르지 않은 것은?

① Although we have to say goodbye for now, we can meet next year.
② Though it rained heavily, we played outside.
③ Even though she had an umbrella, she got wet in the rain.
④ It started to rain though we decided to leave.
⑤ Though I bought it only yesterday, I'll give it to you.

03 다음 빈칸에 알맞은 말이 바르게 짝지어진 것은?

> • _____ he was born in England, he is a Korean boy.
> • It was more beautiful than I _____.

① Even though – had imagined
② Since – had imagined
③ Even though – imagined
④ Since – imagined
⑤ Because – have imagined

04 다음 괄호 안에서 알맞은 말을 고르시오.

(1) When he came home, his son had (finish / finished) homework.
(2) I realized that I (had made / made) a big mistake.
(3) I (had prepared / prepared) to be a musician since I was a kid.
(4) (Although / Because) he was tall, he couldn't touch the ceiling.
(5) (Since / Although) I didn't have lunch today, I had a big dinner.
(6) (Despite / Though) I love snow, I hope it will stop snowing.

05 주어진 문장의 틀린 부분을 찾아, 올바르게 고친 것을 고르시오.

> When I reached home, my brother go to bed and only Mom was awake.

① When I reached home, my brother went to bed and only Mom was awake.
② When I reached home, my brother has gone to bed and only Mom was awake.
③ When I reached home, my brother had gone to bed and only Mom was awake.
④ When I have reached home, my brother went to bed and only Mom was awake.
⑤ When I had reached home, my brother had gone to bed and only Mom was awake.

06 다음 문장의 밑줄 친 부분 중 어법상 어색한 것은?

> ⓐAlthough she ⓑhas been ill ⓒfor a long time, it still ⓓcame as a shock when she eventually ⓔdied.

① ⓐ   ② ⓑ   ③ ⓒ   ④ ⓓ   ⑤ ⓔ

07 빈칸 (A)와 (B)에 알맞은 것으로 바르게 짝지어진 것은?

> Eric was late for the meeting ___(A)___ he ___(B)___ the bus.

      (A)   (B)
① since   has missed
② though   missed
③ because   has missed
④ though   had missed
⑤ because   had missed

08 〈보기〉에서 알맞은 접속사를 골라 다음 빈칸을 채우시오.

> ┤ 보기 ├
> when   though   after   since   unless

(1) You'll miss the bus _____ you walk more quickly.

(2) He achieved success _____ he made lots of efforts.

(3) She hasn't phoned, _____ she said she would.

(4) I still get scared _____ I remember that night.

(5) Yesterday he stayed home from work _____ he got a really bad flu.

09 다음 문장의 빈칸에 알맞은 말은?

> _____ their house was not so nice, they looked happy.

① After   ② Unless
③ If   ④ Though
⑤ Since

10 다음 우리말을 바르게 영작한 것을 고르시오.

> 그 진주는 진짜같이 보여도 가짜예요.

① The pearls are fake, so they look real.
② The pearls are fake, though they look real.
③ The pearls are fake, unless they look real.
④ The pearls are fake since they look real.
⑤ The pearls are fake as they look real.

11 다음 문장의 빈칸에 들어갈 알맞은 말은?

> Isabelle _____ in Rome for 15 years when I met her.

① lives   ② lived
③ living   ④ has lived
⑤ had lived

12 다음 두 문장을 한 문장으로 바꿔 쓰고자 한다. 빈칸에 들어갈 알맞은 말을 쓰시오.

> • Brian started to learn Korean in the year of 2015.
> • Brian gave a speech in Korean at the meeting last weekend.
> = Brian gave a speech in Korean at the meeting last weekend as he _____ it since 2015.

13 다음 밑줄 친 과거완료의 용법이 〈보기〉와 같은 것은?

┌── 보기 ──
Janet <u>had been</u> ill in bed for three days when I visited her.
└──────

① When she got to the station, the train <u>had just left</u> for London.
② Herold <u>had</u> never <u>seen</u> such a big animal till then.
③ Christine <u>had lived</u> in Boston since she got married.
④ I thought that he <u>had lost</u> his bag on the train to New York.
⑤ She asked her to feel the eggs that <u>had become</u> hard.

서답형
14 다음 문장에서 문맥상 어색한 접속사를 바르게 고쳐 다시 쓰시오.

(1) I missed the first bus because I got up early in the morning.
  ➡ _____
    _____

(2) Although I am a student, I will get a discount.
  ➡ _____
    _____

(3) David was doing the dishes since Monica called him.
  ➡ _____
    _____

(4) All of them look tired before they worked hard.
  ➡ _____
    _____

(5) I'll take the job if the pay is much too low.
  ➡ _____
    _____

[15~16] 다음 우리말에 맞게 영작한 것을 고르시오.

15
┌─────────────────────
비록 그것이 사실일지라도, 그는 그것을 믿지 않았다.
└─────────────────────

① Since it was true, he didn't believe it.
② Since he didn't believe it, it was true.
③ Though it was true, he didn't believe it.
④ It was true, though he didn't believe it.
⑤ As though it was true, he didn't believe it.

16
┌─────────────────────
그때 이전에 바다에서 고래를 본 적이 있었니?
└─────────────────────

① Do you ever see a whale in the sea before then?
② Did you ever see a whale in the sea before then?
③ Have you ever seen a whale in the sea before then?
④ Have you ever been seeing a whale in the sea before then?
⑤ Had you ever seen a whale in the sea before then?

17 다음 중 어법상 어색한 것을 고르시오. (2개)

① Since it's very hot outside, I will play soccer.
② Our teacher will edit our video after we finish recording it.
③ I had never been in such a situation, so my face got really red.
④ I remembered that I met him at the party.
⑤ When I arrived at school, class had already begun.

01 시간 흐름에 따른 사건 전개에 맞게 빈칸을 채워 문장을 완성하시오.

> (1) Mom bought a smart phone for me last week.
> → I lost the phone yesterday.
> → I don't have the phone now.
> (2) Kyle bought a flower vase last month.
> → He broke the vase by mistake today.
> → His mom knew the fact later.

(1) Yesterday I lost the smart phone that _____ last week.

(2) Today Kyle's mom knew that Kyle broke the vase by mistake that _____ last month.

02 다음을 when을 이용하여 한 문장으로 연결할 때 빈칸을 알맞게 채우시오. (시제에 유의할 것.)

(1) I wanted to go to Seoul. I arrived at the station. The train already left for Seoul.
➡ When I arrived at the station to go to Seoul, the train _____ for Seoul.

(2) I promised to meet Tom at the bookstore. I went there quite late. He was there but went back to work. So, I couldn't meet him.
➡ When I went to the bookstore to meet Tom, _____ to work.

03 다음 우리말에 맞게 주어진 어구를 바르게 배열하시오.

(1) 비록 집은 파괴되었지만 아무도 다치지 않았습니다. (one, the house, even, no, was, was, hurt, destroyed, though) (접속사로 시작할 것)
➡ _____
_____

(2) 설사 그것이 너의 것이 아니라도 낭비하지 마라. (things, they, yours, even, don't, not, are, waste, if) ('주절+종속절'의 구문으로 작성할 것)
➡ _____
_____

(3) 그는 완전히 새로운 인종을 발견했다는 것을 깨달았다. (he, he, human species, a, discovered, realized, had, whole, new, that)
➡ _____
_____

(4) 나는 그가 왜 그런 어리석은 짓을 했는지 의아했다. (I, he, done, wondered, had, a, thing, stupid, such, why)
➡ _____
_____

04 다음 문장에서 내용에 맞게 잘못된 어휘를 알맞게 고치시오.

(1) Because animals do not speak like humans, some of them actually have a "language."
_____ ➡ _____

(2) As though they are so poor, they seem happy together.
_____ ➡ _____

(3) Despite he often talks big, I love him so much.
_____ ➡ _____

05 그림을 보고, 주어진 어휘를 이용하여 빈칸을 알맞게 채우시오.

(1) I noticed that my sister ＿＿＿＿＿＿ my glasses. (break)

(2) Molly cleaned her living room this afternoon. At night, Mom arrived home. When Mom came home from work, Molly ＿＿＿＿＿＿ her house. (already, clean)

06 알맞은 접속사를 이용하여 주어진 두 문장을 하나의 문장으로 쓰시오. ((1), (3)은 '주절+종속절'의 구문, (2)는 접속사로 시작할 것)

(1) • Horses sleep just like us.
• They do so in a different way.
➡ ＿＿＿＿＿＿＿＿＿＿＿

(2) • The Earth is rotating.
• Two tides occur each day.
➡ ＿＿＿＿＿＿＿＿＿＿＿

(3) • We had lunch.
• We had ice cream as dessert.
➡ ＿＿＿＿＿＿＿＿＿＿＿

07 다음 문장에서 어법상 <u>어색한</u> 것을 바르게 고쳐 다시 쓰시오.

(1) Bella has already done the dishes when he came back home.
➡ ＿＿＿＿＿＿＿＿＿＿＿

(2) Dave never visited Paris until then.
➡ ＿＿＿＿＿＿＿＿＿＿＿

(3) She told me why she left him.
➡ ＿＿＿＿＿＿＿＿＿＿＿

(4) The boy disappeared during walking home from school.
➡ ＿＿＿＿＿＿＿＿＿＿＿

(5) He made his choice, although regretted it later.
➡ ＿＿＿＿＿＿＿＿＿＿＿

(6) Anne was fond of Tim, despite he often annoyed her.
➡ ＿＿＿＿＿＿＿＿＿＿＿

08 다음 두 문장을 알맞은 접속사를 이용하여 한 문장으로 연결하되, 두 사건의 시간차가 드러나도록 쓰시오. ('주절+종속절'의 구문으로 작성할 것)

• Kay didn't recognize any of them.
• She heard of their names.

➡ ＿＿＿＿＿＿＿＿＿＿＿

Reading

Waking Up to an Earthquake

One night in February, after I had gone to bed, an earthquake hit. I
지진이 일어난 것보다 잠자리에 든 것이 먼저 일어난 일이기 때문에 과거완료로 씀.

woke up suddenly because my bed was shaking. I thought my brother

was shaking my bed as a joke. But then I heard the mirror on my desk
　　　　　　　　　　장난으로　　　　　　　　　　지각동사

fall to the floor and break into pieces. I knew it wasn't my brother then,
지각동사(heard)+목적어+목적격보어(원형부정사)

but I still didn't know what exactly was happening.
부정의 조동사 앞에 위치　　　　　　　know의 목적어(간접의문문)

Soon the whole room began to shake violently, and my confusion
= Before long　　　　　　　　　　= shaking

turned to panic. My mom shouted that it was an earthquake and ran
　　　　　　　　　　　명사절을 이끄는 접속사

into my room. Since it was my first time experiencing an earthquake, I
　　　= Because[As]　　be one's first time+-ing: ~하는 게 처음이다

didn't know how to react. I just kept saying, "What should I do?"
　　　= how I should react　　keep ~ing: 계속해서 ~하다

My mom pulled me and my brother out of bed. We ran to the kitchen
　　　　　　　　　　　　　　~의 밖으로

and crawled under the table.

suddenly 갑자기, 급작스럽게

shake 흔들다, 흔들리다

break into pieces 산산조각이 나다

exactly 정확하게

happen (사건이) 일어나다

violently 격렬하게, 심하게

confusion 혼란, 혼동

panic 극심한 공포, 공황

react 반응하다, 반응을 보이다

crawl 기어가다

📎 **확인문제**

● 다음 문장이 본문의 내용과 일치하면 T, 일치하지 않으면 F를 쓰시오.

1 The writer woke up suddenly because her bed was shaking. ☐

2 The writer's brother was shaking her bed as a joke. ☐

3 The mirror on the writer's desk fell to the floor and broke into pieces. ☐

4 The writer's brother shouted that it was an earthquake. ☐

5 The writer didn't experience an earthquake before. ☐

6 The writer pulled her brother out of bed. ☐

I could <u>see the light swinging</u> violently and <u>books falling</u> to the floor.
지각동사(see)+목적어+현재분사   목적어+현재분사

Our family picture dropped from the wall and the glass <u>covering</u> it
앞에 있는 명사 the glass를 수식

broke. A cup tipped over and rolled off the kitchen table. <u>Every second,</u>
= Every moment

I could hear <u>something else</u> in the apartment break. I started <u>to worry</u>
다른 어떤 것   = worrying

that the building would collapse.

Then <u>the shaking seemed to stop.</u> We started crawling toward the
= it seemed that the shaking stopped

door. At that moment, my mom's cell phone rang. <u>It</u> was my dad, <u>who</u>
전화를 한 사람   = and he

was coming home from work.

He shouted, "<u>It</u> stopped! Get out of the building! Take the stairs!
= The shaking

Don't take the elevator! Hurry!" "Where are you? Are you okay?" my

mom asked urgently. My dad answered, "Don't worry. I'm okay. I was

driving <u>home</u> when the shaking started. But I pulled over <u>immediately.</u>
to home(×)   = at once

I'm listening to the radio right now <u>to find</u> out what's <u>going on.</u>"
to부정사의 부사적 용법(목적)   = happening

swing 흔들다, 흔들리다

drop 떨어지다, 쓰러지다

cover 가리다, 덮다

tip over 넘어뜨리다, 넘어지다

roll 굴러가다

collapse 붕괴되다, 무너지다

seem to V …인 것 같다

urgently 긴급하게, 급히

pull over 길 한쪽으로 차를 대다

immediately 즉시, 당장

확인문제

● 다음 문장이 본문의 내용과 일치하면 T, 일치하지 <u>않으면</u> F를 쓰시오.

1 The writer could see the light swinging violently and books falling to the floor. ☐

2 The writer's family picture dropped from the table and the glass covering it broke. ☐

3 The writer started to worry that the building would collapse. ☐

4 When the shaking seemed to be violent, the writer's family started crawling toward the door. ☐

5 The writer's dad was driving home when the shaking started. ☐

6 The writer's mom was listening to the radio to find out what was going on. ☐

We nervously <u>made our way down</u> the stairs and outside. I looked
make one's way: 나아가다, 가다

around. Parts of buildings <u>had fallen</u> and <u>had smashed</u> several cars. We
밖으로 나가기 전에 건물의 일부분이 떨어져 나갔고 몇몇 차들은 박살이 난 것이므로 과거완료로 씀.

went to an open space <u>to avoid</u> more falling pieces. How could all this
to부정사의 부사적 용법(목적)

have happened <u>in a few minutes</u>?
몇 분 만에

Although I <u>had done</u> many earthquake drills in school, I <u>had never</u>
과거(지진이 일어났던 상황)보다 더 이전에 지진 훈련을 했었기 때문에 과거완료로 씀.   과거(지진이 일어났던 상황)보다 더 이전에 지진을 겪으
리라고는 생각해 본 적 없었기 때문에 과거완료로 씀.

<u>thought</u> I'd experience a real earthquake. I still get scared when I

remember that night. I can't forget <u>the panic I felt</u> when the <u>furniture</u>
the panic과 I 사이에 목적격 관계대명사 that[which]이 생략   furnitures(×):
항상 단수로 쓰는 집합명사

was shaking and things were falling to the floor. After that night, I

began <u>to take</u> earthquake drills seriously. I realized <u>that</u> I should be
= taking   목적어를 이끄는 접속사(생략 가능함.)

prepared for the next earthquake, <u>which</u> can occur <u>at any time</u>.
that(×)   언제든

nervously 신경질적으로, 초조하게
smash 박살내다, 때려 부수다
avoid …을 피하다
drill 훈련
seriously 심각하게, 진지하게
occur (일·사건 등이) 일어나다, 발생하다

📎 **확인문제**

• 다음 문장이 본문의 내용과 일치하면 T, 일치하지 <u>않으면</u> F를 쓰시오.

1 The writer's family nervously made their way down the stairs and outside. ☐

2 All the buildings had fallen and had smashed several cars. ☐

3 The writer's family went to an open space to avoid more falling pieces. ☐

4 The writer had never done an earthquake drill in school. ☐

5 The writer had never thought she would experience a real earthquake. ☐

6 The writer realized that she should be prepared for the next earthquake, though it

seldom occurs. ☐

● 우리말을 참고하여 빈칸에 알맞은 말을 쓰시오.

1 _____ _____ to an Earthquake

2 One night in February, after I _____ _____ _____ _____, an earthquake hit.

3 I woke up suddenly because my bed _____ _____.

4 I thought my brother was shaking my bed _____ _____ _____.

5 But then I heard the mirror on my desk _____ _____ _____ _____ and _____ _____ _____.

6 I knew it wasn't my brother then, but I still didn't know _____ _____ _____ _____.

7 Soon the whole room began to shake violently, and my confusion _____ _____ _____.

8 My mom shouted that it was an earthquake and _____ _____ my room.

9 Since it was _____ _____ _____ _____ an earthquake, I didn't know how to react.

10 I just _____ _____, "What should I do?"

11 My mom pulled me and my brother _____ _____ _____.

12 We ran to the kitchen and _____ _____ the table.

13 I could see the light _____ violently and books _____ to the floor.

1	지진에 눈을 뜨는 것
2	2월 어느 날 밤. 내가 잠자리에 든 후에 지진이 일어났다.
3	침대가 흔들렸기 때문에 나는 갑자기 잠에서 깼다.
4	나는 남동생이 장난으로 침대를 흔들고 있다고 생각했다.
5	하지만 그때 나는 내 책상 위에 있던 거울이 바닥으로 떨어져 산산조각이 나는 소리를 들었다.
6	그때 나는 남동생이 그런 것이 아니라는 것을 알았지만, 정확히 무슨 일이 일어나고 있었는지를 여전히 알지 못했다.
7	머지않아 방 전체가 심하게 흔들리기 시작했고 혼란스러움은 공포로 변했다.
8	엄마가 지진이라고 소리를 지르며 내 방으로 뛰어 들어왔다.
9	지진을 경험한 것이 처음이었기 때문에, 나는 어떻게 반응해야 할지 몰랐다.
10	나는 그저 "어떻게 해야 하지?" 라는 말을 반복했다.
11	엄마는 나와 남동생을 침대 밖으로 잡아끌었다.
12	우리는 주방으로 달려가서 식탁 아래로 기어들어 갔다.
13	나는 전등이 심하게 흔들리는 것과 책이 바닥으로 떨어지는 것을 볼 수 있었다.

14 Our family picture dropped from the wall and the glass _____ _____ _____.

15 A cup _____ _____ and _____ _____ the kitchen table.

16 _____ _____, I could hear something else in the apartment break.

17 I started _____ _____ that the building would _____.

18 Then the shaking _____ _____ _____.

19 We started _____ _____ the door.

20 _____ _____ _____, my mom's cell phone rang.

21 It was my dad, who was _____ _____ _____ _____.

22 He shouted, "_____ _____!

23 Get _____ _____ the building!

24 _____ the stairs!

25 _____ _____ the elevator!

26 _____!"

27 "_____ are you?

28 Are you okay?" my mom asked _____.

29 My dad answered, "_____ _____.

30 I'm _____.

14 우리 가족 사진이 벽에서 떨어졌고 사진을 덮고 있던 유리가 깨졌다.

15 컵이 넘어지고 식탁에서 굴러 떨어졌다.

16 매 순간, 나는 아파트에 있는 다른 어떤 것들이 부서지는 소리를 들을 수 있었다.

17 나는 건물이 무너지지는 않을까 하는 걱정이 들기 시작했다.

18 그때 흔들림이 멈추는 것 같았다.

19 우리는 문으로 기어가기 시작했다.

20 그 순간, 엄마의 휴대 전화가 울렸다.

21 전화를 한 사람은 바로 아빠였는데, 직장에서 퇴근하던 중이었다.

22 아빠는 소리쳤다. "지진이 멈췄어요!

23 건물 밖으로 나와요!

24 계단을 이용해요!

25 엘리베이터를 타면 안 돼요!

26 서둘러요!"

27 "어디예요?

28 괜찮아요?"라고 엄마가 다급하게 물었다.

29 아빠가 대답했다. "걱정 말아요.

30 나는 괜찮아요.

31 I _____ _____ _____ when the shaking started.

32 But I _____ _____ immediately.

33 I'm listening to the radio _____ _____ to find out what's _____ _____."

34 We nervously _____ _____ _____ down the stairs and outside.

35 I looked _____.

36 Parts of buildings _____ _____ and _____ _____ several cars.

37 We went to an open space _____ _____ more falling pieces.

38 How _____ all this _____ _____ in a few minutes?

39 Although I had done many _____ _____ in school, I had never thought I'd experience _____ _____ _____.

40 I still _____ _____ when I remember that night.

41 I can't forget _____ _____ _____ _____ when the furniture was shaking and things were falling to the floor.

42 After that night, I began to _____ earthquake _____ _____.

43 I realized that I should _____ _____ _____ the next earthquake, which can occur _____ _____ _____.

---

31 진동이 시작할 때 운전해서 집으로 가던 중이었어요.

32 하지만 즉시 차를 길 한쪽에 댔어요.

33 무슨 일이 일어나는지 알기 위해 지금 라디오를 듣고 있어요."

34 우리는 초조한 마음으로 계단을 내려가서 밖으로 나갔다.

35 나는 주변을 둘러보았다.

36 건물의 일부분이 떨어져 나갔고 몇몇 차들은 박살이 났다.

37 우리는 추가적인 낙하물을 피하기 위해 공터로 갔다.

38 어떻게 이런 일이 몇 분 만에 일어날 수 있단 말인가?

39 비록 학교에서 많은 지진 대피 훈련을 해 왔지만, 내가 실제 지진을 겪으리라고는 전혀 생각해 보지 않았었다.

40 그날 밤을 기억하면 나는 여전히 두려워진다.

41 가구가 흔들리고 물건들이 바닥으로 떨어졌을 때 내가 느꼈던 공포심을 나는 잊을 수가 없다.

42 그날 밤 이후, 나는 지진 대피 훈련에 진지하게 임하기 시작했다.

43 나는 언제든 발생할 수 있는 다음 지진을 대비해야 한다는 것을 깨달았다.

● 우리말을 참고하여 본문을 영작하시오.

1 지진에 눈을 뜨는 것

➡ _____

2 2월 어느 날 밤, 내가 잠자리에 든 후에 지진이 일어났다.

➡ _____

3 침대가 흔들렸기 때문에 나는 갑자기 잠에서 깼다.

➡ _____

4 나는 남동생이 장난으로 침대를 흔들고 있다고 생각했다.

➡ _____

5 하지만 그때 나는 내 책상 위에 있던 거울이 바닥으로 떨어져 산산조각이 나는 소리를 들었다.

➡ _____

6 그때 나는 남동생이 그런 것이 아니라는 것을 알았지만, 정확히 무슨 일이 일어나고 있었는지를 여전히 알지 못했다.

➡ _____

7 머지않아 방 전체가 심하게 흔들리기 시작했고 혼란스러움은 공포로 변했다.

➡ _____

8 엄마가 지진이라고 소리를 지르며 내 방으로 뛰어 들어왔다.

➡ _____

9 지진을 경험한 것이 처음이었기 때문에, 나는 어떻게 반응해야 할지 몰랐다.

➡ _____

10 나는 그저 "어떻게 해야 하지?"라는 말을 반복했다.

➡ _____

11 엄마는 나와 남동생을 침대 밖으로 잡아끌었다.

➡ _____

12 우리는 주방으로 달려가서 식탁 아래로 기어들어 갔다.

➡ _____

13 나는 전등이 심하게 흔들리는 것과 책이 바닥으로 떨어지는 것을 볼 수 있었다.

➡ _____

14 우리 가족 사진이 벽에서 떨어졌고 사진을 덮고 있던 유리가 깨졌다.

➡ _____

15 컵이 넘어지고 식탁에서 굴러 떨어졌다.

➡ _____

16 매 순간, 나는 아파트에 있는 다른 어떤 것들이 부서지는 소리를 들을 수 있었다.

➡ _____

17 나는 건물이 무너지지는 않을까 하는 걱정이 들기 시작했다.

➡ _____

18 그때 흔들림이 멈추는 것 같았다.

➡ _____

19 우리는 문으로 기어가기 시작했다.

➡ _____

20 그 순간, 엄마의 휴대 전화가 울렸다.

➡ _____

21 전화를 한 사람은 바로 아빠였는데, 직장에서 퇴근하던 중이었다.

➡ _____

22 아빠는 소리쳤다. "지진이 멈췄어요!

➡ _____

23 건물 밖으로 나와요!

➡ _____

24 계단을 이용해요!

➡ _____

25 엘리베이터를 타면 안 돼요!

➡ _____

26 서둘러요!"

➡ _____

27 "어디예요?

➡ _____

28 괜찮아요?"라고 엄마가 다급하게 물었다.

➡ _____

29 아빠가 대답했다. "걱정 말아요.

➡ _____

30 나는 괜찮아요.

➡ _____

31 진동이 시작할 때 운전해서 집으로 가던 중이었어요.

➡ _____

32 하지만 즉시 차를 길 한쪽에 댔어요.

➡ _____

33 무슨 일이 일어나는지 알기 위해 지금 라디오를 듣고 있어요."

➡ _____

34 우리는 초조한 마음으로 계단을 내려가서 밖으로 나갔다.

➡ _____

35 나는 주변을 둘러보았다.

➡ _____

36 건물의 일부분이 떨어져 나갔고 몇몇 차들은 박살이 났다.

➡ _____

37 우리는 추가적인 낙하물을 피하기 위해 공터로 갔다.

➡ _____

38 어떻게 이런 일이 몇 분 만에 일어날 수 있단 말인가?

➡ _____

39 비록 학교에서 많은 지진 대피 훈련을 해 왔지만, 내가 실제 지진을 겪으리라고는 전혀 생각해 보지 않았었다.

➡ _____

_____

40 그날 밤을 기억하면 나는 여전히 두려워진다.

➡ _____

41 가구가 흔들리고 물건들이 바닥으로 떨어졌을 때 내가 느꼈던 공포심을 나는 잊을 수가 없다.

➡ _____

42 그날 밤 이후, 나는 지진 대피 훈련에 진지하게 임하기 시작했다.

➡ _____

43 나는 언제든 발생할 수 있는 다음 지진을 대비해야 한다는 것을 깨달았다.

➡ _____

[01~04] 다음 글을 읽고 물음에 답하시오.

One night in February, after I (A)had gone to bed, an earthquake hit. (①) I woke up suddenly because my bed was shaking. (②) But then I heard the mirror on my desk fall to the floor and break ___ⓐ___ pieces. (③) I knew it wasn't my brother then, but I still didn't know what exactly was happening. (④) Soon the whole room began to shake violently, and my confusion turned ___ⓑ___ panic. (⑤) My mom shouted that it was an earthquake and ran into my room. Since it was my first time experiencing an earthquake, I didn't know how to react. I just kept saying, "What should I do?"

01 위 글의 빈칸 ⓐ, ⓑ에 들어갈 말이 바르게 짝지어진 것은?

　　　ⓐ　　ⓑ　　　　　　ⓐ　　ⓑ
① by　– into　　　② into – by
③ for　– by　　　④ for　– into
⑤ into – to

02 위 글의 흐름으로 보아, 주어진 문장이 들어가기에 가장 적절한 곳은?

> I thought my brother was shaking my bed as a joke.

①　　　②　　　③　　　④　　　⑤

03 위 글의 밑줄 친 (A)had gone과 과거완료의 용법이 같은 것을 고르시오.

① I did not tell him at first, for I <u>had</u> never <u>seen</u> him before.
② I <u>had</u> just <u>finished</u> my homework when she came.

③ I couldn't buy it as I <u>had lost</u> my purse.
④ He <u>had been</u> to France twice before he was twenty years old.
⑤ When I visited her, she <u>had been</u> ill for a week.

04 According to the passage, which is NOT true?

① One night in February, the writer had gone to bed before an earthquake hit.
② The writer's brother was shaking the writer's bed as a joke.
③ Before long the whole room began to shake violently.
④ The writer had never experienced an earthquake before.
⑤ The writer didn't know how to react to the earthquake.

[05~07] 다음 글을 읽고 물음에 답하시오.

My mom pulled me and my brother out of bed. We ran to the kitchen and crawled under the table. ⓐI could see the light to swing violently and books to fall to the floor. Our family picture dropped from the wall and the glass covering ⓑit broke. A cup tipped over and rolled off the kitchen table. Every second, I could hear something else in the apartment break. I started to worry that the building would collapse.

05 위 글의 밑줄 친 ⓐ에서 어법상 틀린 부분을 찾아 고치시오. (두 군데)

_____ ➡ _____

_____ ➡ _____

06 위 글의 밑줄 친 ⓑit이 가리키는 것을 본문에서 찾아 쓰시오.

➡ _____

중요

07 다음 중 위 글의 지진 때문에 일어난 일이 <u>아닌</u> 것을 고르시오.

① 전등이 심하게 흔들렸다.
② 책이 바닥으로 떨어졌다.
③ 가족 사진이 벽에서 떨어졌다.
④ 컵이 넘어지고 식탁에서 굴러 떨어졌다.
⑤ 아파트 건물이 무너졌다.

[08~10] 다음 글을 읽고 물음에 답하시오.

Then the shaking seemed to stop. We started crawling toward the door. At that moment, my mom's cell phone rang. It was my dad, who was coming home from work.

He shouted, "It stopped! Get out of the building! Take the stairs! Don't take the elevator! Hurry!" "Where are you? Are you okay?" my mom asked urgently. My dad answered, "Don't worry. I'm okay. I was driving home when the shaking started. But I pulled over immediately. I'm listening to the radio right now ⓐto find out what's going on."

08 아래 〈보기〉에서 위 글의 밑줄 친 ⓐto find와 to부정사의 용법이 같은 것의 개수를 고르시오.

┌─── 보기 ───┐
① He tried to stop smoking.
② There's nothing to stop you from doing it.
③ The policeman ran to stop the flight.
④ I wanted the baby to stop crying.
⑤ You must be crazy to stop the car in the middle of the street.
└───────────┘

① 1개 ② 2개 ③ 3개 ④ 4개 ⑤ 5개

09 위 글의 분위기로 가장 알맞은 것을 고르시오.

① exciting   ② urgent   ③ touching
④ fantastic   ⑤ boring

서답형

10 주어진 영영풀이에 해당하는 단어를 본문에서 찾아 쓰시오.

┌─────────────────────────────────┐
moved to the side of the road and stopped
└─────────────────────────────────┘

➡ _____

[11~14] 다음 글을 읽고 물음에 답하시오.

We nervously made our way down the stairs and outside. I looked around. ⓐParts of buildings fell and smashed several cars. We went to an open space to avoid more falling pieces. ⓑHow could all this have happened in a few minutes?

Although I had done many earthquake drills in school, I had never thought I'd experience a real earthquake. I still get scared when I remember that night. ⓒ가구가 흔들리고 물건들이 바닥으로 떨어졌을 때 내가 느꼈던 공포심을 나는 잊을 수가 없다. After that night, I began to take earthquake drills seriously. I realized that I should be prepared for the next earthquake, which can occur at any time.   <I: a girl>

서답형

11 위 글의 밑줄 친 ⓐ에서 어법상 틀린 부분을 찾아 고치시오. (두 군데)

_____ ➡ _____
_____ ➡ _____

중요

12 위 글의 밑줄 친 ⓑ에서 알 수 있는 글쓴이의 심경으로 가장 알맞은 것을 고르시오.

① excited   ② ashamed
③ disappointed   ④ puzzled
⑤ depressed

서답형

13 위 글의 밑줄 친 ⓒ의 우리말에 맞게 주어진 어휘를 알맞게 배열하시오.

> were falling / when / I / the furniture / can't forget / to the floor / felt / things / and / I / was shaking / the panic / .

➡ _____

_____

중요

14 위 글에 어울리는 속담으로 가장 알맞은 것을 고르시오.

① A friend in need is a friend indeed.
② Prevention is better than cure.
③ Every cloud has a silver lining.
④ Look before you leap.
⑤ Make hay while the sun shines.

15 주어진 글 다음에 이어질 글의 순서로 가장 적절한 것은?

> One night in February, after I had gone to bed, an earthquake hit. I woke up suddenly because my bed was shaking.
>
> (A) I knew it wasn't my brother then, but I still didn't know what exactly was happening. Soon the whole room began to shake violently, and my confusion turned to panic.
>
> (B) I thought my brother was shaking my bed as a joke. But then I heard the mirror on my desk fall to the floor and break into pieces.
>
> (C) My mom shouted that it was an earthquake and ran into my room. Since it was my first time experiencing an earthquake, I didn't know how to react. I just kept saying, "What should I do?"

① (A) – (C) – (B)   ② (B) – (A) – (C)
③ (B) – (C) – (A)   ④ (C) – (A) – (B)
⑤ (C) – (B) – (A)

[16~17] 다음 글을 읽고 물음에 답하시오.

> Then the shaking seemed to stop. We started crawling toward the door. At that moment, my mom's cell phone rang. It was my dad, who was coming home from work.
>
> He shouted, "It stopped! Get out of the building! Take the stairs! Don't take the elevator! Hurry!" "Where are ①you? Are ②you okay?" ③my mom asked urgently. My dad answered, "Don't worry. I'm okay. ④I was driving home when the shaking started. But I pulled over immediately. ⑤I'm listening to the radio right now to find out what's going on."

16 밑줄 친 ①~⑤ 중에서 가리키는 대상이 나머지 넷과 다른 것은?

①   ②   ③   ④   ⑤

중요

17 According to the passage, which is NOT true?

① When the shaking seemed to stop, the writer started crawling toward the door.
② The writer's dad was coming home from work.
③ The writer's dad told the writer's mom to take the elevator.
④ The writer's mom didn't know where the writer's dad was.
⑤ The writer's dad was listening to the radio to find out what was going on.

[18~20] 다음 글을 읽고 물음에 답하시오.

My mom pulled me and my brother out of bed. We ran to the kitchen and crawled under the table. I could see the light swinging violently and books falling to the floor. Our family picture dropped from the wall and the glass ⓐcovering it broke. A cup tipped over and rolled off the kitchen table. Every second, I could hear something else in the apartment break. I started to worry that the building would collapse. <I: a girl>

18 위 글의 밑줄 친 ⓐ를 관계대명사를 사용하여 두 단어로 고치시오.

➡ _____

서답형

19 주어진 영영풀이에 해당하는 단어를 본문에서 찾아 쓰시오.

to fall down very suddenly

➡ _____

20 위 글을 읽고 질문에 답할 수 없는 것을 고르시오.

① What did the writer's mom do?
② Where did the writer take refuge with her mom and her brother?
③ What could the writer see during the earthquake?
④ How long did the earthquake last?
⑤ Why did the writer start to worry that the building would collapse?

[21~23] 다음 글을 읽고 물음에 답하시오.

One night in February, after I ___ⓐ___ to bed, an earthquake hit. I woke up suddenly because my bed was shaking. I thought my brother was shaking my bed as a joke. But then I heard the mirror on my desk fall to the floor and break into pieces. I knew it wasn't my brother then, but I still didn't know what exactly was happening.

Soon the whole room began to shake violently, and my confusion turned to panic. My mom shouted that it was an earthquake and ran into my room. ⓑ지진을 경험한 것이 처음이었기 때문에, I didn't know how to react. I just kept saying, "What should I do?"

21 위 글의 빈칸 ⓐ에 들어갈 알맞은 말을 모두 고르시오.

① have gone   ② would go
③ had gone   ④ go
⑤ went

서답형

22 위 글의 밑줄 친 ⓑ의 우리말에 맞게 주어진 어휘를 이용하여 9단어로 영작하시오.

since, experiencing

➡ _____

_____

23 위 글의 제목으로 알맞은 것을 고르시오.

① Have You Experienced an Earthquake?
② My Brother Likes to Play Jokes on Me
③ Waking Up to an Earthquake
④ Wow! My Room Began Shaking Violently!
⑤ My Mom Ran into My Room in Panic!

[24~26] 다음 글을 읽고 물음에 답하시오.

One night in February, after I had gone to bed, an earthquake hit. I woke up suddenly because my bed was shaking. I thought my brother was shaking my bed as a joke. ⓐBut then I heard the mirror on my desk to fall to the floor and to break into pieces. I knew it wasn't my brother then, but I still didn't know what exactly was happening.

Soon the whole room began to shake violently, and my confusion turned to panic. My mom shouted that it was an earthquake and ran into my room. ⓑSince it was my first time experiencing an earthquake, I didn't know how to react. I just kept saying, "What should I do?" <I: a girl>

서답형

24 위 글의 밑줄 친 ⓐ에서 어법상 틀린 부분을 찾아 고치시오. (두 군데)

_____ ➡ _____

_____ ➡ _____

25 아래 <보기>에서 위 글의 밑줄 친 ⓑSince와 같은 의미로 쓰인 것의 개수를 고르시오.

┌─── 보기 ───┐
① She has moved house six times since she came here.
② Let's do our best since we can expect no help from others.
③ He has written to me once since he left here.
④ Since we're not very busy just now, I can get away from the office.
⑤ Since we live in the computer era, you should get used to personal computers.
└──────────┘

① 1개 ② 2개 ③ 3개 ④ 4개 ⑤ 5개

26 Why didn't the writer know how to react to the earthquake? Answer in English. (9 words)

➡ _____

[27~29] 다음 글을 읽고 물음에 답하시오.

Although I had done many earthquake drills in school, I ⓐhad never thought I'd experience a real earthquake. I still get (A)[scaring / scared] when I remember that night. I can't forget the panic I felt when the furniture was shaking and things were falling to the floor. After that night, I began to take earthquake drills (B)[serious / seriously]. I realized that I should be prepared for the next earthquake, (C)[that / which] can occur at any time. <I: a girl>

중요

27 위 글의 밑줄 친 ⓑhad never thought와 현재완료의 용법이 같은 것을 모두 고르시오.

① I have eaten Pad thai twice.
② They have lived in Seoul since 1998.
③ How many times have you been to Europe?
④ He has not finished his homework yet.
⑤ Have you ever seen such a wonderful scene before?

서답형

28 위 글의 괄호 (A)~(C)에서 문맥이나 어법상 알맞은 낱말을 골라 쓰시오.

➡ (A) _____ (B) _____ (C) _____

서답형

29 다음 빈칸에 알맞은 단어를 넣어 글쓴이가 이번 지진으로 깨달은 점을 완성하시오.

┌──────────────────────┐
The writer realized that she should be _____ _____ the next earthquake, which can occur at any time.
└──────────────────────┘

[01~03] 다음 글을 읽고 물음에 답하시오.

One night in February, after I had gone to bed, an earthquake hit. I woke up suddenly because my bed was shaking. I thought my brother was shaking my bed as a joke. But then I heard the mirror on my desk fall to the floor and break into pieces. ⓐI knew it wasn't my brother then, but I still didn't know what exactly was happened.

Soon the whole room began to shake violently, and my confusion turned to panic. My mom shouted that it was an earthquake and ran into my room. Since it was my first time experiencing an earthquake, I didn't know ⓑhow to react. I just kept saying, "What should I do?"   <I: a girl>

01 Why did the writer wake up suddenly one night in February? Answer in English. (5 words)

➡ _____

02 위 글의 밑줄 친 ⓐ에서 어법상 틀린 부분을 찾아 고치시오.

_____ ➡ _____

03 위 글의 밑줄 친 ⓑhow to react를 다음과 같이 바꿔 쓸 때 빈칸에 들어갈 알맞은 말을 두 단어로 쓰시오.

➡ how _____ _____ react

[04~06] 다음 글을 읽고 물음에 답하시오.

My mom (A)[pulled / pushed] me and my brother out of bed. We ran to the kitchen and crawled under the table. ⓐ나는 전등이 심하게 흔들리는 것과 책이 바닥으로 떨어지는 것을 볼 수 있었다. Our family picture dropped from the

wall and the glass (B)[covering / covered] it broke. A cup tipped over and rolled off the kitchen table. Every second, I could hear something else in the apartment (C)[break / to break]. I started to worry that the building would collapse.   <I: a girl>

04 위 글의 괄호 (A)~(C)에서 문맥이나 어법상 알맞은 낱말을 골라 쓰시오.

➡ (A) _____ (B) _____ (C) _____

05 위 글의 밑줄 친 ⓐ의 우리말에 맞게 주어진 어휘를 알맞게 배열하시오.

violently / the light / and / I / books / to the floor / see / swinging / falling / could / .

➡ _____

_____

06 다음 빈칸 (A)와 (B)에 알맞은 단어를 넣어 글쓴이의 가족이 지진이 났을 때 취한 행동을 완성하시오.

The writer ran to (A)_____ _____ and (B)_____ under the table with her mom and her brother.

[07~10] 다음 글을 읽고 물음에 답하시오.

ⓐThen the shaking seemed to stop. We started crawling toward the door. At that moment, my mom's cell phone rang. It was my dad, who was coming home from work.

He shouted, "ⓑIt stopped! Get out of the building! Take the stairs! Don't take the elevator! Hurry!" "Where are you? Are you okay?" my mom asked urgently. My dad answered, "Don't worry. I'm okay. I was driving home when the shaking started. But I pulled over ©immediately. I'm listening to the radio right now to find out what's going on."

07 위 글의 밑줄 친 ⓐ를 다음과 같이 바꿔 쓸 때 빈칸에 들어갈 알맞은 단어를 쓰시오.

➡ Then _____ seemed that the shaking stopped.

08 위 글의 밑줄 친 ⓑ가 가리키는 것을 본문에서 찾아 쓰시오.

➡ _____

09 위 글의 밑줄 친 ©immediately와 바꿔 쓸 수 있는 말을 쓰시오. (두 단어)

➡ _____ 또는 _____

10 다음 빈칸 (A)와 (B)에 알맞은 단어를 넣어 글쓴이의 아빠에 대한 소개를 완성하시오.

The writer's dad was (A)_____ _____ when the shaking started, but he pulled over immediately. He was (B)_____ _____ _____ _____ right then to find out what was going on.

[11~14] 다음 글을 읽고 물음에 답하시오.

We nervously made our way down the stairs and outside. I looked around. Parts of buildings had fallen and had smashed several cars. We went to an open space to avoid more falling pieces. (A)어떻게 이런 일이 몇 분 만에 일어날 수 있단 말인가?

Although I ___ⓐ___ many earthquake drills in school, I had never thought I'd experience a real earthquake. I still get scared when I remember that night. I can't forget the panic I felt when the furniture was shaking and things were falling to the floor. After that night, I began to take earthquake drills seriously. (B)I realized that I should be prepared for the next earthquake, which can be occurred at any time.   <I: a girl>

11 위 글의 빈칸 ⓐ에 do를 알맞은 형태로 쓰시오.

➡ _____

12 위 글의 밑줄 친 (A)의 우리말에 맞게 주어진 어휘를 이용하여 10 단어로 영작하시오.

how, could, all, have, in

➡ _____

13 위 글의 밑줄 친 (B)에서 어법상 틀린 부분을 찾아 고치시오.

➡ _____ ➡ _____

14 How does the writer feel when she remembers that night? Fill in the blanks (A) and (B) with suitable words.

She still (A)_____ _____, and she can't forget (B)_____ _____ she felt when the furniture was shaking and things were falling to the floor.

After You Read B

R: How did you feel when the earthquake occurred?
접속사 when은 "~할 때"의 의미로 시간의 부사절이다.

W: I began to panic because the whole room was shaking violently.

R: How scary! What did you do next?
How+형용사+(주어+동사)!의 형태로 감탄문이다.

W: We all crawled under the table after my mom got us out of bed.
get A out of B A를 B에서 끌어내다

R: What was happening at the moment?

W: Lots of things were falling to the floor. I heard many things in the
= Many
apartment break.
지각동사 heard의 목적격보어

R: What did you realize after that night?

W: I realized that I should be prepared for the next earthquake. It can occur

at any time!
어느 때고

구문해설 • occur 발생하다 • violently 격렬하게 • scary 무서운 • crawl 기어가다
• realize 깨닫다

Think & Write Step 3

San Andreas

I would like to tell you about the movie *San Andreas*. This movie is set in Los
want to의 공손한 표현   배경으로 하고 있다
Angeles and San Francisco in 2014. The main character, a search-and-rescue
동격
pilot, must search for his missing family during an earthquake. The special
missed(×)
effects used in the disaster scenes are very good. The movie is a little sad
which[that] are used   a few(×)
at times, but the story is very interesting. I give *San Andreas* four stars. Go
= sometimes
and watch it!

구문해설 • would like to: ~하고 싶다 • main character: 주인공
• search-and-rescue pilot: 수색구조 조종사 • missing: 행방불명된
• at times: 가끔(=sometimes)

01 다음 두 문장에 공통으로 알맞은 것을 고르시오.

> • I read a report yesterday _____ the damage from each type of natural disaster.
> • I'm curious _____ how that happened.

① at ② about ③ in
④ of ⑤ for

02 다음 문장의 빈칸에 알맞은 단어를 고르시오.

> Soon the whole room began to shake _____, and my confusion turned to panic.

① violently ② properly ③ recently
④ actually ⑤ exactly

03 다음 대화의 빈칸에 들어갈 말로 적절한 것을 고르시오.

> B: There was a big flood in Europe. Did you hear about it?
> G: No, I didn't. But floods aren't that _____ in winter, are they? I'm curious about how that happened.
> B: Me too. Let's do some online research.

① aware ② missing ③ exact
④ proper ⑤ common

04 다음 영영풀이에 해당하는 단어를 주어진 철자로 시작하여 쓰시오.

> to break apart and fall down suddenly

➡ c_____

[05~07] 다음 대화를 읽고 물음에 답하시오.

> B: Hey, did you hear about the big fires in California?
> G: _____(A)_____
> B: They've destroyed a large number of houses and other buildings.
> G: Are the fires still going on?
> B: Yes, actually the wind has made the fires worse. I hope all the people living there are okay.
> G: So do I. (B)나는 얼마나 많은 사람들이 집을 떠나야 했는지 궁금하다. (curious, had to, how many, leave, I'm, people, about, their homes)
> B: Actually more than 20,000 people had to leave their homes, and about 400 people are missing in that area.
> G: That's terrible. I hope they're somewhere safe.

05 위 대화의 빈칸 (A)에 적절한 것은?

① Really? How did it start?
② Yes. It's not so serious.
③ Well, they stopped at the moment.
④ No, I didn't. How serious are they?
⑤ Of course. I don't know much.

06 밑줄 친 (B)의 우리말에 맞게 주어진 단어를 바르게 배열하시오.

➡ _____
_____

07 위 대화의 내용과 일치하지 <u>않는</u> 것은?

① The fires destroyed a large house.

② The fires are still going on.

③ The fires got worse due to the wind.

④ A lot of people had to leave their homes.

⑤ People missing in that area are about 400.

[08~09] 다음 대화를 읽고 물음에 답하시오.

G: Did you hear that earthquakes are __(A)__ more often in Korea than before?

B: Oh, really? I've never felt an earthquake in Korea.

G: They usually occur in the southern part of Korea, but now they are __(B)__ in other places as well.

B: I didn't know that. I'm curious about why earthquakes have occurred so often in Korea recently.

G: Why don't we do some research to find out?

B: Sounds good, but where do we look first?

G: How about asking our science teacher first? I think she can help us.

B: Okay. Let's go and find her.

08 빈칸 (A)와 (B)에 공통으로 들어가기에 적절한 것은?

① watching   ② increasing

③ occurring   ④ researching

⑤ finding

09 According to the dialogue, what does the boy want to know?

① the time when earthquakes occurred

② the places where earthquakes have occurred

③ the reason why earthquakes have occurred so often in Korea recently

④ the way they do some research

⑤ the person who can help them

[10~11] 다음 대화를 읽고 물음에 답하시오.

G: There seem to be many natural disasters in Korea these days.

B: I agree. ⓐThere was an earthquake in the south last week. ⓑAlso a storm is coming this week.

G: ⓒI'm curious about which type of natural disaster causes the most damage in Korea.

B: ⓓActually I read a report yesterday about the damage from each type of natural disaster. Number one is storms.

G: I see. I guess earthquakes are second.

B: ⓔNo, second is earthquakes, and third is heavy snow.

10 위 대화의 ⓐ~ⓔ 중 흐름상 어색한 문장은?

① ⓐ   ② ⓑ   ③ ⓒ   ④ ⓓ   ⑤ ⓔ

11 위 대화의 내용과 일치하지 <u>않는</u> 것은?

① The girl and the boy think natural disasters are occurring more often in Korea.

② The boy read a report about natural disasters.

③ The girl thinks storms cause the second most damage.

④ The boy says heavy snow causes the third most damage.

⑤ The girl wants to know which type of natural disaster causes the most damage.

[12~13] 다음 대화를 읽고 물음에 답하시오.

B: Mom, what else do we need to put in the __(A)__ survival kit?

W: Well, we need water, some food, and radio.

B: __(B)__, Mom?

W: Oh, make sure that you include batteries for the radio.

12 빈칸 (A)에 들어가기에 적절한 두 단어를 쓰시오.

➡ _____

13 빈칸 (B)에 적절한 말을 두 단어로 쓰시오.

➡ _____

Grammar

14 다음 두 문장이 뜻이 비슷하도록 빈칸에 들어갈 알맞은 것은?

> Sinclare was young but he was regarded as their leader by them.
> = _____, he was regarded as their leader by them.

① Although Sinclare was young
② Since Sinclare was young
③ While Sinclare was young
④ As Sinclare was young
⑤ Unless Sinclare was young

15 다음 문장 중에서 어법상 어색한 것을 고르시오.

① After you say goodbye today, don't ever come back here.
② When I got home, my daughter had finished her homework.
③ When he had arrived at home, they already ate dinner.
④ Mom had gone to work when I woke up.
⑤ Claudia lost the camera that her boy friend had bought for her.

---

16 다음 그림을 참고하여 빈칸에 알맞은 말을 쓰시오.

_____ my dad went to work by car this morning, he came back home on foot.

17 다음 문장의 빈칸에 들어갈 수 없는 것은?

> When Monica went back home, he _____.

① had finished cleaning the house
② had walked the dog
③ had already dinner alone
④ had just gone to bed
⑤ had watered the plants

18 다음 두 문장을 since 또는 although를 이용해 한 문장으로 만드시오. (접속사로 시작할 것)

(1) • It's very hot outside.
　　• I will walk my dog.
　　➡ _____

(2) • They had to paint quickly to capture the effect of light.
　　• They did not sketch their paintings in advance.
　　➡ _____
　　_____

(3) • Most people recognize it as a jewel.
　　• The diamond most directly affects our daily lives as a tool.
　　➡ _____
　　_____

19 다음 ⓐ~ⓕ 중 어법상 옳은 것을 모두 고르시오.

ⓐ I had never eaten *pho* until I have visited Vietnam.

ⓑ I was wearing the dress that my mom had made for me.

ⓒ When I had got home, the TV was turned on.

ⓓ I knew Francesca well since I had seen her before.

ⓔ While playing basketball, Mike broke his leg.

ⓕ Since they are rich, they don't seem happy at all.

➡ _____

20 위 글의 빈칸 ⓐ에 들어갈 알맞은 접속사를 고르시오.

① Though   ② While   ③ Even if

④ Whereas   ⑤ Since

21 위 글의 밑줄 친 (A)의 우리말에 맞게 3 단어로 영작하시오.

➡ _____

22 위 글에서 알 수 있는 글쓴이의 심경 변화로 가장 알맞은 것을 고르시오.

① bored → scared

② nervous → satisfied

③ puzzled → frightened

④ pleased → upset

⑤ confused → bored

Reading

[20~22] 다음 글을 읽고 물음에 답하시오.

One night in February, after I had gone to bed, an earthquake hit. I woke up suddenly because my bed was shaking. I thought my brother was shaking my bed as a joke. But then I heard the mirror on my desk fall to the floor and (A)산산조각이 나다. I knew it wasn't my brother then, but I still didn't know what exactly was happening.

Soon the whole room began to shake violently, and my confusion turned to panic. My mom shouted that it was an earthquake and ran into my room. ___ⓐ___ it was my first time experiencing an earthquake, I didn't know how to react. I just kept saying, "What should I do?"

[23~24] 다음 글을 읽고 물음에 답하시오.

Then the shaking seemed (A)[to stop / stopping]. We started crawling toward the door. At that moment, my mom's cell phone rang. It was my dad, (B)[that / who] was coming home from work.

He shouted, "It stopped! Get out of the building! Take the stairs! Don't take the elevator! Hurry!" "Where are you? Are you okay?" my mom asked urgently. My dad answered, "Don't worry. I'm okay. I was driving (C)[home / to home] when the shaking started. But I pulled over immediately. I'm listening to the radio right now to find out what's ⓐgoing on."

23 위 글의 괄호 (A)~(C)에서 어법상 알맞은 낱말을 골라 쓰시오.

➡ (A) _____ (B) _____ (C) _____

24 위 글의 밑줄 친 ⓐgoing on과 바꿔 쓸 수 있는 한 단어를 h로 시작하여 쓰시오.

➡ _____

[25~26] 다음 글을 읽고 물음에 답하시오.

We nervously made our way down the stairs and outside. I looked around. Parts of buildings had fallen and had smashed several cars. We went to an open space ⓐto avoid more falling pieces. How could all this have happened in a few minutes?

Although I had done many earthquake drills in school, I had never thought I'd experience a real earthquake. I still get scared when I remember that night. I can't forget the panic I felt when the furniture was shaking and things were falling to the floor. After that night, I began to take earthquake drills seriously. I realized that I should be prepared for the next earthquake, which can occur at any time.

<I: a girl>

25 위 글의 밑줄 친 ⓐto avoid와 to부정사의 용법이 다른 것을 모두 고르시오.

① It is good to get up early in the morning.
② Do you have anything delicious to eat?
③ She went to the store to buy some pens.
④ His job is to take pictures.
⑤ He can't be rich to ask me for some money.

26 위 글을 읽고 알 수 없는 것을 고르시오.

① What did the writer see when she made her way down the stairs and outside?
② Where did the writer's family go after they got out of the building?
③ How many earthquake drills had the writer done in school?
④ Had the writer thought she'd experience a real earthquake?
⑤ What did the writer realize after this earthquake?

[27~29] 다음 글을 읽고 물음에 답하시오.

San Andreas
I would like ①telling you about ⓐthe movie *San Andreas*. This movie ②is set in Los Angeles and San Francisco in 2014. The main character, a search-and-rescue pilot, must search for his ③missing family during an earthquake. The special effects ④used in the disaster scenes are very good. The movie is a little sad ⑤at times, but the story is very interesting. I give *San Andreas* four stars. Go and watch it!

27 위 글의 밑줄 친 ①~⑤ 중 어법상 틀린 것을 찾아 고치시오.

_____ 번 ➡ _____

28 위 글의 종류로 알맞은 것을 고르시오.

① article   ② essay   ③ review
④ book report   ⑤ biography

29 위 글을 읽고 ⓐthe movie에 대해 알 수 없는 것을 고르시오.

① 제목   ② 배경
③ 주인공의 직업   ④ 주인공의 나이
⑤ 간략한 줄거리

01 짝지어진 단어의 관계가 같도록 빈칸에 들어갈 알맞은 말을 고르시오.

> destroy : damage = _____ : lately

① recently ② properly ③ urgently
④ nervously ⑤ exactly

02 다음 빈칸에 들어갈 말로 적절한 것은?

> One night in February, after I had gone to bed, _____ hit. I woke up suddenly because my bed was shaking.

① a yellow dust ② an earthquake
③ a heavy rain ④ a heat wave
⑤ a wildfire

03 다음 문장에 공통으로 들어가기에 적절한 것은?

> • A cup tipped over and rolled _____ the kitchen table. Every second, I could hear something else in the apartment break.
> • Never put _____ until tomorrow what you can do.

① around ② under ③ over
④ off ⑤ below

04 주어진 우리말에 맞게 빈칸을 채우시오. (철자가 주어진 경우 그 철자로 시작할 것)

(1) 우리 가족 사진이 벽에서 떨어지고 그것을 덮고 있던 유리가 깨졌다.
➡ Our family picture dropped from the wall and the glass c_____ it broke.

(2) 우리는 초조한 마음으로 계단을 내려가서 밖으로 나갔다.
➡ We nervously _____ _____ _____ down the stairs and outside.

[05~07] 다음 대화를 읽고 물음에 답하시오.

> G: There seem to be many natural disasters in Korea these days. (ⓐ)
> B: I agree. There was an earthquake in the south last week. Also a storm is coming this week. (ⓑ)
> G: I'm curious about _____(A)_____ causes the most damage in Korea. (ⓒ)
> B: Actually I read a report yesterday about the damage from each type of natural disaster. Number one is storms.
> G: I see. (ⓓ)
> B: No, second is heavy rain, and third is heavy snow.
> G: What about earthquakes? (ⓔ)
> B: Based on the report, earthquakes are fourth. But the damage from earthquakes has been increasing recently because they have been happening more often in Korea.
> G: I see. It seems like we have to be prepared for a variety of natural disasters in Korea.

05 ⓐ~ⓔ 중에서 다음 문장이 들어가기에 적절한 곳은?

> I guess earthquakes are second.

① ⓐ ② ⓑ ③ ⓒ ④ ⓓ ⑤ ⓔ

06 위 대화의 빈칸 (A)에 들어가기에 적절한 것은?

① what kind of earthquakes
② which type of natural disaster
③ which season of the year
④ whose report on the disaster
⑤ how many natural disasters

07 위 대화의 내용으로 보아 대답할 수 <u>없는</u> 것은?

① What natural disaster was there last week?

② Which type of natural disaster causes the most damage in Korea?

③ How has the damage from earthquakes been recently?

④ How much damage have storms caused?

⑤ Why has the damage from earthquakes been increasing?

[08~09] 다음 대화를 읽고 물음에 답하시오.

R: How did you feel when the earthquake occurred?

W: ⓐI began to panic because the whole room was shaking violently.

R: ⓑHow scary! What did you do next?

W: ⓒWe all crawled over the table after my mom got us out of bed.

R: What was happening at the moment?

W: ⓓLots of things were falling to the floor. I heard many things in the apartment break.

R: ⓔWhat did you realize after that night?

W: I realized that I should be prepared for the next earthquake. It can occur at any time!

08 밑줄 친 ⓐ~ⓔ 중에서 대화의 흐름으로 보아 어색한 문장을 고르시오.

① ⓐ ② ⓑ ③ ⓒ ④ ⓓ ⑤ ⓔ

---

09 다음 중 위 대화에서 기자가 질문하지 <u>않은</u> 것은?

① What was the feeling of the woman when the earthquake occurred?

② How scary was the earthquake?

③ What did the woman do after the panic?

④ What was happening when the woman crawled?

⑤ What did the woman realize after that night?

---

10 다음 중 어법상 적절한 문장은?

① After she finished her homework, she had gone to bed.

② I had known the story because I have read the book.

③ I couldn't get in the room because I had forget my key.

④ Jin told me how hard he had prepared for the match.

⑤ He carried out all the responsibilities I gave to him.

---

11 빈칸에 알맞은 접속사를 〈보기〉에서 골라 써 넣으시오.

┌─ 보기 ┤
│ though   when   before   if   since │

(1) _____ it was snowing heavily, I stayed home all day.

(2) _____ it is against the law, poor villagers chop down the trees and sell them to make a living.

(3) I can't forget the panic I felt _____ the furniture was shaking and things were falling to the floor.

출제율 100%

12 다음 <보기>에 주어진 단어를 이용하여 문맥에 맞게 문장을 완성하시오.

> ┤ 보기 ├
> happen   take   practice

(1) The teacher notified his students of their results from the test they _____ a few days earlier.

(2) He ran as he _____ and finally won the race.

(3) A reporter asked the man what _____.

출제율 95%

13 다음 빈칸에 들어갈 말을 순서대로 묶은 것은?

> • They achieved more than they _____ at first.
> • _____ he was new to his firm, people didn't know him.

① had expected – Though
② had expected – Since
③ expected – Since
④ expected – Though
⑤ expected – When

[14~16] 다음 글을 읽고 물음에 답하시오.

One night in February, after I had gone to bed, an earthquake hit. I woke up suddenly because my bed was shaking. I thought my brother was shaking my bed as a joke. But then I heard the mirror on my desk fall to the floor and break into pieces. I knew it wasn't my brother then, but ⓐ정확히 무슨 일이 일어나고 있었는지를 여전히 알지 못했다.

ⓑSoon the whole room began to shake violently, and my confusion turned to comfort. My mom shouted that it was an earthquake and ran into my room. Since it was my first time experiencing an earthquake, I didn't know how to react. I just kept saying, "What should I do?"

출제율 95%

14 위 글의 밑줄 친 ⓐ의 우리말에 맞게 주어진 어휘를 알맞게 배열하시오.

> what / still / know / I / was happening / didn't / exactly

➡ _____
_____

출제율 90%

15 위 글의 밑줄 친 ⓑ에서 흐름상 어색한 부분을 찾아 고치시오.

_____ ➡ _____

출제율 100%

16 Which question CANNOT be answered after reading the passage?

① When did the earthquake occur?
② Was the writer still awake when an earthquake hit?
③ What was the writer's brother doing when the earthquake hit?
④ Did the writer experience an earthquake before?
⑤ Did the writer know how to react to an earthquake?

[17~19] 다음 글을 읽고 물음에 답하시오.

(①) We nervously made our way down the stairs and outside. (②) Parts of buildings had fallen and had smashed several cars. (③) We went to an open space to avoid more falling pieces. (④) How could all this have happened _____ⓐ_____ a few minutes? (⑤) Although I had done many earthquake drills in school, I had never thought I'd experience a real earthquake. I still get scared when I remember that night. I can't forget the panic I felt when the furniture was shaking and things were falling to the floor. After that night, I began to take earthquake drills seriously. I realized that I should be prepared _____ⓑ_____ the next earthquake, which can occur at any time.

🖊 출제율 90%

17 위 글의 빈칸 ⓐ와 ⓑ에 들어갈 전치사가 바르게 짝지어진 것은?

① at – for   ② at – to

③ in – for   ④ for – to

⑤ in – on

🖊 출제율 100%

18 위 글의 흐름으로 보아, 주어진 문장이 들어가기에 가장 적절한 곳은?

I looked around.

①   ②   ③   ④   ⑤

🖊 출제율 95%

19 위 글의 주제로 알맞은 것을 고르시오.

① We should know how to avoid more falling pieces.

② We should go to an open space when an earthquake occurs.

③ What could happen in a few minutes?

④ An ounce of prevention is worth a pound of cure.

⑤ We should remember the panic of an earthquake.

[20~21] 다음 글을 읽고 물음에 답하시오.

Haeundae

I would like to tell you about the movie *Haeundae*. This movie is set in Busan, South Korea in 2009. It is a movie about a tsunami that hits the city of Busan. A tsunami researcher warns people, but everyone believes that Korea is safe. Eventually, people realize ⓐthe deadly wave is coming in only ten minutes. It is one of the few South Korean natural disaster movies. It offers some great shots of Haeundae Beach. The best shot in the film is the moment the wave reaches Diamond Bridge near Gwangalli Beach. The movie is full of good special effects! I give *Haeundae* three stars. Go and watch it!

🖊 출제율 100%

20 위 글의 밑줄 친 ⓐthe deadly wave가 가리키는 것을 본문에서 찾아 쓰시오.

➡ _____

🖊 출제율 95%

21 According to the passage, which is NOT true?

① *Haeundae* is set in Busan, South Korea in 2009.

② *Haeundae* is a movie about a tsunami that hits the city of Busan.

③ *Haeundae* is one of the few South Korean natural disaster movies.

④ The best shot in the film is the moment the wave reaches Diamond Bridge near Haeundae Beach.

⑤ *Haeundae* is full of good special effects.

[01~02] 다음 대화를 읽고 물음에 답하시오.

> B: There was a big flood in Europe. Did you hear about it?
> G: No, I didn't. But floods aren't that common in winter, are they? I'm ___(A)___ how that happened.
> B: (B)Me too. Let's do some online research.

01 빈칸 (A)에 들어가기에 적절한 말을 두 단어로 쓰시오.

➡ _____

02 밑줄 친 (B)와 바꿔 쓸 수 있는 말을 쓰시오. (3단어)

➡ _____

03 빈칸에 알맞은 단어를 〈보기〉에서 골라 쓰시오.

┌─ 보기 ─────────────────────┐
│ get   cover   damage   hands │
└──────────────────────────┘

(1) I'm curious about which type of natural disaster causes the most _____ in Korea.

(2) I still _____ scared when I remember that night.

(3) Make sure you place your _____ in the middle of the person's chest.

(4) Make sure that you _____ your mouth with a wet cloth.

04 다음 문장에서 틀린 것을 고쳐 다시 쓰시오.

(1) David has lost his glasses, so he couldn't read anything.

➡ _____

(2) After he moves to a new city, he joined the company baseball team.

➡ _____
_____

(3) In summer, food is easily spoiled because it is kept well.

➡ _____
_____

(4) Our feet remain firmly on the earth since our planet is spinning on its axis.

➡ _____
_____

*spin: 돌다, 뱅뱅 돌다 *axis: 축

05 주어진 단어를 활용하여 빈칸을 완성하시오.

(1) I was shocked to hear that he _____ his job. (quit)

(2) Linda began to tell him that she _____ to a salesman. (marry)

(3) Though _____ it, you must do it. (like)

06 다음 우리말을 주어진 어휘를 이용하여 영작하시오.

(1) 한 남자가 자신의 가게에 강도가 들었다고 경찰에 신고했다. (a man, his store, the police, notify, rob, that)

➡ _____
_____

(2) 비록 손은 없지만, 그녀가 할 수 없는 일은 없습니다. (there, nothing, hands, have, do, cannot, even, 13 단어)

➡ _____
_____

One night in February, after I had gone to bed, an earthquake hit. I (A)[fell asleep / woke up] suddenly (B)[because / because of] my bed was shaking. I thought my brother was shaking my bed as a joke. But then I heard the mirror on my desk fall to the floor and break into pieces. I knew it wasn't my brother then, but I still didn't know what exactly was happening.

Soon the whole room began to shake violently, and my confusion turned to panic. My mom shouted that it was an earthquake and ran into my room. ⓐSince it was my first time experiencing an earthquake, I didn't know (C)[how / what] to react. I just kept saying, "What should I do?"   <I: a girl>

07 위 글의 괄호 (A)~(C)에서 문맥이나 어법상 알맞은 낱말을 골라 쓰시오.

➡ (A) _____ (B) _____ (C) _____

08 위 글의 밑줄 친 ⓐ를 다음과 같이 바꿔 쓸 때 빈칸에 알맞은 단어를 쓰시오.

➡ Since it was the first time that I _____ an earthquake
= Since _____ _____ an earthquake for the first time

09 위 글의 내용과 일치하도록 다음 빈칸 (A)와 (B)에 알맞은 단어를 쓰시오.

When the writer heard the mirror on her desk fall to the floor and break into pieces, she could know that her bed had shaken because of some other reason, not because of (A)_____ _____, but she wasn't sure what was (B)_____.

Then the shaking seemed to stop. We started crawling toward the door. At that moment, my mom's cell phone rang. It was my dad, who was coming home from work.

He shouted, "It stopped! Get out of the building! Take the stairs! ⓐ엘리베이터를 타면 안 돼요! Hurry!" "Where are you? Are you okay?" my mom asked urgently. My dad answered, "Don't worry. I'm okay. I was driving home when the shaking started. But I pulled over immediately. I'm listening to the radio right now ⓑto find out what's going on."   <I: a girl>

10 위 글의 밑줄 친 ⓐ의 우리말에 맞게 4 단어로 영작하시오.

➡ _____

11 위 글의 밑줄 친 ⓑ를 다음과 같이 바꿔 쓸 때 빈칸에 들어갈 알맞은 말을 쓰시오.

➡ _____ _____ _____ find out what's going on
= _____ _____ _____ find out what's going on
= _____ _____ _____ I _____ find out what's going on
= _____ _____ I _____ find out what's going on

12 What did the writer do when the shaking seemed to stop? Answer in English. (6 words)

➡ _____

01 다음 〈보기〉의 표현과 접속사 though를 이용하여 예시와 같이 문장을 완성하시오.

> **보기**
>
> | | | |
> |---|---|---|
> | be twins | eat fast food | like English |
> | play soccer | study hard | rain heavily |
>
> →Tony and Tom are twins though they look different.

(1) I _____ .

(2) He _____ .

(3) She _____ .

(4) They _____ .

02 다음 내용을 바탕으로 영화 비평문을 쓰시오.

> *Title: Haeundae*
>
> Time and Place: Busan, South Korea in 2009
>
> Story: It is a movie about a tsunami that hits the city of Busan. A tsunami researcher warns people, but everyone believes that Korea is safe. Eventually, people realize the deadly wave is coming in only ten minutes.
>
> Reviews: It is one of the few South Korean natural disaster movies. It offers some great shots of Haeundae Beach. The best shot in the film is the moment the wave reaches Diamond Bridge near Gwangalli Beach. The movie is full of good special effects!
>
> Rate the movie! ★★★☆☆

> *Haeundae*
>
> I would like to tell you about the movie *Haeundae*. This movie (A)_____ in Busan, South Korea in 2009. It is a movie about (B)_____ that hits the city of Busan. A tsunami researcher warns people, but everyone believes that Korea is safe. Eventually, people realize the deadly wave is coming (C)_____. It is one of the few South Korean (D)_____. It offers some great shots of Haeundae Beach. The best shot in the film is the moment the wave reaches Diamond Bridge near Gwangalli Beach. The movie is full of good (E)_____! I give *Haeundae* three stars. Go and watch it!

단원별 모의고사

01 다음 짝지어진 단어의 관계가 같도록 빈칸에 알맞은 것을 고르시오.

> whole : partial = _____ : rare

① aware
② prepared
③ common
④ serious
⑤ worse

02 다음 중 각 단어의 영영풀이로 어색하게 짝지어진 것은?

① curious: wanting to know about something
② flood: a very large amount of snow that covers an area that is usually dry
③ common: happening often and to many people or in many places
④ cause: to make something happen, especially something bad
⑤ wildfire: a fire that moves quickly and cannot be controlled

03 다음 중 〈보기〉의 단어를 사용하여 자연스러운 문장을 만들 수 없는 것은?

> ┌─ 보기 ┌─
> made   collapse   react   joke

① I thought my brother was shaking my bed as a _____.
② Soon the whole room began to shake _____.
③ Since it was my first time experiencing an earthquake, I didn't know how to _____.
④ I started to worry that the building would _____.
⑤ We nervously _____ our way down the stairs and outside.

04 다음 문장에 공통으로 들어가기에 적절한 말을 쓰시오.

> • I pulled _____ immediately.
> • He said that _____ 20,000 people had to leave their homes.
> • A cup tipped _____ and rolled off the kitchen table.

➡ _____

[05~06] 다음 대화를 읽고 물음에 답하시오.

> A: In case of a heat wave, what should I do?
> B: Make sure that you drink more water than usual.
> A: _____(A)_____
> B: Make sure that you __(B)__ a cool building immediately.

05 빈칸 (A)에 들어가기에 적절한 말을 고르시오.

① What is it?
② Anything else?
③ Really?
④ How about you?
⑤ Is it necessary?

06 위 대화의 내용으로 보아, 빈칸 (B)에 들어가기에 적절한 것은?

① leave
② exit
③ cause
④ destroy
⑤ move into

[07~09] 다음 대화를 읽고 물음에 답하시오.

> B: Hey, did you hear about the big fires in California?
>
> G: No, I didn't. ⓐHow serious are they?
>
> B: They've destroyed a large number of houses and other buildings.
>
> G: ⓑAre the fires over now?
>
> B: ⓒYes, actually the wind has made the fires worse. I hope all the people living there are okay.
>
> G: (A)나도 마찬가지야. ⓓI'm curious about how many people had to leave their homes.
>
> B: Actually more than 20,000 people had to leave their homes, and about 400 people are missing in that area.
>
> G: ⓔThat's terrible. I hope they're somewhere safe.

07 밑줄 친 (A)에 해당하는 말을 so를 포함하여 3단어의 영어로 쓰시오.

➡ _____

08 위 대화의 ⓐ~ⓔ 중 문맥상 어색한 것은?

① ⓐ   ② ⓑ   ③ ⓒ   ④ ⓓ   ⑤ ⓔ

09 위 대화의 내용과 일치하지 않는 것은?

① The boy and the girl are talking about the big fires in California.
② The fires destroyed many houses and buildings.
③ Due to the wind, the fire got worse.
④ More than 20,000 people had to leave their homes.
⑤ About 400 people were found in that area.

10 Which is grammatically WRONG?

① Although Mina knew the right answer, she didn't let us know.
② Family members gather even though they may live far apart.
③ I had to go and greet him since I didn't want to.
④ When in Rome, do as the Romans do.
⑤ Some dogs have a long tail, while others have a short one.

11 다음 빈칸에 들어갈 말을 순서대로 묶은 것은?

> • I found out that I _____ my purse at the restaurant.
> • Don't eat too much fast food _____ you love them.

① left – when   ② have left – since
③ have left – though   ④ had left – since
⑤ had left – though

12 다음 문장에서 어법상 어색한 것을 바르게 고쳐 다시 쓰시오.

(1) Despite it rained a lot, we enjoyed our holiday.

➡ _____

_____

(2) As though it was cold, I felt very happy today.

➡ _____

(3) Though Laura is very kind, she is loved by all of them.

➡ _____

_____

(4) He learned that he has been chosen to play Harry Potter.

➡ _____

_____

(5) The play already started when we arrived.

➡ _____

13 다음 중 어법상 옳은 문장을 <u>모두</u> 고르시오.

① Winter can have negative effects on many people since it is cold.
② Soon I realized that I left my report at home.
③ Because I had done many earthquake drills in school, I had never thought I'd experience a real earthquake.
④ After I finish the exam, I will go to an amusement park.
⑤ I woke up suddenly though my bed was shaking.

14 위 글의 빈칸 ⓐ에 say를 알맞은 형태로 쓰시오.

➡ _____

15 위 글의 밑줄 친 (A)as와 같은 의미로 쓰인 것을 고르시오.

① They did <u>as</u> I had asked.
② The news came <u>as</u> a shock.
③ He sat watching her <u>as</u> she got ready.
④ <u>As</u> one grows older, one becomes more silent.
⑤ You're <u>as</u> tall as your father.

[14~15] 다음 글을 읽고 물음에 답하시오.

One night in February, after I had gone to bed, an earthquake hit. I woke up suddenly because my bed was shaking. I thought my brother was shaking my bed (A)<u>as</u> a joke. But then I heard the mirror on my desk fall to the floor and break into pieces. I knew it wasn't my brother then, but I still didn't know what exactly was happening.

Soon the whole room began to shake violently, and my confusion turned to panic. My mom shouted that it was an earthquake and ran into my room. Since it was my first time experiencing an earthquake, I didn't know how to react. I just kept ___ⓐ___, "What should I do?"

[16~17] 다음 글을 읽고 물음에 답하시오.

My mom pulled me and my brother out of bed. We ran to the kitchen and crawled under the table. I could see the light ①<u>swinging</u> violently and books ②<u>falling</u> to the floor. Our family picture dropped from the wall and the glass covering it broke. A cup ⓐ <u>tipped</u> over and rolled off the kitchen table. Every ③<u>second</u>, I could hear something else in the apartment ④<u>break</u>. I started ⑤ <u>to worry</u> that the building would collapse.

16 위 글의 밑줄 친 ①~⑤와 바꿔 쓸 수 있는 말로 옳지 <u>않은</u> 것을 고르시오.

① swing   ② fall   ③ moment
④ broken   ⑤ worrying

17 위 글의 밑줄 친 ⓐtip과 같은 의미로 쓰인 것을 고르시오.

① It is in the northern tip of the island.

② I need a useful tip on how to save money.

③ It isn't allowed to leave a tip over $5.

④ He gave the waiter a generous tip.

⑤ The machine may tip over and break the dishes.

[18~19] 다음 글을 읽고 물음에 답하시오.

Then the shaking seemed to stop. We started crawling toward the door. At that moment, my mom's cell phone rang. It was my dad, ⓐwho was coming home from work.

He shouted, "It stopped! Get out of the building! Take the stairs! Don't take the elevator! Hurry!" "Where are you? Are you okay?" my mom asked urgently. My dad answered, "Don't worry. I'm okay. I was driving home when the shaking started. But I pulled over immediately. I'm listening to the radio right now to find out what's going on."

18 위 글의 밑줄 친 ⓐwho를 다음과 같이 바꿔 쓸 때 빈칸에 들어갈 알맞은 말을 두 단어로 쓰시오.

➡ _____

19 위 글의 내용과 일치하도록 다음 빈칸 (A)와 (B)에 알맞은 단어를 쓰시오.

The writer's dad called her mom and told her to get out of the building and take (A)_____ _____ instead of (B)_____ _____.

[20~21] 다음 글을 읽고 물음에 답하시오.

We nervously made our way down the stairs and outside. I looked around. Parts of buildings had fallen and had smashed several cars. We went to an open space to avoid more falling pieces. How could all this have happened in a few minutes?

_____ⓐ_____ I had done many earthquake drills in school, I had never thought I'd experience a real earthquake. I still get scared when I remember that night. I can't forget the panic I felt when the furniture was shaking and things were falling to the floor. After that night, I began to take earthquake drills seriously. I realized that I should be prepared for the next earthquake, which can occur at any time.

<I: a girl>

20 위 글의 빈칸 ⓐ에 들어갈 알맞은 접속사를 고르시오.

① Although ② Because ③ As

④ If ⑤ Since

21 According to the passage, which is NOT true?

① The writer's family nervously made their way down the stairs and outside.

② Parts of buildings had fallen and had smashed several cars.

③ The writer had done many earthquake drills in school.

④ The writer still gets scared when she remembers that night.

⑤ The writer had taken earthquake drills seriously before he experienced a real earthquake.

INSIGHT
on the textbook
교과서 파헤치기

※ 다음 영어를 우리말로 쓰시오.

01 motivate _____

02 confident _____

03 exactly _____

04 perform _____

05 foreign _____

06 furniture _____

07 guess _____

08 own _____

09 treasure _____

10 awesome _____

11 nervous _____

12 improve _____

13 creative _____

14 perfect _____

15 case _____

16 meaningful _____

17 subtitle _____

18 volunteer _____

19 memorize _____

20 culture _____

21 post _____

22 social media _____

23 recommend _____

24 experience _____

25 finally _____

26 responsibility _____

27 talent _____

28 finish _____

29 review _____

30 translation _____

31 vocabulary _____

32 requirement _____

33 weakness _____

34 shelf _____

35 be related to ~ _____

36 get used to ~ _____

37 in any case _____

38 first of all _____

39 take care of _____

40 be struck by _____

41 be proud of ~ _____

42 give up _____

43 spend time -ing _____

Step2

※ 다음 우리말을 영어로 쓰시오.

01 (웹사이트에 정보·사진을) 게시하다 _____

02 보물 _____

03 선반, 책꽂이 _____

04 자막 _____

05 암기하다 _____

06 동기를 부여하다 _____

07 어휘 _____

08 쥐다. 들다 _____

09 자신 있는 _____

10 검토, 후기 _____

11 경험 _____

12 마침내 _____

13 문화 _____

14 추측하다 _____

15 창조적인 _____

16 가구 _____

17 필요조건, 요건 _____

18 재능 _____

19 개선하다, 향상시키다 _____

20 엄청난 _____

21 사례, 경우, 상자 _____

22 의미 있는 _____

23 외국의 _____

24 불안한 _____

25 ~ 자신의; 소유하다 _____

26 완벽한 _____

27 정확하게 _____

28 번역된 것, 번역문 _____

29 공연하다, 수행하다 _____

30 자원봉사자 _____

31 공유하다 _____

32 약점 _____

33 책임감 _____

34 추천하다 _____

35 포기하다 _____

36 ~에 친숙해지다 _____

37 ~을 자랑스러워하다 _____

38 첫째로 _____

39 ~에 익숙해지다 _____

40 ~을 돌보다 _____

41 어쨌든 _____

42 전혀 ~가 아닌 _____

43 ~에 관련되다 _____

※ 다음 영영풀이에 알맞은 단어를 <보기>에서 골라 쓴 후, 우리말 뜻을 쓰시오.

1 _____ : a natural ability to do something well: _____

2 _____ : to entertain an audience by singing, acting, etc.: _____

3 _____ : to advise someone to do something: _____

4 _____ : add a message to an online message board: _____

5 _____ : a long flat narrow board attached to a wall: _____

6 _____ : not having any mistakes, faults, or damage: _____

7 _____ : to have or use something with other people: _____

8 _____ : something that someone needs or asks for: _____

9 _____ : to learn something carefully so that you can remember it exactly:

_____

10 _____ : a group of valuable things such as gold, silver, jewels: _____

11 _____ : a duty to be in charge of someone or something: _____

12 _____ : a careful examination of a situation or process: _____

13 _____ : chairs, tables, beds, etc., that are used to make a room ready for use:

_____

14 _____ : someone who does a job willingly without being paid: _____

15 _____ : feeling sure about your own ability to do things and be successful:

_____

16 _____ : to make someone want to achieve something and make them willing to

work hard in order to do this: _____

보기			
confident	motivate	shelf	volunteer
furniture	talent	perfect	recommend
post	requirement	memorize	treasure
share	perform	responsibility	review

※ 다음 우리말과 일치하도록 빈칸에 알맞은 말을 쓰시오.

해석

Listen & Talk 1 B

G: What _____ you _____ to do _____ _____?

B: I'd _____ to _____ the guitar. I _____ to the song "Cavatina," and I _____ _____ _____ the _____ of the guitar.

G: That's great. _____ are you _____ _____ _____ it?

B: My friend Jinsu is a very _____ guitar _____. I'll _____ _____ _____ _____ me.

Listen & Talk 1 C

B: _____ are you _____?

G: I'm _____ a list of _____ _____ I _____ _____ _____ this year.

B: That's nice. _____ would you _____ _____ do this year?

G: Well, _____ of all, I'd _____ to _____ _____ _____ with my friends _____ summer vacation.

B: That _____ great.

G: _____ _____ you? _____ _____ you _____ _____ _____ this year?

B: I'm _____ of _____ a _____ _____.

G: That's really _____.

Listen & Talk 2 B

B: Hey, Suji! _____ are you _____?

G: Hi, Ben. It's a _____. I'm _____ _____.

B: Wow! I didn't _____ _____ you could _____. _____ did you _____ to _____?

G: I _____ a _____ skateboarding club _____ _____.

B: I _____. So _____ do you _____ it?

G: It's _____ fun! It _____ me _____ new friends, _____.

B: How?

G: I _____ _____ _____ with _____ _____ of the club, and we _____ _____ with _____ _____.

Listen & Talk 2 C

G: Did you _____ this _____ _____? It's _____!

B: Thanks. I _____ _____ _____ _____ _____.

G: Cool! _____ do you _____ it?

B: It was _____ _____ _____, but now I _____ it. I _____ so _____ _____ I _____ _____ something.

G: That's _____. I think you're _____ _____ _____ it.

B: Thanks. I _____ I _____ a new _____. I think it's _____ _____ _____ new things.

G: _____. _____ new _____ lets us _____ new _____.

Listen & Talk 2 D

A: I _____ a _____ last year.

B: _____ _____ you _____ it?

A: I _____ it _____ _____. It _____ me build _____.

Presentation Time Step 1

A: Can you _____ me about _____ of your _____ experiences?

B: I _____ dinner _____ my family last Sunday.

A: _____ did you _____ it?

B: It was _____ _____, but I _____ _____ I could _____ people _____ _____ my _____.

Presentation Time Step 3

Our group _____ _____ dinner for your family. It is a _____ _____ _____ you will learn that _____ for _____ can _____ them happy. After this _____, you will _____ great.

Do It Yourself A

B: My band _____ at the school _____ yesterday.

G: Cool. _____ did you _____ that?

B: It _____ _____, but I _____ some _____.

G: It's okay. I'm _____ you _____ _____.

B: Thanks _____ _____ so. It was my first time _____ the drums _____ _____ _____ so many people.

G: _____ did you _____ _____ that?

B: I was very _____, but I _____ great, _____!

G: That's _____. I'm _____ _____ _____ you.

G: 그 책꽂이를 직접 만들었니? 멋있다!

B: 고마워. 나는 작년에 가구 만들기를 시작했어.

G: 멋있어! 그것이 마음에 드니?

B: 처음에는 어려웠어. 그러나 지금 나는 그것을 아주 좋아해. 무엇인가를 만들고 나면 매우 자신감을 느껴.

G: 좋겠다. 나는 네가 그것을 정말 잘한다고 생각해.

B: 고마워. 나는 새로운 재능을 발견했다고 생각해. 새로운 것을 시도하는 것은 좋다고 생각해.

G: 그렇지. 새로운 경험을 하는 것은 우리에게 새로운 재능을 발견하도록 해.

A: 나는 작년에 달리기를 했어.

B: 그것이 마음에 들었니?

A: 굉장히 좋았어. 그것이 자신감을 가지도록 도와주었어.

A: 너에게 의미 있었던 경험 중 하나를 말해주겠니?

B: 나는 지난 일요일에 가족을 위하여 저녁을 요리했어.

A: 그것이 마음에 들었니?

B: 그것은 쉽지 않았어. 하지만 나는 내가 요리한 것을 가지고 사람을 행복하게 만들 수 있다는 것을 배웠어.

우리 모둠은 여러분의 가족을 위해 저녁을 요리할 것을 추천합니다. 그것은 여러분이 다른 사람을 위해 요리하는 것이 그들을 행복하게 만들 수 있다는 것을 배울 것이기 때문에 의미 있는 경험입니다. 이 경험 이후에 여러분은 기분 좋게 느낄 것입니다.

B: 우리 밴드가 어제 학교 축제에서 연주를 했어.

G: 멋있네. 너는 그것이 마음에 들었니?

B: 나쁘지 않았어. 하지만 내가 몇 가지 실수를 저질렀어.

G: 괜찮아. 네 연주는 확실히 좋았어.

B: 그렇게 말해주니 고마워. 그것이 그토록 많은 사람들 앞에서 처음으로 드럼을 연주한 것이었어.

G: 그것에 대하여 어떻게 느꼈니?

B: 나는 매우 불안했어. 그러나 또한 기분 좋기도 했어.

G: 훌륭하구나. 나는 네가 정말 자랑스러워.

※ 다음 우리말에 맞도록 대화를 영어로 쓰시오.

해석

Listen & Talk 1 B

G: _____

B: _____

_____

G: _____

B: _____

G: 너는 올해 무엇을 하기를 원하니?
B: 나는 기타를 배우고 싶어. 나는 "Cavatina"라는 노래를 들었는데 기타 소리에 감동을 받았어.
G: 좋겠다. 너는 어디에서 그것을 배울 거니?
B: 내 친구 진수가 기타를 매우 잘 쳐. 나는 그에게 가르쳐 달라고 요청할 거야.

Listen & Talk 1 C

B: _____

G: _____

B: _____

G: _____

_____

B: _____

G: _____

B: _____

G: _____

B: 너는 무엇을 하고 있니?
G: 올해 하고 싶은 일의 목록을 작성하고 있는 중이야.
B: 멋있다. 너는 올해 무엇을 하기를 원하니?
G: 음, 우선 여름 방학 동안 친구들과 자원봉사를 하면서 시간을 보내고 싶어.
B: 그거 좋겠다.
G: 너는 어떠니? 너는 올해 무엇을 하고 싶어?
B: 나는 수영 수업 받는 것을 생각하고 있어.
G: 그거 정말 멋있구나.

Listen & Talk 2 B

B: _____

G: _____

B: _____

G: _____

B: _____

G: _____

B: _____

G: _____

B: 안녕, 수지야! 들고 있는 것이 뭐니?
G: 안녕, Ben. 스케이트보드야. 나는 스케이트보드를 타러 가는 중이야.
B: 와우! 네가 스케이트보드를 탈줄 아는지 몰랐어. 스케이트보드는 어떻게 배웠니?
G: 지난달에 지역 스케이트보드 클럽에 가입했어.
B: 알겠다. 너는 그것이 마음에 드니?
G: 정말 재미있어! 그것은 또한 새로운 친구를 사귀도록 도와줘.
B: 어떻게?
G: 나는 클럽의 다른 회원들과 스케이트보드를 타러 가는데, 우리는 서로 방법을 공유해.

Listen & Talk 2 C

G: _____

B: _____

G: _____

B: _____
_____

G: _____

B: _____

G: _____

Listen & Talk 2 D

A: _____

B: _____

A: _____

Presentation Time Step 1

A: _____

B: _____

A: _____

B: _____

Presentation Time Step 3

_____

_____

_____

Do It Yourself A

B: _____

G: _____

B: _____

G: _____

B: _____
_____

G: _____

B: _____

G: _____

G: 그 책꽂이를 직접 만들었니? 멋있다!

B: 고마워. 나는 작년에 가구 만들기를 시작했어.

G: 멋있어! 그것이 마음에 드니?

B: 처음에는 어려웠어. 그러나 지금 나는 그것을 아주 좋아해. 무엇인가를 만들고 나면 매우 자신감을 느껴.

G: 좋겠다. 나는 네가 그것을 정말 잘한다고 생각해.

B: 고마워. 나는 새로운 재능을 발견했다고 생각해. 새로운 것을 시도하는 것은 좋다고 생각해.

G: 그렇지. 새로운 경험을 하는 것은 우리에게 새로운 재능을 발견하도록 해.

A: 나는 작년에 달리기를 했어.

B: 그것이 마음에 들었니?

A: 굉장히 좋았어. 그것이 자신감을 가지도록 도와주었어.

A: 너에게 의미 있었던 경험 중 하나를 말해주겠니?

B: 나는 지난 일요일에 가족을 위하여 저녁을 요리했어.

A: 그것이 마음에 들었니?

B: 그것은 쉽지 않았어. 하지만 나는 내가 요리한 것을 가지고 사람을 행복하게 만들 수 있다는 것을 배웠어.

우리 모둠은 여러분의 가족을 위해 저녁을 요리할 것을 추천합니다. 그것은 여러분이 다른 사람을 위해 요리하는 것이 그들을 행복하게 만들 수 있다는 것을 배울 것이기 때문에 의미 있는 경험입니다. 이 경험 이후에 여러분은 기분 좋게 느낄 것입니다.

B: 우리 밴드가 어제 학교 축제에서 연주를 했어.

G: 멋있네. 너는 그것이 마음에 들었니?

B: 나쁘지 않았어. 하지만 내가 몇 가지 실수를 저질렀어.

G: 괜찮아. 네 연주는 확실히 좋았어.

B: 그렇게 말해주니 고마워. 그것이 그토록 많은 사람들 앞에서 처음으로 드럼을 연주한 것이었어.

G: 그것에 대하여 어떻게 느꼈니?

B: 나는 매우 불안했어. 그러나 또한 기분 좋기도 했어.

G: 훌륭하구나. 나는 네가 정말 자랑스러워.

※ 다음 우리말과 일치하도록 빈칸에 알맞은 것을 골라 쓰시오.

1 _____ a New _____, _____ a New World

A. Language   B. Learn   C. Find

2 _____ Do People Learn _____ _____?

A. Foreign   B. Why   C. Languages

3 _____ students learn new languages _____ _____ school _____.

A. requirements   B. because   C. many   D. of

4 Many _____ learn them _____ _____.

A. fun   B. others   C. for

5 _____ any _____, students everywhere have _____ interesting ways to _____ new languages.

A. case   B. found   C. study   D. in

6 _____ _____ these students and _____ to their _____.

A. ideas   B. let's   C. listen   D. meet

7 I _____ _____!

A. Soccer   B. Love

8 I'm a _____ _____ of a Spanish soccer _____.

A. fan   B. team   C. big

9 I want to _____ _____ with my _____ players.

A. interviews   B. favorite   C. understand

10 _____, it's not _____ _____ I don't know Spanish that _____.

A. because   B. however   C. well   D. easy

11 _____ can I _____ my _____? - Owen, 16

A. Spanish   B. how   C. improve

12 The best _____ to learn a new language is _____ _____ it _____ day.

A. to   B. every   C. way   D. practice

13 I _____ _____ the language of my phone to Spanish, and I have _____ _____ my shopping lists in Spanish! - Julie, 15

A. been   B. changed   C. writing   D. have

14 _____ most important is to _____ _____ _____ the language first.

A. familiar   B. what's   C. with   D. become

15 I _____ _____ Spanish movies _____.

A. watching   B. suggest   C. often

16 It will _____ you get _____ _____ the _____ of the language.

A. sound   B. used   C. help   D. to

17 _____ the people talk _____ fast, _____ _____ Spanish children's movies first. - Inho, 14

A. try   B. if   C. watching   D. too

18 Some words _____ _____ only in soccer, not in _____ _____.

A. every   B. used   C. are   D. day

19 _____ some soccer _____ and _____ it.

A. vocabulary   B. learn   C. memorize

20 Also, _____ _____ you try writing a _____ of a match _____ Spanish?

A. don't   B. in   C. review   D. why

21 It will _____ you _____ your _____ skills. - Rohan, 16

A. writing   B. help   C. improve

22 _____ More _____!

A. Subtitles   B. No

23 DREAM4 _____ _____!

A. back   B. is

24 I'm _____ _____ to see my favorite Korean boy band _____.

A. perform   B. excited   C. so

25 Their _____ and their dancing are _____ _____.

A. just   B. singing   C. perfect

26 I want to understand their songs _____ _____ or _____ though.

A. without   B. translations   C. subtitles

27 _____ _____? - Marisa, 14

A. tips   B. any

28 You _____ _____ friends who are _____ _____ DREAM4 and start a club.

A. find   B. interested   C. should   D. in

29 In my club, we _____ _____ _____.

A. one   B. motivate   C. another

30 We _____ songs and _____ _____.

A. sing   B. together   C. translate

---

15 전 스페인 영화들을 자주 볼 것을 제안하는데요.

16 그것은 당신이 언어의 소리에 익숙해지도록 도울 거예요.

17 만약 사람들이 너무 빨리 말한다면, 어린이를 위한 스페인 영화들을 먼저 보는 것을 시도해 보세요. – 인호, 14세

18 어떤 단어들은 일상생활에서가 아니라 오직 축구에서만 쓰인답니다.

19 몇몇 축구 어휘들을 배우고 기억하세요.

20 또한, 스페인어로 경기에 대한 후기를 써 보는 건 어때요?

21 그것은 당신이 작문 실력을 향상하도록 도울 거예요. – 로한, 16세

22 더는 자막 없이!

23 DREAM4가 돌아왔어요!

24 저는 제가 정말 좋아하는 한국의 젊은 남성 밴드가 공연하는 것을 보는 게 너무 신이 나요.

25 그들의 노래와 춤은 정말 완벽하답니다.

26 그렇지만 자막이나 번역이 없이 그들의 노래를 이해하고 싶어요.

27 어떤 조언들이 있을까요? – 마리사, 14세

28 당신은 DREAM4에 관심이 있는 친구들을 찾아 모임을 시작해야 해요.

29 우리 모임에서 우리는 서로 동기를 부여한답니다.

30 우리는 함께 노래를 번역하고 노래해요.

31 _____ these _____ is fun and really _____ our Korean! - Lori, 15

    A. improves   B. doing   C. things

32 _____ DREAM4 _____ _____ media.

    A. on   B. follow   C. social

33 They often _____ short _____ in Korean about _____ they are _____.

    A. how   B. post   C. doing   D. messages

34 They also post pictures _____ the _____, so you can _____ the posts more _____.- Aishah, 14

    A. easily   B. with   C. messages   D. understand

35 I _____ _____ Korean _____.

    A. watching   B. recommend   C. dramas

36 I've _____ _____ Korean dramas for a _____, and they're really interesting!

    A. watching   B. year   C. been

37 You can use Korean subtitles _____ _____ _____ _____.

    A. help   B. listening   C. with   D. for

38 It's _____ a good idea to _____ _____ the _____ and read them first. - Brandon, 16

    A. subtitles   B. print   C. also   D. out

39 _____ _____ for You?

    A. Works   B. What

40 There are _____ _____ good tips out there, but everyone has their _____ _____ of learning.

    A. of   B. way   C. hundreds   D. own

41 Find _____ keeps you _____; then you will _____ _____ more.

    A. what   B. learning   C. motivated   D. enjoy

42 Remember, every language is hard _____ _____, but a new language can make your world _____ _____!

    A. first   B. bigger   C. at   D. much

31 이런 것들을 하는 것은 재미있고 정말로 우리의 한국어 실력을 향상해요! – 로리, 15세

32 소셜 미디어에서 DREAM4를 팔로하세요.

33 그들은 종종 자신들이 어떻게 지내는지에 대해 한국어로 짧은 메시지를 올려요.

34 그들은 또한 메시지와 함께 사진들을 올려서 당신은 더 쉽게 게시물을 이해할 수 있어요. – 아이샤, 14세

35 저는 한국 드라마들을 볼 것을 추천해요.

36 저는 1년 동안 한국 드라마들을 시청해 왔고, 그것들은 정말 재미있어요!

37 듣기에 도움이 되도록 한국어 자막을 사용할 수 있고요.

38 먼저 자막들을 출력해서 읽는 것도 좋은 생각이랍니다. – 브랜던, 16세

39 무엇이 당신에게 효과가 있는 걸까?

40 세상에는 수백 가지 좋은 조언들이 있지만, 모든 사람이 학습에 대한 그들만의 방법을 가지고 있다.

41 당신에게 계속 동기 부여가 되는 것을 찾아라, 그러면 당신은 학습을 더욱 즐길 것이다.

42 기억해라, 모든 언어는 처음에는 어렵지만, 새로운 언어가 당신의 세상을 더욱 넓혀줄 수 있다!

※ 다음 우리말과 일치하도록 빈칸에 알맞은 것을 골라 쓰시오.

1 Learn _____ _____ _____, _____ a New World

2 _____ Do People _____ _____ _____?

3 Many students _____ new languages _____ _____ _____ _____.

4 Many _____ learn them _____ _____.

5 _____ _____ _____, students everywhere have found interesting _____ _____ _____ new languages.

6 _____ meet these students and _____ _____ _____ _____.

7 I _____ _____!

8 I'm _____ _____ _____ of a _____ soccer team.

9 I want to _____ _____ _____ my favorite players.

10 _____, it's not easy _____ I don't know _____ _____ _____.

11 _____ can I _____ _____ _____ _____? - Owen, 16

12 _____ _____ _____ to learn a new language is _____ _____ _____ every day.

13 I _____ _____ _____ _____ of my phone to Spanish, and I _____ _____ _____ my shopping lists in Spanish! - Julie, 15

14 What's _____ _____ _____ _____ _____ _____ the language first.

1 새로운 언어를 배우고, 새로운 세상을 찾아라

2 왜 사람들은 외국어를 배울까?

3 많은 학생들이 학교 필수 수업이기 때문에 새로운 언어를 배운다.

4 다른 많은 이들은 재미를 위해 그것을 배운다.

5 어떤 경우에도, 모든 곳의 학생들은 새로운 언어를 공부하는 데 흥미로운 방법들을 찾아낸다.

6 이 학생들을 만나서 그들의 생각을 들어보자.

7 저는 축구를 정말 좋아해요!

8 전 스페인 축구 팀의 엄청난 팬이랍니다.

9 저는 제가 정말 좋아하는 선수들의 인터뷰를 이해하고 싶어요.

10 그런데 스페인어를 그렇게 잘 알지 못하기 때문에 그것이 쉽지 않아요.

11 어떻게 하면 제가 스페인어 실력을 늘릴 수 있을까요? – 오언, 16세

12 새로운 언어를 배울 수 있는 가장 좋은 방법은 그 언어를 매일 연습하는 것이랍니다.

13 저는 제 휴대 전화의 설정을 스페인어로 바꿨고, 제가 사야 할 목록을 스페인어로 적어 오고 있어요! – 줄리, 15세

14 가장 중요한 것은 우선 그 언어와 친해지는 것이에요.

15 I _____ _____ _____ movies often.

16 It _____ _____ you _____ _____ _____ the sound of the language.

17 If the people talk _____ _____, _____ _____ Spanish children's movies first. - Inho, 14

18 Some words _____ _____ _____ in soccer, _____ in everyday life.

19 _____ some _____ _____ and _____ it.

20 Also, _____ _____ _____ _____ _____ a review of a match _____ _____?

21 It _____ _____ you _____ _____ _____ _____ _____. - Rohan, 16

22 _____ _____ Subtitles!

23 DREAM4 _____ _____!

24 I'm _____ _____ to see my favorite Korean boy band _____.

25 Their singing and their dancing are _____ _____.

26 I want to understand their songs _____ _____ or _____ _____.

27 _____ _____? - Marisa, 14

28 You _____ _____ friends who _____ _____ _____ DREAM4 and start a club.

29 In my club, we _____ _____ _____.

30 We _____ songs and _____ _____.

15 전 스페인 영화들을 자주 볼 것을 제안하는데요.

16 그것은 당신이 언어의 소리에 익숙해지도록 도울 거예요.

17 만약 사람들이 너무 빨리 말한다면, 어린이를 위한 스페인 영화들을 먼저 보는 것을 시도해 보세요. – 인호, 14세

18 어떤 단어들은 일상생활에서가 아니라 오직 축구에서만 쓰인답니다.

19 몇몇 축구 어휘들을 배우고 기억하세요.

20 또한, 스페인어로 경기에 대한 후기를 써 보는 건 어때요?

21 그것은 당신이 작문 실력을 향상하도록 도울 거예요. – 로한, 16세

22 더는 자막 없이!

23 DREAM4가 돌아왔어요!

24 저는 제가 정말 좋아하는 한국의 젊은 남성 밴드가 공연하는 것을 보는 게 너무 신이 나요.

25 그들의 노래와 춤은 정말 완벽하답니다.

26 그렇지만 자막이나 번역이 없이 그들의 노래를 이해하고 싶어요.

27 어떤 조언들이 있을까요? – 마리사, 14세

28 당신은 DREAM4에 관심이 있는 친구들을 찾아 모임을 시작해야 해요.

29 우리 모임에서 우리는 서로 동기를 부여한답니다.

30 우리는 함께 노래를 번역하고 노래해요.

31 _____ these things is fun and really _____ _____ _____! - Lori, 15

32 _____ DREAM4 _____ _____ _____.

33 They often _____ _____ in Korean about _____ they _____ _____.

34 They also _____ pictures _____ _____ _____, so you can understand the posts _____ _____.- Aishah, 14

35 I _____ _____ Korean dramas.

36 _____ _____ _____ Korean dramas _____ a year, and they're really interesting!

37 You can use _____ _____ _____ _____ _____ _____.

38 It's also a good idea _____ _____ _____ _____ _____ and read them first. - Brandon, 16

39 What _____ _____ You?

40 There are _____ _____ good tips out there, but everyone has _____ _____ _____ of _____.

41 Find _____ _____ you _____; then you will _____ _____ more.

42 Remember, every language is _____ _____ _____, but a new language can _____ your world _____ _____!

---

31 이런 것들을 하는 것은 재미있고 정말로 우리의 한국어 실력을 향상해요! – 로리, 15세

32 소셜 미디어에서 DREAM4를 팔로하세요.

33 그들은 종종 자신들이 어떻게 지내는지에 대해 한국어로 짧은 메시지를 올려요.

34 그들은 또한 메시지와 함께 사진들을 올려서 당신은 더 쉽게 게시물을 이해할 수 있어요. – 아이샤, 14세

35 저는 한국 드라마들을 볼 것을 추천해요.

36 저는 1년 동안 한국 드라마들을 시청해 왔고, 그것들은 정말 재미있어요!

37 듣기에 도움이 되도록 한국어 자막을 사용할 수 있고요.

38 먼저 자막들을 출력해서 읽는 것도 좋은 생각이랍니다. – 브랜던, 16세

39 무엇이 당신에게 효과가 있는 걸까?

40 세상에는 수백 가지 좋은 조언들이 있지만, 모든 사람이 학습에 대한 그들만의 방법을 가지고 있다.

41 당신에게 계속 동기 부여가 되는 것을 찾아라, 그러면 당신은 학습을 더욱 즐길 것이다.

42 기억해라, 모든 언어는 처음에는 어렵지만, 새로운 언어가 당신의 세상을 더욱 넓혀줄 수 있다!

※ 다음 문장을 우리말로 쓰시오.

1 Learn a New Language, Find a New World

➡ _____

2 Why Do People Learn Foreign Languages?

➡ _____

3 Many students learn new languages because of school requirements.

➡ _____

4 Many others learn them for fun.

➡ _____

5 In any case, students everywhere have found interesting ways to study new languages.

➡ _____

6 Let's meet these students and listen to their ideas.

➡ _____

7 I Love Soccer!

➡ _____

8 I'm a big fan of a Spanish soccer team.

➡ _____

9 I want to understand interviews with my favorite players.

➡ _____

10 However, it's not easy because I don't know Spanish that well.

➡ _____

11 How can I improve my Spanish? - Owen, 16

➡ _____

12 The best way to learn a new language is to practice it every day.

➡ _____

13 I have changed the language of my phone to Spanish, and I have been writing my shopping lists in Spanish! - Julie, 15

➡ _____

14 What's most important is to become familiar with the language first.

➡ _____

15 I suggest watching Spanish movies often.

➡ _____

16 It will help you get used to the sound of the language.

➡ _____

17 If the people talk too fast, try watching Spanish children's movies first. - Inho, 14

➡ _____

18 Some words are used only in soccer, not in everyday life.

➡ _____

19 Learn some soccer vocabulary and memorize it.

➡ _____

20 Also, why don't you try writing a review of a match in Spanish?

➡ _____

21 It will help you improve your writing skills. - Rohan, 16

➡ _____

22 No More Subtitles!

➡ _____

23 DREAM4 is back!

➡ _____

24 I'm so excited to see my favorite Korean boy band perform.

➡ _____

25 Their singing and their dancing are just perfect.

➡ _____

26 I want to understand their songs without subtitles or translations though.

➡ _____

27 Any tips? - Marisa, 14

➡ _____

28 You should find friends who are interested in DREAM4 and start a club.

➡ _____

29 In my club, we motivate one another.

➡ _____

30 We translate songs and sing together.

➡ _____

31 Doing these things is fun and really improves our Korean! - Lori, 15

➡ _____

32 Follow DREAM4 on social media.

➡ _____

33 They often post short messages in Korean about how they are doing.

➡ _____

34 They also post pictures with the messages, so you can understand the posts more easily.
- Aishah, 14

➡ _____

35 I recommend watching Korean dramas.

➡ _____

36 I've been watching Korean dramas for a year, and they're really interesting!

➡ _____

37 You can use Korean subtitles for help with listening.

➡ _____

38 It's also a good idea to print out the subtitles and read them first. - Brandon, 16

➡ _____

39 What Works for You?

➡ _____

40 There are hundreds of good tips out there, but everyone has their own way of learning.

➡ _____

41 Find what keeps you motivated; then you will enjoy learning more.

➡ _____

42 Remember, every language is hard at first, but a new language can make your world much bigger!

➡ _____

※ 다음 괄호 안의 단어들을 우리말에 맞도록 바르게 배열하시오.

1 (a / Learn / Language, / New / a / Find / World / New)
➡ _____

2 (Do / Why / Learn / People / Languages? / Foreign)
➡ _____

3 (students / many / new / learn / because / language / school / requirements. / of)
➡ _____

4 (others / many / them / learn / fun. / for)
➡ _____

5 (any / case, / in / everywhere / students / found / have / ways / interesting / study / to / languages. / new)
➡ _____
_____

6 (meet / let's / students / these / and / to / listen / ideas. / their)
➡ _____

7 (Love / I / Soccer!)
➡ _____

8 (a / I'm / fan / big / of / Spanish / a / team. / soccer)
➡ _____

9 (want / I / to / understand / with / interviews / favorite / my / players.)
➡ _____

10 (it's / however, / not / because / easy / don't / I / Spanish / know / well. / that)
➡ _____

11 (can / how / improve / I / Spanish? / my / - / 16 / Owen,)
➡ _____

12 (best / the / to / way / learn / new / a / language / to / is / it / practice / day. / every)
➡ _____

13 (have / I / the / changed / language / my / of / to / phone / Spanish, / and / have / I / writing / been / shopping / my / in / lists / Spanish! / - / 15 / Julie,)
➡ _____
_____

14 (most / what's / important / to / is / familiar / become / with / language / the / first.)
➡ _____

---

1 새로운 언어를 배우고, 새로운 세상을 찾아라

2 왜 사람들은 외국어를 배울까?

3 많은 학생들이 학교 필수 수업이기 때문에 새로운 언어를 배운다.

4 다른 많은 이들은 재미를 위해 그것을 배운다.

5 어떤 경우에도, 모든 곳의 학생들은 새로운 언어를 공부하는데 흥미로운 방법들을 찾아낸다.

6 이 학생들을 만나서 그들의 생각을 들어보자.

7 저는 축구를 정말 좋아해요!

8 전 스페인 축구 팀의 엄청난 팬이랍니다.

9 저는 제가 정말 좋아하는 선수들의 인터뷰를 이3해하고 싶어요.

10 그런데 스페인어를 그렇게 잘 알지 못하기 때문에 그것이 쉽지 않아요.

11 어떻게 하면 제가 스페인어 실력을 늘릴 수 있을까요? – 오언, 16세

12 새로운 언어를 배울 수 있는 가장 좋은 방법은 그 언어를 매일 연습하는 것이랍니다.

13 저는 제 휴대 전화의 설정을 스페인어로 바꿨고, 제가 사야 할 목록을 스페인어로 적어 오고 있어요! – 줄리, 15세

14 가장 중요한 것은 우선 그 언어와 친해지는 것이에요.

15 (suggest / I / watching / movies / often. / Spanish)
➡ _____

16 (will / it / help / get / you / used / the / to / sound / the / of / language.)
➡ _____

17 (the / if / talk / people / fast, / too / watching / try / children's / Spanish / first. / movies / - / 14 / Inho,)
➡ _____

18 (words / some / used / are / in / only / soccer, / in / not / life. / everyday)
➡ _____

19 (some / learn / vocabulary / soccer / and / it. / memorize)
➡ _____

20 (why / also, / don't / try / you / a / writing / review / a / of / match / Spanish? / in)
➡ _____

21 (will / it / you / help / your / improve / skills. / wrting / - / 16 / Rohan,)
➡ _____

22 (More / No / Subtitles!)
➡ _____

23 (is / DREAM4 / back!)
➡ _____

24 (so / I'm / to / excited / see / favorite / my / boy / Korean / perform. / band)
➡ _____

25 (singing / their / and / dancing / their / are / perfect. / just)
➡ _____

26 (want / I / to / their / understand / songs / subtitles / without / or / though. / translations)
➡ _____

27 (tips? / any / - / 14 / Marisa,)
➡ _____

28 (should / you / friends / find / who / interested / are / in / and / DREAM4 / a / club. / start)
➡ _____

29 (my / in / club, / motivate / we / another. / one)
➡ _____

30 (translate / we / songs / and / together. / sing)
➡ _____

15 전 스페인 영화들을 자주 볼 것을 제안하는데요.

16 그것은 당신이 언어의 소리에 익숙해지도록 도울 거예요.

17 만약 사람들이 너무 빨리 말한다면, 어린이를 위한 스페인 영화들을 먼저 보는 것을 시도해 보세요. – 인호, 14세

18 어떤 단어들은 일상생활에서가 아니라 오직 축구에서만 쓰인답니다.

19 몇몇 축구 어휘들을 배우고 기억하세요.

20 또한, 스페인어로 경기에 대한 후기를 써 보는 건 어때요?

21 그것은 당신이 작문 실력을 향상하도록 도울 거예요. - 로한, 16세

22 더는 자막 없이!

23 DREAM4가 돌아왔어요!

24 저는 제가 정말 좋아하는 한국의 젊은 남성 밴드가 공연하는 것을 보는 게 너무 신이 나요.

25 그들의 노래와 춤은 정말 완벽하답니다.

26 그렇지만 자막이나 번역이 없이 그들의 노래를 이해하고 싶어요.

27 어떤 조언들이 있을까요? – 마리사, 14세

28 당신은 DREAM4에 관심이 있는 친구들을 찾아 모임을 시작해야 해요.

29 우리 모임에서 우리는 서로 동기를 부여한답니다.

30 우리는 함께 노래를 번역하고 노래해요.

31 (these / doing / things / fun / is / and / improves / really / Korean! / our / - / 15 / Lori,)

➡ _____

32 (DREAM4 / follow / social / on / media.)

➡ _____

33 (often / they / post / messages / short / Korean / in / how / about / are / they / doing.)

➡ _____

34 (also / they / pictures / post / with / messages, / the / you / so / understand / can / posts / the / easily. / more / - / 14 / Aishah,)

➡ _____

➡ _____

35 (recommend / I / watching / dramas. / Korean)

➡ _____

36 (been / I've / watching / dramas / Korean / a / for / year, / and / really / they're / interesting!)

➡ _____

➡ _____

37 (can / you / Korean / use / for / subtitles / help / listening. / with)

➡ _____

38 (also / it's / good / a / to / idea / out / print / the / and / subtitles / and / them / first. / read / - 16, / Brandon,)

➡ _____

➡ _____

39 (Works / What / You? / for)

➡ _____

40 (are / there / of / hundreds / good / tips / there, / out / everyone / but / their / has / way / own / learning. / of)

➡ _____

➡ _____

41 (what / find / you / keeps / motivated; / you / then / enjoy / will / more. / learning)

➡ _____

42 (every / remember, / language / hard / is / first, / at / but / new / a / language / make / can / world / your / bigger! / much)

➡ _____

➡ _____

31 이런 것들을 하는 것은 재미있고 정말로 우리의 한국어 실력을 향상해요! – 로리, 15세

32 소셜 미디어에서 DREAM4를 팔로하세요.

33 그들은 종종 자신들이 어떻게 지내는지에 대해 한국어로 짧은 메시지를 올려요.

34 그들은 또한 메시지와 함께 사진들을 올려서 당신은 더 쉽게 게시물을 이해할 수 있어요. – 아이샤, 14세

35 저는 한국 드라마들을 볼 것을 추천해요.

36 저는 1년 동안 한국 드라마들을 시청해 왔고, 그것들은 정말 재미있어요!

37 듣기에 도움이 되도록 한국어 자막을 사용할 수 있고요.

38 먼저 자막들을 출력해서 읽는 것도 좋은 생각이랍니다. – 브랜던, 16세

39 무엇이 당신에게 효과가 있는 걸까?

40 세상에는 수백 가지 좋은 조언들이 있지만, 모든 사람이 학습에 대한 그들만의 방법을 가지고 있다.

41 당신에게 계속 동기 부여가 되는 것을 찾아라, 그러면 당신은 학습을 더욱 즐길 것이다.

42 기억해라, 모든 언어는 처음에는 어렵지만, 새로운 언어가 당신의 세상을 더욱 넓혀줄 수 있다!

※ **다음 우리말을 영어로 쓰시오.**

1 ▶ 새로운 언어를 배우고, 새로운 세상을 찾아라

➡ _____

2 ▶ 왜 사람들은 외국어를 배울까?

➡ _____

3 ▶ 많은 학생들이 학교 필수 수업이기 때문에 새로운 언어를 배운다.

➡ _____

4 ▶ 다른 많은 이들은 재미를 위해 그것을 배운다.

➡ _____

5 ▶ 어떤 경우에도, 모든 곳의 학생들은 새로운 언어를 공부하는 데 흥미로운 방법들을 찾아낸다.

➡ _____

6 ▶ 이 학생들을 만나서 그들의 생각을 들어보자.

➡ _____

7 ▶ 저는 축구를 정말 좋아해요!

➡ _____

8 ▶ 전 스페인 축구 팀의 엄청난 팬이랍니다.

➡ _____

9 ▶ 저는 제가 정말 좋아하는 선수들의 인터뷰를 이해하고 싶어요.

➡ _____

10 ▶ 그런데 스페인어를 그렇게 잘 알지 못하기 때문에 그것이 쉽지 않아요.

➡ _____

11 ▶ 어떻게 하면 제가 스페인어 실력을 늘릴 수 있을까요? – 오언, 16세

➡ _____

12 ▶ 새로운 언어를 배울 수 있는 가장 좋은 방법은 그 언어를 매일 연습하는 것이랍니다.

➡ _____

13 ▶ 저는 제 휴대 전화의 설정을 스페인어로 바꿨고, 제가 사야 할 목록을 스페인어로 적어 오고 있어요!

– 줄리, 15세

➡ _____

_____

14 ▶ 가장 중요한 것은 우선 언어와 친해지는 것이에요.

➡ _____

15 전 스페인 영화들을 자주 볼 것을 제안하는데요.

➡ _____

16 그것은 당신이 언어의 소리에 익숙해지도록 도울 거예요.

➡ _____

17 만약 사람들이 너무 빨리 말한다면, 어린이를 위한 스페인 영화들을 먼저 보는 것을 시도해 보세요.
– 인호, 14세

➡ _____

18 어떤 단어들은 일상생활에서가 아니라 오직 축구에서만 쓰인답니다.

➡ _____

19 몇몇 축구 어휘들을 배우고 기억하세요.

➡ _____

20 또한, 스페인어로 경기에 대한 후기를 써 보는 건 어때요?

➡ _____

21 그것은 당신이 작문 실력을 향상하도록 도울 거예요. – 로한, 16세

➡ _____

22 더는 자막 없이!

➡ _____

23 DREAM4가 돌아왔어요!

➡ _____

24 저는 제가 정말 좋아하는 한국의 젊은 남성 밴드가 공연하는 것을 보는 게 너무 신이 나요.

➡ _____

25 그들의 노래와 춤은 정말 완벽하답니다.

➡ _____

26 그렇지만 자막이나 번역이 없이 그들의 노래를 이해하고 싶어요.

➡ _____

27 어떤 조언들이 있을까요? – 마리사, 14세

➡ _____

28 당신은 DREAM4에 관심이 있는 친구들을 찾아 모임을 시작해야 해요.

➡ _____

29 우리 모임에서 우리는 서로 동기를 부여한답니다.

➡ _____

30 우리는 함께 노래를 번역하고 노래해요.

➡ _____

31 이런 것들을 하는 것은 재미있고 정말로 우리의 한국어 실력을 향상해요! – 로리, 15세

➡ _____

32 소셜 미디어에서 DREAM4를 팔로하세요.

➡ _____

33 그들은 종종 자신들이 어떻게 지내는지에 대해 한국어로 짧은 메시지를 올려요.

➡ _____

34 그들은 또한 메시지와 함께 사진들을 올려서 당신은 더 쉽게 게시물을 이해할 수 있어요.

– 아이샤, 14세

➡ _____

_____

35 저는 한국 드라마들을 볼 것을 추천해요.

➡ _____

36 저는 1년 동안 한국 드라마들을 시청해 왔고, 그것들은 정말 재미있어요!

➡ _____

37 듣기에 도움이 되도록 한국어 자막을 사용할 수 있고요.

➡ _____

38 맨 먼저 자막들을 출력해서 읽는 것도 좋은 생각이랍니다. – 브랜던, 16세

➡ _____

39 무엇이 당신에게 효과가 있는 걸까?

➡ _____

40 세상에는 수백 가지 좋은 조언들이 있지만, 모든 사람이 학습에 대한 그들만의 방법을 가지고 있다.

➡ _____

41 당신에게 계속 동기 부여가 되는 것을 찾아라, 그러면 당신은 학습을 더욱 즐길 것이다.

➡ _____

42 기억해라, 모든 언어는 처음에는 어렵지만, 새로운 언어가 당신의 세상을 더욱 넓혀줄 수 있다!

➡ _____

※ 다음 우리말과 일치하도록 빈칸에 알맞은 말을 쓰시오.

After You Read B

1. A: I _____ _____ _____ my Chinese. Do you _____
_____ _____?

2. B: Learn _____ _____ _____ _____ _____ your
interests.

3. C: _____ Chinese dramas _____ _____ _____ is a good
_____ _____ _____ _____ _____ listening.

4. A: Thanks _____ _____!

1. A: 나는 중국어 실력을 늘리고 싶어. 좋은 방법이 있니?
2. B: 관심있는 것들과 관련된 어휘를 배워.
3. C: 중국어 자막이 있는 중국 드라마를 보는 것이 듣기를 잘하게 하는 좋은 방법이야.
4. A: 정말 고마워!

After You Read C

1. _____ _____ _____ a New Language

2. _____: _____ soccer team

3. Wants: _____ _____ the players' _____

4. Useful Tips: • Practice _____ _____ _____.

5. • _____ _____ _____ Spanish.

6. • Learn _____ _____ and write a _____ of a _____
_____ _____.

7. Find _____ keeps you _____; then you will _____ _____
_____.

1. 새로운 언어를 배울 수 있는 방법
2. 관심: 스페인 축구 팀
3. 원하는 것: 선수들의 인터뷰를 이해하기
4. 유용한 조언들: •스페인어를 매일 연습해라.
5. •스페인어와 친해져라.
6. •축구 어휘들을 배우고 스페인어로 경기에 대한 후기를 써 보아라.
7. 당신에게 계속 동기 부여가 되는 것을 찾아라, 그러면 당신은 학습을 더욱 즐길 것이다.

Do It Yourself B

1. I'm _____ _____ _____ _____ my favorite Korean boy
band _____.

2. I want to understand their songs _____ _____ or _____
_____.

3. Any _____? - Marisa

1. 나는 내가 가장 좋아하는 한국의 소년 밴드가 공연하는 것을 보아서 매우 신나요.
2. 그러나 나는 자막이나 번역이 없이 그들의 노래를 이해하고 싶어요.
3. 어떤 조언들이 있을까요? –Marisa

※ **다음 우리말을 영어로 쓰시오.**

After You Read B

1. A: 나는 중국어 실력을 늘리고 싶어. 좋은 방법이 있니?

   ➡ _____

2. B: 관심있는 것들과 관련된 어휘를 배워.

   ➡ _____

3. C: 중국어 자막이 있는 중국 드라마를 보는 것이 듣기를 잘하게 하는 좋은 방법이야.

   ➡ _____

4. A: 정말 고마워!

   ➡ _____

After You Read C

1. 새로운 언어를 배울 수 있는 방법

   ➡ _____

2. 관심: 스페인 축구 팀

   ➡ _____

3. 원하는 것: 선수들의 인터뷰를 이해하기

   ➡ _____

4. 유용한 조언들: •스페인어를 매일 연습해라.

   ➡ _____

5. •스페인어와 친해져라.

   ➡ _____

6. •축구 어휘들을 배우고 스페인어로 경기에 대한 후기를 써 보아라.

   ➡ _____

7. 당신에게 계속 동기 부여가 되는 것을 찾아라, 그러면 당신은 학습을 더욱 즐길 것이다.

   ➡ _____

Do It Yourself B

1. 나는 내가 가장 좋아하는 한국의 소년 밴드가 공연하는 것을 보아서 매우 신나요.

   ➡ _____

2. 그러나 나는 자막이나 번역이 없이 그들의 노래를 이해하고 싶어요.

   ➡ _____

3. 어떤 조언들이 있을까요? – *Marisa*

   ➡ _____

※ 다음 영어를 우리말로 쓰시오.

01 positive _____

02 awesome _____

03 beneficial _____

04 convenient _____

05 similar _____

06 brain _____

07 cell _____

08 damage _____

09 deep sleep _____

10 compared _____

11 walnut _____

12 prevent _____

13 ginger _____

14 risk _____

15 search _____

16 track _____

17 benefit _____

18 contain _____

19 process _____

20 clue _____

21 vision _____

22 increase _____

23 multiple _____

24 wrinkle _____

25 lower _____

26 mirror _____

27 hollow _____

28 improve _____

29 moved _____

30 negative _____

31 sensitive _____

32 chemical _____

33 function _____

34 productive _____

35 a variety of _____

36 in addition _____

37 from now on _____

38 at least _____

39 on the other hand _____

40 come to mind _____

41 not only A but also B _____

42 be divided into _____

43 prevents A from -ing _____

※ 다음 우리말을 영어로 쓰시오.

01 세포 _____

02 유익한 _____

03 처리하다 _____

04 속이 빈 _____

05 호두 _____

06 부정적인 _____

07 엄청난 _____

08 복합적인 _____

09 베개 _____

10 반사하다 _____

11 비교되는 _____

12 긍정적인 _____

13 감동받은 _____

14 손상을 주다 _____

15 주름 _____

16 조사하다 _____

17 단서 _____

18 기능 _____

19 시력 _____

20 화학물질 _____

21 씹다 _____

22 생강 _____

23 생산적인 _____

24 비슷한 _____

25 증가하다 _____

26 건강한 _____

27 이득 _____

28 포함하다 _____

29 뇌 _____

30 개선하다 _____

31 방해하다, 가로 막다 _____

32 낮추다 _____

33 편리한 _____

34 민감한 _____

35 지금부터 _____

36 운동하다 _____

37 게다가 _____

38 반면에 _____

39 계속 ~하다 _____

40 다양한 _____

41 ~로 나뉘어지다 _____

42 A뿐만 아니라 B도 _____

43 생각이 떠오르다 _____

Step3

※ 다음 영영풀이에 알맞은 단어를 <보기>에서 골라 쓴 후, 우리말 뜻을 쓰시오.

1 _____ : feeling that you want or need a drink: _____

2 _____ : having an empty space inside: _____

3 _____ : useful to you because it saves you time: _____

4 _____ : the ability to see: _____

5 _____ : a nut that you can eat, shaped like a human brain: _____

6 _____ : to cut meat, bread, vegetables, etc into thin flat pieces: _____

7 _____ : a cloth bag filled with soft material that you put your head on: _____

8 _____ : always busy doing things, especially physical or mental activities: _____

9 _____ : lines on your face and skin that you get when you are old: _____

10 _____ : the organ inside your head that controls how you think, feel, and move: _____

11 _____ : the possibility that something bad, unpleasant, or dangerous may happen: _____

12 _____ : to become or to make something greater in amount, number, value, etc.: _____

13 _____ : to make something better, or to become better: _____

14 _____ : to bite food into small pieces in your mouth with your teeth to make it easier to swallow: _____

15 _____ : an object, a piece of evidence, or some information that helps the police solve a crime: _____

16 _____ : an advantage that something gives you; a helpful and useful effect that something has: _____

보기			
wrinkle	improve	clue	pillow
chew	thirsty	slice	brain
active	hollow	convenient	risk
vision	increase	walnut	benefit

※ 다음 우리말과 일치하도록 빈칸에 알맞은 말을 쓰시오.

해석

Listen & Talk 1 A

B: _____ you _____ that _____ ice is _____ _____ your _____?

G: No, I _____. _____ is that?

B: It can _____ your teeth. It can also _____ them too _____.

Listen & Talk 1 B

B: You _____ _____. Did you _____ _____ sleep?

G: Yes, I did. I _____ _____ _____ seven hours.

B: Okay. _____ _____ you _____ _____ _____ _____?

G: I _____ _____ _____ after midnight, _____ _____.

B: That's _____ _____ is _____ you _____. _____ you _____ that _____ you go to bed is very important?

G: No, I haven't. _____ is _____?

B: Scientists say that _____ _____ _____ _____ _____ can _____ you _____ _____ the next day.

G: I didn't know that.

B: On the _____ _____, going to bed early can _____ your _____ and help you be more _____. From _____ _____, _____ _____ go to bed _____.

B: 너는 얼음을 씹는 것이 이에 나쁘다는 말을 들어보았니?
G: 아니. 왜 그런데?
B: 그것이 이에 손상을 줄 수 있어. 그것은 또한 이를 너무 예민하게 만들 수 있어.

B: 너 피곤해 보인다. 잠은 충분히 잤니?
G: 응, 그래. 나는 일곱 시간 이상 잤어.
B: 알았어. 너는 언제 잠들었니?
G: 평소처럼 자정이 넘어서 잠들었어.
B: 아마 그것이 너를 피곤하게 만드는 것일 거야. 네가 언제 잠자리에 드는지가 아주 중요하다는 말을 들어본 적이 있니?
G: 아니. 왜 그렇지?
B: 과학자들은 늦게 잠자리에 드는 것은 그 다음날 피곤함을 느끼게 할 수 있다고 말해.
G: 나는 몰랐어.
B: 반면에 일찍 잠자리에 드는 것은 기억력을 향상시키고, 더 생산적이 되도록 도와줄 수 있어. 지금부터는 일찍 자도록 노력해 봐.

Listen & Talk 1 D-1

A: _____ you _____ that _____ by hand is _____ for your _____?

B: Oh, _____?

A: Yes, it _____ your _____.

A: 손으로 글을 쓰는 것이 건강에 좋다는 말을 들어본 적이 있니?
B: 오, 정말?
A: 그래, 그것이 기억력을 높여주는데.

Listen & Talk 2 A

G: What's this?

B: It's a _____ band. It lets me _____ my _____ _____ on my _____.

G: _____ _____ _____ information?

B: It shows _____ _____ I walk _____ the day and _____ _____ I sleep at night.

G: Interesting. I'm _____ that this _____ band can do all that.

G: 이것이 뭐니?
B: 그것은 스마트밴드야. 그것은 나에게 스마트폰으로 건강 정보를 점검할 수 있도록 해줘.
G: 어떤 종류의 정보니?
B: 그것은 내가 낮에 얼마나 멀리 걷는지, 밤에 얼마나 잘 자는지를 보여줘.
G: 흥미롭다. 나는 이 작은 밴드가 그 모든 일을 할 수 있다는 것이 놀라워.

Listen & Talk 2 B

B: _____ are you _____ in the _____ _____?

G: I'm _____ _____.

B: You're _____ out _____ _____?

G: Yes, I'm _____ this online video. It shows me all the _____.

B: _____ me _____. Wow, it's _____ _____ two _____ _____! I'm _____ that so many people _____ _____ this video.

G: I know! These kinds of _____ are becoming _____ right now.

B: It looks very _____. You _____ _____ go _____ to _____.

G: That's right. _____ _____ I love these programs. You should _____ them, _____.

Listen & Talk 2 C

B: What is that? It _____ nice.

G: This is a _____ cup. I _____ it _____ with me.

B: What's _____ _____ it?

G: It's _____. It tells me _____ _____ water _____ two hours.

B: Really? I'm _____ that it can _____ to you.

G: It even _____ me questions _____ "Aren't you _____?"

B: That's so cool! But _____ are you _____ to drink more water?

G: Because _____ a lot of water can _____ your energy and _____ your _____ _____.

B: That's amazing. I should _____ one!

Do It Yourself A

B: Oh, I'm so _____.

G: _____ _____ you eat some snacks _____ dinner?

B: I don't _____ to. I'll _____ _____ dinner.

G: Okay, but _____ you _____ that _____ _____ and _____ is good for your _____?

B: _____? I thought _____ _____ _____ a day was fine.

G: If you keep _____ until dinner, you will _____ too much and _____ quickly. _____ and _____ you _____ _____ like that.

B: I see. Then I'll _____ _____ an apple _____ _____.

B: 너 거실에서 무엇을 하고 있니?
G: 나는 요가를 하는 중이야.
B: 혼자서 운동한다는 말이니?
G: 그래, 이 온라인 비디오를 따라하는 중이야. 그것이 나에게 모든 단계를 보여줘.
B: 어디 보자. 와, 2백만 번이나 시청되었구나! 그렇게 많은 사람이 이 비디오를 보았다니 놀라워.
G: 알아! 이런 종류의 프로그램이 지금 인기를 얻는 중이야.
B: 그것은 매우 편리해 보여. 너는 운동하러 밖에 나갈 필요가 없어.
G: 맞아. 그런 이유로 나는 이런 프로그램을 아주 좋아해. 너도 한번 시도해 봐.

B: 저것이 뭐니? 그것은 좋아 보인다.
G: 이것은 매직 컵이야. 나는 어디든지 그것을 가지고 다녀.
B: 그것은 무엇이 특별하니?
G: 정말 끝내줘. 그것은 두 시간마다 물을 마시라고 나에게 말을 해.
B: 정말? 그것이 너에게 말을 할 수 있다는 것이 놀라워.
G: 심지어 그것은 "목마르지 않니?'와 같은 질문도 해.
B: 정말 멋지구나! 그런데 왜 너는 물을 더 마시려고 애쓰니?
G: 왜냐하면 물을 많이 마시는 것이 에너지를 높여주고, 피가 잘 흐르게 도와줘.
B: 정말 놀랍구나. 하나 사야겠다!

B: 오, 나는 너무 배가 고파.
G: 저녁 먹기 전에 간식을 좀 먹는 것이 어떠니?
B: 나는 그것을 원하지 않아. 나는 저녁식사까지 기다릴 거야.
G: 알았어. 하지만 너는 조금 자주 먹는 것이 건강에 좋다는 말을 들어본 적이 있니?
B: 정말이니? 나는 하루에 세끼 식사하는 것이 좋다고 생각했는데.
G: 만약 네가 저녁식사까지 계속 기다리면 너무 많이 그리고 너무 빨리 먹을 거야. 조금 자주 먹는 것이 네가 그렇게 먹는 것을 막아 줄 거야.
B: 알았어. 그러면 지금 당장 사과를 먹으러 가야겠다.

※ 다음 우리말에 맞도록 대화를 영어로 쓰시오.

해석

Listen & Talk 1 A

B: _____

G: _____

B: _____

B: 너는 얼음을 씹는 것이 이에 나쁘다는 말을 들어보았니?
G: 아니. 왜 그런데?
B: 그것이 이에 손상을 줄 수 있어. 그것은 또한 이를 너무 예민하게 만들 수 있어.

Listen & Talk 1 B

B: _____

G: _____

B: _____

G: _____

B: _____

_____

G: _____

B: _____

G: _____

B: _____

_____

B: 너 피곤해 보인다. 잠은 충분히 잤니?
G: 응, 그래. 나는 일곱 시간 이상 잤어.
B: 알았어. 너는 언제 잠들었니?
G: 평소처럼 자정이 넘어서 잠들었어.
B: 아마 그것이 너를 피곤하게 만드는 것일 거야. 네가 언제 잠자리에 드는지가 아주 중요하다는 말을 들어본 적이 있니?
G: 아니. 왜 그렇지?
B: 과학자들은 늦게 잠자리에 드는 것은 그 다음날 피곤함을 느끼게 할 수 있다고 말해.
G: 나는 몰랐어.
B: 반면에 일찍 잠자리에 드는 것은 기억력을 향상시키고, 더 생산적이 되도록 도와줄 수 있어. 지금부터는 일찍 자도록 노력해 봐.

Listen & Talk 1 D-1

A: _____

B: _____

A: _____

A: 손으로 글을 쓰는 것이 건강에 좋다는 말을 들어본 적이 있니?
B: 오, 정말?
A: 그래, 그것이 기억력을 높여준데.

Listen & Talk 2 A

G: _____

B: _____

G: _____

B: _____

G: _____

G: 이것이 뭐니?
B: 그것은 스마트밴드야. 그것은 나에게 스마트폰으로 건강 정보를 점검할 수 있도록 해줘.
G: 어떤 종류의 정보니?
B: 그것은 내가 낮에 얼마나 멀리 걷는지, 밤에 얼마나 잘 자는지를 보여줘.
G: 흥미롭다. 나는 이 작은 밴드가 그 모든 일을 할 수 있다는 것이 놀라워.

Listen & Talk 2 B

B: _____
G: _____
B: _____
G: _____
B: _____
_____
G: _____
B: _____
G: _____

Listen & Talk 2 C

B: _____
G: _____
B: _____
G: _____
B: _____
G: _____
B: _____
G: _____
B: _____

Do It Yourself A

B: _____
G: _____
B: _____
G: _____
B: _____
G: _____
_____
B: _____

B: 너 거실에서 무엇을 하고 있니?
G: 나는 요가를 하는 중이야.
B: 혼자서 운동한다는 말이니?
G: 그래, 이 온라인 비디오를 따라하는 중이야. 그것이 나에게 모든 단계를 보여줘.
B: 어디 보자. 와, 2백만 번이나 시청되었구나! 그렇게 많은 사람이 이 비디오를 보았다니 놀라워.
G: 알아! 이런 종류의 프로그램이 지금 인기를 얻는 중이야.
B: 그것은 매우 편리해 보여. 너는 운동하러 밖에 나갈 필요가 없어.
G: 맞아. 그런 이유로 나는 이런 프로그램을 아주 좋아해. 너도 한번 시도해 봐.

B: 저것이 뭐니? 그것은 좋아 보인다.
G: 이것은 매직 컵이야. 나는 어디든지 그것을 가지고 다녀.
B: 그것은 무엇이 특별하니?
G: 정말 끝내줘. 그것은 두 시간마다 물을 마시라고 나에게 말을 해.
B: 정말? 그것이 너에게 말을 할 수 있다는 것이 놀라워.
G: 심지어 그것은 "목마르지 않니?'와 같은 질문도 해.
B: 정말 멋지구나! 그런데 왜 너는 물을 더 마시려고 애쓰니?
G: 왜냐하면 물을 많이 마시는 것이 에너지를 높여주고, 피가 잘 흐르게 도와줘.
B: 정말 놀랍구나. 하나 사야겠다!

B: 오, 나는 너무 배가 고파.
G: 저녁 먹기 전에 간식을 좀 먹는 것이 어떠니?
B: 나는 그것을 원하지 않아. 나는 저녁 식사까지 기다릴 거야.
G: 알았어. 하지만 너는 조금 자주 먹는 것이 건강에 좋다는 말을 들어본 적이 있니?
B: 정말이니? 나는 하루에 세끼 식사하는 것이 좋다고 생각했는데.
G: 만약 네가 저녁식사까지 계속 기다리면 너무 많이 그리고 너무 빨리 먹을 거야. 조금 자주 먹는 것이 네가 그렇게 먹는 것을 막아 줄 거야.
B: 알았어. 그러면 지금 당장 사과를 먹으러 가야겠다.

※ 다음 우리말과 일치하도록 빈칸에 알맞은 것을 골라 쓰시오.

1 _____ _____ for Our _____.
A. Bodies   B. Foods   C. Beneficial

2 We all know that a diet _____ a _____ of foods _____ our bodies _____.
A. keeps   B. containing   C. healthy   D. variety

3 But sometimes we are not sure _____ foods are _____ which body _____.
A. for   B. which   C. good   D. parts

4 Nature, _____, gives us a _____ _____.
A. big   B. however   C. clue

5 _____ at the _____ _____.
A. following   B. look   C. examples

6 Each of these foods _____ _____ looks like a certain body part _____ is _____ good for that body part.
A. but   B. not   C. also   D. only

7 Slice open a tomato and _____ it _____ the human _____.
A. with   B. heart   C. compare

8 You will see _____ they _____ _____.
A. that   B. similar   C. look

9 They both have _____ _____ _____ and are red.
A. hollow   B. multiple   C. spaces

10 Researchers say _____ the _____ _____ make tomatoes red _____ good for your heart and _____.
A. blood   B. chemicals   C. are   D. that

11 _____ _____, eating tomatoes can _____ your risk of heart _____.
A. addition   B. disease   C. lower   D. in

12 _____ at the _____ of a _____.
A. shape   B. walnut   C. look

13 Do you _____ _____?
A. anything   B. notice

14 Yes, it's very _____ _____ the _____ of the human _____!
A. to   B. brain   C. similar   D. shape

15 A walnut is _____ _____ two parts, _____ _____ the brain.
A. like   B. divided   C. just   D. into

16 Walnuts also have _____, _____ the _____ has too.
A. brain   B. wrinkles   C. which

17 Studies show that walnuts _____ our brains _____ _____ and _____.
A. stay   B. help   C. active   D. healthy

1 우리 몸에 이로운 음식

2 우리는 다양한 음식을 포함하는 식사가 우리의 몸을 건강하게 유지해 준다는 것을 알고 있다.

3 그러나 때때로 우리는 어떤 음식이 어떤 신체 부위에 좋은지 잘 모를 때가 있다.

4 하지만 자연은 우리에게 확실한 단서를 제시해 준다.

5 다음의 예들을 살펴보자.

6 각각의 이 음식들은 우리 신체의 특정 부분과 비슷해 보일 뿐만 아니라 그 신체 부위에도 좋다.

7 토마토 한 개를 잘라내서 그것을 사람의 심장과 비교해 보자.

8 당신은 그 둘이 비슷해 보인다는 것을 알게 될 것이다.

9 둘 다 여러 개의 빈 공간이 있고 붉은 색이다.

10 연구원들은 토마토를 붉게 만드는 화학 물질이 사람의 심장과 피에 유익하다고 한다.

11 게다가, 토마토를 먹는 것이 심장병에 걸릴 위험성을 낮출 수 있다.

12 호두의 모양을 살펴보자.

13 뭔가를 알아차릴 수 있는가?

14 그렇다, 호두의 모양은 인간의 뇌 형태와 매우 유사하다!

15 호두는 마치 인간의 뇌처럼 두 부분으로 나뉜다.

16 호두에는 또한 주름이 있는데, 이는 인간의 뇌에도 있는 것이다.

17 연구 결과는 호두가 사람의 뇌가 건강하고 활동적인 상태를 유지하는 데 도움을 준다는 것을 보여준다.

18 They are also _____ for _____ Alzheimer's _____.
A. disease   B. good   C. preventing

19 A _____ of carrot _____ _____ the human eye.
A. like   B. slice   C. looks

20 Carrots have some _____ that can make vitamin A, _____ _____ your _____.
A. improves   B. chemicals   C. which   D. vision

21 It helps your eyes _____ light and _____ a clear _____ to the _____.
A. send   B. process   C. brain   D. image

22 So _____ you want _____ _____, eat carrots.
A. eyes   B. if   C. healthy

23 _____ onions is not fun _____ it _____ you _____.
A. makes   B. cutting   C. cry   D. because

24 But _____ _____ one _____.
A. anyway   B. slicing   C. try

25 You can see that the inside _____ _____ _____ _____ a human cell.
A. a   B. like   C. looks   D. little

26 Scientists say that onions contain vitamin B, _____ _____ _____ new, healthy _____.
A. cells   B. helps   C. make   D. which

27 Now, let's _____ _____ _____ ginger.
A. on   B. move   C. to

28 What body part _____ _____ _____ when you see it?
A. to   B. comes   C. mind

29 _____ it _____ a stomach?
A. look   B. doesn't   C. like

30 You may not like ginger's strong _____ or smell, but these come from a special chemical that _____ you from _____ sick and _____ up.
A. feeling   B. taste   C. throwing   D. prevents

31 _____ this _____, ginger can be _____ for your _____.
A. stomach   B. reason   C. good   D. for

32 Isn't it _____ that some foods _____ the body parts _____ they are _____ for?
A. mirror   B. amazing   C. good   D. that

33 Interestingly, there are _____ _____ _____ _____.
A. other   B. many   C. foods   D. such

34 Find _____ _____ as you can and _____ to eat a _____ of them.
A. variety   B. many   C. try   D. as

18 호두는 또한 알츠하이머병을 예방하는 데도 좋다.

19 썰어 놓은 당근의 모양은 사람의 눈과 비슷해 보인다.

20 당근에는 비타민 A를 만들 수 있는 화학 성분이 있는데, 그것이 시력을 개선한다.

21 비타민 A는 눈이 빛을 처리하여 뇌에 선명한 이미지를 보낼 수 있도록 돕는다.

22 그러므로 건강한 눈을 원한다면, 당근을 먹어라.

23 양파를 써는 것은 즐겁지 않은데 왜냐하면 그것이 당신을 울게 만들기 때문이다.

24 그렇지만 어쨌든 하나를 잘라보아라.

25 당신은 양파의 내부가 약간 인간의 세포처럼 보인다는 것을 알 수 있다.

26 과학자들은 양파가 비타민 B를 함유하는데, 이 비타민 B가 새롭고 건강한 세포를 만드는 데 도움이 된다고 주장한다.

27 이제 생강으로 넘어가 보자.

28 생강을 보면 몸의 어떤 부위가 생각나는가?

29 생강이 마치 위장처럼 생기지 않았는가?

30 당신은 어쩌면 생강의 강한 맛과 냄새를 좋아하지 않을지도 모르지만, 이러한 맛과 냄새는 복통과 구토를 예방하는 생강의 특별한 성분에서 나온다.

31 이러한 이유로 생강은 당신의 위장에 좋을 수 있다.

32 어떤 음식이 그 음식이 유익한 신체 부위의 생김새를 반영하고 있다는 점이 놀랍지 않은가?

33 흥미롭게도 그러한 음식은 상당히 많다.

34 가능한 한 그러한 음식을 많이 찾아서 다양한 음식을 먹도록 하라.

※ 다음 우리말과 일치하도록 빈칸에 알맞은 말을 쓰시오.

1 _____ Foods for Our _____

2 We all know _____ a diet _____ a _____ of foods _____ our bodies _____.

3 But sometimes we are not sure which foods _____ _____ _____ which _____ _____.

4 Nature, _____, gives us _____ _____ _____.

5 _____ _____ the _____ examples.

6 _____ _____ these foods _____ _____ looks like a certain body part _____ is _____ good for that body part.

7 _____ open a tomato and _____ it _____ the human heart.

8 You will see _____ they _____ _____.

9 They both have _____ _____ and _____ _____.

10 Researchers say _____ the chemicals _____ make tomatoes red _____ good for your _____ and _____.

11 _____ _____, eating tomatoes can _____ your risk of _____ _____.

12 Look at _____ _____ of a _____.

13 Do you _____ _____?

14 Yes, it's very _____ _____ the _____ of the human brain!

15 A walnut _____ _____ _____ two parts, just _____ the brain.

16 Walnuts also have _____, _____ the brain has too.

17 Studies show that walnuts help our brains _____ _____ and _____.

1 우리 몸에 이로운 음식

2 우리는 다양한 음식을 포함하는 식사가 우리의 몸을 건강하게 유지해 준다는 것을 알고 있다.

3 그러나 때때로 우리는 어떤 음식이 어떤 신체 부위에 좋은지 잘 모를 때가 있다.

4 하지만 자연은 우리에게 확실한 단서를 제시해 준다.

5 다음의 예들을 살펴보자.

6 각각의 이 음식들은 우리 신체의 특정 부분과 비슷해 보일 뿐만 아니라 그 신체 부위에도 좋다.

7 토마토 한 개를 잘라내서 그것을 사람의 심장과 비교해 보자.

8 당신은 그 둘이 비슷해 보인다는 것을 알게 될 것이다.

9 둘 다 여러 개의 빈 공간이 있고 붉은 색이다.

10 연구원들은 토마토를 붉게 만드는 화학 물질이 사람의 심장과 피에 유익하다고 한다.

11 게다가, 토마토를 먹는 것이 심장병에 걸릴 위험성을 낮출 수 있다.

12 호두의 모양을 살펴보자.

13 뭔가를 알아차릴 수 있는가?

14 그렇다, 호두의 모양은 인간의 뇌 형태와 매우 유사하다!

15 호두는 마치 인간의 뇌처럼 두 부분으로 나뉜다.

16 호두에는 또한 주름이 있는데, 이는 인간의 뇌에도 있는 것이다.

17 연구 결과는 호두가 사람의 뇌가 건강하고 활동적인 상태를 유지하는 데 도움을 준다는 것을 보여준다.

18 They are also good for _____ Alzheimer's _____.

19 _____ _____ _____ _____ looks like the human eye.

20 Carrots have some chemicals _____ can make vitamin A, _____ _____ your _____.

21 It _____ your eyes _____ light and _____ a clear image _____ the brain.

22 So _____ you want _____ _____, eat carrots.

23 _____ _____ is not fun _____ it _____ _____ _____ _____.

24 But _____ _____ one _____.

25 You can see that the inside _____ _____ _____ _____ a _____ _____.

26 Scientists say that onions _____ vitamin B, _____ _____ _____ new, healthy cells.

27 Now, let's _____ _____ _____ _____.

28 What body part _____ _____ _____ when you see it?

29 _____ it _____ _____ a stomach?

30 You may not like ginger's _____ _____ or smell, but these _____ _____ a special chemical that _____ you _____ _____ sick and _____ _____.

31 _____ _____ _____, ginger can _____ _____ _____ your stomach.

32 _____ it amazing that some foods _____ the body parts _____ they are good for?

33 Interestingly, there are _____ _____ _____ _____.

34 Find _____ _____ _____ _____ _____ and try to eat _____ _____ _____ them.

18 호두는 또한 알츠하이머병을 예방하는 데도 좋다.

19 썰어 놓은 당근의 모양은 사람의 눈과 비슷해 보인다.

20 당근에는 비타민 A를 만들 수 있는 화학 성분이 있는데, 그것이 시력을 개선한다.

21 비타민 A는 눈이 빛을 처리하여 뇌에 선명한 이미지를 보낼 수 있도록 돕는다.

22 그러므로 건강한 눈을 원한다면, 당근을 먹어라.

23 양파를 써는 것은 즐겁지 않은데 왜냐하면 그것이 당신을 울게 만들기 때문이다.

24 그렇지만 어쨌든 하나를 잘라 보아라.

25 당신은 양파의 내부가 약간 인간의 세포처럼 보인다는 것을 알 수 있다.

26 과학자들은 양파가 비타민 B를 함유하는데, 이 비타민 B가 새롭고 건강한 세포를 만드는 데 도움이 된다고 주장한다.

27 이제 생강으로 넘어가 보자.

28 생강을 보면 몸의 어떤 부위가 생각나는가?

29 생강이 마치 위장처럼 생기지 않았는가?

30 당신은 어쩌면 생강의 강한 맛과 냄새를 좋아하지 않을지도 모르지만, 이러한 맛과 냄새는 복통과 구토를 예방하는 생강의 특별한 성분에서 나온다.

31 이러한 이유로 생강은 당신의 위장에 좋을 수 있다.

32 어떤 음식이 그 음식이 유익한 신체 부위의 생김새를 반영하고 있다는 점이 놀랍지 않은가?

33 흥미롭게도 그러한 음식은 상당히 많다.

34 가능한 한 그러한 음식을 많이 찾아서 다양한 음식을 먹도록 하라.

※ 다음 문장을 우리말로 쓰시오.

1 Beneficial Foods for Our Bodies
➡ _____

2 We all know that a diet containing a variety of foods keeps our bodies healthy.
➡ _____

3 But sometimes we are not sure which foods are good for which body parts.
➡ _____

4 Nature, however, gives us a big clue.
➡ _____

5 Look at the following examples.
➡ _____

6 Each of these foods not only looks like a certain body part but is also good for that body part.
➡ _____

7 Slice open a tomato and compare it with the human heart.
➡ _____

8 You will see that they look similar.
➡ _____

9 They both have multiple hollow spaces and are red.
➡ _____

10 Researchers say that the chemicals that make tomatoes red are good for your heart and blood.
➡ _____

11 In addition, eating tomatoes can lower your risk of heart disease.
➡ _____

12 Look at the shape of a walnut.
➡ _____

13 Do you notice anything?
➡ _____

14 Yes, it's very similar to the shape of the human brain!
➡ _____

15 A walnut is divided into two parts, just like the brain.
➡ _____

16 Walnuts also have wrinkles, which the brain has too.
➡ _____

17 Studies show that walnuts help our brains stay healthy and active.
➡ _____

18 They are also good for preventing Alzheimer's disease.

➡ _____

19 A slice of carrot looks like the human eye.

➡ _____

20 Carrots have some chemicals that can make vitamin A, which improves your vision.

➡ _____

21 It helps your eyes process light and send a clear image to the brain.

➡ _____

22 So if you want healthy eyes, eat carrots.

➡ _____

23 Cutting onions is not fun because it makes you cry.

➡ _____

24 But try slicing one anyway.

➡ _____

25 You can see that the inside looks a little like a human cell.

➡ _____

26 Scientists say that onions contain vitamin B, which helps make new, healthy cells.

➡ _____

27 Now, let's move on to ginger.

➡ _____

28 What body part comes to mind when you see it?

➡ _____

29 Doesn't it look like a stomach?

➡ _____

30 You may not like ginger's strong taste or smell, but these come from a special chemical that prevents you from feeling sick and throwing up.

➡ _____

_____

31 For this reason, ginger can be good for your stomach.

➡ _____

32 Isn't it amazing that some foods mirror the body parts that they are good for?

➡ _____

33 Interestingly, there are many other such foods.

➡ _____

34 Find as many as you can and try to eat a variety of them.

➡ _____

※ 다음 괄호 안의 단어들을 우리말에 맞도록 바르게 배열하시오.

1 (Foods / Beneficial / Our / for / Bodies)
➡ _____

2 (all / we / that / know / diet / a / containing / variety / a / foods / of / keeps / bodies / our / healthy.)
➡ _____

3 (sometimes / but / are / we / sure / not / foods / which / are / for / good / body / which / parts.)
➡ _____

4 (however, / nature, / us / gives / big / clue. / a)
➡ _____

5 (at / look / the / examples. / following)
➡ _____

6 (of / each / foods / these / only / not / like / looks / certain / a / body / but / part / also / is / good / that / for / part. / body)
➡ _____

7 (open / slice / tomato / a / and / it / compare / the / with / heart. / human)
➡ _____

8 (will / you / that / see / they / similar. / look)
➡ _____

9 (both / they / multiple / have / spaces / hollow / and / red. / are)
➡ _____

10 (say / researchers / that / chemicals / the / that / tomatoes / make / are / red / for / good / heart / your / blood. / and)
➡ _____

11 (addition, / in / tomatoes / eating / lower / can / risk / your / heart / of / disease.)
➡ _____

12 (at / look / shape / the / of / walnut. / a)
➡ _____

13 (you / do / anything? / notice)
➡ _____

14 (yes, / very / it's / to / similar / the / of / shape / the / brain! / human)
➡ _____

15 (walnut / a / divided / is / two / into / parts, / like / just / brain. / the)
➡ _____

16 (also / walnuts / wrinkles, / have / the / which / has / brain / too.)
➡ _____

17 (show / studies / that / help / walnuts / brains / our / healthy / stay / active. / and)
➡ _____

1 우리 몸에 이로운 음식

2 우리는 다양한 음식을 포함하는 식사가 우리의 몸을 건강하게 유지해 준다는 것을 알고 있다.

3 그러나 때때로 우리는 어떤 음식이 어떤 신체 부위에 좋은지 잘 모를 때가 있다.

4 하지만 자연은 우리에게 확실한 단서를 제시해 준다.

5 다음의 예들을 살펴보자.

6 각각의 이 음식들은 우리 신체의 특정 부분과 비슷해 보일 뿐만 아니라 그 신체 부위에도 좋다.

7 토마토 한 개를 잘라내서 그것을 사람의 심장과 비교해 보자.

8 당신은 그 둘이 비슷해 보인다는 것을 알게 될 것이다.

9 둘 다 여러 개의 빈 공간이 있고 붉은 색이다.

10 연구원들은 토마토를 붉게 만드는 화학 물질이 사람의 심장과 피에 유익하다고 한다.

11 게다가, 토마토를 먹는 것이 심장병에 걸릴 위험성을 낮출 수 있다.

12 호두의 모양을 살펴보자.

13 뭔가를 알아차릴 수 있는가?

14 그렇다. 호두의 모양은 인간의 뇌 형태와 매우 유사하다!

15 호두는 마치 인간의 뇌처럼 두 부분으로 나뉜다.

16 호두에는 또한 주름이 있는데, 이는 인간의 뇌에도 있는 것이다.

17 연구 결과는 호두가 사람의 뇌가 건강하고 활동적인 상태를 유지하는 데 도움을 준다는 것을 보여준다.

18 (are / they / good / also / preventing / for / disease. / Alzheimer's)
➡ _____

19 (slice / a / carrot / of / like / looks / human / eye. / the)
➡ _____

20 (have / carrots / chemicals / some / can / that / vitamin / make / A, / improves / which / vision. / your)
➡ _____

21 (helps / it / eyes / your / light / process / and / a / send / image / clear / to / brain. / the)
➡ _____

22 (if / so / want / you / eyes, / healthy / carrots. / eat)
➡ _____

23 (onions / cutting / not / is / because / fun / makes / it / cry. / you)
➡ _____

24 (try / but / one / slicing / anyway.)
➡ _____

25 (can / you / see / the / that / looks / inside / like / little / a / cell. / human / a)
➡ _____

26 (say / scientists / onions / that / vitamin / contain / B, / helps / which / new, / make / cells. / healthy)
➡ _____

27 (let's / now / on / move / ginger. / to)
➡ _____

28 (body / what / comes / part / mind / to / you / when / it? / see)
➡ _____

29 (it / doesn't / like / look / stomach? / a)
➡ _____

30 (may / you / like / not / strong / ginger's / taste / smell, / or / but / come / these / from / special / a / chemical / prevents / that / from / you / feeling / and / sick / up. / throwing)
➡ _____

31 (this / for / reason, / can / ginger / be / for / good / stomach. / your)
➡ _____

32 (it / isn't / that / amazing / foods / some / mirror / body / the / parts / they / that / good / for? / are)
➡ _____

33 (there / interestingly / many / are / other / foods. / such)
➡ _____

34 (as / find / many / you / as / can / try / and / eat / to / a / of / them. / variety)
➡ _____

※ 다음 우리말을 영어로 쓰시오.

1 우리 몸에 이로운 음식

➡ _____

2 우리는 다양한 음식을 포함하는 식사가 우리의 몸을 건강하게 유지해 준다는 것을 알고 있다.

➡ _____

3 그러나 때때로 우리는 어떤 음식이 어떤 신체 부위에 좋은지 잘 모를 때가 있다.

➡ _____

4 하지만 자연은 우리에게 확실한 단서를 제시해 준다.

➡ _____

5 다음의 예들을 살펴보자.

➡ _____

6 각각의 이 음식들은 우리 신체의 특정 부분과 비슷해 보일 뿐만 아니라 그 신체 부위에도 좋다.

➡ _____

7 토마토 한 개를 잘라내서 그것을 사람의 심장과 비교해 보자.

➡ _____

8 당신은 그 둘이 비슷해 보인다는 것을 알게 될 것이다.

➡ _____

9 둘 다 여러 개의 빈 공간이 있고 붉은 색이다.

➡ _____

10 연구원들은 토마토를 붉게 만드는 화학 물질이 사람의 심장과 피에 유익하다고 한다.

➡ _____

11 게다가, 토마토를 먹는 것이 심장병에 걸릴 위험성을 낮출 수 있다.

➡ _____

12 호두의 모양을 살펴보자.

➡ _____

13 뭔가를 알아차릴 수 있는가?

➡ _____

14 그렇다, 호두의 모양은 인간의 뇌 형태와 매우 유사하다!

➡ _____

15 호두는 마치 인간의 뇌처럼 두 부분으로 나뉜다.

➡ _____

16 호두에는 또한 주름이 있는데, 이는 인간의 뇌에도 있는 것이다.

➡ _____

17 연구 결과는 호두가 사람의 뇌가 건강하고 활동적인 상태를 유지하는 데 도움을 준다는 것을 보여준다.

➡ _____

18 호두는 또한 알츠하이머병을 예방하는 데도 좋다.

➡ _____

19 썰어 놓은 당근의 모양은 사람의 눈과 비슷해 보인다.

➡ _____

20 당근에는 비타민 A를 만들 수 있는 화학 성분이 있는데, 그것이 시력을 개선한다.

➡ _____

21 비타민 A는 눈이 빛을 처리하여 뇌에 선명한 이미지를 보낼 수 있도록 돕는다.

➡ _____

22 그러므로 건강한 눈을 원한다면, 당근을 먹어라.

➡ _____

23 양파를 써는 것은 즐겁지 않은데 왜냐하면 그것이 당신을 울게 만들기 때문이다.

➡ _____

24 그렇지만 어쨌든 하나를 잘라 보아라.

➡ _____

25 당신은 양파의 내부가 약간 인간의 세포처럼 보인다는 것을 알 수 있다.

➡ _____

26 과학자들은 양파가 비타민 B를 함유하는데, 이 비타민 B가 새롭고 건강한 세포를 만들어 내는 데 도움이 된다고 주장한다.

➡ _____

27 이제 생강으로 넘어가 보자.

➡ _____

28 생강을 보면 몸의 어떤 부위가 생각나는가?

➡ _____

29 생강이 마치 위장처럼 생기지 않았는가?

➡ _____

30 당신은 어쩌면 생강의 강한 맛과 냄새를 좋아하지 않을지도 모르지만, 이러한 맛과 냄새는 복통과 구토를 예방하는 생강의 특별한 성분에서 나온다.

➡ _____

➡ _____

31 이러한 이유로 생강은 당신의 위장에 좋을 수 있다.

➡ _____

32 어떤 음식이 그 음식이 유익한 신체 부위의 생김새를 반영하고 있다는 점이 놀랍지 않은가?

➡ _____

33 흥미롭게도 그러한 음식은 상당히 많다.

➡ _____

34 가능한 한 그러한 음식을 많이 찾아서 다양한 음식을 먹도록 하라.

➡ _____

※ 다음 우리말과 일치하도록 빈칸에 알맞은 말을 쓰시오.

Presentation Time

1. _____ you _____ that swimming _____ _____ _____ your back?

2. Our group _____ _____ _____ _____ swimming together _____ _____ and _____ at World Sports Park.

3. We are _____ it will _____ _____ _____ _____.

1. 수영을 하는 것이 허리에 좋다는 말을 들어본 적이 있니?
2. 우리 모둠은 매주 화요일과 목요일에 World Sports Park에 함께 수영을 가기로 계획을 세웠어.
3. 우리는 그것이 우리가 건강하게 지내는 데 도움이 될 것이라고 확신하고 있어.

Wrap Up READING

1. Eat Chicken Sandwiches, _____ _____

2. A chicken sandwich is a _____ _____ _____ I _____.

3. I'd _____ _____ _____ _____ some of its ingredients that _____ _____ _____ our health.

4. First, chicken breast is meat _____ a lot of _____ and _____ _____.

5. Onions _____ _____ _____ vitamin B.

6. Also, walnuts _____ _____ _____ _____ _____.

7. So _____ _____ _____ _____ a chicken sandwich this weekend?

1. 치킨 샌드위치를 먹고 더 건강해 지세요
2. 치킨 샌드위치는 제가 추천하는 건강에 좋은 음식입니다.
3. 저는 건강에 좋은 그것의 재료 몇 가지에 대해 이야기하고 싶습니다.
4. 먼저 닭 가슴살은 많은 단백질을 가지고 있고 지방은 거의 없는 고기입니다.
5. 양파는 비타민 B를 많이 포함하고 있습니다.
6. 또한, 호두는 뇌에 좋습니다.
7. 그러니, 이번 주말에 치킨 샌드위치를 드시는 것이 어떠세요?

Culture Link

1. Yoga _____ _____

2. Indian people _____ yoga _____ _____ _____ their minds, bodies, _____, and _____.

3. They use it _____ _____ themselves _____ _____ _____ _____.

1. 인도의 요가
2. 인도 사람들은 그들의 마음, 신체, 생각과 감정을 더 잘 이해하기 위해 요가를 한다.
3. 그들은 자신들을 더 건강한 삶으로 인도하기 위해 그것을 사용한다.

※ 다음 우리말을 영어로 쓰시오.

Presentation Time

1. 수영을 하는 것이 허리에 좋다는 말을 들어본 적이 있니?
➡ _____

2. 우리 모둠은 매주 화요일과 목요일에 World Sports Park에 함께 수영을 가기로 계획을 세웠어.
➡ _____

3. 우리는 그것이 우리가 건강하게 지내는 데 도움이 될 것이라고 확신하고 있어.
➡ _____

Wrap Up READING

1. 치킨 샌드위치를 먹고 더 건강해 지세요
➡ _____

2. 치킨 샌드위치는 제가 추천하는 건강에 좋은 음식입니다.
➡ _____

3. 저는 건강에 좋은 그것의 재료 몇 가지에 대해 이야기하고 싶습니다.
➡ _____

4. 먼저 닭 가슴살은 많은 단백질을 가지고 있고 지방은 거의 없는 고기입니다.
➡ _____

5. 양파는 비타민 B를 많이 포함하고 있습니다.
➡ _____

6. 또한, 호두는 뇌에 좋습니다.
➡ _____

7. 그러니, 이번 주말에 치킨 샌드위치를 드시는 것이 어떠세요?
➡ _____

Culture Link

1. 인도의 요가
➡ _____

2. 인도 사람들은 그들의 마음, 신체, 생각과 감정을 더 잘 이해하기 위해 요가를 한다.
➡ _____

3. 그들은 자신들을 더 건강한 삶으로 인도하기 위해 그것을 사용한다.
➡ _____

※ 다음 영어를 우리말로 쓰시오.

01	recently	
02	aware	
03	cause	
04	panic	
05	collapse	
06	smash	
07	damage	
08	exit	
09	avoid	
10	serious	
11	wildfire	
12	worse	
13	properly	
14	common	
15	affect	
16	nervously	
17	missing	
18	earthquake	
19	exactly	
20	destroy	
21	heavy rain	

22	whole	
23	crawl	
24	flood	
25	immediately	
26	include	
27	natural disaster	
28	mention	
29	tap	
30	confusion	
31	urgently	
32	occur	
33	reaction	
34	violently	
35	based on~	
36	as well	
37	get a discount	
38	a variety of	
39	in case of ~	
40	a large number of	
41	tip over	
42	pull over	
43	break into pieces	

※ 다음 우리말을 영어로 쓰시오.

01 격렬하게 _____

02 초래하다 _____

03 반응 _____

04 혼란, 혼동 _____

05 더 나쁜 _____

06 제대로, 적절하게 _____

07 최근에 _____

08 파괴하다 _____

09 흔한 _____

10 손상 _____

11 실종된 _____

12 가슴 _____

13 붕괴되다, 무너지다 _____

14 불안하게 _____

15 재난 _____

16 홍수 _____

17 지진 _____

18 (일·사건 등이) 발생하다 _____

19 기어가다 _____

20 세게 부딪치다 _____

21 폭염 _____

22 극심한 공포 _____

23 정확하게 _____

24 포함하다 _____

25 특수 효과 _____

26 갑자기 _____

27 나가다, 퇴장하다 _____

28 영향을 주다 _____

29 두들기다 _____

30 긴급하게 _____

31 즉시 _____

32 실제로 _____

33 폭우 _____

34 심각한 _____

35 길 한쪽으로 차를 대다 _____

36 ~의 한 가운데 _____

37 다양한 _____

38 넘어지다, 기울어지다 _____

39 ~의 경우에 _____

40 ~에 바탕을 둔 _____

41 매우 많은 _____

42 집어넣다 _____

43 굴러 떨어지다 _____

※ 다음 영영풀이에 알맞은 단어를 <보기>에서 골라 쓴 후, 우리말 뜻을 쓰시오.

1 _____ : to leave a place: _____

2 _____ : wanting to know about something: _____

3 _____ : correctly, or in a way that is considered right: _____

4 _____ : happening often and to many people or in many places: _____

5 _____ : to hit something violently and very hard: _____

6 _____ : to break apart and fall down suddenly: _____

7 _____ : a fire that moves quickly and cannot be controlled: _____

8 _____ : to make something happen, especially something bad: _____

9 _____ : a very large amount of water that covers an area that is usually dry: _____

10 _____ : to make someone or something part of a larger group: _____

11 _____ : a sudden shaking of the Earth's surface that often causes a lot of damage: _____

12 _____ : to move along on your hands and knees with your body close to the ground: _____

13 _____ : to move backward or forward or from side to side while hanging from a fixed point: _____

14 _____ : to do an action or activity that usually requires training or skill: _____

15 _____ : to damage something so badly that it no longer exists or cannot be used or repaired: _____

16 _____ : a sudden event such as a flood, storm, or accident which causes great damage or suffering: _____

보기

smash	earthquake	properly	exit
cause	include	collapse	wildfire
destroy	common	crawl	disaster
perform	curious	flood	swing

대화문 Test

※ 다음 우리말과 일치하도록 빈칸에 알맞은 말을 쓰시오.

Listen & Talk 1 A

B: There _____ a big _____ in Europe. Did you _____ _____ it?

G: No, I didn't. But _____ aren't that _____ in winter, _____ they? I'm _____ about _____ that _____.

B: Me too. _____ do some online _____.

Listen & Talk 1 B

G: There _____ _____ _____ many _____ _____ in Korea _____ _____.

B: I agree. There was an _____ in the _____ last week. Also a _____ is coming this week.

G: I'm _____ about _____ _____ _____ _____ _____ causes the _____ _____ in Korea.

B: Actually I read a _____ yesterday about the _____ from _____ _____ of _____ _____. Number one is _____.

G: I see. I _____ earthquakes are _____.

B: No, second is _____ rain, and third is _____ _____.

G: _____ about earthquakes?

B: _____ _____ the report, _____ are fourth. But the _____ from earthquakes has _____ _____ recently _____ they have _____ _____ more often in Korea.

G: I see. It _____ _____ we have to be _____ for a _____ of _____ _____ in Korea.

Listen & Talk 1 C

B: Hey, did you _____ _____ the big _____ in California?

G: No, I didn't. _____ _____ are they?

B: They've _____ a large _____ _____ _____ and _____ _____.

G: _____ the fires still _____ _____?

B: Yes, _____ the wind has made the fires _____. I hope all the people _____ _____ are okay.

G: _____ _____ I. I'm _____ _____ how many people had to _____ their homes.

B: _____ _____ _____ 20,000 people had to _____ their _____, and about 400 people are _____ in that area.

G: That's _____. I hope they're _____ _____.

B: 유럽에 큰 홍수가 있었어. 그것에 대해 들었니?
G: 아니. 하지만 겨울에는 홍수가 그렇게 흔하지 않아, 그렇지 않니? 나는 어떻게 그런 일이 일어났는지 궁금해.
B: 나도 그래. 온라인 검색을 해보자.

G: 요즈음 한국에서 많은 자연 재해가 있는 것 같아.
B: 동의해. 지난주에 남부에서 지진이 있었어. 또한 이번 주에는 태풍이 올 거야.
G: 나는 어떤 종류의 자연 재해가 한국에서 가장 큰 피해를 주는지 궁금해.
B: 사실 나는 어제 각 유형의 자연 재해로 인한 피해에 관한 보고서를 읽었어. 첫 번째가 폭풍이야.
G: 그렇구나. 지진이 두 번째인 것 같아.
B: 아니야. 두 번째는 폭우이고 세 번째는 폭설이야.
G: 지진은?
B: 보고서에 따르면, 지진은 네 번째야. 하지만 최근 한국에서 지진이 더 자주 일어나기 때문에 지진으로 인한 피해가 증가하고 있어.
G: 그렇구나. 한국에서는 다양한 자연 재해에 대비를 해야 할 것 같아.

B: 안녕. 너 캘리포니아에서 일어난 큰 화재에 대해 들었니?
G: 아니. 얼마나 심각하니?
B: 많은 집들과 다른 건물들을 파괴했어.
G: 아직도 화재가 진행되고 있니?
B: 그래. 사실 바람이 화재를 더 악화시켰어. 나는 거기 사는 모든 사람들이 괜찮기를 바라.
G: 나도 그래. 얼마나 많은 사람들이 집을 떠나야 했는지 궁금해.
B: 사실 2만 명 이상이 집을 떠나야 했고, 약 400명이 실종되었어.
G: 끔찍하구나. 나는 그들이 안전한 곳에 있기를 바라.

Listen & Talk 2 A

B: Mom, _____ _____ do we _____ _____ _____ _____
the _____ _____ _____ _____?

W: Well, we need _____, some food, and _____.

B: _____ _____, Mom?

W: Oh, _____ _____ that you _____ _____ for the _____.

Listen & Talk 2 B

W: _____ CPR _____ can _____ someone's life. _____ are the _____ for _____ CPR. First, check that the person _____ help. _____ the person and shout, "_____ you okay?" If there's no _____, call 119 for help. Second, _____, look, and _____ _____ _____. If the person's not _____, begin CPR. Make _____ you _____ your _____ _____ the middle of the person's _____. Use your body _____ to press _____ on the chest. After 30 presses, give the person two _____. _____ _____ CPR _____ _____ _____.

Listen & Talk 2 D

A: _____ _____ _____ a fire, _____ should I _____?

B: _____ _____ that you _____ your mouth with a _____ _____.

A: Anything _____?

B: _____ _____ _____ you _____ the building _____.

Do It Yourself A

G: Did you _____ that earthquakes are _____ more _____ in Korea than _____?

B: Oh, _____? I've _____ _____ an earthquake in Korea.

G: They _____ _____ in the _____ part of Korea, but now they are occurring in _____ _____ _____ _____.

B: I didn't know that. I'm _____ about _____ earthquakes have _____ so often in Korea _____.

G: _____ _____ we do some _____ to find out?

B: Sounds good, but where _____ we look first?

G: _____ _____ _____ our science teacher first? I think she can _____ us.

B: Okay. _____ go and _____ her.

※ 다음 우리말에 맞도록 대화를 영어로 쓰시오.

해석

Listen & Talk 1 A

B: _____

G: _____

_____

B: _____

B: 유럽에 큰 홍수가 있었어. 그것에 대해 들었니?

G: 아니. 하지만 겨울에는 홍수가 그렇게 흔하지 않아, 그렇지 않니? 나는 어떻게 그런 일이 일어났는지 궁금해.

B: 나도 그래. 온라인 검색을 해보자.

Listen & Talk 1 B

G: _____

B: _____

_____

G: _____

_____

B: _____

G: _____

B: _____

G: _____

B: _____

_____

G: _____

_____

G: 요즈음 한국에서 많은 자연 재해가 있는 것 같아.

B: 동의해. 지난주에 남부에서 지진이 있었어. 또한 이번 주에는 태풍이 올 거야.

G: 나는 어떤 종류의 자연 재해가 한국에서 가장 큰 피해를 주는지 궁금해.

B: 사실 나는 어제 각 유형의 자연 재해로 인한 피해에 관한 보고서를 읽었어. 첫 번째가 폭풍이야.

G: 그렇구나. 지진이 두 번째인 것 같아.

B: 아니야. 두 번째는 폭우이고 세 번째는 폭설이야.

G: 지진은?

B: 보고서에 따르면, 지진은 네 번째야. 하지만 최근 한국에서 지진이 더 자주 일어나기 때문에 지진으로 인한 피해가 증가하고 있어.

G: 그렇구나. 한국에서는 다양한 자연 재해에 대비를 해야 할 것 같아.

Listen & Talk 1 C

B: _____

G: _____

B: _____

G: _____

B: _____

_____

G: _____

B: _____

_____

G: _____

B: 안녕. 너 캘리포니아에서 일어난 큰 화재에 대해 들었니?

G: 아니. 얼마나 심각하니?

B: 많은 집들과 다른 건물들을 파괴했어.

G: 아직도 화재가 진행되고 있니?

B: 그래. 사실 바람이 화재를 더 악화시켰어. 나는 거기 사는 모든 사람들이 괜찮기를 바라.

G: 나도 그래. 얼마나 많은 사람들이 집을 떠나야 했는지 궁금해.

B: 사실 2만 명 이상이 집을 떠나야 했고, 약 400명이 실종되었어.

G: 끔찍하구나. 나는 그들이 안전한 곳에 있기를 바라.

Listen & Talk 2 A

B: _____

W: _____

B: _____

W: _____

Listen & Talk 2 B

W: _____

_____

_____

_____

_____

_____

Listen & Talk 2 D

A: _____

B: _____

A: _____

B: _____

Do It Yourself A

G: _____

B: _____

G: _____

_____

B: _____

_____

G: _____

B: _____

G: _____

B: _____

B: 엄마, 자연 재해 생존 장비에 무엇을 더 넣어야 할까요?

W: 글쎄. 우리는 물, 약간의 식량 그리고 라디오가 필요해.

B: 다른 것은요, 엄마?

W: 오, 라디오 건전지를 반드시 포함하도록 해.

W: 제대로 심폐소생술을 수행하는 것은 누군가의 생명을 구할 수 있습니다. 여기 적절한 심폐소생술을 위한 단계가 있습니다. 첫째, 그 사람이 도움을 필요로 하는지 확인하십시오. 그 사람을 두드리며 "괜찮으세요?"라고 큰소리로 외치세요. 반응이 없으면 119에 전화를 걸어 도움을 요청하세요. 둘째, 호흡을 하는지 듣고, 보고, 느끼세요. 그 사람이 숨을 쉬지 않으면 심폐소생술을 시작하세요. 손을 반드시 그 사람의 가슴 가운데에 놓도록 하세요. 가슴을 더 세게 누르기 위해 체중을 이용하세요. 30번 누른 후, 그 사람에게 두 번 바람을 불어 넣으시오. 도움이 올 때까지 심폐소생술을 계속하세요.

A: 화재가 발생하면 어떻게 해야 하나요?

B: 반드시 젖은 천으로 입을 가리도록 해.

A: 다른 것은 뭐가 있을까요?

B: 즉시 건물 밖으로 나가도록 해야 해.

G: 한국에서 지진이 전보다 자주 일어나고 있다는 말을 들었니?

B: 오, 정말? 나는 한국에서 지진을 느껴본 적이 없어.

G: 보통 지진이 한국의 남부에서 발생하지만, 이제는 다른 지역에서도 발생하고 있어.

B: 그건 몰랐어. 나는 왜 최근에 한국에서 지진이 그렇게 자주 발생하는지 궁금해.

G: 알아내기 위해 조사를 해보는 게 어떨까?

B: 좋은 것 같아. 하지만 먼저 어디에서 찾아야 하지?

G: 먼저 과학 선생님께 여쭤보면 어떨까? 나는 선생님께서 우리를 도울 수 있을 거라고 생각해.

B: 알았어. 가서 선생님을 찾아보자.

※ 다음 우리말과 일치하도록 빈칸에 알맞은 것을 골라 쓰시오.

1 _____ _____ to an _____
  A. Up   B. Waking   C. Earthquake

2 One night _____ February, after I _____ _____ to bed, an earthquake _____ .
  A. hit   B. gone   C. in   D. had

3 I _____ _____ suddenly _____ my bed was _____ .
  A. because   B. up   C. shaking   D. woke

4 I _____ my brother was _____ my bed _____ a _____ .
  A. as   B. joke   C. shaking   D. thought

5 But then I _____ the mirror on my desk _____ to the floor and _____ into _____ .
  A. break   B. fall   C. pieces   D. heard

6 I knew it wasn't my brother then, but I still didn't know _____ _____ _____ _____ .
  A. exactly   B. what   C. happening   D. was

7 Soon the _____ room began to shake _____ , and my confusion _____ to _____ .
  A. violently   B. whole   C. panic   D. turned

8 My mom _____ that it was an _____ and _____ _____ my room.
  A. into   B. shouted   C. ran   D. earthquake

9 _____ it was my first time _____ an earthquake, I didn't know _____ to _____ .
  A. how   B. since   C. react   D. experiencing

10 I _____ _____ _____ , "What should I do?"
  A. saying   B. kept   C. just

11 My mom _____ me and my brother _____ _____ _____ .
  A. out   B. pulled   C. of   D. bed

12 We _____ to the kitchen and _____ _____ the table.
  A. crawled   B. ran   C. under

13 I could see the light _____ violently and books _____ to the _____ .
  A. falling   B. swinging   C. floor

1 지진에 눈을 뜨는 것

2 2월 어느 날 밤, 내가 잠자리에 든 후에 지진이 일어났다.

3 침대가 흔들렸기 때문에 나는 갑자기 잠에서 깼다.

4 나는 남동생이 장난으로 침대를 흔들고 있다고 생각했다.

5 하지만 그때 나는 내 책상 위에 있던 거울이 바닥으로 떨어져 산산조각이 나는 소리를 들었다.

6 그때 나는 남동생이 그런 것이 아니라는 것을 알았지만, 정확히 무슨 일이 일어나고 있었는지를 여전히 알지 못했다.

7 머지않아 방 전체가 심하게 흔들리기 시작했고 혼란스러움이 공포로 변했다.

8 엄마가 지진이라고 소리를 지르며 내 방으로 뛰어 들어왔다.

9 지진을 경험한 것이 처음이었기 때문에, 나는 어떻게 반응해야 할지 몰랐다.

10 나는 그저 "어떻게 해야 하지?"라는 말을 반복했다.

11 엄마는 나와 남동생을 침대 밖으로 잡아끌었다.

12 우리는 주방으로 달려가서 식탁 아래로 기어들어 갔다.

13 나는 전등이 심하게 흔들리는 것과 책이 바닥으로 떨어지는 것을 볼 수 있었다.

14 Our family picture _____ from the wall and the glass _____ it _____.

A. covering   B. dropped   C. broke

15 A cup _____ _____ and _____ _____ the kitchen table.

A. off   B. tipped   C. rolled   D. over

16 _____ _____, I could hear _____ _____ in the apartment break.

A. second   B. else   C. every   D. something

17 I started _____ _____ that the building would _____.

A. to   B. collapse   C. worry

18 Then the shaking _____ _____ _____.

A. to   B. seemed   C. stop

19 We started _____ _____ the _____.

A. door   B. toward   C. crawling

20 _____ that _____, my mom's cell phone _____.

A. moment   B. rang   C. at

21 It was my dad, who was _____ _____ _____ _____.

A. home   B. work   C. coming   D. from

22 He _____, "It _____!

A. stopped   B. shouted

23 _____ _____ _____ the building!

A. out   B. get   C. of

24 _____ the _____!

A. stairs   B. take

25 _____ _____ the elevator!

A. take   B. don't

26 Hurry!"

27 "_____ _____ you?

A. are   B. where

28 Are you _____?" my mom _____ _____.

A. urgently   B. okay   C. asked

29 My dad _____, "_____ _____.

A. worry   B. answered   C. don't

30 _____ _____.

A. okay   B. I'm

14 우리 가족 사진이 벽에서 떨어졌고 사진을 덮고 있던 유리가 깨졌다.

15 컵이 넘어지고 식탁에서 굴러 떨어졌다.

16 매 순간, 나는 아파트에 있는 다른 어떤 것들이 부서지는 소리를 들을 수 있었다.

17 나는 건물이 무너지지는 않을까 하는 걱정이 들기 시작했다.

18 그때 흔들림이 멈추는 것 같았다.

19 우리는 문으로 기어가기 시작했다.

20 그 순간, 엄마의 휴대 전화가 울렸다.

21 전화를 한 사람은 바로 아빠였는데, 직장에서 퇴근하던 중이었다.

22 아빠는 소리쳤다. "지진이 멈췄어요!

23 건물 밖으로 나와요!

24 계단을 이용해요!

25 엘리베이터를 타면 안 돼요!

26 서둘러요!"

27 "어디예요?

28 괜찮아요?"라고 엄마가 다급하게 물었다.

29 아빠가 대답했다. "걱정 말아요.

30 나는 괜찮아요.

31 I was _____ _____ when the _____ started.

   A. home   B. shaking   C. driving

32 But I _____ _____ _____.

   A. over   B. pulled   C. immediately

33 I'm listening to the radio _____ _____ to find out what's _____ _____."

   A. now   B. on   C. right   D. going

34 We nervously _____ our _____ the stairs and _____.

   A. way   B. outside   C. made   D. down

35 I _____ _____.

   A. around   B. looked

36 _____ of buildings had _____ and _____ _____ several cars.

   A. smashed   B. fallen   C. parts   D. had

37 We went to an _____ space to _____ more _____.

   A. falling   B. open   C. avoid   D. pieces

38 How _____ all this _____ _____ in a _____ minutes?

   A. few   B. have   C. happened   D. could

39 _____ I had done many earthquake _____ in school, I had never _____ I'd experience a _____ earthquake.

   A. real   B. drills   C. thought   D. although

40 I still _____ _____ when I _____ that night.

   A. scared   B. remember   C. get

41 I can't _____ the _____ I _____ when the furniture was shaking and things were _____ to the floor.

   A. falling   B. felt   C. panic   D. forget

42 After that night, I began to _____ earthquake _____ _____.

   A. drills   B. take   C. seriously

43 I _____ that I should be _____ for the next earthquake, which can _____ at any _____.

   A. occur   B. prepared   C. realized   D. time

31 진동이 시작할 때 운전해서 집으로 가던 중이었어요.

32 하지만 즉시 차를 길 한쪽에 댔어요.

33 무슨 일이 일어나는지 알기 위해 지금 라디오를 듣고 있어요."

34 우리는 초조한 마음으로 계단을 내려가서 밖으로 나갔다.

35 나는 주변을 둘러보았다.

36 건물의 일부분이 떨어져 나갔고 몇몇 차들은 박살이 났다.

37 우리는 추가적인 낙하물을 피하기 위해 공터로 갔다.

38 어떻게 이런 일이 몇 분 만에 일어날 수 있단 말인가?

39 비록 학교에서 많은 지진 대피 훈련을 해 왔지만, 내가 실제 지진을 겪으리라고는 전혀 생각해 보지 않았었다.

40 그날 밤을 기억하면 나는 여전히 두려워진다.

41 가구가 흔들리고 물건들이 바닥으로 떨어졌을 때 내가 느꼈던 공포심을 나는 잊을 수가 없다.

42 그날 밤 이후, 나는 지진 대피 훈련에 진지하게 임하기 시작했다.

43 나는 언제든 발생할 수 있는 다음 지진을 대비해야 한다는 것을 깨달았다.

※ 다음 우리말과 일치하도록 빈칸에 알맞은 말을 쓰시오.

1 _____ _____ to an _____

2 One night _____ February, after I _____ _____ _____ _____, an earthquake _____.

3 I woke up suddenly because my bed _____ _____.

4 I thought my brother _____ _____ my bed _____ _____ _____.

5 But then I _____ the mirror on my desk _____ _____ _____ _____ and _____ _____ _____.

6 I knew it wasn't my brother _____, but I _____ _____ know _____ _____ _____ _____.

7 Soon the whole room began _____ _____ _____, and my _____ _____ _____ _____.

8 My mom _____ _____ it was an earthquake and _____ _____ my room.

9 Since it was _____ _____ _____ _____ an earthquake, I didn't know _____ _____ _____.

10 I just _____ _____, "What should I do?"

11 My mom _____ me and my brother _____ _____ _____.

12 We _____ _____ the kitchen and _____ _____ the table.

13 I could _____ the light _____ _____ and books _____ _____ the floor.

1 지진에 눈을 뜨는 것

2 2월 어느 날 밤, 내가 잠자리에 든 후에 지진이 일어났다.

3 침대가 흔들렸기 때문에 나는 갑자기 잠에서 깼다.

4 나는 남동생이 장난으로 침대를 흔들고 있다고 생각했다.

5 하지만 그때 나는 내 책상 위에 있던 거울이 바닥으로 떨어져 산산조각이 나는 소리를 들었다.

6 그때 나는 남동생이 그런 것이 아니라는 것을 알았지만, 정확히 무슨 일이 일어나고 있었는지를 여전히 알지 못했다.

7 머지않아 방 전체가 심하게 흔들리기 시작했고 혼란스러움은 공포로 변했다.

8 엄마가 지진이라고 소리를 지르며 내 방으로 뛰어 들어왔다.

9 지진을 경험한 것이 처음이었기 때문에, 나는 어떻게 반응해야 할지 몰랐다.

10 나는 그저 "어떻게 해야 하지?"라는 말을 반복했다.

11 엄마는 나와 남동생을 침대 밖으로 잡아끌었다.

12 우리는 주방으로 달려가서 식탁 아래로 기어들어 갔다.

13 나는 전등이 심하게 흔들리는 것과 책이 바닥으로 떨어지는 것을 볼 수 있었다.

14 Our family picture _____ from the wall and the glass _____
_____ _____ .

15 A cup _____ _____ and _____ _____ the kitchen table.

16 _____ _____ , I could _____ something else in the apartment
_____ .

17 I started _____ _____ that the building would _____ .

18 Then the _____ _____ _____ _____ .

19 We started _____ _____ the door.

20 _____ _____ _____ , my mom's cell phone _____ .

21 It was my dad, who was _____ _____ _____ _____ .

22 He _____ , " _____ _____ !

23 _____ _____ _____ the building!

24 _____ the _____ !

25 _____ _____ the elevator!

26 _____ !"

27 " _____ are you?

28 Are you _____ ?" my mom _____ _____ .

29 My dad _____ , " _____ _____ .

30 I'm _____ .

14 우리 가족 사진이 벽에서 떨어
졌고 사진을 덮고 있던 유리가
깨졌다.

15 컵이 넘어지고 식탁에서 굴러
떨어졌다.

16 매 순간, 나는 아파트에 있는 다
른 어떤 것들이 부서지는 소리
를 들을 수 있었다.

17 나는 건물이 무너지지는 않을까
하는 걱정이 들기 시작했다.

18 그때 흔들림이 멈추는 것 같았다.

19 우리는 문으로 기어가기 시작했다.

20 그 순간, 엄마의 휴대 전화가 울
렸다.

21 전화를 한 사람은 바로 아빠였
는데, 직장에서 퇴근하던 중이
었다.

22 아빠는 소리쳤다. "지진이 멈췄
어요!

23 건물 밖으로 나와요!

24 계단을 이용해요!

25 엘리베이터를 타면 안 돼요!

26 서둘러요!"

27 "어디예요?

28 괜찮아요?"라고 엄마가 다급하
게 물었다.

29 아빠가 대답했다. "걱정 말아요.

30 나는 괜찮아요.

31 I _____ _____ _____ when the _____ started.

32 But I _____ _____ _____.

33 I'm listening to the radio _____ _____ to _____ _____ what's _____ _____."

34 We _____ _____ _____ _____ down the stairs and _____.

35 I _____ _____.

36 _____ _____ buildings _____ _____ and _____ _____ several cars.

37 We went to an open space _____ _____ more _____ _____.

38 How _____ all this _____ _____ in _____ _____ minutes?

39 _____ I had done many _____ _____ in school, I had never thought I'd _____ _____ _____ _____ _____.

40 I still _____ _____ when I _____ that night.

41 I _____ _____ _____ _____ _____ _____ when the furniture was shaking and things _____ _____ _____ the floor.

42 _____ that night, I began to _____ earthquake _____ _____.

43 I _____ that I should _____ _____ _____ the next earthquake, which can _____ _____ _____ _____.

31 진동이 시작할 때 운전해서 집으로 가던 중이었어요.

32 하지만 즉시 차를 길 한쪽에 댔어요.

33 무슨 일이 일어나는지 알기 위해 지금 라디오를 듣고 있어요."

34 우리는 초조한 마음으로 계단을 내려가서 밖으로 나갔다.

35 나는 주변을 둘러보았다.

36 건물의 일부분이 떨어져 나갔고 몇몇 차들은 박살이 났다.

37 우리는 추가적인 낙하물을 피하기 위해 공터로 갔다.

38 어떻게 이런 일이 몇 분 만에 일어날 수 있단 말인가?

39 비록 학교에서 많은 지진 대피 훈련을 해 왔지만, 내가 실제 지진을 겪으리라고는 전혀 생각해 보지 않았었다.

40 그날 밤을 기억하면 나는 여전히 두려워진다.

41 가구가 흔들리고 물건들이 바닥으로 떨어졌을 때 내가 느꼈던 공포심을 나는 잊을 수가 없다.

42 그날 밤 이후, 나는 지진 대피 훈련에 진지하게 임하기 시작했다.

43 나는 언제든 발생할 수 있는 다음 지진을 대비해야 한다는 것을 깨달았다.

※ 다음 문장을 우리말로 쓰시오.

1 Waking Up to an Earthquake

➡ _____

2 One night in February, after I had gone to bed, an earthquake hit.

➡ _____

3 I woke up suddenly because my bed was shaking.

➡ _____

4 I thought my brother was shaking my bed as a joke.

➡ _____

5 But then I heard the mirror on my desk fall to the floor and break into pieces.

➡ _____

6 I knew it wasn't my brother then, but I still didn't know what exactly was happening.

➡ _____

7 Soon the whole room began to shake violently, and my confusion turned to panic.

➡ _____

8 My mom shouted that it was an earthquake and ran into my room.

➡ _____

9 Since it was my first time experiencing an earthquake, I didn't know how to react.

➡ _____

10 I just kept saying, "What should I do?"

➡ _____

11 My mom pulled me and my brother out of bed.

➡ _____

12 We ran to the kitchen and crawled under the table.

➡ _____

13 I could see the light swinging violently and books falling to the floor.

➡ _____

14 Our family picture dropped from the wall and the glass covering it broke.

➡ _____

15 A cup tipped over and rolled off the kitchen table.

➡ _____

16 Every second, I could hear something else in the apartment break.

➡ _____

17 I started to worry that the building would collapse.

➡ _____

18 Then the shaking seemed to stop.

➡ _____

19 We started crawling toward the door.

➡ _____

20 At that moment, my mom's cell phone rang.

➡ _____

21 It was my dad, who was coming home from work.

➡ _____

22 He shouted, "It stopped!

➡ _____

23 Get out of the building!

➡ _____

24 Take the stairs!

➡ _____

25 Don't take the elevator!

➡ _____

26 Hurry!"

➡ _____

27 "Where are you?

➡ _____

28 Are you okay?" my mom asked urgently.

➡ _____

29 My dad answered, "Don't worry.

➡ _____

30 I'm okay.

➡ _____

31 I was driving home when the shaking started.

➡ _____

32 But I pulled over immediately.

➡ _____

33 I'm listening to the radio right now to find out what's going on."

➡ _____

34 We nervously made our way down the stairs and outside.

➡ _____

35 I looked around.

➡ _____

36 Parts of buildings had fallen and had smashed several cars.

➡ _____

37 We went to an open space to avoid more falling pieces.

➡ _____

38 How could all this have happened in a few minutes?

➡ _____

39 Although I had done many earthquake drills in school, I had never thought I'd experience
a real earthquake.

➡ _____

40 I still get scared when I remember that night.

➡ _____

41 I can't forget the panic I felt when the furniture was shaking and things were falling to the floor.

➡ _____

42 After that night, I began to take earthquake drills seriously.

➡ _____

43 I realized that I should be prepared for the next earthquake, which can occur at any time.

➡ _____

※ 다음 괄호 안의 단어들을 우리말에 맞도록 바르게 배열하시오.

1 (Up / Walking / to / Earthquake / an)

➡ _____

2 (night / one / February, / in / I / after / gone / had / bed, / to / an / hit. / earthquake)

➡ _____

3 (woke / I / up / because / suddenly / bed / my / shaking. / was)

➡ _____

4 (thought / I / brother / my / shaking / was / bed / my / a / as / joke.)

➡ _____

5 (then / but / heard / I / mirror / the / my / on / desk / to / fall / floor / the / and / into / pieces. / break)

➡ _____

6 (knew / I / wasn't / it / brother / my / then, / I / but / still / know / didn't / exactly / what / happening. / was)

➡ _____

7 (the / soon / whole / began / room / shake / to / violently, / and / confusion / my / to / turned / panic.)

➡ _____

8 (mom / my / that / shouted / was / it / earthquake / an / and / into / ran / room. / my)

➡ _____

9 (it / since / was / first / my / time / an / experiencing / earthquake, / didn't / I / how / know / react. / to)

➡ _____

10 (just / I / saying, / kept / should / "what / do?" / I)

➡ _____

11 (mom / my / me / pulled / and / brother / my / of / out / bed.)

➡ _____

12 (ran / we / the / to / kitchen / and / under / crawled / table. / the)

➡ _____

13 (could / I / the / see / swinging / light / and / violently / books / to / falling / floor. / the)

➡ _____

---

1 지진에 눈을 뜨는 것

2 2월 어느 날 밤, 내가 잠자리에 든 후에 지진이 일어났다.

3 침대가 흔들렸기 때문에 나는 갑자기 잠에서 깼다.

4 나는 남동생이 장난으로 침대를 흔들고 있다고 생각했다.

5 하지만 그때 나는 내 책상 위에 있던 거울이 바닥으로 떨어져 산산조각이 나는 소리를 들었다.

6 그때 나는 남동생이 그런 것이 아니라는 것을 알았지만, 정확히 무슨 일이 일어나고 있었는지를 여전히 알지 못했다.

7 머지않아 방 전체가 심하게 흔들리기 시작했고 혼란스러움은 공포로 변했다.

8 엄마가 지진이라고 소리를 지르며 내 방으로 뛰어 들어왔다.

9 지진을 경험한 것이 처음이었기 때문에, 나는 어떻게 반응해야 할지 몰랐다.

10 나는 그저 "어떻게 해야 하지?"라는 말을 반복했다.

11 엄마는 나와 남동생을 침대 밖으로 잡아끌었다.

12 우리는 주방으로 달려가서 식탁 아래로 기어들어 갔다.

13 나는 전등이 심하게 흔들리는 것과 책이 바닥으로 떨어지는 것을 볼 수 있었다.

14 (family / our / dropped / picture / the / from / wall / and / glass / the / covering / broke. / it)
➡ _____

15 (cup / a / over / tipped / and / off / rolled / kitchen / the / table.)
➡ _____

16 (second, / every / could / I / something / hear / else / the / in / break. / apartment)
➡ _____

17 (started / I / worry / to / the / that / building / collapse. / would)
➡ _____

18 (the / then / seemed / shaking / stop. / to)
➡ _____

19 (started / we / toward / crawling / door. / the)
➡ _____

20 (that / at / moment, / mom's / my / phone / cell / rang.)
➡ _____

21 (was / it / dad, / my / was / who / home / coming / work. / from)
➡ _____

22 (shouted, / he / stopped! / "it)
➡ _____

23 (out / get / the / of / building!)
➡ _____

24 (the / take / stairs!)
➡ _____

25 (take / don't / elevator! / the)
➡ _____

26 (hurry!")
➡ _____

27 (are / "where / you?)
➡ _____

28 (you / are / okay?" / mom / my / urgently. / asked)
➡ _____

29 (dad / my / "don't / answered, / worry)
➡ _____

30 (okay. / I'm)
➡ _____

14 우리 가족 사진이 벽에서 떨어졌고 사진을 덮고 있던 유리가 깨졌다.

15 컵이 넘어지고 식탁에서 굴러 떨어졌다.

16 매 순간, 나는 아파트에 있는 다른 어떤 것들이 부서지는 소리를 들을 수 있었다.

17 나는 건물이 무너지지는 않을까 하는 걱정이 들기 시작했다.

18 그때 흔들림이 멈추는 것 같았다.

19 우리는 문으로 기어가기 시작했다.

20 그 순간, 엄마의 휴대 전화가 울렸다.

21 전화를 한 사람은 바로 아빠였는데, 직장에서 퇴근하던 중이었다.

22 아빠는 소리쳤다. "지진이 멈췄어요!

23 건물 밖으로 나와요!

24 계단을 이용해요!

25 엘리베이터를 타면 안 돼요!

26 서둘러요!"

27 "어디예요?

28 괜찮아요?"라고 엄마가 다급하게 물었다.

29 아빠가 대답했다. "걱정 말아요.

30 나는 괜찮아요.

31 (was / I / home / driving / when / shaking / the / started.)
➡ _____

32 (I / but / over / pulled / immediately.)
➡ _____

33 (listening / I'm / the / to / right / radio / now / find / to / out / going / what's / on.")
➡ _____

34 (nervously / we / our / made / down / way / stairs / the / outside. / and)
➡ _____

35 (looked / I / around.)
➡ _____

36 (of / parts / buildings / fallen / had / and / smashed / had / cars. / several)
➡ _____

37 (went / we / an / to / open / to / space / avoid / falling / more / pieces.)
➡ _____

38 (could / how / this / all / happened / have / a / in / few / minutes?)
➡ _____

39 (I / although / done / had / earthquake / many / in / drills, / school, / had / I / thought / never / experience. / I'd / real / a / earthquake.)
➡ _____
_____

40 (still / I / scared / get / I / when / that / remember / night.)
➡ _____

41 (can't / I / the / forget / panic / felt / I / the / when / was / furniture / shaking / and / were / things / to / falling / floor. / the)
➡ _____
_____

42 (that / after / night, / began / I / take / to / drills / earthquake / seriously.)
➡ _____

43 (realized / I / that / I / be / should / prepared / the / for / earthquake, / next / can / which / at / occur / time. / any)
➡ _____
_____

31 진동이 시작할 때 운전해서 집으로 가던 중이었어요.

32 하지만 즉시 차를 길 한쪽에 댔어요.

33 무슨 일이 일어나는지 알기 위해 지금 라디오를 듣고 있어요."

34 우리는 초조한 마음으로 계단을 내려가서 밖으로 나갔다.

35 나는 주변을 둘러보았다.

36 건물의 일부분이 떨어져 나갔고 몇몇 차들은 박살이 났다.

37 우리는 추가적인 낙하물을 피하기 위해 공터로 갔다.

38 어떻게 이런 일이 몇 분 만에 일어날 수 있단 말인가?

39 비록 학교에서 많은 지진 대피 훈련을 해 왔지만, 내가 실제 지진을 겪으리라고는 전혀 생각해 보지 않았었다.

40 그날 밤을 기억하면 나는 여전히 두려워진다.

41 가구가 흔들리고 물건들이 바닥으로 떨어졌을 때 내가 느꼈던 공포심을 나는 잊을 수가 없다.

42 그날 밤 이후, 나는 지진 대피 훈련에 진지하게 임하기 시작했다.

43 나는 언제든 발생할 수 있는 다음 지진을 대비해야 한다는 것을 깨달았다.

※ 다음 우리말을 영어로 쓰시오.

1 지진에 눈을 뜨는 것

➡ _____

2 2월 어느 날 밤, 내가 잠자리에 든 후에 지진이 일어났다.

➡ _____

3 침대가 흔들렸기 때문에 나는 갑자기 잠에서 깼다.

➡ _____

4 나는 남동생이 장난으로 침대를 흔들고 있다고 생각했다.

➡ _____

5 하지만 그때 나는 내 책상 위에 있던 거울이 바닥으로 떨어져 산산조각이 나는 소리를 들었다.

➡ _____

6 그때 나는 남동생이 그런 것이 아니라는 것을 알았지만, 정확히 무슨 일이 일어나고 있었는지를 여전히 알지 못했다.

➡ _____

7 머지않아 방 전체가 심하게 흔들리기 시작했고 혼란스러움은 공포로 변했다.

➡ _____

8 엄마가 지진이라고 소리를 지르며 내 방으로 뛰어 들어왔다.

➡ _____

9 지진을 경험한 것이 처음이었기 때문에, 나는 어떻게 반응해야 할지 몰랐다.

➡ _____

10 나는 그저 "어떻게 해야 하지?"라는 말을 반복했다.

➡ _____

11 엄마는 나와 남동생을 침대 밖으로 잡아끌었다.

➡ _____

12 우리는 주방으로 달려가서 식탁 아래로 기어들어 갔다.

➡ _____

13 나는 전등이 심하게 흔들리는 것과 책이 바닥으로 떨어지는 것을 볼 수 있었다.

➡ _____

14 우리 가족 사진이 벽에서 떨어졌고 사진을 덮고 있던 유리가 깨졌다.

➡ _____

15 컵이 넘어지고 식탁에서 굴러 떨어졌다.

➡ _____

16 매 순간, 나는 아파트에 있는 다른 어떤 것들이 부서지는 소리를 들을 수 있었다.

➡ _____

17 나는 건물이 무너지지는 않을까 하는 걱정이 들기 시작했다.

➡ _____

18 그때 흔들림이 멈추는 것 같았다.

➡ _____

19 우리는 문으로 기어가기 시작했다.

➡ _____

20 그 순간, 엄마의 휴대 전화가 울렸다.

➡ _____

21 전화를 한 사람은 바로 아빠였는데, 직장에서 퇴근하던 중이었다.

➡ _____

22 아빠는 소리쳤다, "지진이 멈췄어요!

➡ _____

23 건물 밖으로 나와요!

➡ _____

24 계단을 이용해요!

➡ _____

25 엘리베이터를 타면 안 돼요!

➡ _____

26 서둘러요!"

➡ _____

27 "어디예요?

➡ _____

28 괜찮아요?"라고 엄마가 다급하게 물었다.

➡ _____

29 아빠가 대답했다, "걱정 말아요.

➡ _____

30 나는 괜찮아요.

➡ _____

31 진동이 시작할 때 운전해서 집으로 가던 중이었어요.

➡ _____

32 하지만 즉시 차를 길 한쪽에 댔어요.

➡ _____

33 무슨 일이 일어나는지 알기 위해 지금 라디오를 듣고 있어요."

➡ _____

34 우리는 초조한 마음으로 계단을 내려가서 밖으로 나갔다.

➡ _____

35 나는 주변을 둘러보았다.

➡ _____

36 건물의 일부분이 떨어져 나갔고 몇몇 차들은 박살이 났다.

➡ _____

37 우리는 추가적인 낙하물을 피하기 위해 공터로 갔다.

➡ _____

38 어떻게 이런 일이 몇 분 만에 일어날 수 있단 말인가?

➡ _____

39 비록 학교에서 많은 지진 대피 훈련을 해 왔지만, 내가 실제 지진을 겪으리라고는 전혀 생각해 보지 않았었다.

➡ _____

_____

40 그날 밤을 기억하면 나는 여전히 두려워진다.

➡ _____

41 가구가 흔들리고 물건들이 바닥으로 떨어졌을 때 내가 느꼈던 공포심을 나는 잊을 수가 없다.

➡ _____

42 그날 밤 이후, 나는 지진 대피 훈련에 진지하게 임하기 시작했다.

➡ _____

43 나는 언제든 발생할 수 있는 다음 지진을 대비해야 한다는 것을 깨달았다.

➡ _____

※ 다음 우리말과 일치하도록 빈칸에 알맞은 말을 쓰시오.

After You Read B

1. R: How did you feel _____ the _____ _____?
2. W: I _____ _____ panic _____ the whole room _____ _____ _____.
3. R: _____ _____! What did you do next?
4. W: We _____ _____ under the table after my mom _____ _____ _____ _____ _____.
5. R: What was _____ _____ _____ _____?
6. W: _____ _____ things _____ _____ to the floor. I _____ many things in the apartment _____.
7. R: What _____ you _____ after that night?
8. W: I realized that I _____ _____ _____ _____ the next earthquake. It _____ _____ _____ _____ _____!

1. R: 지진이 일어났을 때 어떻게 느끼셨습니까?
2. W: 방 전체가 심하게 흔들렸기 때문에 공포에 사로잡히기 시작했어요.
3. R: 얼마나 무서웠을까! 그 다음에 무엇을 했나요?
4. W: 어머니가 우리를 침대에서 끌어내린 후, 우리는 식탁 아래로 기어갔어요.
5. R: 그 순간에 무슨 일이 일어나고 있었나요?
6. W: 많은 것들이 바닥으로 떨어지고 있었어요. 나는 아프트 안에 있는 많은 것들이 깨지는 소리를 들었어요.
7. R: 그날 밤 이후에 무엇을 깨달았나요?
8. W: 나는 내가 다음번 지진에 대비해야 한다는 것을 깨달았어요. 지진은 언제든지 일어날 수 있어요!

Think & Write Step 3

San Andreas

1. I _____ _____ _____ _____ you about the movie *San Andreas*.
2. This movie _____ _____ _____ Los Angeles and San Francisco _____ 2014.
3. The _____ _____, a search-and-rescue _____, must search for his _____ family _____ an earthquake.
4. The _____ _____ _____ in the _____ _____ are very good.
5. The movie is _____ _____ sad _____ _____, but the story is very interesting.
6. I give *San Andreas* four stars. _____ and _____ _____!

San Andreas
1. 저는 영화 San Andreas에 대해 말하고 싶습니다.
2. 이 영화의 배경은 2014년 Los Angeles와 San Francisco입니다.
3. 수색구조 조종사인 주인공은 지진이 일어난 동안 행방불명된 그의 가족을 찾아야 합니다.
4. 재난 장면에 사용된 특수효과는 매우 좋습니다.
5. 이 영화는 가끔 약간 슬프지만, 이야기는 매우 재미있습니다.
6. 저는 San Andreas에게 별 4개를 줍니다. 가서 보세요!

※ 다음 우리말을 영어로 쓰시오.

After You Read B

1. R: 지진이 일어났을 때 어떻게 느끼셨습니까?
   ➡ _____

2. W: 방 전체가 심하게 흔들렸기 때문에 공포에 사로잡히기 시작했어요.
   ➡ _____

3. R: 얼마나 무서웠을까! 그 다음에 무엇을 했나요?
   ➡ _____

4. W: 어머니가 우리를 침대에서 끌어내린 후, 우리는 식탁 아래로 기어갔어요.
   ➡ _____

5. R: 그 순간에 무슨 일이 일어나고 있었나요?
   ➡ _____

6. W: 많은 것들이 바닥으로 떨어지고 있었어요. 나는 아프트 안에 있는 많은 것들이 깨지는 소리를 들었어요.
   ➡ _____

7. 그날 밤 이후에 무엇을 깨달았나요?
   ➡ _____

8. W: 나는 내가 다음번 지진에 대비해야 한다는 것을 깨달았어요. 지진은 언제든지 일어날 수 있어요!
   ➡ _____

Think & Write Step 3

San Andreas

1. 저는 영화 *San Andreas*에 대해 말하고 싶습니다.
   ➡ _____

2. 이 영화의 배경은 2014년 Los Angeles와 San Francisco입니다.
   ➡ _____

3. 수색구조 조종사인 주인공은 지진이 일어난 동안 행방불명된 그의 가족을 찾아야 합니다.
   ➡ _____

4. 재난 장면에 사용된 특수효과는 매우 좋습니다.
   ➡ _____

5. 이 영화는 가끔 약간 슬프지만, 이야기는 매우 재미있습니다.
   ➡ _____

6. 저는 *San Andreas*에게 별 4개를 줍니다. 가서 보세요!
   ➡ _____

영어 기출 문제집

적중100

1학기

정답 및 해설

능률 | 김성곤

중 3

영어 기출 문제집

영어 기출 문제집

적중100

1학기

정답 및 해설

능률 | 김성곤

중 3

적중100

Lesson 1

A Life Full of Experiences

시험대비 실력평가   p.08

01 ②   02 ①   03 ③   04 ①
05 ②   06 meaningful

01 내용상 '~에 익숙해지다'에 해당하는 'get used to'가 적절하다.

02 '벽에 붙은 길고 평평한 좁은 판자'는 '선반(shelf)'을 가리킨다.

03 산꼭대기까지 올라가는 것은 중간에 포기하지 않는 것을 의미한다. look up 찾아보다 run up 늘리다 give up 포기하다 hang up 전화를 끊다 fill up 채우다

04 'own'은 '자기 자신의'라는 의미로 소유격을 강조한다.

05 ① practice 연습하다 ② changed 바꾸다 ③ familiar 친숙한 ④ match 경기, 시합 ⑤ suggest 제안하다

06 명사 experiences를 수식하는 형용사 meaningful이 적절하다.

서술형 시험대비   p.09

01 memorize 02 (1) case   (2) confident
(3) motivated   (4) watching   03 requirement
04 (f)inish   05 get
06 (1) joined   (2) talents   (3) review   (4) subtitles
    (5) experiences

01 memory: 기억 memorize: 암기하다

02 (1) 어쨌든 = in any case (2) confident 자신감 있는 (3) 동기 부여된 = motivated (4) ~을 시도해 보다 = try ~ing

03 학생들은 '학교의 요구 사항' 때문에 새로운 언어를 배운다. require 요구하다 requirements 요구 사항, 의무

04 주어진 단어는 동의어 관계이다. finish 끝내다 complete 완성하다

05 • 너는 다른 문화에 익숙해져야 한다. get used to ~ ~에 익숙해지다 • 중국어 자막이 있는 중국 드라마를 보는 것은 듣기를 더 잘하게 되는 좋은 방법이다. get better at ~ ~을 더 잘하게 되다

06 (1) 가입했다 = joined (2) 재능 = talent (3) 평론 = review (4) 자막 = subtitle (5) 새로운 경험 new experiences

교과서 Conversation

핵심 Check   p.10~11

1 What, like   2 (C) → (A) → (B)
3 ③

03 '스케이트보드를 어떻게 배웠느냐?'는 질문에 (B) 클럽에 가입해서 배웠다고 대답하고 (C) '그것이 마음에 드니?'라고 물어보자 (A) '그것이 재미있고 친구를 사귀는 데 도움이 된다.'고 대답한다.

교과서 대화문 익히기

Check(√) True or False   p.12

1 F   2 T   3 T   4 F   5 F

교과서 확인학습   p.14~15

Listen & Talk 1 B
would, like / like, learn, listened, was struck, sound / Where, going, good, player, ask

Listen & Talk 1 C
What, doing / writing, things that, do / What, like / first, like, spend, volunteering, during / sounds / What about, What, like / thinking, taking, class / cool

Listen & Talk 2 B
What, holding / skateboard, skateboarding / know that, How, learn, skateboard / joined, local, last month / see, how, like / really, helps, make / go skateboarding, members, share tips

Listen & Talk 2 C
make, shelf yourself, amazing / started making furniture / How, like / hard, love, feel, confident, making / great, really good at / guess, found, talent, good, try / Exactly, Having, experiences, find

Listen & Talk 2 D
ran, race / How, like / liked, helped, confidence

Presentation Time Step 1
tell, one, meaningful / cooked, for / How, like / not easy, that, make, happy, cooking

Presentation Time Step 3
recommends cooking, meaningful experience because, cooking, others, make, experience, feel

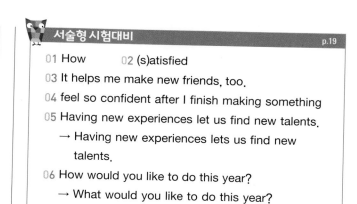
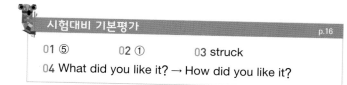

performed, festival / How, like / wasn't bad, made,
mistakes / sounded fine / for saying, playing, front /
feel / nervous, felt / awesome, so proud

시험대비 기본평가
p.16

01 ⑤　　　　02 ①　　　　03 struck

04 What did you like it? → How did you like it?

01 밑줄 친 부분은 상대방에게 만족이나 불만족에 대해 묻는 표현이다.

02 would you like 다음에는 to부정사가 온다.

03 수동태이므로 strike의 과거분사 struck가 적절하다.

04 만족을 물어볼 때는 'How did you like it?'이라고 한다.

시험대비 실력평가
p.17~18

01 ③　　　02 ②　　　03 ⑤　　　04 ②
05 ⑤　　　06 ③　　　07 ②
08 I'm so proud of you.　　09 ⑤　　　10 ④
11 ③

01 Bill이 요리한 경험을 만족스러워하는지를 물어보는 것이 이어지는 대답과 자연스럽게 연결된다.

02 주어진 문장은 'I learned that I could make people happy with my cooking.'이다.

03 ⑤ Lina가 Bill에게 질문한 이유는 이 대화에서 언급되지 않았다.

04 자신이 가지고 있는 것이 skateboard라고 소개하는 것으로 보아 '들고 있는 것'에 대한 질문이 있었다고 생각할 수 있다.

05 ① skateboarding을 배우는 것은 수지이고, 수지는 club에서 배워서, 클럽 회원들과 tip을 공유한다.

06 이 글의 필자는 학교 축제에서 드럼을 연주했다.

07 앞에 나온 내용에 대하여 감사하다는 반응을 보이는 것으로 보아 칭찬하는 내용이 적절하다.

08 자랑스러워하다 = be proud of, take pride in

09 소년이 연주에서 실수를 했다는 것은 나와 있지만 정확하게 몇 번인지는 나와 있지 않다.

10 ④ 상대방의 의견이나 의도를 물어보는 말로 'What about you?'가 자연스럽다.

11 상대방이 잘한다고 생각하면서 '안됐다.'고 말하는 것은 어색하다. 'That's great.'가 적절하다.

01 How　　　　02 (s)atisfied

03 It helps me make new friends, too.

04 feel so confident after I finish making something

05 Having new experiences let us find new talents.
　→ Having new experiences lets us find new talents.

06 How would you like to do this year?
　→ What would you like to do this year?

01 스케이트보드를 배운 방법을 묻고 있어서 how가 적절하다.

02 만족을 물어보는 'How do you like it?'은 'Are you satisfied with it?'으로 바꾸어 쓸 수 있다.

03 새로운 친구를 사귀다 = make new friends

04 매우 자신감을 느낀다 = feel so confident 무엇인가를 만들고 난 후 = after I finish making something

05 주어가 동명사이므로 단수 동사로 받는다.

06 상대가 바라는 것을 물어볼 때는 'What would you like to do?'라고 물어본다.

핵심 Check
p.20~21

1 (1) studying　(2) liked　(3) celebrating
2 (1) what　(2) what　(3) What

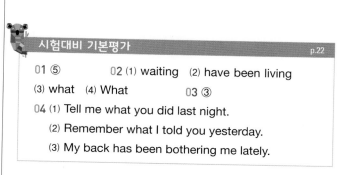
01 ⑤　　　　02 (1) waiting　(2) have been living
(3) what　(4) What　　　　03 ③

04 (1) Tell me what you did last night.
　(2) Remember what I told you yesterday.
　(3) My back has been bothering me lately.

01 the thing(s) which[that]는 선행사를 포함하는 관계대명사 what으로 바꿔 쓸 수 있다.

02 (1) 한 시간 동안 계속 그녀를 기다리고 있는 것이므로 현재완료진행형이 적절하다. (2) 10년 동안 살아오고 있는 것이므로 현재완료진행형이 적절하다. (3) is의 보어와 bought의 목적어 역할을 할 수 있는 what이 적절하다. (4) do의 목적어와 is의 주어 역할을 할 수 있는 what이 적절하다.

3

03 그저께부터 눈이 오기 시작하여 현재까지 계속 진행되고 있으므로 현재완료진행형이 적절하다.

04 (1), (2) the thing(s) which[that]로 쓰일 수 있는 선행사를 포함하는 관계대명사 what을 이용한다. (3) 과거의 어느 때부터 시작되어 현재까지 계속 진행되고 있음을 나타내는 현재완료진행형을 이용한다.

p.23~25

시험대비 실력평가

01 ④　　02 ③　　03 ⑤
04 (1) been wearing　(2) for　(3) since　(4) what
　　(5) that　　　　　　05 ①
06 ②　　07 ④　　08 that → what
09 Prices have been increasing steadily for months.
10 ②, ③　　11 ④　　12 ③　　13 ⑤
14 ③
15 (1) The man has been taking care of the children for a few years.
　　(2) Melina taught English at the school two years ago.
　　(3) She has been reading a book since 3 p.m..
　　(4) Ron has been watching the play for two hours.
　　(5) This is the movie which[that] I want to see.
　　(6) Let me look at what you took with your camera in Canada.
16 ④　　17 ②, ③　　18 ⑤

01 ① He has been planting apple trees since 2010. ② I've been looking for this book for an hour. ③ Megan has been writing letters all day long. ⑤ He has been reading the book for about two hours.

02 understand와 says의 목적어 역할을 할 수 있도록 that을 what으로 고쳐야 한다.

03 8살 이래로 계속 발레를 배워 오고 있는 것이므로 현재완료진행형이 적절하다. 동사 is의 보어와 bought의 목적어 역할을 할 수 있는 것은 what이다.

04 (1) 현재완료진행형은 'have[has] been+동사원형-ing'의 형태이다. (2), (3) 현재완료진행형에서 since는 '시간'을 나타내는 명사(구)와 함께 쓰이고 for는 '기간'을 나타내는 명사(구)와 함께 쓰인다. (4) eat의 목적어가 없으므로 what이 이끄는 절이 sell의 목적어가 되도록 해야 한다. (5) 선행사 all이 있으므로 관계대명사 that이 적절하다. all을 없애고, what만 써도 어법상 바른 문장이다.

05 for의 목적어와 is의 주어 역할을 할 수 있는 What이 적절하다.

06 현재완료진행형에서 since는 '시간'을 나타내는 명사(구)와 함께

쓰이고, for는 '기간'을 나타내는 명사(구)와 함께 쓰인다.

07 현재완료진행형은 'have[has] been+동사원형-ing'의 형태이며 과거를 나타내는 어구와 함께 쓰이지 않는다. ②번은 know가 진행형으로 쓰이지 않는 동사임에 유의한다.

08 what is called: 소위, 이른바

09 현재완료진행형을 이용하여 쓴다.

10 what이 관계대명사인지 의문사인지 구분하는 문제로 보통 의문사 what은 '무엇을, 무엇이 ~인(한)지'로, 관계대명사 what은 '~하는 것'으로 해석한다. ① 의문대명사 ② 관계대명사 ③ 관계대명사 ④ 의문대명사 ⑤ 의문대명사

11 과거 어느 때부터 시작되어 현재까지 계속 진행되고 있음을 나타내는 현재완료진행형이 적절하다.

12 ③번은 선행사(the person)가 있으므로 who나 that이 들어가야 하고, 나머지는 선행사가 없으므로 what이 적절하다.

13 the things which[that]의 역할을 하는 what을 이용하여 나타내도록 한다.

14 내용상 현재완료진행형(have[has] been+동사원형-ing)을 이용한다.

15 (1) 현재완료진행형은 'have[has] been+동사원형-ing'의 형태이다. (2) 현재완료진행형은 과거를 나타내는 어구와 함께 쓰이지 않는다. (3), (4) 현재완료진행형에서 since는 '시간'을 나타내는 명사(구)와 함께 쓰이고 for는 '기간'을 나타내는 명사(구)와 함께 쓰인다. (5) the movie가 선행사로 나왔으므로 what이 아니라 which나 that을 써야 한다. (6) look at과 took의 목적어 역할을 할 수 있는 what으로 고쳐야 한다.

16 ① 현재완료진행형은 과거를 나타내는 어구와 함께 쓰이지 않는다. ④ the book이라는 선행사가 있으므로 what을 that으로 고쳐야 한다.

17 understand와 said의 목적어 역할을 할 수 있는 what이 적절하며 what은 the thing(s) that으로 바꿔 쓸 수 있다.

18 선행사가 없고 to의 목적어와 is의 주어 역할을 해야 하므로 관계대명사 what이 적절하다.

p.26~27

서술형 시험대비

01 (1) Oliver has been waiting for his friend since one o'clock.
　　(2) James has been doing yoga for an hour.
　　(3) I have been taking tennis lessons over the last 5 years.
02 (1) You don't think that I know what you're doing.
　　(2) What I want to do most is to go to a concert.
　　(3) They have been thinking of him as an Italian for years.

03 (1) What she wants to receive

   (2) what I want to

04 (1) for (2) since

05 (1) Find what keeps you motivated.

   (2) It made me think what I liked.

   (3) What you said made me surprised.

   (4) What is done cannot be undone.

06 (1) lived → living (2) since → for (3) for → since

   (4) That → What (5) that → what (6) what → that

   (7) That → What

07 (1) Harold has been reading the book since this morning.

   (2) Taehee has been talking on the phone for two hours.

08 (1) They have been living here for four generations.

   (2) Scientists have been studying Saturn's rings.

   (3) The movie has been showing for three months.

   (4) Don't forget what you promised the other day.

01 과거에 시작하여 지금까지 계속되고 있는 것이므로 현재완료진행형을 이용한다.

02 (1)~(2) 선행사를 포함하는 관계대명사 what을 이용하여 배열한다. what이 선행사를 포함하므로 문장에서 두 가지의 역할을 함에 유의한다. (3) 과거 어느 때부터 시작되어 현재까지 계속 진행되고 있음을 나타내는 현재완료진행형 구문을 이용한다.

03 선행사를 포함하는 관계대명사 what을 이용한다.

04 (1) 현재완료진행형에서 since는 '시간'을 나타내는 명사(구)와 함께 쓰이고, for는 '기간'을 나타내는 명사(구)와 함께 쓰인다.

05 the thing(s) which[that]의 역할을 하는 what을 이용하여 하나의 문장으로 쓴다.

06 (1) 계속 살아오고 있는 것이므로 현재완료진행형으로 나타낸다. (2), (3) 현재완료진행형에서 since는 '시간'을 나타내는 명사(구)와 함께 쓰이고 for는 '기간'을 나타내는 명사(구)와 함께 쓰인다. (4) do의 목적어와 is의 주어 역할을 해야 하므로 That을 What으로 고친다. (5) tell의 직접목적어와 saw의 목적어 역할을 할 수 있도록 that을 what으로 고친다. (6) the only one이라는 선행사가 있으므로 what을 that으로 고친다. (7) did의 목적어와 was의 주어 역할을 해야 하므로 That을 What으로 고친다.

07 과거 어느 때부터 시작되어 현재까지 계속 진행되고 있음을 나타내는 현재완료진행형으로 쓰고, 현재완료진행형에서 since는 '시간'을 나타내는 명사(구)와 함께 쓰이고 for는 '기간'을 나타내는 명사(구)와 함께 쓰인다.

08 (1)~(3) 과거 어느 때부터 시작되어 현재까지 계속 진행되고 있음을 나타내는 현재완료진행형을 이용한다. (4) forget의 목적어와 promise의 목적어 역할을 할 수 있는 what을 이용한다.

Reading 교과서

확인문제   p.28

1 T 2 F 3 T 4 F 5 T 6 F

확인문제   p.29

1 T 2 F 3 T 4 F 5 T 6 F

확인문제   p.30

1 T 2 F 3 T 4 F 5 T 6 F

교과서 확인학습 A   p.31~33

01 a New Language   02 Foreign Languages

03 because of school requirements

04 for fun   05 In any case

06 listen to their ideas   07 Love

08 a big fan

09 understand interviews

10 However, Spanish that well

11 improve my Spanish   12 to practice it

13 have changed the language, have been writing

14 become familiar with   15 suggest watching

16 get used to   17 try watching

18 are used

19 soccer vocabulary, memorize

20 why don't you, in Spanish

21 improve your writing skills

22 No More   23 is back

24 so excited   25 just perfect

26 without subtitles, translations

27 Any tips   28 are interested in

29 one another

30 translate, sing together

31 Doing, improves our Korean

32 on social media   33 post short messages

34 with the messages, more easily

35 recommend watching   36 I've been watching

37 for help with listening   38 print out the subtitles

39 Works

40 hundreds of, their own way

41 what, motivated

42 at first, much bigger

1 Learn a New Language, Find a New World

2 Why Do People Learn Foreign Languages?

3 Many students learn new languages because of school requirements.

4 Many others learn them for fun.

5 In any case, students everywhere have found interesting ways to study new languages.

6 Let's meet these students and listen to their ideas.

7 I Love Soccer!

8 I'm a big fan of a Spanish soccer team.

9 I want to understand interviews with my favorite players.

10 However, it's not easy because I don't know Spanish that well.

11 How can I improve my Spanish? – Owen, 16

12 The best way to learn a new language is to practice it every day.

13 I have changed the language of my phone to Spanish, and I have been writing my shopping lists in Spanish! – Julie, 15

14 What's most important is to become familiar with the language first.

15 I suggest watching Spanish movies often.

16 It will help you get used to the sound of the language.

17 If the people talk too fast, try watching Spanish children's movies first. – Inho, 14

18 Some words are used only in soccer, not in everyday life.

19 Learn some soccer vocabulary and memorize it.

20 Also, why don't you try writing a review of a match in Spanish?

21 It will help you improve your writing skills. – Rohan, 16

22 No More Subtitles!

23 DREAM4 is back!

24 I'm so excited to see my favorite Korean boy band perform.

25 Their singing and their dancing are just perfect.

26 I want to understand their songs without subtitles or translations though.

27 Any tips? – Marisa, 14

28 You should find friends who are interested in DREAM4 and start a club.

29 In my club, we motivate one another.

30 We translate songs and sing together.

31 Doing these things is fun and really improves our Korean! – Lori, 15

32 Follow DREAM4 on social media.

33 They often post short messages in Korean about how they are doing.

34 They also post pictures with the messages, so you can understand the posts more easily. – Aishah, 14

35 I recommend watching Korean dramas.

36 I've been watching Korean dramas for a year, and they're really interesting!

37 You can use Korean subtitles for help with listening.

38 It's also a good idea to print out the subtitles and read them first. – Brandon, 16

39 What Works for You?

40 There are hundreds of good tips out there, but everyone has their own way of learning.

41 Find what keeps you motivated; then you will enjoy learning more.

42 Remember, every language is hard at first, but a new language can make your world much bigger!

01 What

02 It will help you improve your writing skills.

| 03 ② | 04 ② | 05 ① | 06 ②, ④ |

07 (A) Why   (B) because of   (C) found

| 08 new languages | | 09 ④ |

| 10 how they are doing | | 11 ⑤ |

12 comments → pictures

| 13 (A) following   (B) Korean dramas | | 14 ③, ④ |

| 15 are used | 16 ③ | 17 to do | 18 ⑤ |

| 19 ③ | 20 ②, ⑤ | 21 ④ |

22 (A) school requirements   (B) for fun

| 23 ② | 24 ①, ④ / ②, ⑤ | | 25 ② |

| 26 ⓐ: ①, ②, ④   ⓑ: ③, ⑤ | 27 If you | 28 ⑤ |

| 29 Spanish | | 30 ② |

01 선행사를 포함한 관계대명사 What을 쓰는 것이 적절하다.

02 help는 5형식 문장에서 목적격보어에 to부정사나 원형부정사를 둘 다 쓸 수 있는 준사역동사이지만, 8단어로 영작하라고 했으므로 원형부정사를 쓰는 것이 적절하다.

03 이 글은 스페인어 구사 능력을 향상시키는 법에 관해 조언하는 글이므로, 주제로는 ②번이 적절하다.

04 앞에 나오는 내용과 상반되는 내용이 뒤에 이어지므로

However가 가장 적절하다. ① 그러므로, ③ 게다가, ④ 즉, 다시 말해, ⑤ 예를 들어

05 ①: 스페인의(형용사), ②~⑤: 스페인어(명사)

06 ⓑ와 ②, ④: 계속 용법, ①, ⑤: 경험 용법, ③: 완료 용법

07 (A) 이 글은 사람들이 외국어를 배우는 이유를 설명하는 글이므로, '왜' 사람들은 외국어를 배우는가?가 적절하다. (B) because+절(주어+동사), because of+명사구, (C) 흥미로운 방법들을 '찾아낸다'고 해야 하므로 found가 적절하다. find-found-found: 찾다, found-founded-founded: 설립하다

08 '새로운 언어들'을 가리킨다.

09 '모든 곳의 학생들은 새로운 언어를 공부하는 데 흥미로운 방법들을 찾아낸다. 이 학생들을 만나서 그들의 생각을 들어보자.'라고 했으므로, ④번이 적절하다.

10 간접의문문(의문사+주어+동사)의 순서로 쓰는 것이 적절하다.

11 ⓐ와 ⑤: 가주어, ① 비인칭 주어(거리), ② 가목적어, ③ 문장의 어떤 부분을 강조할 때 쓰는 대명사, ④ 비인칭 주어(막연한 상황)

12 DREAM4의 멤버들은 메시지와 함께 '사진들'을 올려서 당신은 더 쉽게 게시물을 이해할 수 있다. comment: 논평, 해설, 설명

13 아이샤는 소셜 미디어에서 DREAM4를 '팔로할' 것을 추천하고, 브랜던은 '한국 드라마들'을 볼 것을 추천한다. recommend는 동명사를 목적어로 취한다.

14 (A)와 ③, ④: 관계대명사, ① 의문형용사(무슨), 어떤, ② 감탄문에 쓰인 의문형용사(얼마나), ⑤ 의문대명사(무엇)

15 어떤 단어들은 일상생활에서가 아니라 오직 축구에서만 '쓰인다'고 해야 하므로, 수동태로 쓰는 것이 적절하다.

16 이 글은 마리사가 자막이나 번역이 없이 DREAM4의 노래를 이해하려고 조언을 구하는 내용이므로, 제목으로는 ③번 '더는 자막 없이!'가 적절하다.

17 진주어를 to부정사로 바꿔 쓰는 것이 적절하다.

18 로리의 모임에 몇 명의 회원이 있는지는 대답할 수 없다. ① Because she can see her favorite Korean boy band perform. ② DREAM4. ③ No. ④ She recommends that Marisa should start a club with friends who are also interested in DREAM4.

19 ⓐ와 ①, ②, ④, ⑤: 어쨌든, ③ by the way: 그런데(대화에서 화제를 바꿀 때 씀)

20 ⓑ와 ②, ⑤: 형용사적 용법, ①, ③: 부사적 용법, ④: 명사적 용법

21 이 글은 사람들이 외국어를 배우는 이유를 설명하는 글이므로, 제목으로는 ④번 '왜 사람들은 외국어를 배울까?'가 적절하다.

22 많은 학생들이 '학교 필수 수업'이기 때문에 혹은 '재미를 위해' 새로운 언어를 배운다.

23 ⓐ change A to B: A를 B로 바꾸다, ⓑ in: 언어, 재료 등을 나타냄

24 (A)와 ①, ④: 형용사적 용법, (B)와 ②, ⑤: 명사적 용법, ③: 부사적 용법

25 오언은 자신이 정말 좋아하는 선수들의 인터뷰를 이해하고 싶지만, 스페인어를 그렇게 잘 알지 못하기 때문에 그것이 쉽지 않다고 했다.

26 ⓐ와 ①, ②, ④: 동명사, ⓑ와 ③, ⑤: 현재분사

27 명령문, and ~ = If you …로 고칠 수 있다. ⓒ의 경우, 세미콜론이 and의 뜻을 나타낸다.

28 very는 원급을 강조하는 말이고, 나머지는 다 비교급을 강조한다.

29 soccer team을 수식하는 형용사 Spanish로 쓰는 것이 적절하다. Spanish: 스페인의(형용사)

30 주어진 문장의 However에 주목한다. ②번 앞에 나오는 내용과 상반되는 내용이 However 뒤에 이어지므로 ②번이 적절하다.

서술형 시험대비 p.42~43

01 to understand interviews with my favorite players
02 have been writing
03 (A) soccer   (B) understand   (C) Spanish
04 what
05 (A) interesting   (B) read   (C) motivated
06 (A) Korean subtitles   (B) printing out   (C) reading
07 to watch → watching   08 get used to the sound
09 (A) soccer vocabulary   (B) in Spanish
10 (A) is   (B) are   (C) is
11 Translating songs and singing together
12 motivate

01 '내가 정말 좋아하는 선수들의 인터뷰를 이해하는 것'을 가리킨다.

02 과거에 시작된 일이 현재에도 계속 진행 중임을 나타낼 때 쓰이는 현재완료 진행형으로 쓰는 것이 적절하다.

03 흥미: 스페인 '축구' 팀, 원하는 것: 선수들의 인터뷰를 '이해하기', 유용한 조언: 매일 '스페인어'를 연습하기

04 선행사를 포함한 관계대명사 what을 쓰는 것이 적절하다.

05 (A) 감정을 나타내는 동사는 감정을 유발할 때 현재분사를 쓰는 것이 적절하므로 interesting이 적절하다. (B) 진주어 to print와 병렬 구문이 되도록 (to) read로 쓰는 것이 적절하다. (C) 당신이 계속 '동기 부여가 되는 것'이므로 motivated가 적절하다.

06 그는 듣기에 도움이 되도록 '한국어 자막'을 사용할 것과 맨 먼저 자막들을 '출력해서' '읽을' 것을 추천한다.

07 suggest는 목적어로 to부정사가 아니라 동명사를 취하는 동사이다.

08 get used to: ~에 익숙해지다

09 로한은 오언에게 몇몇 '축구 어휘들'을 배우고 기억할 것을 제안한다. 로한은 또한 '스페인어로' 경기에 대한 후기를 써 볼 것을

7

제안한다.

10 (A) DREAM4는 밴드의 이름이므로 단수 취급하여 is가, (B) 주어가 Their singing and their dancing이므로 are가, (C) 주어가 동명사 Doing이므로 is가 적절하다.

11 '함께 노래를 번역하고 노래하는 것'을 가리킨다. Doing에 맞춰 동명사 형태로 답하는 것이 적절하다.

12 로리와 그녀의 친구들은 한국어를 배우고 실력을 향상시키려고 각각의 모임 친구에게 '동기를 부여하고', 함께 노래를 번역하고 노래한다. 영영풀이: 동기를 제공하다

01 ②   **02** ⑤   **03** ①
04 (1) spend   (2) through   **05** ①   **06** ②
07 I'm thinking of taking a swimming class.
08 What
09 I was struck by the sound of the guitar.
10 ③   **11** ⑤   **12** ⑤   **13** ①
14 ④   **15** ①, ③, ④   **16** has been cooking for
17 (1) what she painted
    (2) his son what looked really nice
    (3) believe what they want to believe
18 ②   **19** ⓒ, ⓓ, ⓕ   **20** ④
21 The best way to learn a new language is to
    practice it every day.
22 ①   **23** ①, ⑤   **24** ③   **25** ③
26 with → without
27 pictures with the messages
28 ago, watching
29 ⓑ Korean dramas
    ⓒ to print out the subtitles and read them first

01 주어진 단어는 동의어 관계이다. improve 개선하다 – develop 발달시키다 complete 완성하다 finish 끝내다 recommend 추천하다 translate 번역하다 perform 공연하다

02 새로운 언어를 배우는 방법으로 축구를 좋아하는 경우 축구에 사용되는 어휘를 배워서 그것을 암기하는 것이다.

03 바람을 물어보는 표현은 'would like to'를 사용하는 것이 자연스럽다.

04 (1) (시간을) 쓰다 = spend (2) ~을 통해서 = through

05 이어지는 대답에 앞으로 할 일이 나와 있는 것으로 보아 앞으로의 바람이나 계획을 묻는 질문이 적절하다.

06 자신의 바람을 말하고 이어서 상대의 바람을 묻는 대화이므로 '너는 어떠니?'에 해당하는 'What about you?'가 적절하다.

07 나는 ~을 생각하고 있다: I am thinking of ~, 수영 수업을 받는 것: taking a swimming class

08 앞으로의 바람을 묻는 질문은 'What would you like to ~?' 이다.

09 나는 ~에 감동을 받았다. = I was struck by ~., 기타 소리 = the sound of the guitar

10 ③ 소년이 듣고 감동을 받은 노래는 'Cavatina'이었다.

11 (C) 의미 있는 경험을 묻는 말에 요리한 경험으로 대답하고, (B) 그 대답을 듣고 만족하는지를 묻고 (A) 거기에 대한 대답으로 자신이 배운 것을 말한다.

12 스케이트보드 클럽에 가입했다는 내용으로 보아 스케이트보드 타는 방법을 어떻게 배웠는지를 묻는 질문이 적절하다.

13 상대방이 마음에 드는지를 물어볼 때는 'How did you like that?'이라고 한다.

14 현재완료진행형에서 since는 '시간'을 나타내는 명사(구)와 함께 쓰이고, for는 '기간'을 나타내는 명사(구)와 함께 쓰인다.

15 ① Please tell me what you bought for Jane's birthday. ③ My mom has been growing vegetables since last year. 또는 My mom grew vegetables last year. ④ Long time ago, they believed that the earth was flat.

16 과거 어느 때부터 시작되어 현재까지 계속 진행되고 있음을 나타내는 현재완료진행형을 이용한다. '기간'을 나타내는 an hour 가 있으므로 for를 쓴다.

17 선행사를 포함한 관계대명사 what(= the thing(s) which[that])을 이용한다.

18 ②에는 know의 목적어가 되는 명사절을 이끄는 that이 적절하다. 나머지는 모두 what이 적절하다.

19 ⓐ what → that ⓑ that → what ⓔ for → since ⓖ has been snowing → snowed 또는 last week → since last week

20 ⓐ와 ④: 지시부사(수량·정도를 나타내는 형용사·부사를 수식한다.) ① 지시대명사, ② 관계대명사, ③, ⑤: 접속사

21 The best way를 주어로 해서 쓰는 것이 적절하다.

22 ⓐ become familiar with: ~와 친해지다 ⓑ get used to: ~에 익숙해지다

23 (A)와 ②, ③, ④: 동명사, ①, ⑤: 현재분사

24 만약 사람들이 너무 빨리 말한다면, 어린이를 위한 스페인 영화들을 먼저 보는 것을 시도해 보라고 했다.

25 ⓐ와 ③, ⑤: 부사적 용법, ①, ④: 형용사적 용법, ②: 명사적 용법

26 자막이나 번역이 '없이' 그들의 노래를 이해하고 싶다고 해야 하므로 without이 적절하다.

27 그들은 또한 '메시지와 함께 사진들을' 올려서 당신은 더 쉽게 게시물을 이해할 수 있다.

28 현재완료진행형은 과거에 시작된 일이 현재에도 계속 진행 중임을 나타낼 때 쓴다.

29 ⓑ '한국 드라마들', ⓒ It은 가주어로서 진주어인 to부정사 이하의 내용을 가리킨다.

p.50~53

01 ①　　　02 ⑤　　　03 ①

04 I think you're really good at it.

05 Having new experiences lets us to find new talents. → Having new experiences lets us find new talents.

06 What would you like to do this year?　　07 ④

08 ②　　　09 ①　　　10 ④, ⑤　　　11 what

12 ②　　　13 ③　　　14 ②

15 ⓑ Spanish　　ⓓ some soccer vocabulary

16 but　　　17 who[that]　　　18 ③

19 improve → improves

20 He has been watching them for a year.

21 ⑤　　　22 ②

23 (1) to try Andong-jjimdak

　　(2) to make my own Hahoe mask and learn how to dance the *talchum*

　　(3) to visit Hahoe Village

24 ③

01 주어진 단어는 반의어 관계이다. weakness 약점 strength 강점 remember 기억하다 forget 잊어버리다 realize 깨닫다 motivate 동기부여하다 join 가입하다 convince 확신시키다

02 ⑤ 'having some mistakes, faults, or damage'는 '실수, 결점, 손상이 있는'이라는 뜻으로 '불완전한'에 해당한다.

03 G의 물음을 보아 이 대화에서는 가구 만들기가 주제인 것을 알 수 있다.

04 be good at ~ = ~을 잘하다

05 사역동사 let의 목적격보어는 원형부정사이다.

06 '무엇을 하고 싶니?' = 'What would you like to do?'

07 "I'm thinking of taking a swimming class."를 보면 소년은 올해 수영을 배우고 싶어한다는 것을 알 수 있다.

08 ① 이번 주에 소년이 무엇을 할지는 언급되지 않았다. ② 소녀는 여름 방학에 자원봉사를 가려고 한다. ③ 소년이 소녀의 계획을 묻는 이유는 나오지 않았다. ④ 대화의 장소는 알 수 없다. ⑤ 자원봉사 가는 방법은 언급되지 않았다.

09 첫 번째 문장에서는 두 개의 is의 주어 역할을 할 수 있는 관계대명사 what이 적절하다. 두 번째 문장에서는 3 p.m.이라는 시간을 나타내는 명사가 있으므로 since가 적절하다.

10 ① It has been snowing for three days. ② She cleaned her room last night. ③ He has been building his house for two months.

11 관계대명사 what은 선행사를 포함한 관계대명사로 the thing(s) which[that]를 나타낸다.

12 현재완료진행형은 과거의 명백한 시점을 나타내는 ~ ago와 함께 쓰이지 않는다.

13 현재완료진행형은 'have[has] been+동사원형-ing'의 형태로 어떤 상태나 행위가 과거 어느 때부터 시작되어 현재까지 계속 진행되고 있음을 나타내거나, 현재까지 계속적으로 반복되고 있다는 것을 나타낸다.

14 ⓐ와 ①, ⑤: 명사적 용법, ②: 형용사적 용법, ③, ④: 부사적 용법

15 ⓑ '스페인어', ⓓ '몇몇의 축구 어휘'를 가리킨다.

16 not A but B = B, not A: A가 아니라 B

17 선행사 friends를 수식하는 주격 관계대명사 who[that]를 쓰는 것이 적절하다.

18 (A)와 ③: (문장 끝이나 중간에서 단독으로) 그렇지만[하지만] (부사), 나머지는 모두 접속사이다

19 주어가 동명사 Doing이므로 improves로 고치는 것이 적절하다.

20 브랜던은 '1년' 동안 한국 드라마들을 시청해 왔다.

21 모든 언어는 처음에는 '어렵지만', 새로운 언어가 당신의 세상을 더욱 넓혀줄 수 있다.

22 ②번 다음 문장의 also에 주목한다. 주어진 문장에 이어 추가 설명을 하는 것이므로 ②번이 적절하다.

23 (1) 안동 찜닭 먹기, (2) 하회탈을 만들고 탈춤 추는 법을 배우기, (3) 하회 마을 방문하기

24 ③ '하회탈 만드는 법'은 알 수 없다. ① 안동, ② 안동 찜닭, ④ 탈춤, ⑤ 하회 마을

p.54~55

01 (i)mprove

02 Watching Chinese dramas with Chinese subtitles is a good way to get better at listening.

03 (1) (s)truck　　(2) (t)aking　　(3) (s)hare

04 (1) This is what I wanted to buy.

　　(2) I enjoyed what you cooked for me last night.

　　(3) Do you remember what Bella wore at the party last night?

05 (1) The alarm has been ringing for 5 minutes.

　　(2) Mary has been chatting with her friends since two o'clock.

　　(3) He has been writing a book since last month.

06 (1) The report showed what I wanted to know.

　　(2) He silently agreed with much of what she had said.

　　(3) I never believe what I read in the newspaper.

　　(4) Mom has been shopping for weeks.

(5) Someone has been stealing candies from the kitchen.

(6) This movie is what many people have been waiting for.

07 What's most important is to become familiar with the language first.

08 how[what] about

09 (A) Spanish movies　(B) the sound

10 Korean　　11 (A) subtitles　(B)translations

01 이어지는 대화 내용에서 중국어를 잘하도록 방법을 설명하는 것으로 보아 중국어를 잘할 수 있도록 하는 방법을 물어보았다는 것을 알 수 있다.

02 중국어 자막이 있는 중국 드라마 보는 것 = watching Chinese dramas with Chinese subtitles 듣기를 더 잘하다 = get better at listening

03 (1) 감동 받다 = be struck (2) 수업을 듣다 = take a class (3) 공유하다 = share

04 what은 선행사를 포함한 관계대명사로 '~하는 것'으로 해석하며, the thing(s) which[that]를 나타낸다.

05 현재완료진행형에서 since는 '시간'을 나타내는 명사(구)와 함께 쓰이고 for는 '기간'을 나타내는 명사(구)와 함께 쓰인다.

06 (1)~(3) 선행사를 포함한 관계대명사 what을 이용한다. (4)~(6) 어떤 상태나 행위가 과거 어느 때부터 시작되어 현재까지 계속 진행되고 있음을 나타내거나, 현재까지 계속적으로 반복되고 있다는 것을 나타내는 현재완료진행형을 이용한다.

07 선행사를 포함한 관계대명사 What을 주어로 해서 쓰는 것이 적절하다.

08 why don't you+동사원형 ~? = how[what] about ~ing?: ~하는 게 어때?

09 인호는 스페인 영화들을 보는 것이 그 언어의 '소리'에 익숙해지는 것에 도움이 될 것이기 때문에 '스페인 영화들'을 자주 볼 것을 제안한다.

10 Korean: 한국어(명사), 한국의(형용사)

11 마리사는 자신이 정말 좋아하는 한국의 젊은 남성 밴드인 DREAM4의 노래를 '자막'이나 '번역'이 없이 이해할 수 있는 방법에 대한 조언을 구한다.

창의사고력 서술형 문제　　p.56

|모범답안|

01 (1) She has been swimming for half an hour.

(2) I have been working here since 2018.

(3) They have known her for two years.

(4) It has been raining since last night.

02 (1) What I bought at the bookstore was the Little Prince.

(2) What he likes the most is to play the guitar.

(3) I like what she gave me yesterday.

03 (A) Andong　(B) Andong-jjimdak
(C) Hahoe mask　(D) the *talchum*
(E) Hahoe Village

01 과거에서 현재까지 진행 중인 일에는 현재완료진행형을 사용한다. 단, 진행형이 불가능한 know와 같은 상태 동사의 경우 현재완료(have/has known)를 사용한다. 또한 날씨를 나타낼 때는 비인칭 주어 it을 사용한다.

단원별 모의고사　　p.57~60

01 ③　　　02 (i)mperfect　　　03 ④

04 Learn vocabulary what is related to your interests.
→ Learn vocabulary which[that] is related to your interests.

05 ①

06 Having new experiences lets us find new talents.

07 ③　　　08 (C) → (A) → (D) → (B)

09 ④　　　10 ⑤

11 (1) has been listening to the music for 2 hours
(2) has been cooking bulgogi since 6:00 p.m.

12 ②　　　13 ④

14 (1) This ring is what my mom gave me.
(2) You can look up what you need on the computer.
(3) Is this the thing that you were looking for?
(4) Russia has belonged to such a category.

15 ③, ⑤

16 Because he doesn't know Spanish that well.

17 (1) 휴대 전화의 설정을 스페인어로 바꿨다.
(2) 사야 할 목록을 스페인어로 적어 오고 있다.

18 ⓐ Watching Spanish movies often
ⓒ Writing a review of a match in Spanish

19 People use some words only in soccer

20 to perform → perform　　　21 ③

22 watching　　　23 subtitles

01 ① how to ~ = 어떻게 ~하는지 ② a very good guitar player = 뛰어난 기타 연주자 ③ take a swimming class = 수영 수업을 듣다 ④ go camping = 캠핑을 가다 ⑤ understand 이해하다

02 주어진 단어는 반의어 관계이다. perfect 완벽한 imperfect 불완전한

03 ④ 여기서 'talent'는 '재능'이라는 뜻이다.

04 관계대명사 what은 선행사가 없을 때 사용한다. 선행사 vocabulary가 있을 때 관계대명사는 which 또는 that을 쓴다.

05 앞에 나온 'It was hard'와 대조적으로 만들기는 어려웠다는 내용과는 상반되는 내용이 들어가야 한다.

06 새로운 경험을 하는 것 = having new experiences 우리에게 ~을 발견하도록 해준다 = lets us find ~

07 'I think it's good to try new things.'를 보면 가구 만들기에 대하여 긍정적인 태도를 가지고 있다는 것을 알 수 있다.

08 (C) 금년에 무엇을 할 것이냐는 질문을 하고 자원봉사를 하면서 시간을 보내겠다는 말에 (A) 좋은 일이라고 응답한다. (D) 상대방은 어떤 계획을 가지고 있는지 묻고 (B) 수영을 하겠다는 바람을 나타낸다.

09 ④ 그것이 마음에 들었느냐는 질문에 많이 좋아할 것이라는 대답은 어색하다.

10 금년에 무엇을 할 것이냐는 질문에 (C) 기타를 배우고 싶다고 대답하자 (B) 어디서 배울 것이냐는 물음에 (A) 친구에게 배울 것이라고 대답한다.

11 현재완료진행형에서 since는 '시간'을 나타내는 명사(구)와 함께 쓰이고 for는 '기간'을 나타내는 명사(구)와 함께 쓰인다.

12 과거 어느 때부터 시작되어 현재까지 계속 진행되고 있음을 나타내는 현재완료진행형을 이용한다.

13 첫 번째 빈칸에는 with의 목적어와 have의 목적어 역할을 할 수 있는 what이 적절하고 두 번째 빈칸에는 all이라는 선행사가 있으므로 that이 적절하다.

14 (1) that을 is의 주어와 gave의 직접목적어 역할을 할 수 있는 what으로 고치는 것이 적절하다. (2) that을 look up과 need의 목적어 역할을 할 수 있는 what으로 고치는 것이 적절하다. (3) what = the thing that[which] (4) 진행형으로 쓸 수 없는 동사인 belong은 현재완료형으로 상태의 계속을 표현한다.

15 ① I could not understand what the teacher talked about. ② Judy has had the hairpin for 10 years. ④ This dress is what she bought last weekend.

16 오언은 '스페인어를 그렇게 잘 알지 못하기 때문에' 그가 정말 좋아하는 선수들의 인터뷰를 이해하는 데 어려움을 겪는다.

17 줄리는 '휴대 전화의 설정을 스페인어로 바꿨고 사야 할 목록을 스페인어로 적어 오고 있다.'

18 ⓐ 스페인 영화들을 자주 보는 것, ⓒ 스페인어로 경기에 대한 후기를 써 보는 것

19 생략되어 있는 by people의 people을 주어로 해서 능동태로 고치는 것이 적절하다.

20 지각동사 see+목적어+원형부정사 또는 현재분사

21 'DREAM4에 관심이 있는 친구들을 찾는 것'은 로리가 조언을 한 내용이다.

22 recommend는 동명사를 목적어로 취한다.

23 subtitle: [주로 복수로] (영화나 텔레비전 화면의) 자막, 영화나 TV 프로그램의 외국어 대화의 번역

Take Care of Yourself

시험대비 실력평가 p.64

| 01 ① | 02 ⑤ | 03 ⑤ | 04 ① |
| 05 ③ | 06 ② | | |

01 얼음이 이를 너무 민감하게 하는 것은 손상을 주는 것으로 damage가 적절하다. clean 깨끗하게 하다 produce 생산하다 lower 낮추다 check 검토하다

02 ⑤ "taste or smell"은 "맛이나 냄새"라는 뜻이다.

03 '건강을 유지하기 위하여 너는 규칙적으로 운동을 할 필요가 있다.'가 적절하다.

04 '머리를 올려놓는 부드러운 물질로 채워진 포대'는 'pillow 베개'이다.

05 (1) look like ~처럼 보이다 (2) just like 마치 ~처럼 (3) like 좋아하다

06 ① clue 단서 ② reason 이유 ③ preventing 예방하는 것 ④ shape 형태 ⑤ lower 낮추다

서술형 시험대비 p.65

01 meaningful 　　　　02 (p)roductive
03 (1) healthy (2) advice (3) what (4) usual
04 (1) term (2) chewing (3) compare (4) shape
05 (t)hirsty
06 Some foods mirror the body parts that they are good for.
07 walk, sleep

01 명사 experiences를 수식하는 형용사가 필요하다. mean 의미하다 meaningful 의미 있는

02 주어진 단어는 동의어 관계이다. improve 개선하다 develop 발전하다 productive 생산적인 – profitable 이득이 되는

03 (1) healthy 건강한 (2) advice 충고 (3) what ~인 것 (4) as usual 평소처럼

04 (1) 용어 term (2) 씹는 것 chewing (3) 비교하다 compare (4) 형태 shape

05 '음료를 원하거나 필요하다고 느끼는' 것은 '목마른 thirsty'이다.

06 몇몇 음식들은 ~ 신체 부위의 생김새를 반영한다 Some foods mirror the body parts ~

07 문맥상 낮에 측정하는 것은 걷기이고, 밤에 측정하는 것은 잠이다.

Conversation

핵심 Check p.66~67

| 1 ② | 　　　　2 ② |

01 상대방이 알고 있는지 물어보는 사실에 대하여 왜 그러냐고 다시 묻는 것으로 보아, 상대방이 물어본 사실을 모르고 있었다는 것을 알 수 있다.

02 작은 스마트 밴드가 여러 가지 역할을 하는 것에 대하여 놀라움을 나타내는 표현이 적절하다.

교과서 대화문 익히기

Check(√) True or False p.68

1 T 2 F 3 F 4 T

교과서 확인학습 p.70~71

Listen & Talk 1 A
Have, heard, chewing, teeth / Why / damage, make, sensitive

Listen & Talk 1 B
look, get enough / slept for over / When did, go / went to bed, as usual / what, making, Have, when / Why, that / going to bed late, feel tired / other, improve, memory, productive, now

Listen & Talk 1 D-1
Have, writing, good, health / really / improves

Listen & Talk 2 A
smart, check, health, smartphone / kind / how far how well / surprised, small

Listen & Talk 2 B
What, living / doing yoga / working, yourself / following, steps / Let, been watched, surprised, have watched / programs, popular / convenient, out, exercise / That's why, try

Listen & Talk 2 C
looks / magic, everywhere / special / awesome, drink, every / surprised, talk / asks, thirsty / why, trying / drinking, increase, help, flow / buy

Do It Yourself A
hungry / don't, before / want, wait / eating, often, health / Really, eating / waiting, eat, too, Eating little, often, from eating / eat, right

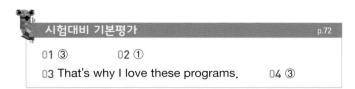

시험대비 기본평가   p.72

01 ③   02 ①

03 That's why I love these programs.   04 ③

---

01 앞에 나온 소개의 내용이 대단해서 놀랐다는 반응이 적절하다.

02 ②~⑤는 상대가 물어본 것을 몰랐을 때 하는 말이고, ①은 알고 있다는 말이다.

03 그런 이유로 ~하다 = That's why ~, 내가 이 프로그램을 아주 좋아한다 = I love these programs

04 ① 소녀가 혼자 요가를 한다. ② 소녀가 온라인 비디오를 따라 하고 있다. ④ 소녀는 많은 사람이 비디오를 본 것을 알고 있다. ⑤ 비디오 덕택에 소녀는 밖에 나갈 필요가 없다.

시험대비 실력평가   p.73~74

01 ④   02 as usual   03 ②

04 ③ eat little and often is good for your health

    → eating little and often is good for your health

05 ①   06 go → to go   07 ②

08 why   09 increase   10 ②   11 ⑤

---

01 ④ '~ 동안'이라는 의미의 전치사가 필요하다.

02 평소처럼 = as usual

03 ② 소녀가 늦게 잠을 자는 이유를 묻는 질문은 대답할 수가 없다.

04 ③ that 절의 주어가 되는 동명사가 되어야 자연스러운 문장이 될 수 있다.

05 자기 전에 휴대전화를 사용하는 것이 잠을 잘자는 것에 좋지 않다는 내용의 구체적인 대답이 나와야 한다.

06 'made a plan'은 '계획을 세웠다'의 의미로 여기에 사용된 made는 사역동사가 아니다. 사역동사의 목적격보어는 원형부정사를 쓰지만, 사역동사가 아니기 때문에 to부정사가 되어야 한다.

07 ⓑ 소녀이 'Really? I'm surprised that it can talk to you.' 라고 말을 하는 것은 위에 주어진 문장을 듣고 보여주는 반응이기 때문에 주어진 문장의 위치는 ⓑ가 적절하다.

08 이어지는 대화에 이유를 나타내는 Because가 있으므로 이유를 물어보는 의문사 why가 적절하다.

09 '어떤 것의 크기, 양, 수 등을 크게 하다'의 의미를 나타내는 단어는 increase(증가시키다)이다.

10 ② magic cup은 두 시간마다 물을 마시도록 해준다.

11 자신이 yoga video program을 사용해 보고 좋은 점을 친구에게 소개하는 내용이다. 자신이 경험한 좋은 점을 추천하는 의미에서 ⓔYou should try them, too.가 적절하다.

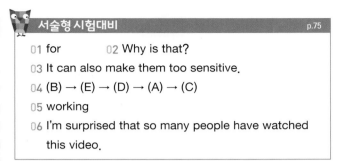

서술형 시험대비   p.75

01 for   02 Why is that?

03 It can also make them too sensitive.

04 (B) → (E) → (D) → (A) → (C)

05 working

06 I'm surprised that so many people have watched this video.

---

01 be bad for ~ = ~에 나쁘다

02 상대가 소개한 내용을 모르고 있었는데 그것의 이유를 설명하는 내용이 이어지는 것으로 보아 앞의 내용에 대한 이유를 물어보는 것이 적절하다.

03 '~을 …하게 만들다'는 'make+목적어+형용사'의 구문을 이용한다.

04 배가 고프다는 말에 (B) 간식을 권하고, (E) 간식을 원하지 않는다는 대답에 그 반대의 상황을 설명하고 (D) 자신의 생각을 말하고, (A) 적게 자주 먹는 것이 더 낫다는 설명을 듣고 (C) 그것을 시도해 보겠다는 대답이 이어진다.

05 요가를 하고 있으므로 운동하는 지를 묻는 말이 적절하다.

06 ~라는 사실에 놀랐다 = I'm surprised that ~

교과서

Grammar

핵심 Check   p.76~77

1 (1) who   (2) which   (3) which

2 (1) filled   (2) carrying   (3) having

시험대비 기본평가   p.78

01 ②   02 (1) known   (2) painted   (3) wearing

(4) sleeping   03 ③

04 (1) I began to read the book, which was very interesting.

(2) The boy watching TV is Jane's son.

(3) He bought a smart phone made in Korea.

---

01 some books를 선행사로 하는 계속적 용법의 목적격 관계대명사 which가 와야 한다. that이나 what은 계속적 용법의 관계대명사로 쓸 수 없다.

02 (1) 사실이 알려지는 것이므로 수동의 의미를 갖는 과거분사가 적절하다. (2) 그림이 그려지는 것이므로 수동의 의미를 갖는 과거분사가 적절하다. (3) 모자를 소녀가 쓰는 것이므로 능동의 의미를 갖는 현재분사가 적절하다. (4) 아기가 잠을 자는 것이므로 진행의 의미를 갖는 현재분사가 적절하다.

03 계속적 용법의 관계대명사에서 선행사가 Ms. Green으로 사람이고 lives의 주어가 필요한 주격이므로 who를 쓰는 것이 적절하다.

04 (1) 우리말 해석이 순차적으로 되어 있으므로 관계대명사의 계속적 용법을 이용한다. (2) TV를 보고 있는 것이므로 진행의 의미를 갖는 현재분사를 이용한다. (3) 스마트폰이 만들어지는 것이므로 수동의 의미를 갖는 과거분사를 이용한다.

시험대비 실력평가　　　　　　p.79~81

01 ②　　　　02 ③　　　　03 ①
04 (1) who　(2) which　(3) which　(4) playing
　　(5) posted　(6) barking
05 ⑤　　　　06 ④　　　　07 ③
08 (1) who　(2) which　(3) who　(4) which
09 ②　　　　10 ①　　　　11 ②　　　　12 which
13 ⑤　　　　14 ①　　　　15 ②
16 (1) I didn't like the students, who ran here and
　　　there in the library.
　　(2) I put the picture on the wall, which made me
　　　remember my best friend.
　　(3) There was a little baby crying on the bed.
　　(4) People all over the world love to eat food made
　　　out of potatoes.
17 ①, ④　　　　18 ③
19 (1) Kim Yuna who is[was] loved by many Koreans
　　　was a famous figure skater.
　　(2) People in Germany want to buy smart phones
　　　which are made in Korea.

01 ② 관계대명사 that은 계속적 용법으로 사용할 수 없다. that → who / jail: 교도소, 감옥

02 ③ 감동을 주는 이야기이므로 과거분사가 아니라 현재분사로 고쳐야 한다. touched → touching

03 첫 번째 빈칸에는 영화를 보는 것이므로 능동의 뜻을 갖는 현재분사가 적절하다. 두 번째 빈칸에는 선행사가 사람이고 주어 역할을 하는 계속적 용법이므로 who가 적절하다.

04 (1) 선행사가 Ms. Chalsey로 사람이고 주어 역할을 하는 계속적 용법이므로 who가 적절하다. (2) 선행사가 사물이고 주어 역할을 하는 계속적 용법이므로 which가 적절하다. (3) 선행사가 앞의 절 전체(He said nothing)이므로 which가 적절하다. (4) flute를 연주하는 것이므로 진행의 뜻을 갖는 현재분사가 적절하다. (5) 기사가 게시되는 것이므로 수동의 뜻을 갖는 과거분사가 적절하다. (6) 개가 짖는 것이므로 진행의 뜻을 갖는 현재분사가 적절하다. 현재분사가 앞에서 수식하는 경우이다. fiercely: 맹렬히, 지독히

05 ⑤번은 과거완료에 쓰였고 나머지는 모두 앞에 나오는 명사를 수식하고 있다.

06 계속적 용법의 관계대명사는 '접속사+대명사'로 바꾸어 쓸 수 있다. '이것은 노인과 바다'인데 Hemingway가 썼다.'라는 것으로, 적절한 접속사는 and이다.

07 그림이 그려진 것이므로 수동의 뜻을 갖는 과거분사가 적절하다.

08 계속적 용법에는 선행사가 사람이면 who, 동물이나 사물이면 which를 쓴다.

09 분사에 다른 어구(여기서는 for me)가 함께 있을 때는 뒤에서 명사를 수식한다.

10 앞에 콤마가 있는 관계대명사의 계속적 용법에는 that을 쓰지 않는다.

11 노래가 불려지고 사랑받는 것이므로 과거분사가 적절하며 이것은 '주격 관계대명사+be동사'가 생략된 것으로 볼 수 있다.

12 계속적 용법의 관계대명사는 '접속사+대명사'로 바꾸어 쓸 수 있다.

13 ⑤ 안경을 끼고 있는 것이므로 진행의 의미를 가지는 현재분사 wearing이 되어야 한다.

14 앞에 콤마(,)가 있으므로 관계대명사의 계속적 용법으로 seen의 목적어 역할을 할 수 있는 whom이 적절하다.

15 첫 번째 빈칸에는 카레가 제공되는 것이므로 수동의 뜻을 갖는 과거분사가 적절하다. 두 번째 빈칸에는 가방을 들고 있는 것이므로 진행의 뜻을 갖는 현재분사가 적절하다.

16 (1) 선행사가 사람이므로 which가 아니라 who를 써야 한다. (2) 계속적 용법에는 that을 쓰지 않는다. (3) 아기가 우는 것이므로 진행의 의미를 갖는 현재분사 crying이 되어야 한다. (4) 음식이 감자로 만들어지는 것이므로 수동의 의미를 갖는 과거분사 made가 되어야 한다.

17 ① 계속적 용법에는 that을 쓰지 않는다. ④ 별명이 붙여지는 것이므로 수동의 의미를 갖는 과거분사 nicknamed가 되어야 한다.

18 ③ 계속적 용법이므로 that을 쓰면 안 된다.

19 분사가 명사를 뒤에서 수식하는 경우에는 그 앞에 '주격 관계대명사+be동사'가 생략된 것으로 생각할 수 있다.

서술형 시험대비　　　　　　p.82~83

01 (1) who　(2) which　(3) who　(4) which
02 (1) The novel written by an unknown author was
　　　made into a movie last year.
　　(2) Korea ranked 10th place, which was ahead of
　　　India and Brazil.
　　(3) The man who is walking his dog is a friend of
　　　mine.
03 (1) A lot of people like cars which[that] are made
　　　in Korea.
　　(2) The man who[that] is reading a book at the
　　　table is my father.

(3) The little girl who[that] is holding the woman's hand is crying loudly.

04 해석: (1) Jacob은 농부인 아들 두 명이 있다.
(2) Jacob은 아들 두 명이 있는데, 그들 모두 농부이다.
차이: (1)은 관계대명사의 한정적 용법으로 선행사를 수식하는 형용사 역할을 하며 '농부인 아들 두 명'으로 해석한다. 아들이 몇 명인지 모르는데 그 중에 농부인 아들이 두 명이라는 의미이며, (2)는 관계대명사가 계속적 용법으로 쓰였으며 아들이 두 명뿐이다.

05 (1) baking   (2) written

06 (1) singing and dancing   (2) planted

07 (1) wrapped, wrapping   (2) lying

08 (1) The new library can hold many people, which made them happy.
(2) Ella carried a box, which looked very heavy for her.
(3) I like Jane, who is kind and wise.

09 (1) who → which   (2) which → who
(3) that → who   (4) The sleeping in the bed baby → The baby sleeping in the bed
(5) making → made   (6) sold → selling

01 (1) 앞의 선행사(사람)를 부연 설명하는 관계대명사의 계속적 용법이므로 who를 쓴다. (2) 앞의 선행사(사물)를 부연 설명하는 관계대명사의 계속적 용법이므로 which를 쓴다. (3) who와 which는 모두 계속적 용법에 쓰일 수 있고 선행사가 사람이면 who, 동물이나 사물이면 which를 쓴다. (4) which는 앞 문장 전체를 선행사로 받을 수 있다.

02 (1) 소설이 씌어진 것이므로 수동의 뜻을 갖는 과거분사를 이용한다. (2) 앞에 있는 절을 선행사로 하는 관계대명사 which를 이용한다. (3) 개를 산책시키고 있는 것이므로 능동의 뜻을 갖는 현재분사를 이용한다. 명사를 뒤에서 수식하는 경우, '주격 관계대명사+be 동사'가 생략된 것으로 생각한다.

03 분사가 명사를 뒤에서 수식하는 경우에는 그 앞에 '주격 관계대명사+be동사'가 생략된 것으로 생각할 수 있다.

05 (1) 빵을 굽는 것이므로 현재분사를 이용한다. (2) 메시지가 씌어진 것이므로 과거분사를 이용한다.

06 (1) 진행의 뜻을 갖는 현재분사를, (2) 수동의 뜻을 갖는 과거분사를 이용한다.

07 (1) 첫 번째 빈칸에는 box를 뒤에서 수식하는 과거분사(싸여 있는 상자)가 적절하며, 두 번째 빈칸에는 포장지(wrapping paper)로 동명사(싸여 있는 상자)가 적절하다. (2) 똬리를 튼 채로 누워 있는 뱀이므로 현재분사가 적절하다. coil: (여러 겹으로 둥글게 감아 놓은) 고리[사리], a snake's coils: 뱀의 똬리

08 (1) 앞에 나온 절 전체를 선행사로 받는 which를 이용한다. (2) 사물을 선행사로 받는 which를 이용한다. (3) 계속적 용법의 관계대명사는 '접속사(and, but, for, though 등)+대명사'로 고쳐 쓸 수 있다. 여기서는 'for(= because)+she'로 생각할 수 있다.

09 (1) 선행사가 사물이므로 which로 나타낸다. (2) 선행사가 사람이므로 who로 나타낸다. (3) 계속적 용법의 관계대명사로는 that을 쓰지 않는다. (4) 분사에 다른 어구(목적어나 보어, 수식 어구 등)가 함께 있을 때는 뒤에서 명사를 수식한다. (5) 차가 만들어지는 것이므로 과거분사로 고친다. (6) 가게에서 장난감을 파는 것이므로 현재분사로 고친다.

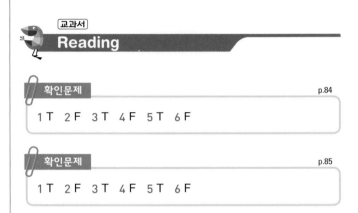

교과서
Reading

확인문제   p.84

1 T   2 F   3 T   4 F   5 T   6 F

확인문제   p.85

1 T   2 F   3 T   4 F   5 T   6 F

교과서 확인학습 A   p.86~87

01 Beneficial
02 containing, keeps, healthy
03 are good for   04 a big clue
05 following   06 not only, but, also
07 compare, with   08 look similar
09 multiple hollow spaces 10 that, that, are
11 In addition, lower   12 the shape
13 anything   14 similar to
15 is divided into   16 which
17 stay healthy   18 preventing
19 A slice of carrot   20 that, which
21 process, send, to   22 healthy eyes
23 Cutting onions, makes you cry
24 try slicing   25 looks a little like
26 which helps make   27 move on to
28 comes to mind   29 Doesn't
30 strong taste, come from, prevents, from feeling, throwing
31 For this reason   32 mirror, that
33 many other such foods 34 as many as you can

1 Beneficial Foods for Our Bodies

2 We all know that a diet containing a variety of foods keeps our bodies healthy.

3 But sometimes we are not sure which foods are good for which body parts.

4 Nature, however, gives us a big clue.

5 Look at the following examples.

6 Each of these foods not only looks like a certain body part but is also good for that body part.

7 Slice open a tomato and compare it with the human heart.

8 You will see that they look similar.

9 They both have multiple hollow spaces and are red.

10 Researchers say that the chemicals that make tomatoes red are good for your heart and blood.

11 In addition, eating tomatoes can lower your risk of heart disease.

12 Look at the shape of a walnut.

13 Do you notice anything?

14 Yes, it's very similar to the shape of the human brain!

15 A walnut is divided into two parts, just like the brain.

16 Walnuts also have wrinkles, which the brain has too.

17 Studies show that walnuts help our brains stay healthy and active.

18 They are also good for preventing Alzheimer's disease.

19 A slice of carrot looks like the human eye.

20 Carrots have some chemicals that can make vitamin A, which improves your vision.

21 It helps your eyes process light and send a clear image to the brain.

22 So if you want healthy eyes, eat carrots.

23 Cutting onions is not fun because it makes you cry.

24 But try slicing one anyway.

25 You can see that the inside looks a little like a human cell.

26 Scientists say that onions contain vitamin B, which helps make new, healthy cells.

27 Now, let's move on to ginger.

28 What body part comes to mind when you see it?

29 Doesn't it look like a stomach?

30 You may not like ginger's strong taste or smell, but these come from a special chemical that prevents you from feeling sick and throwing up.

31 For this reason, ginger can be good for your stomach.

32 Isn't it amazing that some foods mirror the body parts that they are good for?

33 Interestingly, there are many other such foods.

34 Find as many as you can and try to eat a variety of them.

---

01 ②, ⑤   02 (A) for   (B) looks   (C) is

03 ②   04 ⑤

05 makes → make, is → are   06 ①

07 ③   08 ④   09 and it   10 ②

11 ②   12 protecting → preventing

13 (A) two parts   (B) wrinkles   14 ③

15 (A) special chemical   (B) throwing up

16 Cutting onions   17 ③

18 to make

19 ① onion   ② a human cell   ③ Vitamin B

20 ④   21 as   22 some foods

23 ②, ③   24 keeps our bodies healthy

25 (A) look like   (B) good for

26 생강의 강한 맛과 냄새   27 ⑤

---

01 ⓐ와 ②, ⑤: 현재분사, ①, ③, ④: 동명사

02 (A) 어떤 음식이 어떤 신체 부위에 '좋은지' 잘 모를 때가 있다고 해야 하므로 for가 적절하다. be good at: ~을 잘하다, be good for: ~에 좋다, (B) Each가 주어이므로 looks가 적절하다. (C) Each가 주어이므로 is가 적절하다.

03 ② '때때로' 우리는 어떤 음식이 어떤 신체 부위에 좋은지 잘 모를 때가 있다.

04 앞에 나오는 내용에 추가하는 내용이 뒤에 이어지므로 In addition이 가장 적절하다. ① 대신에, ② 그러나 ③ 그런데도, 그럼에도 불구하고, ④ 다른 한편으로는, 반면에 ⑤ 게다가

05 선행사가 the chemicals이므로 make로, 주어가 the chemicals이므로 are로 고치는 것이 적절하다.

06 이 글은 토마토 한 개를 갈라서 보면 사람의 심장과 비슷해 보이고, 토마토를 먹는 것이 심장에 좋다는 글이므로, 제목으로는 ① 번 '당신의 심장과 닮은 음식이 당신의 심장에 좋다.'가 적절하다.

07 ③ 토마토를 붉게 만드는 화학물질이 무엇인지는 대답할 수 없다. ① A tomato. ② They both have multiple hollow spaces and are red. ④ Yes. ⑤ Yes.

08 뒤에 비타민 A는 눈이 빛을 처리하여 뇌에 선명한 이미지를 보낼 수 있도록 돕는다는 말이 이어지므로, 비타민 A가 '시력'을 개선한다고 하는 것이 적절하다.

09 which는 계속적 용법의 주격 관계대명사로, and it으로 바꿔 쓸 수 있다.

10 '당근에 비타민 A의 효능을 낮출 수 있는 화학 성분이 있다'는 말은 위 글의 내용과 일치하지 않는다.

11 주어진 문장의 Yes에 주목한다. ②번 앞 문장의 질문에 대한 답에 해당하므로 ②번이 적절하다.

12 알츠하이머병을 '예방하는 데'도 좋다고 해야 하므로, preventing으로 고쳐야 한다. protect: 보호하다, prevent: 예방하다, 막다

13 그것들은 '두 부분'으로 나뉘어 있고, '주름'이 있다.

14 ⓐ move on to: (새로운 일·주제로) 넘어가다, come to mind: 생각이 떠오르다, 생각나다, ⓑ come from: ~에서 나오다, prevent A from ~ing: A가 ~하는 것을 막다

15 생강의 '특별한 성분'이 복통과 '구토'를 예방하기 때문이다.

16 '양파를 써는 것'을 가리킨다..

17 ③: 그런데(대화에서 화제를 바꿀 때 씀), ⓑ와 나머지 모두: '어쨌든'

18 help+원형부정사 또는 to부정사

19 음식: '양파', 유사한 신체 부위: '인간의 세포', 혜택: 이 음식 안의 '비타민 B'가 새롭고 건강한 세포를 만드는 것을 돕는다.

20 (A)의 however가 (C)의 내용과 상반되는 내용을 이끄는 것이므로 (C) 다음에 (A)가 이어지고 (B)의 these foods가 (A)의 the following examples의 음식들을 가리키는 것이므로 (A) 다음에 (B)가 와야 한다. 그러므로 (C)-(A)-(B)의 순서가 적절하다.

21 as+원급+as+주어+can: 가능한 한 ~한

22 '어떤 음식들'을 가리킨다.

23 (B)와 ②, ③: 명사적 용법, ①, ⑤: 부사적 용법, ④: 형용사적 용법

24 keep+목적어+목적격보어(형용사)

25 우리 신체의 특정 부분과 '비슷해 보이는' 몇몇 음식들은 그 신체 부위들에 '좋다.'

26 '생강의 강한 맛과 냄새'를 가리킨다.

27 어떻게 특별한 성분이 복통과 구토를 예방하는지는 알 수 없다. ① A stomach. ② Yes. ③ Yes. ④ It comes from a special chemical.

서술형 시험대비 p.94~95

01 which[that] contains 02 (A) similar (B) good
03 looks → looks like 04 mirror
05 possible 06 carrots 07 brain → eye

08 (A) improves (B) process light (C) clear image
09 ⓐ to ⓑ into   10 and, them
11 (A) Walnuts (B) our brains
12 ⓐ feeling ⓑ throwing
13 strong taste, smell
14 (A) a[the] tomato (B) human heart
15 the chemicals that make tomatoes red are good for your heart and blood

01 주격 관계대명사 which 또는 that을 사용하는 것이 적절하다.

02 어떤 음식들의 모양들은 그 음식들이 '유익한' 우리 신체의 특정 부분의 모양들과 자연적으로 '유사'하다. be good for: ~에 좋다

03 뒤에 명사가 있으므로 looks like로 고쳐야 한다. look+형용사, look like+명사

04 '그 음식이 유익한 신체 부위의 생김새를 반영하고 있는 몇몇 음식'을 가리킨다.

05 as + 원급 + as + 주어 + can[could] = as + 원급 + as possible: 가능한 한 …한

06 당근에 있는 화학 성분이 비타민 A를 만들고 그것이 시력을 개선한다고 했으므로, 건강한 눈을 원한다면, '당근'을 먹으라고 하는 것이 적절하다.

07 썰어 놓은 당근의 모양은 사람의 '눈'과 비슷해 보인다.

08 비타민 A는 시력을 '개선하고', 눈이 '빛을 처리하여' 뇌에 '선명한 이미지'를 보낼 수 있도록 돕는다.

09 ⓐ be similar to: ~와 유사하다, ⓑ be divided into: ~로 나뉘다

10 which는 계속적 용법의 목적격 관계대명사로, and ~ them으로 바꿔 쓸 수 있다.

11 '호두'는 알츠하이머병을 예방하는 데도 좋을 뿐만 아니라 '사람의 뇌'가 건강하고 활동적인 상태를 유지하는 데 도움을 준다.

12 전치사 from 다음에 동명사로 쓰는 것이 적절하다.

13 생강의 '강한 맛'이나 '냄새' 때문이다.

14 잘라낸 '토마토'와 '사람의 심장'을 가리킨다.

15 관계대명사 that[which]을 보충하면 된다.

영역별 핵심문제 p.97~101

01 ③   02 ②   03 ①   04 ①
05 ⑤   06 ③   07 your body
08 ②   09 ④   10 ②   11 ④
12 소년이 낮에 얼마나 멀리 걷는지 그리고 밤에 얼마나 잘 자는지 보여준다.
13 ④   14 ⑤   15 ①, ③
16 with whom
17 (1) which are (2) who is   18 ②

01 ③ midnight = 자정

02 ① 알아차리다 notice ② ~으로 나뉘다 be divided into ③ 유지하다 stay ④ 포함하다 contain ⑤ 다양한 a variety of

03 호두는 뇌를 건강하게 한다고 했으므로 알츠하이머를 예방하는 데 유익하다고 해야 한다.

04 damage 손상을 주다 harm 손상시키다 chew 씹다 contain 포함하다 improve 개선하다 compare 비교하다

05 (C) 이백만 번을 보았다는 사실에 알고 있다는 대답과 그 이유를 덧붙인다. (A) 비디오의 장점으로 밖에 나갈 필요가 없다는 언급에 (B) 동의하는 표현이 따라온다.

06 compared to: ~와 비교하여 compare A to B: A를 B에 비교하다

07 it은 인칭대명사로 앞에 언급된 단수명사를 받는다.

08 ② 'A lot of teens have a negative body image.'를 보면 청소년들은 자신에 대한 부정적인 신체 이미지를 가지고 있다는 것을 알 수 있다.

09 'I'll wait until dinner.'라고 말하는 것으로 보아 먹고 싶지 않다는 내용이 들어가야 한다.

10 하루 세 번 식사하는 것보다는 조금씩 자주 먹는 것이 낫다는 내용이다.

11 ④ 이 대화에서는 a smart band가 별도의 장치인지 smartphone에 탑재되어 있는 앱인지가 밝혀지지 않았다.

13 ④ 이어지는 설명으로 보았을 때 'I didn't know that.'이 적절하다.

14 Our art room을 선행사로 하는 계속적 용법의 주격 관계대명사 which가 와야 한다. that은 계속적 용법의 관계대명사로 쓸 수 없다.

15 ① The injured man was lying on the ground. ③ This is the most expensive car made in England.

16 앞에 콤마(,)가 있는 관계대명사의 계속적 용법을 이용한다. 함께 쓰레기를 주운 것이므로 전치사 with와 목적격이므로 whom을 쓴다.

17 분사가 명사를 뒤에서 수식하는 경우에는 그 앞에 '주격 관계대명사+be동사'가 생략된 것으로 생각할 수 있다.

18 계속적 용법의 관계대명사는 '접속사(and, but, for, though 등)+대명사'로 고쳐 쓸 수 있다. 여기서는 though이 적절하다.

19 ⓑ baking → baked ⓓ jumped → jumping ⓕ that → who

20 앞에 나오는 내용과 상반되는 내용이 뒤에 이어지므로 however가 가장 적절하다. ① 그러므로, ② 게다가, ④ 비슷하게, ⑤ 예를 들어

21 keeps의 목적격보어이므로, 형용사 healthy로 고치는 것이 적절하다. healthily: 건강하게(부사), healthy: 건강한

22 not only[just/merely/simply] A but also B: A뿐만 아니라 B도, ③ mainly: 주로, ⑤ mostly: 주로

23 관계대명사 that은 계속적 용법으로 쓸 수 없으므로 which로 바꾸는 것이 적절하다.

24 호두와 인간의 뇌에 주름이 있는 이유는 대답할 수 없다. ① The shape of the human brain. ② They are divided into two parts. ④ A walnut. ⑤ A walnut.

25 ⓐ와 ①, ②, ⑤: 동명사, ③, ④: 현재분사

26 (A) 동명사 Cutting이 주어이므로 is가 적절하다. (B) '사역동사 make+목적어+원형부정사'이므로 cry가 적절하다. (C) a few 뒤에는 셀 수 있는 명사 복수가 와야 하므로 a little이 적절하다.

27 try ~ing: 시험 삼아 ~해 보다

28 이 글은 위장과 유사하게 생긴 생강의 효능을 설명한 글이므로, 요지로는 ②번 '위장과 닮은 생강이 위장에 좋다'가 적절하다.

29 '구토'를 예방한다고 해야 하므로, throwing up으로 고치는 것이 적절하다. overeat: 과식하다, throw up: …을 토하다

01 주어진 단어는 반의어 관계이다. prevent 가로 막다 allow 허용하다 accept 받아들이다 refuse 거부하다

02 "prevent A from ~ing"는 "keep A from ~ing" "stop A from ~ing"로 "A가 ~하지 못하게 막다"는 뜻이다.

03 '생각, 느낌, 행동을 조절하는 머릿속에 있는 기관'은 'brain 뇌'이다.

04 (1) 씹는 것 chewing (2) 인기 있는 popular (3) 속이 빈 hollow (4) 처리하다 process

05 (A) 이어지는 대답으로 7시간 잔다는 것을 통해서 잠의 양에 대

한 질문임을 알 수 있다. (B) 대답에 'after midnight'는 시간을 가리킨다.

06 이어지는 설명에 그 기능이 나와 있으므로 질문은 기능이나 특징을 물어보는 것이어야 한다.

07 놀라움을 나타낼 수 있는 amazed가 적절하다. worried 걱정하는 pleased 즐거워하는 frightened 겁먹은 convinced 확신하는

08 'help+목적어+(to) 부정사'의 구문이 되어야 한다.

09 'so many people have watched this video.'를 보면 앞에 나온 말을 많은 사람이 시청한 것과 어울리는 "Wow, it's been watched two milion times!"가 되어야 한다.

10 놀라움을 나타내는 "I'm surprised that ~."은 "How could it be possible that ~?" "I can't believe that ~." "It's surprising ~."으로 바꿔 쓸 수 있다.

11 모두 관계대명사 who가 적절하지만 ④번은 선행사가 앞선 절 전체이므로 which가 적절하다.

12 ① I found a box filled with many letters at the basement. ② I bought a new laptop manufactured in Korea. ④ Mom bought me a new camera, with which I took lots of photos. ⑤ Sumin loves her new cap, which she bought on sale. basement: 지하실

13 계속적 용법의 관계대명사는 '접속사(and, but, for, though 등)+대명사'로 바꿔 쓸 수 있다. in good shape: (몸의) 상태가 좋은

14 소나기를 만나서 늦은 것이므로 수동의 뜻을 갖는 과거분사가 적절하다. shower: 소나기

15 첫 번째 문장에서는 "iron horse"라고 불리는 것이므로 과거분사가 적절하다. 두 번째 문장에서는 선행사가 사물이고 계속적 용법이므로 which가 적절하다. consecutive: 연속적인

16 토마토를 붉게 만드는 화학 물질이 사람의 심장과 피에 유익하다고 했으므로, 토마토를 먹는 것이 '심장병'에 걸릴 위험성을 낮출 수 있다고 하는 것이 적절하다. ① 복통

17 hollow 속이 빈, 텅 빈, ① vacant: 빈

18 (B)와 ②, ⑤: 접속사, (C)와 ①, ③, ④: 주격 관계대명사

19 a slice of: 한 조각

20 help+목적어+원형부정사 또는 to부정사

21 음식: '당근', 유사한 신체 부위: 눈, 혜택: 그들은 '시력'을 개선한다.

22 ⓐ에는 접속사 that, ⓑ에는 관계대명사 that이 적절하다.

23 (A)와 ③: 가주어, ①, ⑤: 앞에 이미 언급되었거나 현재 이야기되고 있는 것을 가리키는 인칭대명사(그것), ② 가목적어, ④ 비인칭 주어

24 위 글은 ④ '추천하는 글'이다. ① (책·연극·영화 등에 대한) 논평[비평], 감상문, ② 독후감, ③ 요약, 개요, ⑤ 수필

25 ⓐ 다음의 내용을 쓰면 된다.

26 why don't you+동사원형 ~? = how[what] about ~ing?: ~하는 게 어때?

01 (h)ealth

02 how far I walk during the day and how well I sleep at night

03 (s)urprised   **04** compared

05 (1) shape   (2) clue   (3) contain

06 (1) I want to meet Jon Kim, who is my favorite actor, in person someday.

(2) Have you read the book, *The Last Leaf*, which was written by O. Henry?

07 (1) The men giving out flyers are wearing caps.

(2) The soldier injured in the war was lying on the bed.

(3) Last week I bought a new computer, which I like a lot.

08 (1) He got married to Huong, who is from Vietnam.

(2) She wanted to buy the dress, which was too expensive.

(3) The flower planted in the garden grew up very fast.

09 clue   **10** various   **11** as well as

12 (A) similar   (B) that   (C) lower

13 (A) hollow spaces   (B) red

14 The chemicals that make tomatoes red.

01 하루 동안 걷는 거리와 밤에 잠을 잘 자는지 등의 정보는 건강(health) 정보이다.

02 동사 shows에 이어지는 목적어로 간접의문문이 되어서 'how far ~ and how well ~'의 형태가 되어야 한다.

03 놀라움을 나타내는 surprised가 적절하다.

04 주어진 문장의 청소년이 다른 사람과 비교되는 상황을 나타내므로 과거분사 compared가 적절하다.

05 (1) 모양 shape (2) 단서 clue (3) 포함하다 contain

06 (1) 선행사가 사람이므로 who를 이용한다. (2) 선행사가 사물이므로 which를 이용한다.

07 (1) 전단지(flyers)를 주는 것이므로 현재분사가 적절하다. (2) 수동의 의미이므로 과거분사가 적절하다. (3) 계속적 용법에는 that을 사용하지 않는다. which가 적절하다.

08 (1), (2) 계속적 용법의 관계대명사를 이용한다. (3) 꽃이 심겨진 것이므로 과거분사를 이용한다.

09 clue: 단서, 실마리, 문제나 수수께끼에 대한 답을 발견하도록 도와주는 것

10 a variety of = various: 여러 가지의, 각양각색의, 다양한

11 not only A but also B = B as well as A: A뿐만 아니라 B도

12 (A) 그 둘이 '비슷해' 보인다고 해야 하므로 similar가 적절하다. (B) 선행사(the chemicals)가 있으므로 that이 적절하다. (C) 심장병에 걸릴 위험성을 '낮출 수 있다'고 해야 하므로

lower가 적절하다.

13 둘 다 여러 개의 '빈 공간'이 있고 '붉은 색'이다.

14 토마토를 사람의 심장과 피에 유익하게 만드는 것은 '토마토를 붉게 만드는 화학 물질'이다.

창의사고력 서술형 문제   p.108

|모범답안|

01 Accept / praise / compare

02 (1) written in English
   (2) covered with fallen leaves
   (3) sitting on the corner

03 (A) Fruit yogurt salad   (B) bananas
   (C) lower blood pressure   (D) vitamin C
   (E) bones

01 accept 수용하다, 받아들이다 compare 비교하다

단원별 모의고사   p.109~112

01 ①   02 ③   03 ①

04 working   05 ②   06 ④

07 that is making you tired → what is making you tired

08 Scientists say that going to bed late can make you feel tired the next day.

09 ②   10 ①

11 (1) parked   (2) parking   12 ⑤   13 ①

14 (1) I can't find the books, which Evelyn gave to me.
   (2) She is my friend, Sophia, who is from Hungary.
   (3) I got a C in my test, which made my mom disappointed.
   (4) The girl cleaning the room is my sister. 또는 The girl who is cleaning the room is my sister.
   (5) You can find a nice beach covered with white sand.

15 containing

16 which foods are good for which body parts

17 ②   18 ③

19 (A) heart   (B) heart   (C) blood

20 ①, ③   21 ④   22 Vitamin A does.

01 compare 비교하다 improve 향상시키다 lower 낮추다 check 검토하다 prevent 가로막다

02 질문의 내용이 잠이 든 시간이기 때문에 대답도 잠잔 시간을 나타내는 말이 적절하다.

03 '내부에 빈 공간을 가진'에 해당하는 단어는 'hollow 속이 빈'이다. sensitive 민감한 productive 생산적인 positive 긍정적

인 moved 감동 받은

04 "운동하다"는 "work out"이고 be동사에 이어지는 현재분사를 써서 "~하고 있다"에 해당하는 현재진행시제가 되도록 하여야 한다.

05 "That's why I love these programs."를 보면 위 질문에 대한 대답은 "It looks very convenient. You don't have to go out to exercise."에서 찾을 수 있다.

06 ④ "It's no wonder."는 당연함을 나타내는 말로 "4월에 눈이 온다."고 할 때는 놀라움을 나타내는 "It's surprising."이 어울린다.

07 '너를 피곤하게 만드는 것'은 'what is making you tired'라고 한다. 선행사 없이 명사절을 유도하는 what이 적절하다.

08 과학자들이 ~라고 말한다 = Scientists say that ~, 늦게 자는 것 = going to bed late, 너를 다음날 피곤하게 느끼도록 만들 수 있다 = can make you feel tired the next day

09 ① 소년이 충분한 잠을 자지 않았는지는 알 수 없다. ③ 소녀는 자정 이후에 잠들었다. ④ 언제 자는 가는 중요하다. ⑤ 소년의 말은 듣고 소녀는 일찍 자려고 할 것이다.

10 (A) 하루 세 번 먹는 것과 대조적으로 조금씩 자주 먹는 것이 되어야 한다. (B) 하루 세 번 먹으려고 배가 고파도 계속 기다리면 나중에는 과식을 하게 된다는 내용이 자연스럽다.

11 (1) 차가 주차된 것이므로 수동의 뜻을 갖는 과거분사를 이용한다. (2) 차를 주차하는 것이므로 능동의 뜻을 갖는 현재분사를 이용한다.

12 관계대명사의 계속적 용법으로 첫 번째 빈칸에는 선행사가 사람이므로 who를 이용하고, 두 번째 빈칸에는 선행사가 사물이므로 which를 이용한다.

13 which는 앞 문장 전체를 선행사로 받을 수 있으므로 접속사 and와 it 대신에 쓸 수 있다.

14 (1) 관계대명사의 계속적 용법으로 that을 쓰지 않으며 관계대명사는 접속사와 대명사의 역할을 하므로 목적어로 쓰인 them을 삭제해야 한다. (2) 계속적 용법이므로 that을 who로 고치는 것이 적절하다. (3) 관계대명사의 계속적 용법으로 what을 쓰지 않으며 앞에 나오는 절을 선행사로 받는 which가 적절하다. (4) 현재분사가 뒤에서 명사를 수식하도록 하거나 '주격 관계대명사+be동사'가 되도록 해야 한다. (5) 해변이 모래로 덮인 것이므로 과거분사가 적절하다.

15 앞의 명사 a diet를 수식하는 현재분사 containing이 적절하다.

16 for를 보충하면 된다.

17 주어진 문장의 they에 주목한다. ②번 앞 문장의 it과 the human heart를 가리키므로 ②번이 적절하다.

18 ②, ③ 현재분사, ⑧와 ①, ④, ⑤는 동명사

19 음식: 토마토, 유사한 신체 부위: '심장', 혜택: 그들은 '심장'과 '피'에 유익하다.

20 (A)와 ①, ③: ~와 닮다, ~와 비슷[유사]하다, ② ~을 찾다, ④ A slice of carrot and the human eye are alike.라고 쓸 수 있다. ⑤ ~을 돌보다

21 ⑤와 ④: 처리하다(동사), 나머지는 다 '과정'(명사)

22 시력을 개선하도록 돕는 비타민은 '비타민 A'이다.

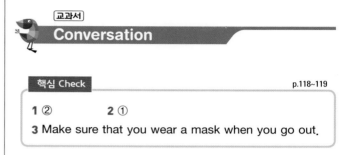

Always Aware, Always Prepared

시험대비 실력평가   p.116

01 ①   02 ⑤   03 ②   04 ④
05 ④   06 (t)raining

01 주어진 단어는 동의어 관계이다. damage 손상(=harm) exact 정확한 correct 정확한

02 내용상 자동차를 운전하던 사람이 방송을 듣기 위해서 차를 멈춰 세운 상황으로 "길 한쪽으로 차를 대다"에 해당하는 'pull over'가 적절하다.

03 ① 홍수 - 대개는 건조한 한 지역을 덮는 많은 양의 물 ② 지진 (earthquake) - 많은 손상을 가져오는 지표면의 갑작스러운 흔들림 ③ 재난 - 큰 손상이나 고통을 초래하는 홍수, 폭풍 또는 사고와 같은 갑작스러운 사건 ④ 흔한 – 많은 장소나 많은 사람에게 자주 일어나는 ⑤ 나가다, 퇴장하다 - 어떤 장소를 떠나다

04 ④ exit는 '출구; 나가다'라는 뜻이다. '들어가다'는 'enter'이다.

05 ① crawl 기어가다 ② based on ~에 바탕을 둔 ③ destroy 파괴되다 ④ shaking 흔들림 ⑤ ring 울리다

06 'drill 훈련'과 동의어 관계에 있는 것은 'training 훈련'이다.

서술형 시험대비   p.117

01 properly   02 out   03 (c)ollapse
04 (1) exactly   (2) pulled, out of   (3) In case of
05 include
06 (1) made our way   (2) scared   (3) seriously
07 (d)estroy   08 (e)nter

01 perform을 수식하는 'proper 적절한'의 부사 'properly'가 올바른 형태이다.

02 황사에서 마스크를 쓰는 것은 밖에 나갈 때이다. 밖에 나가다 = go out 무슨 일이 일어났는지 알아보기 위해 라디오를 듣고 있기 때문에 "알아내다 find out"이 적절하다.

03 collapse: 붕괴되다, 무너지다

04 (1) 정확하게 exactly (2) A를 끌어내다 pull A out of ~ (3) ~의 경우에 in case of ~

05 주어진 단어는 반의어 관계이다. destroy 파괴하다 construct 건설하다 include 포함하다 exclude 제외하다

06 (1) make one's way ~로 가다 (2) scared 겁먹은 (3)

---

seriously 진지하게

07 '어떤 것을 더 이상 존재하지 않거나 사용할 수 없거나 수리할 수 없도록 심하게 손상시키다'는 '파괴하다 destroy'에 해당한다.

08 "exit 나가다"의 반대말은 "enter"이다.

교과서 Conversation

핵심 Check   p.118~119

1 ②   2 ①
3 Make sure that you wear a mask when you go out.

01 (B) 한국의 산불에 대한 궁금증을 나타내자 그것에 대한 대답을 하고 (A) 다시 언제 일어났는지 질문을 하니까 (C) 2005년에 일어났다고 대답한다.

02 '반드시 ~해라.'의 의미로 'Make sure ~' 또는 'Be sure ~'를 쓴다.

03 '반드시 ~해라'의 의미로 'Make sure that ~'을 이용한다.

교과서 대화문 익히기

Check(√) True or False   p.120

1 T   2 F   3 F   4 T

교과서 확인학습   p.122~123

Listen & Talk 1 A

was, flood, hear / floods, common, are, curious, how / research

Listen & Talk 1 B

seem, natural disasters, these / earthquake, south, storm / curious, which, natural disaster, most damage / report, damage, each type / guess, second / heavy, snow / What / Based, earthquakes, damage, been increasing, because, been / seems like, prepared, variety, natural disasters

Listen & Talk 1 C

hear about, fires / serious / destroyed, houses, other / Are, going on / actually, worse, living there / So do, curious, leave / Actually, leave, missing / terrible, somewhere

Listen & Talk 2 A

what else, put in, survival kit / water, radio / Anything / make, include, radio

Listen & Talk 2 B

Performing, save, Here, steps, proper, needs, Tap, Are, reaction, listen, feel, breathing, sure, place, in, chest, weight, harder, breaths, help

Listen & Talk 2 D

In case, what, do / Make, cover, wet / else / exit, immediately

Do It Yourself A

hear, occurring, often, before / really, felt / usually, southern, other places / curious, why, occurred / research / do / How about, help / Let's, find

---

시험대비 기본평가 p.124

01 ①　　　02 ②

03 make sure that you include batteries for the radio

01 이어지는 문장에 화재의 상황에 대한 소개가 있으므로 화재 상황에 대한 질문이 빈칸에 들어가는 것이 적절하다.

02 화재가 난 경우의 주의사항에 추가하는 내용이므로 주의사항을 알려주는 표현인 'Make sure'가 적절하다.

03 '반드시 ~해라'는 'Make sure that 주어+동사'이다.

시험대비 실력평가 p.125~126

01 actually　　02 ③　　03 ②

04 ②　　05 It, that, are　06 prepared　07 ⑤

08 ①　　09 ④　　10 ④

01 문맥상 actual의 부사형이 와야 한다.

02 "~에 대하여 궁금하다"의 의미는 "I'm curious about ~" 또는 "I wonder ~"이다.

03 바람이 산불을 악화시키기는 했지만 바람 때문에 산불이 났다는 언급은 없다.

04 자연 재해가 가져오는 손상의 정도를 구체적으로 설명하는 것은 보고서를 읽었기 때문이므로 순서를 나열하기 전에 주어진 문장이 들어가야 한다.

05 There seem to ~는 It seems that ~ 구문으로 바꿔 쓸 수 있다.

06 be동사의 보어가 되는 형용사형으로 고쳐야 한다.

07 왜 한국에서 지진이 더 자주 일어나는지는 언급되지 않았다.

08 한국에서는 많은 산불이 일어난다는 말을 들었다고 말하자 (A) 양양에서 큰 산불이 있었다고 대답하고 (C) 그것이 언제 일어났는지 궁금하다고 말하자. (B) 2005년에 일어났다고 대답한다.

09 'I think she can help us.'를 보면 과학 선생님께 질문하자는 'How about asking our science teacher first?'가 적절하다.

10 지진이 더 자주 일어나는 것에 대하여 조사를 해보자고 하는 것으로 보아 두 사람은 지진의 빈도가 늘어난 이유를 알지 못하고 있다고 해야 한다.

서술형 시험대비 p.127

01 I'm curious about　　02 What[How] about

03 It seems like we have to be prepared for a variety of natural disasters in Korea.

04 reaction

05 Make sure you place your hands in the middle of the person's chest.

06 We should start when the person is not breathing.

01 궁금하다는 의미로 curious를 써서 "I'm curious about"가 적절하다.

02 앞에 나온 폭우, 폭설 이외에 지진에 대한 궁금증을 나타내어 "지진은 어떻습니까?"의 의미로 'What about ~?'나 'How about ~?'가 적절하다.

03 '~인 것 같다'는 'It seems like ~'이다.

04 심폐소생술을 수행하기 전에 확인하는 단계에서 상대가 반응이 없을 때 119에 도움을 요청한다.

05 반드시 ~하도록 해라 = Make sure ~, 손을 ~의 가슴 가운데에 놓다 = put your hands in the middle of one's chest

06 그 사람이 숨을 쉬지 않을 때 심폐소생술을 시작해야 한다.

교과서

Grammar

핵심 Check p.128~129

1 (1) had done　(2) had finished　(3) had

2 (1) Although　(2) since　(3) after

시험대비 기본평가 p.130

01 ⑤　　　02 (1) had already started

(2) had lied　(3) Although　(4) since　　03 ③

04 (1) Until last year, Linda had never visited Paris.

(2) Although he was rich, people thought he was poor.

(3) I couldn't sleep last night since I was so afraid.

---

22 정답 및 해설

01 주절의 동사가 recognized로 과거이고 그녀를 본 것은 그 이전의 사실이므로 과거완료를 써야 한다.

02 (1) 방문한 것보다 그가 출발한 것이 앞서는 것이므로 과거완료가 적절하다. (2) 거짓말을 한 것(앞선 사실)을 시인하는 것이므로 과거완료가 적절하다. (3) 앞과 뒤의 절의 내용이 상반되므로 Although가 적절하다. (4) 뒤의 절이 이유를 나타내고 있으므로 since가 적절하다.

03 첫 문장과 두 번째 문장이 원인과 결과를 언급하는 것으로 보아 원인이 되는 문장에 접속사 since를 쓰는 것이 적절하다.

04 (1) 경험을 나타내는 과거완료를 이용한다. (2) 서로 상반되는 내용이 나오므로 although를 이용한다. (3) 원인과 결과를 나타내는 since를 이용한다.

시험대비 실력평가   p.131~133

01 ②   02 ④   03 ①
04 (1) finished   (2) had made   (3) had prepared
    (4) Although   (5) Since   (6) Though
05 ③   06 ②   07 ⑤
08 (1) unless   (2) after   (3) though   (4) when
    (5) since
09 ④   10 ②   11 ⑤
12 had learned   13 ③
14 (1) I missed the first bus though[although] I got up early in the morning.
    (2) Since[As, Because] I am a student, I will get a discount.
    (3) David was doing the dishes when[as] Monica called him.
    (4) All of them look tired after they worked hard.
    (5) I'll take the job unless the pay is much too low.
15 ③   16 ⑤   17 ①, ④

01 They talked about the accident that had happened there a few hours before.

02 We decided to leave though it started to rain.

03 첫 번째 빈칸에는 서로 상반되는 내용이 나오므로 양보절을 이끄는 Even though가 적절하다. 두 번째 빈칸에는 상상했던 것이 실제 보아서 아름다운 것보다 앞선 시제이므로 과거완료가 적절하다.

04 (1) 과거완료는 'had+과거분사'의 형태이므로 finished가 적절하다. (2) 깨달은 시점보다 실수한 시점이 앞서므로 had made가 적절하다. (3) since(~ 이래로)가 있으므로 had prepared가 적절하다. (4) 서로 상반되는 내용이 나오므로 Although가 적절하다. (5) 이끌리는 절이 뒤에 나오는 주절의 이유가 되므로 Since가 적절하다. (6) despite는 전치사이므로 뒤에 (대)명사나 동명사가 나온다. Though가 적절하다.

05 도착했을 때 이미 잠자러 간 것이므로 과거완료로 써야 하고 엄마는 깨어 있는 것이므로 같은 과거로 쓴다.

06 그녀가 죽은 것보다 앞서 일어난 일이므로 ⓑ의 has been은 had been으로 고쳐야 한다.

07 버스를 놓친 것이 이유이므로 since나 because가 적절하고 그것이 회의에 늦은 것보다 앞선 시제이므로 과거완료가 적절하다.

08 (1) 조건의 unless가 적절하다. (2) 시간의 전후 관계를 나타내는 after가 적절하다. (3) 서로 상반되는 내용이 나오므로 though가 적절하다. (4) 시간의 부사절을 이끄는 when이 적절하다. (5) 집에 있게 된 이유를 나타내는 since가 적절하다.

09 서로 상반되는 내용이 나오므로 양보절을 이끄는 Though가 적절하다.

10 서로 상반되는 내용이 나오므로 양보절을 이끄는 though가 적절하다.

11 내가 그녀를 만나기 전에 로마에서 살아온 것이므로 과거완료가 적절하다.

12 2015년에 배우기 시작했으므로 2015년 이래로 배워 왔다고 과거완료로 나타낼 수 있다.

13 <보기>는 계속 용법이다. ① 완료, ② 경험, ③ 계속, ④ 결과, ⑤ 대과거

14 (1) 앞 절과 뒤 이은 절의 내용이 원인과 결과가 아니라 상반되는 내용이므로 though 정도로 양보절을 이끌도록 하는 것이 적절하다. (2) 앞 절과 뒤 이은 절의 내용이 상반되는 내용이 아니라 원인과 결과로 볼 수 있으므로 Since 정도로 고치는 것이 적절하다. (3) 앞 절과 뒤 이은 절의 내용이 원인과 결과가 아니므로 when 정도로 고치는 것이 적절하다. (4) 시간의 순서상 일을 한 후에 피곤해 보였다고 하는 것이 적절하다. (5) 내용상 if가 아니라 unless(= if ~ not)가 적절하다.

15 양보의 접속사 though(비록 ~일지라도)를 이용한다.

16 '그때 이전'이므로 과거완료로 본 적이 있는지를 나타내는 것이 적절하다.

17 ① Although it's very hot outside, I will play soccer. ④ I remembered that I had met him at the party.

서술형 시험대비   p.134~135

01 (1) Mom had bought for me   (2) he had bought
02 (1) had already left   (2) he had gone back
03 (1) Even though the house was destroyed,
    (2) Don't waste things even if they are not yours.
    (3) He realized that he had discovered a whole new human species.
    (4) I wondered why he had done such a stupid thing.

04 (1) Because → Though[Although]

  (2) As though → Even though

  (3) Despite → Though[Although]

05 (1) had broken   (2) had already cleaned

06 (1) Horses sleep just like us though[although] they do so in a different way.

  (2) Since[Because, As] the Earth is rotating, two tides occur each day.

  (3) We had ice cream as dessert after we had lunch.

07 (1) Bella had already done the dishes when he came back home.

  (2) Dave had never visited Paris until then.

  (3) She told me why she had left him.

  (4) The boy disappeared while walking home from school.

  (5) He made his choice, although he regretted it later.

  (6) Anne was fond of Tim, though[although] he often annoyed her.

08 Kay didn't recognize any of them, though[although] she had heard of their names.

---

01 각각 과거보다 앞선 시제에 행한 것을 나타내는 과거완료를 이용한다.

02 (1) 과거완료의 완료 용법을 이용한다. (2) 과거완료의 결과 용법을 이용한다.

03 (1) Even though가 양보절을 이끌도록 한다. (2) even if가 양보절을 이끌도록 한다. (3) 발견한 것이 깨달은 것보다 앞서므로 과거완료를 이용한다. (4) 어리석은 짓을 한 것이 의아해 하는 것보다 앞서므로 과거완료를 이용한다.

04 (1) 이유를 이끄는 것이 아니라 양보절을 이끄는 것으로 Though로 고치는 것이 적절하다. (2) even though: 비록 … 일지라도, as though: 마치 …인 것처럼 (3) Despite는 전치사로 뒤에 (대)명사나 동명사가 나오므로 Though로 고친다.

05 과거의 어느 시점보다 먼저 일어난 일이나 상태를 나타내는 과거완료(대과거)를 이용한다.

06 내용에 맞게 (1)에는 양보를 나타내는 접속사, (2)에는 이유를 나타내는 접속사, (3)에는 시간의 순서를 나타내는 접속사를 이용한다.

07 (1) 그가 집에 돌아왔을 때보다 Bella가 설거지를 끝낸 시점이 앞서므로 과거완료가 적절하다. (2) until then으로 보아 그때까지의 경험을 나타내는 과거완료가 적절하다. (3) 그를 떠난 후에 나에게 말하는 것이므로 떠난 것을 과거완료로 쓰는 것이 적절하다. (4) 접속사 while 뒤에 '주어+be동사'가 생략된 형태이다. 전치사 during이 아니라 while이 적절하다. (5) although는 접속사이므로 뒤에 '주어+동사'가 있는 절이 나와

야 한다. (6) despite는 전치사이므로 양보절을 이끄는 though 등으로 고친다.

08 서로 상반되는 내용이 이어지므로 양보절을 이끄는 접속사를 사용하고, 앞선 일에는 과거완료를 쓴다.

Reading

확인문제					p.136
1 T	2 F	3 T	4 F	5 T	6 F

확인문제					p.137
1 T	2 F	3 T	4 F	5 T	6 F

확인문제					p.138
1 T	2 F	3 T	4 F	5 T	6 F

교과서 확인학습 A   p.139~141

01 Waking Up	02 had gone to bed
03 was shaking	04 as a joke
05 fall to the floor, break into pieces	
06 what exactly was happening	
07 turned to panic	08 ran into
09 my first time experiencing	10 kept saying
11 out of bed	12 crawled under
13 swinging, falling	14 covering it broke
15 tipped over, rolled off	16 Every second
17 to worry, collapse	18 seemed to stop
19 crawling toward	20 At that moment
21 coming home from work	22 It stopped
23 out of	24 Take
25 Don't take	26 Hurry
27 Where	28 urgently
29 Don't worry	30 okay
31 was driving home	32 pulled over
33 right now, going on	34 made our way
35 around	
36 had fallen, had smashed	37 to avoid
38 could, have happened	
39 earthquake drills, a real earthquake	
40 get scared	41 the panic I felt
42 take, drills seriously	
43 be prepared for at any time	

1 Waking Up to an Earthquake

2 One night in February, after I had gone to bed, an earthquake hit.

3 I woke up suddenly because my bed was shaking.

4 I thought my brother was shaking my bed as a joke.

5 But then I heard the mirror on my desk fall to the floor and break into pieces.

6 I knew it wasn't my brother then, but I still didn't know what exactly was happening.

7 Soon the whole room began to shake violently, and my confusion turned to panic.

8 My mom shouted that it was an earthquake and ran into my room.

9 Since it was my first time experiencing an earthquake, I didn't know how to react.

10 I just kept saying, "What should I do?"

11 My mom pulled me and my brother out of bed.

12 We ran to the kitchen and crawled under the table.

13 I could see the light swinging violently and books falling to the floor.

14 Our family picture dropped from the wall and the glass covering it broke.

15 A cup tipped over and rolled off the kitchen table.

16 Every second, I could hear something else in the apartment break.

17 I started to worry that the building would collapse.

18 Then the shaking seemed to stop.

19 We started crawling toward the door.

20 At that moment, my mom's cell phone rang.

21 It was my dad, who was coming home from work.

22 He shouted, "It stopped!

23 Get out of the building!

24 Take the stairs!

25 Don't take the elevator!

26 Hurry!"

27 "Where are you?

28 Are you okay?" my mom asked urgently.

29 My dad answered, "Don't worry.

30 I'm okay.

31 I was driving home when the shaking started.

32 But I pulled over immediately.

33 I'm listening to the radio right now to find out what's going on."

34 We nervously made our way down the stairs and outside.

35 I looked around.

36 Parts of buildings had fallen and had smashed several cars.

37 We went to an open space to avoid more falling pieces.

38 How could all this have happened in a few minutes?

39 Although I had done many earthquake drills in school, I had never thought I'd experience a real earthquake.

40 I still get scared when I remember that night.

41 I can't forget the panic I felt when the furniture was shaking and things were falling to the floor.

42 After that night, I began to take earthquake drills seriously.

43 I realized that I should be prepared for the next earthquake, which can occur at any time.

01 ⑤   02 ②   03 ③   04 ②

05 to swing → swing 또는 swinging,
to fall → fall 또는 falling

06 our family picture   07 ⑤   08 ②

09 ②   10 pulled over

11 fell → had fallen, smashed → had smashed

12 ④

13 I can't forget the panic I felt when the furniture was shaking and things were falling to the floor.

14 ②   15 ②   16 ③   17 ③

18 which[that] covered   19 collapse

20 ④   21 ③, ⑤

22 Since it was my first time experiencing an earthquake   23 ③

24 to fall → fall[falling], to break → break[breaking]

25 ③

26 Because it was her first time experiencing an earthquake.

27 ①, ③, ⑤   28 (A) scared   (B) seriously   (C) which

29 prepared for

01 ⓐ break into pieces: 산산조각이 나다, ⓑ turn to: (바람·조수·형세 등이) ~으로 변하다, 방향을 바꾸다

02 주어진 문장의 'my brother was shaking my bed'에 주목한다. ②번 앞 문장의 'my bed was shaking'의 원인을 설명하는 것이므로 ②번이 적절하다.

03 (A)와 ③: 대과거 용법(결과 용법으로 보는 것도 가능함), ①, ④: 경험 용법, ②: 완료 용법, ⑤: 계속 용법

04 글쓴이는 처음에는 남동생이 장난으로 침대를 흔들고 있다고 생각했지만, 곧 '남동생이 그런 것이 아니라는 것을 알았다'고 했다.

05 지각동사(see)+목적어+현재분사(원형부정사도 가능함.)

06 '우리 가족 사진'을 가리킨다.

07 '나는 건물이 무너지지는 않을까 하는 걱정이 들기 시작했다.'라고만 되어 있다.

08 ⓐ와 ③, ⑤: 부사적 용법, ①, ④: 명사적 용법, ②: 형용사적 용법

09 ② 긴급한, ① 신나는, 흥미진진한, ③ 감동적인, ④ 환상적인, ⑤ 지루한

10 pull over: (차량·운전자가) (정차하거나 다른 차가 지나가도록) 길 한쪽으로 빠지다[차를 대다]

11 건물의 일부분이 떨어져 나갔고 몇몇 차들이 박살이 난 것이 계단을 내려가서 밖으로 나간 것보다 먼저 일어난 일이므로 과거완료로 쓰는 것이 적절하다.

12 '어떻게 이런 일이 몇 분 만에 일어날 수 있단 말인가?'에서, 글쓴이의 혼란스럽고 어리둥절한 심경을 알 수 있다. puzzled: 어리둥절해하는, 얼떨떨한, ② 부끄러운, ③ 실망한, ⑤ 우울한

13 the panic과 I felt 사이에 목적격 관계대명사 that[which]이 생략되어 있다.

14 이 글은 글쓴이가 지진을 겪은 뒤에 언제든 발생할 수 있는 다음 지진을 대비해야 한다는 것을 깨달았다는 내용의 글이므로, 어울리는 속담으로는 ②번 '예방이 치료보다 낫다.'가 적절하다. ① 어려울 때 친구가 진정한 친구이다. ③ 모든 구름의 뒤편은 은빛으로 빛난다.(괴로움 뒤에는 기쁨이 있다.) ④ 잘 생각해 보고 행동하라(돌다리도 두드려 보고 건너라). ⑤ 해가 비칠 때 건초를 말려라.(기회를 잘 이용하라.)

15 (A)의 'I knew it wasn't my brother then'은 (B)의 첫 문장에 대한 글쓴이의 생각을 바로잡는 것이므로 (B) 다음에 (A)가 이어지고 (C)에서 엄마의 지진이라는 소리에 글쓴이가 상황을 알게 되는 것이므로 (A) 다음에 (C)가 와야 한다. 그러므로 (B)-(A)-(C)의 순서가 적절하다.

16 ③은 글쓴이의 엄마를 가리키고, 나머지는 다 글쓴이의 아빠를 가리킨다.

17 필자의 아빠는 엘리베이터를 타면 안 된다고 말했다.

18 주격 관계대명사 which[that]를 사용하여 과거시제로 고치는 것이 적절하다.

19 지진이 얼마나 오래 계속되었는지는 알 수 없다. ① She pulled the writer and her brother out of bed. ② They took refuge under the kitchen table. take refuge 피난하다, 대피하다, ③ She could see the light swinging violently and books falling to the floor. ⑤ Because every second, she could hear something else in the apartment break.

21 지진이 일어나기 전에 잠자리에 든 것이 먼저 일어난 일이기 때

문에 과거완료로 쓰는 것이 적절하다. 또한, after처럼 시간의 전후 관계를 분명히 알 수 있는 접속사가 있는 경우에는 과거완료 대신 과거시제로 써도 무방하다.

22 be one's first time+-ing: ~하는 게 처음이다

23 위 글은 글쓴이가 처음 겪는 지진 때문에 잠에서 깨어 공포를 느끼는 내용이므로, 제목으로는 '지진에 눈을 뜨는 것'이 적절하다. ② play a joke on: ~에게 장난을 치다, ⑤ in panic: 당황하여

24 지각동사(heard)+목적어+원형부정사(현재분사도 가능함.)

25 ⓑ와 ②, ④, ⑤: [이유를 나타내어] …이므로, …이니까, ①, ③: …한 이래로

26 '지진을 경험한 것이 처음이었기' 때문이다.

27 ⓑ와 ①, ③, ⑤: 경험 용법, ② 계속 용법, ④ 완료 용법

28 (A) 감정을 나타내는 동사는 수식받는 명사가 감정을 느끼게 되는 경우에 과거분사를 써야 하므로 scared가 적절하다. (B) take를 수식하므로 부사 seriously가 적절하다. (C) 관계대명사 that은 계속적용법으로 쓸 수 없으므로 which가 적절하다.

29 글쓴이는 언제든 발생할 수 있는 다음 지진을 '대비해야 한다'는 것을 깨달았다.

서술형 시험대비
p.150~151

01 Because her bed was shaking.

02 happened → happening   03 I should

04 (A) pulled   (B) covering   (C) break

05 I could see the light swinging violently and books falling to the floor.

06 (A) the kitchen   (B) crawled   07 it

08 the shaking   09 at once, right away

10 (A) driving home   (B) listening to the radio

11 had done

12 How could all this have happened in a few minutes?

13 be occurred → occur

14 (A) gets scared   (B) the panic

---

01 '침대가 흔들렸기 때문에' 갑자기 잠에서 깼다.

02 happen은 수동태로 쓸 수 없으므로 happening으로 고치는 것이 적절하다.

03 의문사+to부정사 = 의문사+'주어+should'+동사원형으로 바꿔 쓸 수 있다.

04 (A) 침대 밖으로 '잡아끌었다'고 해야 하므로 pulled가 적절하다. pull: 끌다, 당기다, push: 밀다, (B) 사진을 '덮고 있던' 유리라고 해야 하므로 covering이 적절하다. (C) '지각동사(hear)+목적어+원형부정사'로 써야 하므로 break가 적절하다.

05 지각동사(see)+목적어+현재분사

06 글쓴이는 엄마와 남동생과 함께 '주방'으로 달려가서 식탁 아래

로 '기어들어 갔다.'

07 'seemed to부정사'를 'it seemed that 주어+동사'로 바꿔 쓸 수 있다.

08 '흔들림'을 가리킨다.

09 immediately = at once = right away: 즉시, 당장, 현재시제일 때는 right now도 가능함.

10 글쓴이의 아빠는 진동이 시작할 때 '운전해서 집으로 가던' 중이었지만, 즉시 차를 길 한쪽에 댔다. 그는 무슨 일이 일어나는지 알기 위해 바로 그 때 '라디오를 듣고 있었다.'

11 과거(지진이 일어났던 상황)보다 더 이전에 지진 훈련을 했었기 때문에 과거완료로 쓰는 것이 적절하다.

12 이런 일이 일어난 것이 공터로 간 것보다 먼저 일어난 일이므로 과거완료로 써야 하는데, 가능성을 나타내기 위해 쓰인 could 뒤에서 have happened로 바뀐 것이다.

13 occur는 수동태로 쓸 수 없으므로, be occurred를 occur로 고치는 것이 적절하다.

14 그녀는 여전히 '두려워지고', 가구가 흔들리고 물건들이 바닥으로 떨어졌을 때 그녀가 느꼈던 '공포심'을 잊을 수가 없다.

영역별 핵심문제

01 ②　　　02 ①　　　03 ⑤
04 (c)ollapse　　　05 ④
06 I'm curious about how many people had to leave their homes
07 ①　　08 ③　　09 ③　　10 ⑤
11 ③　　12 natural disaster
13 Anything else　　14 ①　　15 ③
16 Though[Although, Even though]　　17 ③
18 (1) Although it's very hot outside, I will walk my dog.
　　(2) Since they had to paint quickly to capture the effect of light, they did not sketch their paintings in advance.
　　(3) Although most people recognize it as a jewel, the diamond most directly affects our daily lives as a tool.
19 ⓑ, ⓓ, ⓔ　　20 ⑤　　21 break into pieces
22 ③　　23 (A) to stop　(B) who　(C) home
24 happening　　25 ①, ②, ④
26 ③　　27 ①, to tell　28 ③　　29 ④

---

01 a report about: ~에 관한 보고서 be curious about ~에 관하여 궁금하다

02 violently 격렬하게 properly 적절하게 recently 최근에 actually 실제로 exactly 정확히

03 aware 인식하는 missing 실종된 exact 정확한 proper 적절

한 common 흔한

04 '갑자기 부서지거나 무너지다'에 해당하는 것은 '붕괴하다 collapse'이다.

05 이어지는 대화로 보아 소녀는 산불에 대해 알고 있지 않아서 산불에 대해 질문을 하는 상황이 적절하다.

06 '나는 ~에 대해 궁금하다'는 'I'm curious about ~'이다. 얼마나 많은 사람이 집을 떠나야 했는지 = how many people had to leave their homes

07 ① 'a large number of houses'는 '매우 많은 주택'이라는 뜻으로 '하나의 큰 주택'은 아니다.

08 지진의 발생에 관한 글로 "발생하다"는 뜻의 occur를 현재진행의 시제에 맞게 "occurring"으로 써야 한다.

09 "I'm curious about why earthquakes have occurred so often in Korea recently."를 보면 소년은 한국에서 지진이 최근에 더 자주 발생하는 원인에 대하여 궁금증을 가지고 있다는 것을 알 수 있다.

10 ⑤ 지진이 두 번째라는 추측에 대하여 아니라고 대답했으므로 지진이 아닌 다른 것을 언급해야 한다.

11 "I guess earthquakes are second."를 통해서 소녀는 지진이 두 번째로 많은 피해를 야기시킨다고 추측하고 있다는 것을 알 수 있다.

12 비상 상황에 사용할 물품을 준비하는 것으로 보아 자연 재난 상황에 사용할 생존 장비를 꾸리는 것을 알 수 있다.

13 반드시 건전지를 포함하라는 것으로 보아 앞에 나온 것에 대하여 추가로 준비할 것에 대한 질문이 있었음을 알 수 있다.

14 although로 이끌리는 절은 주절과 상반되는 내용이 나온다.

15 When he arrived at home, they had already eaten dinner. 도착하기 전에 이미 먹은 것이므로 도착한 것은 과거로, 먹은 것은 과거완료로 써야 한다.

16 아침에 차로 갔다가 걸어서 집에 돌아온 그림이므로 양보절을 이끄는 접속사가 적절하다.

17 already로 보아 과거완료가 나와야 한다.

18 내용에 맞게 (1), (3)에는 서로 상반되는 내용이 나오므로 although를, (2)에는 이유를 나타내고 있으므로 since를 이용한다.

19 ⓐ have visited → visited ⓒ had got → got, was → had been ⓕ Since → Though

20 지진을 경험한 것이 처음이었기 '때문에', 나는 어떻게 반응해야 할지 몰랐다고 하는 것이 적절하다. since는 이유를 나타내는 부사절을 이끄는 접속사로 '… 때문에'라는 의미이다. ③ …에도 불구하고, ④ 그런데, …한데, …에 반해서

21 break into pieces: 산산조각이 나다

22 후반부의 'my confusion turned to panic(혼란스러움은 공포로 변했다)'을 통해 'puzzled'와 'frightened'를 찾을 수 있다. puzzled: 어리둥절해하는, frightened: 겁먹은, 무서워

27

하는, ① scared: 겁먹은, ② nervous: 초조한, satisfied: 만족한, ④ pleased: 기쁜, 기뻐하는, upset: 속상한, ⑤ confused: 혼란스러워 하는

23 (A) seem to부정사: ~인 것 같다. (B) that은 계속적 용법으로 쓸 수 없으므로 who가 적절하다. (C) home은 부사이므로 to 없이 쓰는 것이 적절하다.

24 What's going on? = What's happening?: 무슨 일이야?

25 ⓐ와 ③, ⑤: 부사적 용법, ①, ④: 명사적 용법, ②: 형용사적 용법

26 글쓴이가 학교에서 지진 대피 훈련을 몇 번 했는지는 알 수 없다. ① She saw that parts of buildings had fallen and had smashed several cars. ② They went to an open space. ④ No. ⑤ She realized that she should be prepared for the next earthquake, which can occur at any time.

27 would like to부정사: ~하고 싶다

28 위 글은 '영화 비평문'이다. review (책·연극·영화 등에 대한) 논평[비평], 감상문, ① (신문·잡지의) 글, 기사, ② 수필, ④ 독후감, ⑤ 전기

29 '주인공의 나이'는 알 수 없다. ① San Andreas. ② Los Angeles and San Francisco in 2014. ③ A search-and-rescue pilot. ⑤ It's about the search for the missing family during an earthquake.

단원별 예상문제

p.158~161

01 ①	02 ②	03 ④	
04 (1) (c)overing (2) made our way			
05 ④	06 ②	07 ④	08 ③
09 ②	10 ④		
11 (1) Since (2) Though (3) when			
12 (1) had taken (2) had practiced			
(3) had happened		13 ②	
14 I still didn't know what exactly was happening 또는 I still didn't know exactly what was happening			
15 comfort → panic	16 ③	17 ③	
18 ②	19 ④	20 a tsunami	
21 ④			

01 주어진 단어는 동의어 관계이다. destroy 파괴하다 damage 손상을 입히다 recently 최근에 lately 최근에

02 침대가 흔들리는 것으로 보아 지진이 난 것을 알 수 있다.

03 컵이 넘어지고, 식탁에서 물건이 떨어지는 등의 상황에서 "굴러 떨어지다"는 "roll off"가 적절하다. 오늘 할 일을 내일로 미루지 마라 put off 미루다

04 (1) covering 덮고 있는 (2) make one's way 가다

05 'No, second is heavy rain'은 제시문의 추측이 잘못되었음을 알려주는 것이므로 주어진 문장은 ⓓ가 적절하다.

06 이어지는 설명에 피해를 입히는 자연재해의 종류가 나열되어 있는 것으로 보아 자연재해의 종류에 대하여 궁금해하는 것이 적절하다.

07 ④ 태풍이 가져온 손해가 얼마나 큰지는 소개되지 않았다.

08 지진이 났을 때는 탁자 밑으로 대피를 해야 하기 때문에 "over the table"을 "under the table"로 바꾸어야 한다.

09 대화 속의 "How scary!"는 놀라움에 공감하는 의미의 감탄문으로 질문의 내용은 아니다.

10 ① After she (had) finished her homework, she went to bed. ② I knew the story because I had read the book. ③ I couldn't get in the room because I had forgotten my key. ⑤ He carried out all the responsibilities I had given to him.

11 (1) 이유를 나타내고 있으므로 Since (2) 상반되는 내용이므로 Though (3) 시간의 부사절을 이끄는 when이 적절하다.

12 각각 한 시제 앞선 일에 대한 것이므로 과거완료 시제로 쓰는 것이 적절하다.

13 첫 번째 문장에서는 예상한 것이 성취한 것보다 앞선 시제이므로 과거완료 had expected가 적절하다. 두 번째 문장에서는 다음에 이어지는 절의 이유에 해당하므로 Since가 적절하다.

14 부정문에서 still은 부정어 앞에 위치한다. exactly가 was happening을 수식하는 것이 아니라 의문사 what을 수식하고 있고, 이런 경우에는, 의문사 바로 앞이나 뒤에 위치하는 것이 정상적인 어순이다.

15 머지않아 방 전체가 심하게 흔들리기 시작했다고 했으므로, 혼란스러움은 '공포'로 변했다라고 하는 것이 적절하다. comfort: 안락, 편안

16 지진이 일어났을 때 필자의 동생이 무엇을 하고 있었는지는 대답할 수 없다. ① It occurred one night in February. ② No. ④ No. ⑤ No.

17 ⓐ in a few minutes: 몇 분 만에, ⓑ be prepared for: ~에 대비하고 있다

18 주어진 문장의 looked around에 주목한다. ②번 뒤에 주변을 둘러본 상황이 이어지고 있으므로 ②번이 적절하다.

19 이 글은 글쓴이가 지진을 겪은 뒤에 언제든 발생할 수 있는 다음 지진을 대비해야 한다는 것을 깨달았다는 내용의 글이므로, 주제로는 ④번이 적절하다. 예방은 치료약보다 낫다; 유비무환이다. (좋지 않은 일이 일어나기 전에 예방하는 편이 그 결과에 대처하는 것보다 쉽고 유효하다.)

20 '쓰나미'를 가리킨다.

21 near Haeundae Beach를 near Gwangalli Beach로 고쳐야 한다.

01 curious about　　　　　02 So am I.

03 (1) damage　(2) get　(3) hands　(4) cover

04 (1) David had lost his glasses, so he couldn't read anything.

(2) After he (had) moved to a new city, he joined the company baseball team.

(3) In summer, food is easily spoiled unless it is kept well.

(4) Our feet remain firmly on the earth though[although] our planet is spinning on its axis.

05 (1) had quit　(2) had been married

(3) you do not like

06 (1) A man notified the police that his store had been robbed.

(2) Even though she does not have hands, there is nothing she cannot do.

07 (A) woke up　(B) because　(C) how

08 experienced / I experienced

09 (A) her brother　(B) happening

10 Don't take the elevator!

11 in order to / so as to / in order that, may[can] / so that, may[can]

12 She started crawling toward the door.

01 함께 조사를 해보자는 제안을 하는 것으로 보아 궁금증을 나타내는 "I'm curious about ~"가 되는 것이 적절하다.

02 '~도 마찬가지이다'의 의미로 동의를 나타내는 표현은 'So +주어+동사.'이다.

03 (1) 손상, 손해 damage (2) 겁먹다 get scared (3) 두 손을 올려놓다 place one's hands (4) 씌우다[가리다] cover

04 (1) 안경을 잃어버린 것이 앞선 일이므로 과거완료로 나타낸다. (2) 앞선 일이므로 과거완료로 나타낸다. After가 있으므로 단순히 과거로 고쳐도 좋다. (3) 조건을 나타내는 내용이므로 unless로 고치는 것이 적절하다. (4) 상반되는 내용이 나오므로 since를 though로 고치는 것이 적절하다.

05 (1) 충격을 받기 전에 그가 그만 둔 것이므로 과거완료를 이용한다. (2) 결혼한 것을 말하는 것이므로 과거완료를 이용한다. to가 있으므로 수동태로 써야 하는 것에 주의한다. (3) though는 앞이나 뒤의 절의 내용과 상반되는 내용을 이끈다.

06 (1) 가게에 강도가 든 것이므로 수동태로 써야 하며, 강도가 든 것이 신고하는 시점보다 앞서므로 과거완료로 써야 한다. (2) even이 있으므로 양보절을 이끄는 even though를 이용한다.

07 (A) '잠에서 깼다'고 해야 하므로 woke up이 적절하다. fall asleep: 잠들다, (B) 뒤에 절이 이어지므로 because가 적절하

다. because of+명사구, (C) '어떻게' 반응해야 할지 몰랐다고 해야 하므로 how가 적절하다.

08 be one's first time+-ing = be the first time+that+주어+동사: ~하는 게 처음이다, for the first time: 처음으로

09 글쓴이가 책상 위에 있던 거울이 바닥으로 떨어져 산산조각이 나는 소리를 들었을 때, 침대가 흔들렸던 것이 '남동생' 때문이 아니라 어떤 다른 이유 때문이었다는 것은 알 수 있었지만, 무슨 일이 '일어나고' 있었는지를 확신하지 못했다.

10 take the elevator: 엘리베이터를 타다

11 부사적 용법의 목적을 나타내는 to부정사는 in order[so as] to부정사나 in order that[so that] ~ may[can]로 바꿔 쓸 수 있다.

12 그녀는 문으로 기어가기 시작했다.

|모범답안|

01 (1) often eat fast food though it is not good for the health

(2) likes English though he is not good at it

(3) studies hard though her grades are not good

(4) played soccer though it rained outside

02 (A) is set　(B) a tsunami

(C) in only ten minutes

(D) natural disaster movies　(E) special effects

01 ③　　02 ②　　03 ②　　04 over
05 ②　　06 ⑤　　07 So do I.　08 ②
09 ⑤　　10 ③　　11 ⑤

12 (1) Though[Although] it rained a lot, we enjoyed our holiday.

(2) Even though it was cold, I felt very happy today.

(3) Since[As/Because] Laura is very kind, she is loved by all of them.

(4) He learned that he had been chosen to play Harry Potter.

(5) The play had already started when we arrived..

13 ①, ④　　14 saying　　15 ②　　16 ④
17 ⑤　　　　18 and he
19 (A) the stairs　(B) the elevator
20 ①　　21 ⑤

29

01 주어진 단어는 반의어 관계이다. whole 전체의 partial 부분의 common 흔한 rare 드문

02 ② flood는 'a very large amount of water that covers an area 한 지역을 덮는 아주 많은 양의 물'이라고 해야 한다.

03 ① 장난삼아 as a joke ② 격렬하게 violently ③ 반응하다 react ④ 붕괴하다 collapse ⑤ 가다 make one's way

04 • pull over 길 한쪽으로 차를 대다 • over ~ ~ 이상 • tip over 넘어지다

05 폭염에 대한 주의 사항을 이야기하고 이어서 또 다른 주의 사항을 더하는 것으로 보아 앞에 제시된 것 이외에 또 다른 것이 있는지 묻는 말이 적절하다.

06 더위에 대한 대응 방안으로 폭염이 왔을 때는 시원한 건물로 들어가는 것이 적절한 방법이다.

07 "~도 마찬가지이다"는 "So+동사+주어."이다. 앞의 문장에 be동사가 있으면 be동사를 쓰고, 일반동사가 있을 때는 do/does/did를 쓴다.

08 ⓑ "Yes, actually the wind has made the fires worse." 라는 대답으로 보아 "산불이 끝났니?"가 아니라 "여전히 산불이 계속되니?"에 해당하는 "Are the fires still going on?"이 적절하다.

09 ⑤ "About 400 people are missing in that area."는 그 지역에서 400명 정도가 실종되었다는 의미이기 때문에 찾을 수 없었다.

10 I had to go and greet him though I didn't want to. 내용상 주절과 종속절이 서로 상반되므로 though가 적절하다.

11 첫 번째 빈칸에는 식당에 둔 것이 알게 된 것보다 앞서므로 과거완료를 이용하고, 두 번째 빈칸에는 서로 상반되는 내용이 나오므로 though를 이용한다.

12 (1) Despite 다음에는 '구'가 나오고 Though[Although] 다음에는 '절'이 나온다. (2) As though: 마치 …인 것처럼 Even though: 비록 …일지라도, 설사 …이라고 할지라도 (3) 뒤에 나오는 절의 이유가 나오고 있으므로 이유를 나타내는 절을 이끄는 Since나 As, Because 등이 적절하다. (4) 알기 전에 먼저 선택된 것이므로 과거완료로 쓰는 것이 적절하다. (5) 도착하기 전에 시작된 것이므로 과거완료로 쓰는 것이 적절하다.

13 ② Soon I realized that I had left my report at home. ③ Although I had done many earthquake drills in school, I had never thought I'd experience a real earthquake. ⑤ I woke up suddenly because[as] my bed was shaking.

14 keep ~ing: 계속해서 ~하다

15 (A)와 ②: (자격·기능 등이) …로(서)(전치사) ① …하는 대로(접속사) ③ …하는 동안에(접속사) ④ [비례] …함에 따라, … 할수록(접속사) ⑤ as ~ as …에서, 앞의 as가 지시부사, 뒤의 as는 접속사

16 ①과 ②: 지각동사(see)+목적어+현재분사 또는 원형부정사 ③ every second ＝ every moment: 매 순간 ④ 지각동

사(hear)+목적어+원형부정사 또는 현재분사로 써야 하므로 breaking으로 고치는 것이 적절하다. ⑤ start는 to부정사와 동명사를 모두 목적어로 취하는 동사이다.

17 ⓐ와 ⑤: 기울어지다, tip over 넘어뜨리다, 넘어지다 ① (뾰족한) 끝 ② (실용적인, 작은) 조언 ③, ④: 팁, 봉사료

18 계속적 용법의 주격 관계대명사는 '접속사+주어'로 바꿔 쓸 수 있다.

19 글쓴이의 아빠는 엄마에게 전화해서 건물 밖으로 나오라고 말했고, '엘리베이터' 대신 '계단'을 이용하라고 말했다.

20 앞의 내용과 상반되고 대조적인 내용이 주절에 이어지므로 Although가 가장 적절하다.

21 글쓴이는 지진을 겪은 이후부터 지진 대피 훈련에 진지하게 임하기 시작했다.

교과서 파헤치기

Lesson 1

01 동기를 부여하다	02 자신 있는	03 정확하게
04 공연하다, 수행하다		05 외국의
06 가구	07 추측하다	08 ~ 자신의; 소유하다
09 보물	10 엄청난	11 불안한
12 개선하다, 향상시키다		13 창조적인
14 완벽한	15 사례, 경우, 상자	16 의미 있는, 중요한
17 자막	18 자원봉사자; 자원봉사하다	
19 암기하다	20 문화	
21 (웹사이트에 정보·사진을) 올리다[게시하다]		
22 소셜 미디어	23 추천하다	24 경험
25 마침내	26 책임감	27 재능
28 끝내다	29 검토, 후기	
30 번역[통역](된 것), 번역문		31 어휘
32 필요조건, 요건	33 약점	34 선반, 책꽂이
35 ~에 관련되다	36 ~에 익숙해지다	37 어쨌든
38 첫째로	39 ~을 돌보다	40 ~에 감동받다
41 ~을 자랑스러워하다		42 포기하다
43 ~하면서 시간을 보내다		

01 post	02 treasure	03 shelf
04 subtitle	05 memorize	06 motivate
07 vocabulary	08 hold	09 confident
10 review	11 experience	12 finally
13 culture	14 guess	15 creative
16 furniture	17 requirement	18 talent
19 improve	20 awesome	21 case
22 meaningful	23 foreign	24 nervous
25 own	26 perfect	27 exactly
28 translation	29 perform	30 volunteer
31 share	32 weakness	33 responsibility
34 recommend	35 give up	
36 become familiar with ~		37 be proud of ~
38 first of all	39 get used to ~	40 take care of
41 in any case	32 not ~ at all	43 be related to ~

1 talent, 재능   2 perform, 공연하다
3 recommend, 추천하다
4 post, (웹사이트에 정보·사진을) 올리다[게시하다]
5 shelf, 선반   6 perfect, 완벽한
7 share, 공유하다   8 requirement, 필요조건, 요건
9 memorize, 암기하다   10 treasure, 보물
11 responsibility, 책임감   12 review, 검토
13 furniture, 가구   14 volunteer, 자원봉사자
15 confident, 자신 있는   16 motivate, 동기를 부여하다

Listen & Talk 1 B

would, like, this year / like, learn, listened, was struck by, sound / Where, going to learn / good, player, ask him to teach

Listen & Talk 1 C

What, doing / writing, things that, want to do / What, like to / first, like, spend time volunteering, during / sounds / What about, What would, like to do / thinking, taking, swimming class / cool

Listen & Talk 2 B

What, holding / skateboard, going skateboarding / know that, skateboard, How, learn, skateboard / joined, local, last month / see, how, like / really, helps, make, too / go skateboarding, other members, share tips, one another

Listen & Talk 2 C

make, shelf yourself, amazing / started making furniture last year / How, like / hard at first, love, feel, confident after, finish making / great, really good at / guess, found, talent, good to try / Exactly, Having, experiences, find, talents

Listen & Talk 2 D

ran, race / How did, like / liked, a lot, helped, confidence

Presentation Time Step 1

tell, one, meaningful / cooked, for / How, like / not easy, learned that, make, happy with, cooking

Presentation Time Step 3

recommends cooking, meaningful experience because, cooking, others, make, experience, feel

Do It Yourself A

performed, festival / How, like / wasn't bad, made, mistakes / sure, sounded fine / for saying, playing, in front of / How, feel about / nervous, felt, too / awesome, so proud of

Listen & Talk 1 B

G: What would you like to do this year?

B: I'd like to learn the guitar. I listened to the song "Cavatina," and I was struck by the sound of the guitar.

G: That's great. Where are you going to learn it?

B: My friend Jinsu is a very good guitar player. I'll ask him to teach me.

Listen & Talk 1 C

B: What are you doing?

G: I'm writing a list of things that I want to do this year.

B: That's nice. What would you like to do this year?

G: Well, first of all, I'd like to spend time volunteering with my friends during summer vacation.

B: That sounds great.

G: What about you? What would you like to do this year?

B: I'm thinking of taking a swimming class.

G: That's really cool.

Listen & Talk 2 B

B: Hey, Suji! What are you holding?

G: Hi, Ben. It's a skateboard. I'm going skateboarding.

B: Wow! I didn't know that you could skateboard. How did you learn to skateboard?

G: I joined a local skateboarding club last month.

B: I see. So how do you like it?

G: It's really fun! It helps me make new friends, too.

B: How?

G: I go skateboarding with other members of the club, and we share tips with one another.

Listen & Talk 2 C

G: Did you make this shelf yourself? It's amazing!

B: Thanks. I started making furniture last year.

G: Cool! How do you like it?

B: It was hard at first, but now I love it. I feel so confident after I finish making something.

G: That's great. I think you're really good at it.

B: Thanks. I guess I found a new talent. I think it's good to try new things.

G: Exactly. Having new experiences lets us find new talents.

Listen & Talk 2 D

A: I ran a race last year.

B: How did you like it?

A: I liked it a lot. It helped me build confidence.

Presentation Time Step 1

A: Can you tell me about one of your meaningful experiences?

B: I cooked dinner for my family last Sunday.

A: How did you like it?

B: It was not easy, but I learned that I could make people happy with my cooking.

Presentation Time Step 3

Our group recommends cooking dinner for your family. It is a meaningful experience because you will learn that cooking for others can make them happy. After this experience, you will feel great.

Do It Yourself A

B: My band performed at the school festival yesterday.

G: Cool. How did you like that?

B: It wasn't bad, but I made some mistakes.

G: It's okay. I'm sure you sounded fine.

B: Thanks for saying so. It was my first time playing the drums in front of so many people.

G: How did you feel about that?

B: I was very nervous, but I felt great, too!

G: That's awesome. I'm so proud of you.

01 Learn, Language, Find

02 Why, Foreign Languages

03 Many, because of, requirements

04 others, for fun   05 In, case, found, study

06 Let's meet, listen, ideas 07 Love Soccer

08 big fan, team

09 understand interviews, favorite

10 However, easy because, well

11 How, improve, Spanish

12 way, to practice, every

13 have changed, been writing

14 What's, become familiar with

15 suggest watching, often

16 help, used to, sound   17 If, too, try watching

18 are used, every day

19 Learn, vocabulary, memorize

20 why don't, review, in   21 help, improve, writing

22 No, Subtitles   23 is back

24 so excited, perform   25 singing, just perfect

26 without subtitles, translations

27 Any tips

28 should find, interested in

29 motivate one another

30 translate, sing together

31 Doing, things, improves 32 Follow, on social

33 post, messages, how, doing

34 with, messages, understand, easily

35 recommend watching, dramas

36 been watching, year

37 for help with listening

38 also, print out, subtitles

39 What Works

40 hundreds of, own way

41 what, motivated, enjoy learning

42 at first, much bigger

01 a New Language, Find

02 Why, Learn Foreign Languages

03 learn, because of school requirements

04 others, for fun

05 In any case, ways to study

06 Let's, listen to their ideas

07 Love Soccer   08 a big fan, Spanish

09 understand interviews with

10 However, because, Spanish that well

11 How, improve my Spanish

12 The best way, to practice it

13 have changed the language, have been writing

14 most important is to become familiar with

15 suggest watching Spanish

16 will help, get used to   17 too fast, try watching

18 are used only, not

19 Learn, soccer vocabulary, memorize

20 why don't you try writing, in Spanish

21 will help, improve your writing skills

22 No More   23 is back

24 so excited, perform   25 just perfect

26 without subtitles, translations though

27 Any tips

28 should find, are interested in

29 motivate one another

30 translate, sing together

31 Doing, improves our Korean

32 Follow, on social media

33 post short messages, how, are doing

34 post, with the messages, more easily

35 recommend watching

36 I've been watching, for

37 Korean subtitles for help with listening

38 to print out the subtitles

39 Works for

40 hundreds of, their own way, learning

41 what keeps, motivated, enjoy learning

42 hard at first, make, much bigger

1 새로운 언어를 배우고, 새로운 세상을 찾아라

2 왜 사람들은 외국어를 배울까?

3 많은 학생들이 학교 필수 수업이기 때문에 새로운 언어를 배운다.

4 다른 많은 이들은 재미를 위해 그것을 배운다.

5 어떤 경우에도, 모든 곳의 학생들은 새로운 언어를 공부하는 데 흥미로운 방법들을 찾아낸다.

6 이 학생들을 만나서 그들의 생각을 들어보자.

7 저는 축구를 정말 좋아해요!

8 전 스페인 축구 팀의 엄청난 팬이랍니다.

9 저는 제가 정말 좋아하는 선수들의 인터뷰를 이해하고 싶어요.

10 그런데 스페인어를 그렇게 잘 알지 못하기 때문에 그것이 쉽지 않아요.

11 어떻게 하면 제가 스페인어 실력을 늘릴 수 있을까요? – 오언, 16세

12 새로운 언어를 배울 수 있는 가장 좋은 방법은 그 언어를 매일 연습하는 것이랍니다.

13 저는 제 휴대 전화의 설정을 스페인어로 바꿨고, 제가 사야 할 목록을 스페인어로 적어 오고 있어요! – 줄리, 15세

14 가장 중요한 것은 우선 언어와 친해지는 것이에요.

15 나는 전 스페인 영화들을 자주 볼 것을 제안하는데요.

16 그것은 당신이 언어의 소리에 익숙해지도록 도울 거예요.

17 만약 사람들이 너무 빨리 말한다면, 어린이를 위한 스페인 영화들을 먼저 보는 것을 시도해 보세요. – 인호, 14세

18 어떤 단어들은 일상생활에서가 아니라 오직 축구에서만 쓰인답니다.

19 몇몇 축구 어휘들을 배우고 기억하세요.

20 또한, 스페인어로 경기에 대한 후기를 써 보는 건 어때요?

21 그것은 당신이 작문 실력을 향상하도록 도울 거예요. – 로한, 16세

22 더는 자막 없이!

23 DREAM4가 돌아왔어요!

24 저는 제가 정말 좋아하는 한국의 젊은 남성 밴드가 공연하는 것을 보는 게 너무 신이 나요.

25 그들의 노래와 춤은 정말 완벽하답니다.

26 그렇지만 자막이나 번역이 없이 그들의 노래를 이해하고 싶어요.

27 어떤 조언들이 있을까요? – 마리사, 14세

28 당신은 DREAM4에 관심이 있는 친구들을 찾아 모임을 시작해야 해요.

29 우리 모임에서 우리는 서로 동기를 부여한답니다.

30 우리는 함께 노래를 번역하고 노래해요.

31 이런 것들을 하는 것은 재미있고 정말로 우리의 한국어 실력을 향상해요! – 로리, 15세

32 소셜 미디어에서 DREAM4를 팔로우하세요.

33 그들은 종종 자신들이 어떻게 지내는지에 대해 한국어로 짧은 메시지를 올려요.

34 그들은 또한 메시지와 함께 사진들을 올려서 당신은 더 쉽게 게시물을 이해할 수 있어요. – 아이샤, 14세

35 저는 한국 드라마들을 볼 것을 추천해요.

36 저는 1년 동안 한국 드라마들을 시청해 왔고, 그것들은 정말 재미있어요!

37 듣기에 도움이 되도록 한국어 자막을 사용할 수 있고요.

38 맨 먼저 자막들을 출력해서 읽는 것도 좋은 생각이랍니다. – 브랜던, 16세

39 무엇이 당신에게 효과가 있는 걸까?

40 세상에는 수백 가지 좋은 조언들이 있지만, 모든 사람이 학습에 대한 그들만의 방법을 가지고 있다.

41 당신에게 계속 동기 부여가 되는 것을 찾아라, 그러면 당신은 학습을 더욱 즐길 것이다.

42 기억해라, 모든 언어는 처음에는 어렵지만, 새로운 언어가 당신의 세상을 더욱 넓혀줄 수 있다!

본문 TEST Step 4-Step 5
p.18~23

1 Learn a New Language, Find a New World

2 Why Do People Learn Foreign Languages?

3 Many students learn new languages because of school requirements.

4 Many others learn them for fun.

5 In any case, students everywhere have found interesting ways to study new languages.

6 Let's meet these students and listen to their ideas.

7 I Love Soccer!

8 I'm a big fan of a Spanish soccer team.

9 I want to understand interviews with my favorite players.

10 However, it's not easy because I don't know Spanish that well.

11 How can I improve my Spanish? – Owen, 16

12 The best way to learn a new language is to practice it every day.

13 I have changed the language of my phone to Spanish, and I have been writing my shopping lists in Spanish! – Julie, 15

14 What's most important is to become familiar with the language first.

15 I suggest watching Spanish movies often.

16 It will help you get used to the sound of the language.

17 If the people talk too fast, try watching Spanish children's movies first. – Inho, 14

18 Some words are used only in soccer, not in everyday life.

19 Learn some soccer vocabulary and memorize it.

20 Also, why don't you try writing a review of a match in Spanish?

21 It will help you improve your writing skills. – Rohan, 16

22 No More Subtitles!

23 DREAM4 is back!

24 I'm so excited to see my favorite Korean boy band perform.

25 Their singing and their dancing are just perfect.

26 I want to understand their songs without subtitles or translations though.

27 Any tips? – Marisa, 14

28 You should find friends who are interested in DREAM4 and start a club.

29 In my club, we motivate one another.

30 We translate songs and sing together.

31 Doing these things is fun and really improves our Korean! – Lori, 15

32 Follow DREAM4 on social media.

33 They often post short messages in Korean about how they are doing.

34 They also post pictures with the messages, so you can understand the posts more easily. – Aishah, 14

35 I recommend watching Korean dramas.

36 I've been watching Korean dramas for a year, and they're really interesting!

37 You can use Korean subtitles for help with listening.

38 It's also a good idea to print out the subtitles and read them first. – Brandon, 16

39 What Works for You?

40 There are hundreds of good tips out there, but everyone has their own way of learning.

41 Find what keeps you motivated; then you will enjoy learning more.

42 Remember, every language is hard at first, but a new language can make your world much bigger!

After You Read B

1. want to improve, have any tips
2. vocabulary which is related to
3. Watching, with Chinese subtitles, way to get better at
4. a lot

After You Read C

1. How to Learn
2. Interests, Spanish
3. To understand, interviews
4. Spanish every day
5. Become familiar with
6. soccer vocabulary, review, match in Spanish
7. what, motivated, enjoy learning more

Do It Yourself B

1. so excited to see, perform
2. without subtitles, translations though
3. tips

After You Read B

1. A: I want to improve my Chinese. Do you have any tips?
2. B: Learn vocabulary which is related to your interests.
3. C: Watching Chinese dramas with Chinese subtitles is a good way to get better at listening.
4. A: Thanks a lot!

After You Read C

1. How to Learn a New Language
2. Interests: Spanish soccer team
3. Wants: To understand the players' interviews
4. Useful Tips: • Practice Spanish every day.
5. • Become familiar with Spanish.
6. • Learn soccer vocabulary and write a review of a match in Spanish.
7. Find what keeps you motivated; then you will enjoy learning more.

Do It Yourself B

1. I'm so excited to see my favorite Korean boy band perform.
2. I want to understand their songs without subtitles or translations though.
3. Any tips? - *Marisa*

Lesson 2

01 긍정적인	02 엄청난	03 유익한
04 편리한	05 비슷한	06 뇌
07 세포	08 손상을 주다	09 숙면
10 비교되는	11 호두	12 방해하다, 가로 막다
13 생강	14 위험	15 조사하다
16 진행과정을 추적하다		17 이득
18 포함하다	19 처리하다	20 단서
21 시력	22 증가하다	23 복합적인
24 주름	25 낮추다	26 반사하다
27 속이 빈	28 개선하다	29 감동받은
30 부정적인	31 민감한	32 화학물질
33 기능	34 생산적인	35 다양한
36 게다가	37 지금부터	38 적어도
39 반면에	40 생각이 떠오르다	
41 A뿐만 아니라 B도		42 ~로 나뉘어지다
43 A가 ~하지 못하게 하다		

01 cell	02 beneficial	03 process
04 hollow	05 walnut	06 negative
07 awesome	08 multiple	09 pillow
10 mirror	11 compared	12 positive
13 moved	14 damage	15 wrinkle
16 search	17 clue	18 function
19 vision	20 chemical	21 chew
22 ginger	23 productive	24 similar
25 increase	26 healthy	27 benefit
28 contain	29 brain	30 improve
31 prevent	32 lower	33 convenient
34 sensitive	35 from now on	36 work out
37 in addition	38 on the other hand	
39 keep -ing	40 a variety of	41 be divided into
42 not only A but also B		43 come to mind

1 thirsty, 목마른   2 hollow, 속이 빈   3 convenient, 편리한
4 vision, 시력   5 walnut, 호두   6 slice, 얇게 자르다
7 pillow, 베개   8 active, 활발한   9 wrinkle, 주름
10 brain, 뇌   11 risk, 위험   12 increase, 증가하다
13 improve, 개선하다   14 chew, 씹다   15 clue, 실마리
16 benefit, 이익

Listen & Talk 1 A

Have, heard, chewing, bad for, teeth / haven't Why / damage, make, sensitive

Listen & Talk 1 B

look tired, get enough / slept for over / When did, go to bed / went to bed, as usual / probably what, making, tired, Have, heard, when / Why, that / going to bed late, make, feel tired / other hand, improve, memory, productive, now on, try to, earlier

Listen & Talk 1 D-1

Have, heard, writing, good, health / really / improves, memory

Listen & Talk 2 A

smart, check, health information, smartphone / What kind of / how far, during, how well / surprised, small

Listen & Talk 2 B

What, doing, living room / doing yoga / working, by yourself / following, steps / Let, see, been watched, million times, surprised, have watched / programs, popular / convenient, don't have to, out, exercise / That's why, try, too

Listen & Talk 2 C

looks / magic, carry, everywhere / special about / awesome, to drink, every / surprised, talk / asks, like, thirsty / why, trying / drinking, increase, help, blood flow / buy

Do It Yourself A

hungry / Why don't, before / want, wait until / have, eating little, often, health / Really, eating three meals / waiting, eat, too, Eating little, often prevents, from eating / go eat, right now

Listen & Talk 1 A

B: Have you heard that chewing ice is bad for your teeth?

G: No, I haven't. Why is that?

B: It can damage your teeth. It can also make them too sensitive.

Listen & Talk 1 B

B: You look tired. Did you get enough sleep?

G: Yes, I did. I slept for over seven hours.

B: Okay. When did you go to bed?

G: I went to bed after midnight, as usual.

B: That's probably what is making you tired. Have you heard that when you go to bed is very important?

G: No, I haven't. Why is that?

B: Scientists say that going to bed late can make you feel tired the next day.

G: I didn't know that.

B: On the other hand, going to bed early can improve your memory and help you be more productive. From now on, try to go to bed earlier.

Listen & Talk 1 D-1

A: Have you heard that writing by hand is good for your health?

B: Oh, really?

A: Yes, it improves your memory.

Listen & Talk 2 A

G: What's this?

B: It's a smart band. It lets me check my health information on my smartphone.

G: What kind of information?

B: It shows how far I walk during the day and how well I sleep at night.

G: Interesting. I'm surprised that this small band can do all that.

Listen & Talk 2 B

B: What are you doing in the living room?

G: I'm doing yoga.

B: You're working out by yourself?

G: Yes, I'm following this online video. It shows me all the steps.

B: Let me see. Wow, it's been watched two million times! I'm surprised that somany people have watched this video.

G: I know! These kinds of programs are becoming popular right now.

B: It looks very convenient. You don't have to go out to exercise.

G: That's right. That's why I love these programs. You should try them, too.

Listen & Talk 2 C

B: What is that? It looks nice.

G: This is a magic cup. I carry it everywhere with me.

B: What's special about it?

G: It's awesome. It tells me to drink water every two hours.

B: Really? I'm surprised that it can talk to you.

G: It even asks me questions like "Aren't you thirsty?"

B: That's so cool! But why are you trying to drink more water?

G: Because drinking a lot of water can increase your energy and help your blood flow.

B: That's amazing. I should buy one!

Do It Yourself A

B: Oh, I'm so hungry.

G: Why don't you eat some snacks before dinner?

B: I don't want to. I'll wait until dinner.

G: Okay, but have you heard that eating little and often is good for your health?

B: Really? I thought eating three meals a day was fine.

G: If you keep waiting until dinner, you will eat too much and too quickly. Eating little and often prevents you from eating like that.

B: I see. Then I'll go eat an apple right now.

본문 TEST Step 1 · p.33~34

01 Beneficial Foods, Bodies

02 containing, variety, keeps, healthy

03 which, good for, parts　04 however, big clue

05 Look, following examples　06 not only, but, also

07 compare, with, heart　08 that, look similar

09 multiple hollow spaces

10 that, chemicals that, are, blood

11 In addition, lower, disease

12 Look, shape, walnut　13 notice anything

14 similar to, shape, brain

15 divided into, just like

16 wrinkles, which, brain

17 help, stay healthy, active

18 good, preventing, disease

19 slice, looks like

20 chemicals, which improves, vision

21 process, send, image, brain

22 if, healthy eyes

23 Cutting, because, makes, cry

24 try slicing, anyway　25 looks a little like

26 which helps make, cells　27 move on to

28 comes to mind　29 Doesn't, look like

30 taste, prevents, feeling, throwing

31 For, reason, good, stomach

32 amazing, mirror, that, good

33 many other such foods　34 as many, try, variety

본문 TEST Step 2 · p.35~36

01 Beneficial, Bodies

02 that, containing, variety, keeps, healthy

03 are good for, body parts　04 however, a big clue

---

05 Look at, following

06 Each of, not only, but, also

07 Slice, compare, with　08 that, look similar

09 multiple hollow spaces, are red

10 that, that, are, heart, blood

11 In addition, lower, heart disease

12 the shape, walnut　13 notice anything

14 similar to, shape　15 is divided into, like

16 wrinkles, which　17 stay healthy, active

18 preventing, disease

19 A slice of carrot

20 that, which improves, vision

21 helps, process, send, to　22 if, healthy eyes

23 Cutting onions, because, makes you cry

24 try slicing, anyway

25 looks a little like, humam cell

26 contain, which helps make

27 move on to ginger　28 comes to mind

29 Doesn't, look like

30 strong taste, come from, prevents, from feeling, throwing up

31 For this reason, be good for

32 Isn't, mirror, that

33 many other such foods

34 as many as you can, a variety of

본문 TEST Step 3 · p.37~38

1 우리 몸에 이로운 음식

2 우리는 다양한 음식을 포함하는 식사가 우리의 몸을 건강하게 유지해 준다는 것을 알고 있다.

3 그러나 때때로 우리는 어떤 음식이 어떤 신체 부위에 좋은지 잘 모를 때가 있다.

4 하지만 자연은 우리에게 확실한 단서를 제시해 준다.

5 다음의 예들을 살펴보자.

6 각각의 이 음식들은 우리 신체의 특정 부분과 비슷해 보일 뿐만 아니라 그 신체 부위에도 좋다.

7 토마토 한 개를 잘라내서 그것을 사람의 심장과 비교해 보자.

8 당신은 그 둘이 비슷해 보인다는 것을 알게 될 것이다.

9 둘 다 여러 개의 빈 공간이 있고 붉은 색이다.

10 연구원들은 토마토를 붉게 만드는 화학 물질이 사람의 심장과 피에 유익하다고 한다.

11 게다가, 토마토를 먹는 것이 심장병에 걸릴 위험성을 낮출 수 있다.

12 호두의 모양을 살펴보자.

13 뭔가를 알아차릴 수 있는가?

14 그렇다, 호두의 모양은 인간의 뇌 형태와 매우 유사하다!

15 호두는 마치 인간의 뇌처럼 두 부분으로 나뉜다.

16 호두에는 또한 주름이 있는데, 이는 인간의 뇌에도 있는 것이다.

17 연구 결과는 호두가 사람의 뇌가 건강하고 활동적인 상태를 유지하는 데 도움을 준다는 것을 보여준다.

18 호두는 또한 알츠하이머병을 예방하는 데도 좋다.

19 썰어 놓은 당근의 모양은 사람의 눈과 비슷해 보인다.

20 당근에는 비타민 A를 만들 수 있는 화학 성분이 있는데, 그것이 시력을 개선한다.

21 비타민 A는 눈이 빛을 처리하여 뇌에 선명한 이미지를 보낼 수 있도록 돕는다.

22 그러므로 건강한 눈을 원한다면, 당근을 먹어라.

23 양파를 써는 것은 즐겁지 않은데 왜냐하면 그것이 당신을 울게 만들기 때문이다.

24 그렇지만 어쨌든 하나를 잘라 보아라.

25 당신은 양파의 내부가 약간 인간의 세포처럼 보인다는 것을 알 수 있다.

26 과학자들은 양파가 비타민 B를 함유하는데, 이 비타민 B가 새롭고 건강한 세포를 만들어 내는 데 도움이 된다고 주장한다.

27 이제 생강으로 넘어가 보자.

28 생강을 보면 몸의 어떤 부위가 생각나는가?

29 생강이 마치 위장처럼 생기지 않았는가?

30 당신은 어쩌면 생강의 강한 맛과 냄새를 좋아하지 않을지도 모르지만, 이러한 맛과 냄새는 복통과 구토를 예방하는 생강의 특별한 성분에서 나온다.

31 이러한 이유로 생강은 당신의 위장에 좋을 수 있다.

32 어떤 음식이 그 음식이 유익한 신체 부위의 생김새를 반영하고 있다는 점이 놀랍지 않은가?

33 흥미롭게도 그러한 음식은 상당히 많다.

34 가능한 한 그러한 음식을 많이 찾아서 다양한 음식을 먹도록 하라.

본문 TEST Step 4-Step 5 · p.39~42

1 Beneficial Foods for Our Bodies

2 We all know that a diet containing a variety of foods keeps our bodies healthy.

3 But sometimes we are not sure which foods are good for which body parts.

4 Nature, however, gives us a big clue.

5 Look at the following examples.

6 Each of these foods not only looks like a certain body part but is also good for that body part.

7 Slice open a tomato and compare it with the human heart.

8 You will see that they look similar.

9 They both have multiple hollow spaces and are red.

10 Researchers say that the chemicals that make tomatoes red are good for your heart and blood.

11 In addition, eating tomatoes can lower your risk of heart disease.

12 Look at the shape of a walnut.

13 Do you notice anything?

14 Yes, it's very similar to the shape of the human brain!

15 A walnut is divided into two parts, just like the brain.

16 Walnuts also have wrinkles, which the brain has too.

17 Studies show that walnuts help our brains stay healthy and active.

18 They are also good for preventing Alzheimer's disease.

19 A slice of carrot looks like the human eye.

20 Carrots have some chemicals that can make vitamin A, which improves your vision.

21 It helps your eyes process light and send a clear image to the brain.

22 So if you want healthy eyes, eat carrots.

23 Cutting onions is not fun because it makes you cry.

24 But try slicing one anyway.

25 You can see that the inside looks a little like a human cell.

26 Scientists say that onions contain vitamin B, which helps make new, healthy cells.

27 Now, let's move on to ginger.

28 What body part comes to mind when you see it?

29 Doesn't it look like a stomach?

30 You may not like ginger's strong taste or smell, but these come from a special chemical that prevents you from feeling sick and throwing up.

31 For this reason, ginger can be good for your stomach.

32 Isn't it amazing that some foods mirror the body parts that they are good for?

33 Interestingly, there are many other such foods.

34 Find as many as you can and try to eat a variety of them.

구석구석지문 TEST Step 1 · p.43

Presentation Time

1. Have, heard, is good for

2. made a plan to go, every Tuesday, Thursday

3. sure, help us stay healthy

Wrap Up READING

1. Be Healthier
2. healthy food that, recommend
3. like to talk about, are good for
4. with, protein, little fat
5. contain lots of
6. are good for the brain
7. why don't you try

Culture Link

1. in India
2. practice, to better understand, thoughts, emotions
3. to guide, to a healthier life

구석구석지문 TEST Step 2   p.44

Presentation Time

1. Have you heard that swimming is good for your back?
2. Our group made a plan to go swimming together every Tuesday and Thursday at World Sports Park.
3. We are sure it will help us stay healthy.

Wrap Up READING

1. Eat Chicken Sandwiches, Be Healthier
2. A chicken sandwich is a healthy food that I recommend.
3. I'd like to talk about some of its ingredients that are good for our health.
4. First, chicken breast is meat with a lot of protein and little fat.
5. Onions contain lots of vitamin B.
6. Also, walnuts are good for the brain.
7. So why don't you try a chicken sandwich this weekend?

Culture Link

1. Yoga in India
2. Indian people practice yoga to better understand their minds, bodies, thoughts, and emotions.
3. They use it to guide themselves to a healthier life.

단어 TEST Step 1   p.45

01 최근에	02 인식하는	03 초래하다
04 극심한 공포, 공황	05 붕괴되다, 무너지다	
06 세게 부딪치다	07 손상	08 나가다, 퇴장하다
09 피하다	10 심각한	11 들불, 산불
12 더 나쁜	13 제대로, 적절하게	14 흔한
15 영향을 주다	16 불안하게	17 실종된
18 지진	19 정확하게	20 파괴하다
21 폭우	22 전체의	23 기어가다
24 홍수	25 즉시	26 포함하다
27 자연 재해	28 언급하다	29 두들기다
30 혼란, 혼동	31 긴급하게	
32 (일·사건 등이) 일어나다, 발생하다		33 반응
34 격렬하게, 심하게	35 ~에 바탕을 둔	
36 역시 또한	37 할인을 받다	38 다양한
39 ~의 경우에	40 매우 많은	
41 넘어지다, 기울어지다		
42 길 한쪽으로 차를 대다		43 산산조각이 나다

단어 TEST Step 2   p.46

01 violently	02 cause	03 reaction
04 confusion	05 worse	06 properly
07 recently	08 destroy	09 common
10 damage	11 missing	12 chest
13 collapse	14 nervously	15 disaster
16 flood	17 earthquake	18 occur
19 crawl	20 smash	21 heat wave
22 panic	23 exactly	24 include
25 special effect	26 suddenly	27 exit
28 affect	29 tap	30 urgently
31 immediately	32 actually	33 heavy rain
34 serious	35 pull over	36 in the middle of
37 a variety of	38 tip over	39 in case of ~
40 based on ~	41 a large number of	
42 put in	43 roll off	

단어 TEST Step 3   p.47

1 exit, 나가다, 퇴장하다   2 curious, 호기심이 많은
3 properly, 제대로, 적절하게   4 common, 흔한
5 smash, 세게 부딪치다   6 collapse, 붕괴되다
7 wildfire, 산불, 들불   8 cause, 초래하다

9 flood, 홍수　10 include, 포함하다

11 earthquake, 지진　12 crawl, 기어가다

13 swing, 흔들리다　14 perform, 수행하다

15 destroy, 파괴하다　16 disaster, 재난

Listen & Talk 1 A

was, flood, hear about / floods, common, are, curious, how, happened / Let's, research

Listen & Talk 1 B

seem to be, natural disasters, these days / earthquake, south, storm / curious, which type of natural disaster, most damage / report, damage, each type, natural disaster, storms / guess, second / heavy, heavy snow / What / Based on, earthquakes, damage, been increasing, because, been happening / seems like, prepared, variety, natural disasters

Listen & Talk 1 C

hear about, fires / How serious / destroyed, number of houses, other buildings / Are, going on / actually, worse, living there / So do, curious about, leave / Actually more than, leave, homes, missing / terrible, somewhere safe

Listen & Talk 2 A

what else, need to put in, natural disaster survival kit / water, radio / Anything else / make sure, include batteries, radio

Listen & Talk 2 B

Performing, properly, save, Here, steps, proper, needs, Tap, Are, reaction, listen, feel for breathing, breathing, sure, place, hands in, chest, weight, harder, breaths, keep doing, until help arrives

Listen & Talk 2 D

In case of, what, do / Make sure, cover, wet cloth / else / Make sure that, exit, immediately

Do It Yourself A

hear, occurring, often, before / really, never felt / usually occur, southern, other places as well / curious, why, occurred, recently / Why don't, research / do / How about asking, help / Let's, find

Listen & Talk 1 A

B: There was a big flood in Europe. Did you hear about it?

G: No, I didn't. But floods aren't that common in winter, are they? I'm curious about how that happened.

B: Me too. Let's do some online research.

Listen & Talk 1 B

G: There seem to be many natural disasters in Korea these day.

B: I agree. There was an earthquake in the south last week. Also a storm is coming this week.

G: I'm curious about which type of natural disaster causes the most damage in Korea.

B: Actually I read a report yesterday about the damage from each type of natural disaster. Number on is storms.

G: I see. I guess earthquakes are second.

B: No, second is heavy rain, and third is heavy snow.

G: What about earthquakes?

B: Based on the report, earthquakes are fourth. But the damage from earthquakes has been increasing recently because they have been happening more often in Korea.

G: I see. It seems like we have to be prepared for a variety of natural disasters in Korea.

Listen & Talk 1 C

B: Hey, did you hear about the big fires in California?

G: No, I didn't. How serious are they?

B: They've destroyed a large number of houses and other buildings.

G: Are the fires still going on?

B: Yes, actually the wind has made the fires worse. I hope all the people living there are okay.

G: So do I. I'm curious about how many people had to leave their homes.

B: Actually more than 20,000 people had to leave their homes, and about 400 people are missing in that area.

G: That's terrible. I hope they're somewhere safe.

Listen & Talk 2 A

B: Mom, what else do we need to put in the natural disaster survival kit?

W: Well, we need water, some food, and radio.

B: Anything else, Mom?

W: Oh, make sure that you include batteries for the radio.

W: Performing CPR properly can save someone's life. Here are the steps for proper CPR. First, check that the person needs help. Tap the person and shout, "Are you okay?" If there's no reaction, call 119 for help. Second, listen, look, and feel for breathing. If the person's not breathing, begin CPR. Make sure you place your hands in the middle of the person's chest. Use your body weight to press harder on the chest. After 30 presses, give the person two breaths. Keep doing CPR until help arrives.

A: In case of a fire, what should I do?

B: Make sure that you cover your mouth with a wet cloth.

A: Anything else?

B: Make sure that you exit the building immediately.

G: Did you hear that earthquakes are occurring more often in Korea than before?

B: Oh, really? I've never felt an earthquake in Korea.

G: They usually occur in the southern part of Korea, but now they are occurring in other places as well.

B: I didn't know that. I'm curious about why earthquakes have occurred so often in Korea recently.

G: Why don't we do some research to find out?

B: Sounds good, but where do we look first?

G: How about asking our science teacher first? I think she can help us.

B: Okay. Let's go and find her.

01 Waking Up, Earthquake

02 in, had gone, hit

03 woke up, because, shaking

04 thought, shaking, as, joke

05 heard, fall, break, pieces

06 what exactly was happening

07 whole, violently, turned, panic

08 shouted, earthquake, ran into

09 Since, experiencing, how, react

10 just kept saying

11 pulled, out of bed

12 ran, crawled under

13 swinging, falling, floor

14 dropped, covering, broke

15 tipped over, rolled off

16 Every second, something else

17 to worry, collapse

18 seemed to stop

19 crawling toward, door

20 At, moment, rang

21 coming home from work

22 shouted, stopped   23 Get out of

24 Take, stairs   25 Don't take

27 Where are

28 okay, asked urgently

29 answered, Don't worry   30 I'm okay

31 driving home, shaking

32 pulled over immediately

33 right now, going on

34 made, way down, outside

35 looked around

36 Parts, fallen, had smashed

37 open, avoid, falling pieces

38 could, have happened, few

39 Although, drills, thought, real

40 get scared, remember

41 forget, panic, felt, falling

42 take, drills seriously

43 realized, prepared, occur, time

01 Waking Up, Earthquake

02 in, had gone to bed, hit

03 was shaking

04 was shaking, as a joke

05 heard, fall to the floor, break into pieces

06 then, still didn't, what exactly was happening

07 to shake violently, confusion turned to panic

08 shouted that, ran into

09 my first time experiencing, how to react

10 kept saying

11 pulled, out of bed

12 ran to, crawled under

13 see, swinging violently, falling to

14 dropped, covering it broke

15 tipped over, rolled off

16 Every second, hear, break

17 to worry, collapse

18 shaking seemed to stop

19 crawling toward

20 At that moment, rang

21 coming home from work

22 shouted, It stopped

23 Get out of

24 Take, stairs 　　25 Don't take

26 Hurry 　　27 Where

28 okay, asked urgently

29 answered, Don't worry 　　30 okay

31 was driving home, shaking

32 pulled over immediately

33 right now, find out, going on

34 nervously made our way, outside

35 looked around

36 Parts of, had fallen, had smashed

37 to avoid, falling pieces

38 could, have happened, a few

39 Although, earthquake drills, experience a real earthquake

40 get scared, remember

41 can't forget the panic I felt, were falling to

42 After, take, drills seriously

43 realized, be prepared for, occur at any time

본문 TEST Step 3　　　　　p.58~60

1 지진에 눈을 뜨는 것

2 2월 어느 날 밤, 내가 잠자리에 든 후에 지진이 일어났다.

3 침대가 흔들렸기 때문에 나는 갑자기 잠에서 깼다.

4 나는 남동생이 장난으로 침대를 흔들고 있다고 생각했다.

5 하지만 그때 나는 내 책상 위에 있던 거울이 바닥으로 떨어져 산산조각이 나는 소리를 들었다.

6 그때 나는 남동생이 그런 것이 아니라는 것을 알았지만, 정확히 무슨 일이 일어나고 있었는지를 여전히 알지 못했다.

7 머지않아 방 전체가 심하게 흔들리기 시작했고 혼란스러움은 공포로 변했다.

8 엄마가 지진이라고 소리를 지르며 내 방으로 뛰어 들어왔다.

9 지진을 경험한 것이 처음이었기 때문에, 나는 어떻게 반응해야 할지 몰랐다.

10 나는 그저 "어떻게 해야 하지?"라는 말을 반복했다.

11 엄마는 나와 남동생을 침대 밖으로 잡아끌었다.

12 우리는 주방으로 달려가서 식탁 아래로 기어들어 갔다.

13 나는 전등이 심하게 흔들리는 것과 책이 바닥으로 떨어지는 것을 볼 수 있었다.

14 우리 가족 사진이 벽에서 떨어졌고 사진을 덮고 있던 유리가 깨졌다.

15 컵이 넘어지고 식탁에서 굴러 떨어졌다.

16 매 순간, 나는 아파트에 있는 다른 어떤 것들이 부서지는 소리를 들을 수 있었다.

---

17 나는 건물이 무너지지는 않을까 하는 걱정이 들기 시작했다.

18 그때 흔들림이 멈추는 것 같았다.

19 우리는 문으로 기어가기 시작했다.

20 그 순간, 엄마의 휴대 전화가 울렸다.

21 전화를 한 사람은 바로 아빠였는데, 직장에서 퇴근하던 중이었다.

22 아빠는 소리쳤다, "지진이 멈췄어요!

23 건물 밖으로 나와요!

24 계단을 이용해요!

25 엘리베이터를 타면 안 돼요!

26 서둘러요!"

27 "어디예요?

28 괜찮아요?"라고 엄마가 다급하게 물었다.

29 아빠가 대답했다, "걱정 말아요.

30 나는 괜찮아요.

31 진동이 시작할 때 운전해서 집으로 가던 중이었어요.

32 하지만 즉시 차를 길 한쪽에 댔어요.

33 무슨 일이 일어나는지 알기 위해 지금 라디오를 듣고 있어요."

34 우리는 초조한 마음으로 계단을 내려가서 밖으로 나갔다.

35 나는 주변을 둘러보았다.

36 건물의 일부분이 떨어져 나갔고 몇몇 차들은 박살이 났다.

37 우리는 추가적인 낙하물을 피하기 위해 공터로 갔다.

38 어떻게 이런 일이 몇 분 만에 일어날 수 있단 말인가?

39 비록 학교에서 많은 지진 대피 훈련을 해 왔지만, 내가 실제 지진을 겪으리라고는 전혀 생각해 보지 않았었다.

40 그날 밤을 기억하면 나는 여전히 두려워진다.

41 가구가 흔들리고 물건들이 바닥으로 떨어졌을 때 내가 느꼈던 공포심을 나는 잊을 수가 없다.

42 그날 밤 이후, 나는 지진 대피 훈련에 진지하게 임하기 시작했다.

43 나는 언제든 발생할 수 있는 다음 지진을 대비해야 한다는 것을 깨달았다.

본문 TEST Step 4 - Step 5　　　　　p.61~66

1 Waking Up to an Earthquake

2 One night in February, after I had gone to bed, an earthquake hit.

3 I woke up suddenly because my bed was shaking.

4 I thought my brother was shaking my bed as a joke.

5 But then I heard the mirror on my desk fall to the floor and break into pieces.

6 I knew it wasn't my brother then, but I still didn't know what exactly was happening.

7 Soon the whole room began to shake violently, and my confusion turned to panic.

8 My mom shouted that it was an earthquake and ran into my room.

9 Since it was my first time experiencing an earthquake, I didn't know how to react.

10 I just kept saying, "What should I do?"

11 My mom pulled me and my brother out of bed.

12 We ran to the kitchen and crawled under the table.

13 I could see the light swinging violently and books falling to the floor.

14 Our family picture dropped from the wall and the glass covering it broke.

15 A cup tipped over and rolled off the kitchen table.

16 Every second, I could hear something else in the apartment break.

17 I started to worry that the building would collapse.

18 Then the shaking seemed to stop.

19 We started crawling toward the door.

20 At that moment, my mom's cell phone rang.

21 It was my dad, who was coming home from work.

22 He shouted, "It stopped!

23 Get out of the building!

24 Take the stairs!

25 Don't take the elevator!

26 Hurry!"

27 "Where are you?

28 Are you okay?" my mom asked urgently.

29 My dad answered, "Don't worry.

30 I'm okay.

31 I was driving home when the shaking started.

32 But I pulled over immediately.

33 I'm listening to the radio right now to find out what's going on."

34 We nervously made our way down the stairs and outside.

35 I looked around.

36 Parts of buildings had fallen and had smashed several cars.

37 We went to an open space to avoid more falling pieces.

38 How could all this have happened in a few minutes?

39 Although I had done many earthquake drills in school, I had never thought I'd experience a real earthquake.

40 I still get scared when I remember that night.

41 I can't forget the panic I felt when the furniture was shaking and things were falling to the floor.

42 After that night, I began to take earthquake drills seriously.

43 I realized that I should be prepared for the next earthquake, which can occur at any time.

After You Read B

1. when, earthquake occurred

2. began to, because, was shaking violently

3. How scary

4. all crawled, got us out of bed

5. happening at the moment

6. Lot's of, were falling, heard, break

7. did, realize

8. should be prepared for, can occur at any time

Think & Write Step 3

1. would like to tell

2. is set in, in

3. main character, pilot, missing, during

4. special effects used, disaster scenes

5. a little, at times

6. Go, watch it

After You Read B

1. R: How did you feel when the earthquake occurred?

2. W: I began to panic because the whole room was shaking violently.

3. R: How scary! What did you do next?

4. W: We all crawled under the table after my mom got us out of bed.

5. R: What was happening at the moment?

6. W: Lots of things were falling to the floor. I heard many things in the apartment break.

7. R: What did you realize after that night?

8. W: I realized that I should be prepared for the next earthquake. It can occur at any time!

Think & Write Step 3

1. I would like to tell you about the movie *San Andreas*.

2. This movie is set in Los Angeles and San Francisco in 2014.

3. The main character, a search-and-rescue pilot, must search for his missing family during an earthquake.

4. The special effects used in the disaster scenes are very good.

5. The movie is a little sad at times, but the story is very interesting.

6. I give *San Andreas* four stars. Go and watch it!

MEMO

적중100

영어 기출 문제집

정답 및 해설

능률 | 김성곤